A History of Social Welfare and Social Work in the United States

A
History
of
Social Welfare
—and—
Social Work
—in the—
United States
James Leiby

Columbia University Press

New York

Library of Congress Cataloging in Publication Data

Leiby, James.
  A history of social welfare and social work in the
United States, 1815–1972.

  Bibliography: p.
  Includes index.
  1. Public welfare—United States—History.
2. Social service—United States—History. I. Title.
HV91.L37   361 .973   78-3774
ISBN 0-231-03352-4

Columbia University Press
New York   Guildford, Surrey
Copyright © 1978 Columbia University Press
All rights reserved
Printed in the United States of America
9 8 7 6 5 4 3

To Oscar Handlin

Contents

A History of Social Welfare and Social Work in the United States

Introduction

THIS BOOK IS an introduction to the history of social welfare and social work in the United States. Its purposes are to show how policies and agencies came into being and changed over the years and how they gave form to general notions about personal and social problems. I hope that readers may feel a sympathy between their own aspirations and these efforts and that they may also see how the circumstances of intervention in social problems have changed.

The term *social welfare* came into currency shortly after 1900 as a euphemism for the older phrase "charity and correction."[1] In the nineteenth century people thought of this range of institutions as an organized provision for the "dependent, defective, and delinquent classes." "Dependent" meant, in this formula, those who had insufficient income and no relatives who were able or felt obliged to support them, and therefore had to fall on charity, whether private or public; they were also called *paupers*. "Defective" meant the physically and mentally handicapped or disabled—blind, crippled, or insane, for example—who needed both the means of life and some personal help or supervision. "Delinquent" referred to people who

1. The term *social welfare* was imported from England, where it connoted a democratic sensibility that resented the older forms of charity. See, for example, the article by Charles Stewart Loch, the leader of the London Charity Organization Society, " 'A Social Democracy' and 'Social Welfare,' " *Charity Organization Review* [London], 27 (June 1910), 286–95, and his later comment, in a discussion: " 'Social Welfare' was a new name, but 'Charity' was a larger and grander one, coming deep out of the history of our lives, and he would not barter it for a dozen 'Social Welfares.' 'Charity' included 'Social Welfare' and instead of abandoning it because of its alleged unpopularity one should set oneself to make people realize the nobility of its significance." *Ibid.*, 28 (July 1910), 71. See also Helen Bosanquet, *Social Work in London 1869 to 1912: A History of the Charity Organization Society* (London: John Murray, 1914), pp. 92–94.

1

misbehaved to such an extent they were thought to require social control.

These definitions imply a formal organization set up by one class of people—sponsors, whether public or private—to deal with another class that is supposed to need help or perhaps "correction." Accordingly, my historical analysis is intended to identify these various groups of sponsors and users and to locate them in the changing social structure, as well as to trace the development of particular agencies and programs.

Because the social-welfare institutions that concern us most today are responses to conditions of life in big cities with an industrial base and a market economy, my story begins in the years 1815–1845, when the producing classes, as the Jacksonians called them, were mostly farmers and artisans, and when society was significantly more homogeneous than it had been before or would be again until the 1950s. The problems agitated by humanitarian reformers in those years, which often involved the dependent, defective, and delinquent, were serious, as were the pessimistic reflections of some critics of the democratic social order that was emerging at the time. But the massive immigration of the years after 1845, crowding into the growing industrial cities of the Northeast and their counterparts toward the west, caused problems and evils of a different order. It is a central fact of this history that, as the process of urbanization and industrialization took place in community after community, practical decisions about welfare institutions were made mostly by local philanthropists or officials who got together with their current situation in mind; however, their local social problems were parts of a general process and therefore were not likely to yield to piecemeal solutions. In this respect the term *social welfare* sometimes connoted, not very clearly, a recognition of human interdependence in a society in which social action was fragmented, a sense of mutual responsibilities and goals among its classes and parts, and of the need for common policies to realize them. The profession of social work, in its peculiar American elaboration, was also in part an effort to establish a common interest and aspiration in a society that often seemed too divided to act in its own behalf.

Of course there had been since the founding of the Republic, even from the beginning of the European nation-state, ideas about a national sovereign and policies deliberately formulated for the common weal. These notions were the stuff of political theory and especially of "political economy," or simply economics, as it came to be called in the nineteenth century. Various schools of thought laid down doctrines that prescribed for the general well-being, for individual and social justice, and for the production and distribution of the "wealth of nations." These policies had direct implications for the administration of charity to the able-bodied unemployed. During the nineteenth century many utopians and some revolutionaries advanced schemes to reorganize society so as to obtain the rewards of modern industry without its penalties. In the twentieth century, however, people with a more pragmatic temper brought forth the range of programs for "income maintenance" and the extensive services for prevention and rehabilitation that linked the tradition of "charity and correction" (on its religious base) with that of political economy (and social science generally) in the welfare state.

The initiative and momentum for modern welfare policies and practices came from diverse elements and in varying circumstances. These included organized philanthropists of a religious inclination; business and professional people who could recognize an enlightened self-interest in social justice; working-class people, and more recently ethnic minorities, who had much to gain from mutual aid or some public provision; and professional administrators or practitioners, who offered their technical insights. These partisans have often been at odds, even within their own groups, and powerless against the apathy or hostility of a majority. On the other hand, individuals and groups who were befuddled or frustrated in one direction could turn elsewhere; problems that did not yield to one attack might give way to another.

The historical interpretations that I offer are frankly provisional, an effort to sketch the big picture before we know much about its several parts. Few leaders in social welfare have biographies; the private papers of others, when studied, will doubtless bring out relationships that are now unimagined. Few agencies or policies have been described in an analytical way; anyone who has tried to trace the history of a bureaucracy or a policy learns how much events depend on contingencies and personalities that seem to defy generalization. My own research has been mostly in state welfare institutions in New Jersey and California; in this work I was impressed more by the differences than by the similarities in their development. (To a large extent distinctive patterns of settlement explain the variations, but the difference in size between the two states also had an influence.) Historians have written a great deal about politics, including state and local politics, but they have largely ignored the service functions of government that are central to my story. Historians of labor have focused mostly on unions or industries, not on the lives of working people or their communities. It is reasonable to suppose that most people who needed help turned to their family or neighbors, and that formal institutions served relatively few, but we have no definite generalizations on how families managed for theselves. Until we develop social indicators and other tests, we have only impressionistic views of what difference helping actually made in people's lives, and of course there is something inherently subjective about human needs and satisfactions and sentiments like "security," let alone well-being. Obviously the federal programs of the Depression years and later were a major change toward universality and standardization, and our knowledge of economic and social affairs was increased very greatly, but these data are too massive and too recent to be comprehended as yet in a very critical historical perspective.

The organization is as follows: Chapters 1–3 summarize the relevant social and intellectual history of the decades before industrialization; chapter 4 describes the poor law, the fundamental provision for public aid, and chapter 5 the early attempts to develop special and rational institutions for particular problems. Chapters 6–8 sketch in the years 1845–1900, during which the difficult circumstances of industrial and urban life became prominent. Chapter 6 lays out the general character of private and public responses, chapter 7 the early effort to rationalize and improve these around the work of the state boards of charities, and chapter 8 the critical-minded private and urban efforts that came into focus in the charity organization societies and settlement houses. The call for a profession of social work first sounded among the sponsors of these efforts, particularly the charity organization societies. Chapter 9 discusses developments during the "progressive years," 1900–1919, emphasizing the influence of science on political thought, particularly the vision of a welfare state, and on professionalism in social service. Chapter 10 describes the disillusion with political solutions that arose during the 1920s, but brings out the hopes of many leaders for a sort of welfare state under the direction of private or voluntary agencies. Chapters 11 and 12 explain the significance of the Social Security Act of 1935; chapter 11 looks backward to the agitation for modern forms of social insurance and public assistance and their slow progress in the United States, and chapter 12 puts the act into this context and also that of the New Deal efforts for recovery and reform.

After World War II the development of American institutions for social welfare was largely a matter of federal initiatives. Chapter 13 discusses the evolution of income maintenance programs—social insurance and public assistance—during the years 1945–1960, when conservatives dominated Congress and, after 1952, the White House; it notes the surprising revival of a sort of private welfare state in these years. Chapter 14 gives an account of the "direct services," as they came to be called during this period; it shows how, in that rather conservative climate, scientific and professional ideas were nevertheless a dynamic of change. Chapters 15 and 16 cover the years since 1961, when President Kennedy advanced a more liberal policy toward social welfare. They include the remarkable legislation of the years 1965–1966 under President Johnson, a period equal in importance, in my opinion, to the New Deal, and then the conservative reaction that began in 1967 and was carried forward by President Nixon. Nixon tried in several ways to reform our social-welfare policies and administration, but his efforts foundered on the strength of the opposition and the demoralization caused by the Watergate scandal. Chapter 17 concludes with some reflections on the problem of professional identification in social work.

My goal in this story is to draw attention to the main social forces and ideas at work at any given time and to their influence on the main features of contemporary policies and programs. Accordingly, I have sacrificed most of the technical and statistical details that usually fill books on social welfare, even introductory surveys. Those who pursue the reading mentioned in the bibliographical essay will soon realize the intellectual challenge of the subject. Lay readers may think there is still too much to grasp; experts on particular parts of the subject will, I hope, sympathize with the way I have tried to generalize and simplify matters that are complicated at best and often obscure.

Chapter

1

American Society, 1815–1845:
The Rural Democracy

CONTEMPORARY WELFARE institutions are a response to the conditions and risks of industrial labor in a market economy, but industrial nations have responded in different ways as a result of their particular historical traditions and circumstances. It happens that industrialization in the United States began at a peculiar point in our general history, when it seemed that the nation was about to realize a truly democratic social structure, when religious and secular ideas about social welfare pointed in the same direction, and when a vision of progress colored the scene. In time the social structure grew in unexpected ways and the progressive ideas began to seem reactionary, so that it requires a sympathetic reconstruction to show why they were once convincing, why they remained convincing among certain groups of people or in certain places, and why they are still worth pondering.

The urban-industrial style of life, which today has brought practically all Americans under the sway of its mass culture, began in a few scattered towns in a society that was agrarian, although it was already notably different from the more traditional agrarian societies of Europe. It took four or five generations for the new way of life to spread across the country. Occasionally, as in the case of San Francisco, a metropolis sprang into being and a hinterland grew up around it. More often, a crossroads market became the center of a specialized region. Before 1845 the characteristic interests and problems of urban-industrial life appeared in few places and not at all clearly; they came into view in the matrix of a rural democracy that seemed to embody essential norms of American life and provided a framework for our ideas about social welfare and its appropriate institutions.

The year 1815 is significant because it marked the resumption of peaceful relations with Europe and is consequently a benchmark not only in American economic development but also in the history of immigration to our shores. It was then forty years since relations between the United States and Europe had been disturbed, first by the Revolution, then by the uncertainty that lasted until the adoption of the Constitution in 1789, and then by the European wars of the French Revolution, which lasted until 1815. These crises had broken up the framework of colonial trade and immigration. The African slave trade was legally ended in 1808, for example, and in the nineteenth century European immigrants came as free agents rather than as indentured servants.

In its isolation from Europe during the years 1775–1815, the nation underwent internal changes that reinforced the movement, evident already in the colonial period, toward social and political democracy. The population increased by an astonishing three and a half times. Most of this growth was "natural," a result of early marriages and big families; only a small portion was due to immigration. Settlers moved up the valleys of the Atlantic seacoast, across the Appalachians (or around their southern tip), and into the great valleys of the Ohio and Mississippi rivers. The movement, well under way in 1815, rushed forward after the conclusion of hostilities and the signing of treaties with the Indians. By 1845 the population had more than doubled again, so that it almost equaled that of the British Isles, and it was spreading over a land area (including Texas, Oregon, and California, soon to be annexed) that was roughly equal to all of Europe. The ethnic character of its citizens (inhabitants of African or Indian descent were rarely citizens) was essentially that of the colonial settlers, very much mixed during these decades of isolation. Immigration during the years 1815–1845 was moderate and did not alter the basic ethnic mixture. In those days no one spoke of a "melting pot" in which different European nationalities were blended, but in fact the mixture was more homogeneous than it had ever been before, such that Alexis de Tocqueville, the penetrating commentator of the 1830s, could conceive of the "Anglo-Americans" as a distinctive group and make this concept a foundation of his discussion.

There were some trappers, lumbermen, and miners among the settlers who occupied the continental domain, but most were farmers. Economic growth, measured by the increase of per capita production, suffered during the War of 1812 and was slow for many years thereafter. (It took steady increments of production simply to keep up with the growing population, of course.) With the return of peace, British manufacturers undersold most of the "infant industries" that had sprung up during the years of isolation. Farmers were settling the less productive land facing the Atlantic, and those who moved west of the Appalachians had to open to cultivation the forest and prairie and devise ways to bring their crops to market. By 1845, however, the new western croplands and pastures were yielding their wealth and manufactures had a firm footing; nationwide markets were coming into being; growth was jumping ahead. But in these formative years the farmer, whether east or west, north or south, had to adapt to rapidly changing markets. This meant going beyond subsistence agriculture to find cash crops. Some farmers were also trappers, loggers, or fishermen; others went into market gardening and dairy farming or worked at home manufactures, the precursors of the factory system. Most were in the land-clearing business, increasing and improving their holdings. Except for the southern plantations, which were important but relatively few in number, the typical farmer was a self-employed proprietor who, if his property was too large for him to manage by himself, might rent to neighbors or employ them as hired men.

Towns served the farmers as commercial and social centers. Their typical residents were self-employed artisan-shopkeepers, merchants, and workers in transporation—teamsters, sailors, or craftsmen. There were also in the towns a large number of hired men—apprentices, clerks, casual laborers—who were not self-employed but might realistically look forward to self-employment. There were conspicuous degrees of wealth and honor among townsmen, but much free and easy association between masters and men, and nothing like the host of proletarians and paupers who had for generations been the scandal of great European cities. In the towns, even more than on the farms, one could find economic change and speculative opportunity.

Throughout the country and the society, movement, economic

growth, progress were in the air. In the search for prizes there was a degree of social and economic equality that was striking to European travelers, accustomed as they were to aristocratic societies, and what tendencies there were toward inequality were hedged about by three notable conditions: family estates were usually divided equally among the children; basic education and literacy were increasingly available; and citizens enjoyed universal manhood suffrage—one man, one vote, or if it came to the worst, one man, one gun.

Arising in these circumstances of social equality and change was a remarkable sense of a common situation and destiny. Many people thought the United States was in the vanguard of an equalitarian democratic revolution that would, in time, sweep aside the world's kings and aristocrats and advance the common people to their proper role in social progress. This thought brought Tocqueville and other travelers to study and comment. The desire to make society more democratic inspired many reforms in the years 1815–1845. So did the sober wish to make democracy more edifying and responsible, for many people had reservations about majority rule and licentious vulgarity. The elaboration of free public schools and the heroic advances of the evangelical churches in these years testified to a feeling that more discipline was needed, that the individual and society that were called to improve themselves had indeed much to improve. Meanwhile new popular newspapers, magazines, and lyceums were a material basis for an unprecedented literary flowering that, in its enduring spokesmen, pulled together common interests and values and expressed them in ways that later generations would recognize as classic: James Fenimore Cooper, Ralph Waldo Emerson, and in the 1850s, Herman Melville, Walt Whitman, and many others provided both eloquent testimony to and sharp criticism of democracy in America.

There were variations in this common culture, between New England, the Middle Atlantic states, and the South, and between settled regions and those near the frontier. Moreover, there were two large groups of people who were excluded from it: Indians, who lived mostly along and beyond the frontier of settlement, and Negroes, who lived mostly on southern plantations. These groups presented a difficult moral problem because, in theory at least, Anglo-Americans believed that all men were God's children and, hence, brothers, and that according to natural law they were essentially equal. In fact, however, it was thought that Indians and Africans did not have the historical and cultural background that united the diverse kinds of Europeans and that they had no great eagerness to learn European ways, if, indeed, they had the ability.

Differing as they did from European settlers, Indians and Negroes had little else in common. The Indians were aboriginal inhabitants, few in number and sharply divided among tribes and confederations of tribes. They might have been reduced to slavery or forced labor, but they clung to their pagan liberty and tribal ways. They were looked upon as separate nations: relations with them came under the head of diplomacy and war, and policy was first to push them west, then to segregate them on reservations, where it was thought they might, with some help and oversight, become self-sufficient in a more European style.

Regarding the Africans the problem was more complicated. There were many more of them—they accounted for one-sixth of the population in 1840—and they were mostly slaves on flourishing plantations. They were a powerful economic interest for their masters and at the same time an economic threat to "free labor"—the majority of Americans. Their situation became the object of an antislavery movement that, because of its political implications, grew into the most hotly debated cause of the period.

Some antislavery leaders, associates of William Lloyd Garrison, took a radical religious stand. In their view slaveholding was a personal sin. Their calling was to dramatize its evil with prophetic vehemence, to make people aware of it and to bring about a change of heart, so that slaveholders and others would resolve to treat Africans as their spiritual and civil equals. Many Americans agreed that slavery was wrong and evil, but they recognized that it was an established social institution and that slaveowners did, according to law, have a property right in their slaves. These people (who later found a leader in Abraham Lincoln) tended to favor having the government buy up the slaves and set them free. But this would have been very expensive; it seemed to some to be a compromise with sin; and in any case the Anglo-Americans were not willing to associate with freedmen as social equals. Accordingly, they thought the emancipated slaves should be returned to Africa. A colonization society was established for that purpose, and this society founded the African nation of Liberia.

Colonization did not appeal to the most militant antislavery reformers or to many free blacks, who thought it compromised the moral issue of whether people of African descent were to be treated as equal children of God. Meanwhile the slaveholders also took a moral view. Disagreeing with the widespread notion that slavery was wrong, they argued that it was a positive good. Like most people, north and south, they recognized a difference between the progressive civilization of Western Europe and the primitive barbarism of Africa. The fundamental cultural difference, it appeared, was Protestant Christianity. On the plantations, they said, Africans were being taught the discipline and aspirations of a Christian and progressive society. Moreover, as wards of a paternalistic master, they were more secure and better treated than the lowest class of free workers, who had to compete savagely to gain employment from their capitalist masters. Ironically, the defenders of slavery were the most critical observers of the predicament of free labor in a market economy.

As a practical matter, then, the plight of Indians and blacks did not enter into anyone's thinking about social-welfare institutions in these formative years. Reformers who contemplated the problems of the dependent, defective, and delinquent classes assumed that they were dealing with people who shared the Anglo-American culture, who had somehow stepped out of ordinary social roles and consequently needed charity or correction. Indians and Africans came from entirely different cultures, primitive and barbaric by European standards. People recognized that there was a common humanity between them and the Europeans, but it was in fact much qualified by distance in terms of both culture and "progress." As we might put it today, the relationship between races (and cultures) was different from that between deviants and the culture in which they were raised. It was thought that the relationship between races and cultures was properly structured by the benign solicitude of the great white father for his wards on the Indian reservations, or by the conscientious oversight of the benevolent planter (and his wife) for their wards in the slave quarters, or by the zeal of the evangelist for any of God's heathen children.

Nevertheless there was, behind these rationalizations of European (or racial) superiority, a more generous vision of a true human dignity and equality, extending not just to the unfortunate and outcast members of one's own society but beyond, to people of quite different cultures. It haunted the Anglo-Americans then, and it haunts them still.

Chapter

2

Religious Ideas About Social Welfare,

1815–1845

RELIGIOUS IDEAS WERE the most important intellectual influence on American welfare institutions in the nineteenth century. People interested in charity and correction usually professed a religious motive and claimed a religious sanction. Clergymen were prominent in both administration and reform.

Less clear than these direct efforts, but more fundamental, is the way religious doctrine framed the general view of human life. Many Anglo-Americans were militant Protestants who read the Bible carefully and took it literally. In their thinking, the Golden Rule and charity were by no means the whole of religion. A Jew, Confucian, or Deist might affirm the Golden Rule and practice it. Christians believed what Jews, Confucians, or Deists did not: that Jesus saves. The heart of their religion was (and is) an explanation of the vicissitudes of life and how one could find salvation among them. It is necessary, therefore, to describe the relationship between salvation and charity.

According to the Bible, pious Christians thought, there is a purpose and meaning to the universe. God created it to glorify himself. The wonder of creation, its majesty and beauty, is a representation of God's power. As the culmination of his labors, the crown of creation, God created man. Like God, man could act according to his preferences, and he was expected to glorify his Creator by freely worshiping Him. But, the Bible says, Adam and Eve were tempted away from worshiping and glorifying God, so God became angry and cursed man, punished him, and sent him out of paradise. Thereafter man had to make his living by the sweat of his brow and his women had to bring forth children in pain. From time to time God laid His wrath upon sinful man: for example, in the Flood He drowned everyone but the family of Noah and the creatures on the ark.

But God planned and promised to redeem certain people. His Son, Jesus Christ, was the redeemer. Redemption would come on a great judgment day. The dead would come to life again, and they and the living would come before Him. Some would go to heaven and eternal bliss, worshiping God; the rest would go to hell and suffer for their sins.

This story, summarized in the Apostle's Creed or one of its variations, is the core of Christian orthodoxy, a core on which Catholics and Protestants can agree, however they disagree about details and interpretations. Its teaching about life is pessimistic. While Creation has many enjoyable features—many blessings of God—it is also a vale of suffering and tears. As the Lord's Prayer (*Paternoster*) puts it, men are dependent on God for the means of life ("Give us this day our daily bread"). They sin and feel guilty "'Forgive us our trespasses"). They are surrounded by moral danger ("Lead us not into temptation; But deliver us from evil"). Physical gratifications and mental satisfactions are likely to be doubtful, partial, and temporary. Frustration, pain, and ultimately death are inevitable.

But if anxiety, pain, and grief are the really enduring facts of existence, there is still meaning to them. Life on earth is a preparation for eternal life. It is a discipline, a proving ground, a pilgrim's progress (as a very popular tale was named) in which the pilgrim, like Job in the Bible, has to maintain his faith in God and his hope and courage in the most trying situations. Circumstances do not shape character in this view; they test and reveal it. The crucial factor of character is the personal response of the individual, his faithful seeking out and following God's will, in which he comes to feel that he is among those God has chosen for salvation.

Beyond this drama of personal faith and commitment is a social dimension, for the unhappy state of affairs on earth is contrasted with the ideal of heaven, the city of man with the city of God ("Thy kingdom come, Thy will be done on earth as it is in heaven"). To do God's will is not only to fortify one's conscience and courage but also to arrange a social life that will inhibit sin and quicken virtue and worship.

The monastic movement in the Christian tradition is an example of these ideas pushed to an extreme. People who wanted to live a truly religious life withdrew from the world into separate communities, where they could devote themselves to religious service without worldly distractions. They gave up any claim to private property (the vow of poverty); the monastic community supplied their needs for food, shelter, and clothing very simply from its common stock. They gave up the pleasures of sex and the rewards or distractions of family life (the vow of chastity). They submitted entirely to the will of God as formulated in their order and by their superior (the vow of obedience). They performed strenuous exercises to mortify the flesh and humble the spirit, to cultivate saintly endurance, zeal, insight, and perseverance. Ironically, because of their strong morale and social organization, these communities that deliberately rejected the world, the flesh, and the devil often were among the most efficient and constructive powers in Christian Europe.

Protestants of the sort that settled and dominated America rejected the traditional monastic orders. One reason was that the monks and nuns were strong partisans of the pope, another that they sometimes lapsed from their calling to the point of scandal. Moreover, Protestants were dubious about the notion that there were properly two grades of religious life, an everyday kind for those who could not or would not aspire to anything better and another kind for enthusiasts who would withdraw to a monastery. Instead, they thought, the saints might properly remain in everyday life but elevate it by their zeal. "To monasticize the world" was the core of what Max Weber later identified as "the Protestant ethic."

Instead of taking vows of poverty, chastity, and obedience, these Protestants took a generally ascetic view of everyday life. Private property, even wealth, was not bad, so long as one was not unduly preoccupied by money-getting, recognized that the blessing came from God, and acted as a steward of these material things in His name. Sex was good, as long as it was within the bounds of holy matrimony. Obedience was not to some vicar of God but to the authority of the individual's own conscience, suitably informed by the Bible and continually examined.

The Protestant belief that ultimately every man is his own priest had important consequences for the organization of the church, but it did not lead at first to religious liberty. Protestants assumed that good men, rightly informed, would agree on the implications of the Bible. They had a strong communal spirit: once the saints got together they not only ran out dissenters but also brought the ungodly into line. Puritan settlements in New England are the best examples of the Protestants' ideas in practice, their deliberate effort to set up "A city on a hill" that would inspire all Christendom.

By 1815 this dream of religious unity and an organized Christian commonwealth had faded, however. Religion still had tax support in part of New England, but that was soon lost, and American congregations became entirely voluntary and self-supporting. Denominations tended to grow along class lines. Some clergymen and congregations appealed to the rich, others to particular ethnic groups. Many people were unchurched and only nominal Christians. For them, evangelists worked out a style of sensational revivalist preaching that emphasized their emotional needs and responses, and the importance of religious conversion in helping them direct their lives. The 1830s were a high tide in this revival, which made the Baptists, Methodists, and similar churches the largest sects in the nation. The revivalists never succeeded in their hope of converting the whole country and never made deep inroads into many established denominations. But their continuing success and appeal, though limited mostly to rural communities and the lower middle class, testified to the relevance of their doctrine.

In the history of American social welfare this revivalist spirit is important because it emphasized the personal and inward-looking side of the Christian tradition. It tended to see adversity as a test of or challenge to character, a consequence of bad habits, perhaps, and it looked for a personal response to remedy the situation. The response properly began, it was thought, with trust in God; where there was trust in God there was a potent will, resourceful and ingenious; where there was a will there was a way to become self-sufficient or socially useful, or at least to minimize one's dependency or difficulty. From this viewpoint it is easy to interpret social problems as defects in personal morality rather than in social organization: if everyone, fortunate or unfortunate, would only act like a good Christian, any problem could be solved. It is plausible to argue that if people lack good will, if they do not really want to help and do not really want to be helped, any scheme of helping is likely to fail; therefore the heart or will is important. This insight lies behind the modern social worker's emphasis on self-determination. It is also true, however, that a narrowly moralistic view blinds one to the impersonal factors of human thought and action. The moralistic view of slaveholding as a personal sin, for example, was self-defeating because it ignored the institutional supports of slavery and the obvious cultural differences between Africans and Europeans. So were analogous efforts to interpret poverty, crime, or even illness as simply results of sinful behavior.

Even more important in the history of social welfare were the secular implications of the Protestant ethic, which gave a peculiar stimulus and sanction to the "spirit of capitalism," in Max Weber's phrase, and to the American economy, which so plainly embodied it. The monks and nuns had felt that every task that helped the community function, even the most humble, was as necessary and valuable in the eyes of God as every other task, and they had also scrutinized such tasks rationally to see whether they were in fact necessary or well done. These attitudes gave dignity to productive labor and support to innovation and a critical view of workmanship. The Protestant reformers applied this religious doctrine of vocation, the idea that God laid a worthy task upon everyone, to everyday jobs. Common sense had generally recognized and praised competence in everyday tasks, of course, but this conventional approval was often bound to traditional ways of doing things. What the religious doctrine of vocation added was a more zealous attitude, which linked the task to God's will, and a more rational and innovative spirit of workmanship or commerce. In general, it praised the qualities that were adaptive in a market economy and appealed to people who were inclined to meet the challenge of a market economy.

This combination of religious piety and temporal diligence was soon unbalanced. It had been difficult for the monks to maintain their religious vocation, despite their very strong commitment and communal controls. The Protestant similarly found it hard to maintain an agonized conscience about his salvation; the word *revival* implies a renewal of something that has been lost, and evangelists knew from experience how today's converts might backslide tomorrow. Workmanlike diligence or businesslike enterprise may also falter, but then the discipline of the market brings punishments or rewards, degrees of failure or success. Moreover, good work or good business is a source of both self-respect and the respect of others. There are always risks of loss in a market economy, but there are also openings for gain, particularly when the economy is changing and growing. Gain won by honorable application increases one's self-respect and the respect of others, and brings the advantages of more wealth. So the pious notion that diligence in one's calling was a form of divine service gave way to the notion that a good religious character led to economic success.

One man who made this transition, whom Max Weber chose as an example of the Protestant ethic, was Benjamin Franklin. Grandson of an early settler of Massachusetts, he was born in Boston in 1706. He was apprenticed to a printer and became the leading publisher in the colonies and then a famous scientist, diplomat, and founding father of the Republic. In his autobiography he attributed his success largely to devising and practicing "the art of virtue." He tells how he carefully scheduled his day to balance his responsibilities and allow for self-improvement. He made a list of thirteen virtues—temperance, silence, order, resolution, frugality, industry, sincerity, justice, moderation, cleanliness, tranquility, chastity, and humility—and concentrated on each for one week of a thirteen-week cycle, which he repeated four times a year, with a scorecard to show his progress. There is a monkish quality about his persistent self-examination and ascetic self-discipline. At the same time, Franklin had a strong public spirit. He looked upon his printing and publishing as a public service. He was quick to organize for mutual aid or the common good—a library, a hospital, a better system of cleaning streets—and he never took a profit from such important inventions as the Franklin stove (a superior space heater) or the bifocal lens for eyeglasses.

Franklin's conscientious, even compulsive, striving to improve himself and society, his belief in perfectibility, was plainly part of his Puritan heritage, but his own strictly religious views moved far from Christian orthodoxy. Like many men of the eighteenth century, he became a Deist; he rejected what seemed to be fanciful and superstitious parts of the Bible story and tried to interpret religion in a rational or scientific way. In this view religion was important as a social control, a guide to morality, and Franklin came to think that religious commandments were right not because they came from God but because they had in fact proved wise and beneficial. As he said, "Early to bed and early to rise"—the ascetic self-discipline of the Protestant ethic—"makes a man healthy, wealthy, and wise." Health, wealth, and wisdom are wordly goals; Franklin did not mention the saintliness, the salvation that was the goal of Christian orthodoxy, although he himself continued to believe in God and heaven.

Eighteenth-century Deism did not have much appeal to the common people of America in the generations after Franklin—it did not address their emotional needs, as Christian orthodoxy and especially revivalism somehow did—but Franklin became a famous sage partly because of his teaching that good conduct is good business and that there are rational ways to go about improving self and society.

Many historians have argued that the Protestant ethic has weakened our sense of social justice and hampered our social legislation. This is partly because it directs attention to failures of personal responsibility rather than to problems of social organization, but also because it furnishes a plausible rationale for the unequal distribution of wealth. If workers are trustworthy and enterprising, it is held, they are likely to prosper in the long run. If they are unreliable, distracted, or lazy, they are likely to fail in their work. Accordingly, prosperity may indicate good character and poverty some personal fault. Self-respect and social status thus relate to money-making. Franklin's most popular book, next to his autobiography, is a collection of lively aphorisms from *Poor Richard's Almanac* entitled "The Way to Wealth," which linked diligence, prudence, money, and success. Franklin himself stopped working as soon as he had made his fortune so that he could spend his time on science and public service, but it was easy for his admirers in the nineteenth century to make money-getting an end in itself or a means to conspicuous snobbery.

At a deeper level the indictment of the Protestant ethic criticizes an ascetic inclination to subordinate human life to some superhuman end, as if personality and social relations were mere instruments to manipulate in a rational way toward the glory of God or the glory of the nation-state or simply wealth. Because people are looked upon as impersonal instruments, it is said, it is possible to justify their suffering and even their exploitation by some elite that controls the social organization. Or it is said that people take an obsessive view of work, chain themselves and their families to their jobs, and sacrifice their finer inclinations to acquisitiveness.

These arguments are partly true, but they are based on observations wrenched out of historical context. The main historical effect of the Protestant ethic on American social welfare has been to call forth the motivation and energy that have led to our unexampled economic development and national wealth; a study of the welfare problems of less developed nations brings out how important such human responses are. Amid increasing wealth, large parts of the work force in the United States perceived the situation as actually affording opportunities and gratifications that suited them. There was neither the pervasive hardship of primitive economies nor much sense of class oppression such as beset much of the West-European proletariat. It seems impossible to separate the benefits of modern industry and society from the kinds of motivation and rationality that have historically been necessary to its rise; the strains and costs, individual and social, may best be reduced or modified if seen in the context of their function in bringing about the benefits.

Undoubtedly there is an impersonal and instrumental quality to modern technology, whether material or social, that appears to have its roots in our religious tradition. There is a correspondence between the monk in the monastery, the prisoner in the penitentiary, the soldier in the army, and the worker in the factory. Individuals may be viewed as interchangeable parts in a social machinery that has a more or less specific and rationalized function. But of course members of a primitive tribe are also interchangeable parts in a social organization that is much more prescriptive and comprehensive than modern associations that are functionally specific. Indeed, tribesmen can scarcely conceive the individual as a person separate from his tribal roles. The notion of the individual as separate and self-conscious, with unique interests and gifts, a *person* as well as part of a social organization—this notion also has deep religious roots in Christian culture, in the belief in a personal union with God or Christ and a personal salvation and immortality. If the idea of human life as an instrument in some collective enterprise has the sanction of our religious tradition, so does the idea of an individual person, separate, self-conscious, and free to seek and do the bidding of his Father in Heaven.

These considerations bear upon the doctrine of charity. If, as the Bible said, God created the world as a paradise for men, and if mankind was descended from common parents, it followed that all men might claim a share in God's bounty. If one gained property only with the help of God, which was certainly the case, the rich were fortunate stewards who were obliged to manage their wealth as their Master wished. Old Testament and New are full of demands to share with the widow, the orphan, the aged, the sick, the dependent and forlorn. There is also a strong current of suspicion of the rich and of those who grind the faces of the poor.

To the general view that men ought to share their common inheritance, Christianity added a special urgency. Perhaps the most quoted scriptural passage (Matt. 25:34–40) prophesies the coming day of judgment, when Christ the King is about to separate the sheep from the goats. Christ says to those on his right hand,

> "Come, blessed of my Father, inherit the kingdom prepared for you.
> . . . For I was ahungered, and ye gave me meat: I was thirsty and ye
> gave me drink: I was a stranger, and ye took me in:
>   Naked, and ye clothed me: I was sick, and ye visited me: I was in
> prison, and ye came unto me."

The righteous are surprised, and ask (the accent should fall on "thee'),

> "Lord, when saw we thee ahungered, and fed thee? or thirsty, and gave
> thee drink?
>   When saw we thee a stranger, and took thee in? or naked, and
> clothed thee?
>   Or when saw we thee sick, or in prison, and came unto thee?"

And Jesus answers,

> "Verily I say unto you, Inasmuch as ye have done it unto one of the
> least of these my brethren, ye have done it unto me."

The point is not simply that charity is an evidence of righteousness and a sign of grace, but that Christ Himself is present in "the least of these my brethren." Clergymen preaching charity sermons would sometimes dramatize the lesson by presenting to their congregation a particularly repulsive wretch and asking, Would they turn their back on the Christ, the divine element, in him? So the Christian duty of charity was related not only to salvation but in a very concrete way to the belief that there is a dignity—something precious and worthy—about all humans, however lowly or loathsome they may seem to be. The divine spark gives "the least of these" a potential for merit and service.

Taken literally, this doctrine might have justified a very radical sharing of property, holding goods in common as the family does, or the monastery. But in fact clergymen recognized many practical limitations on the obligation of charity. No one had to give away the necessities of his life, for example—only the superfluities—and necessities were defined to include what was consumed in the conventional style of life of one's social class. The church accepted inequalities of wealth in society as the will of God, and even saw in them a benefit and opportunity: if there were no needy, how could the benevolent be charitable? There were charitable priorities: a person's family and neighbors had a stronger claim than those who were more remote. Finally, charity was by no means uncritical; a Christian was obliged to recognize and love the Christ in the sinner, but also to hate and correct the sin. From the start, Protestant reformers were inclined to be strict about abuses of charity: they were particularly critical of the "mendicant orders" of monks who begged for a living, as it were, not to mention the lay beggars who swarmed in European cities. God decreed that people should be poor and in need, according to the Protestant ethic, but not that they should be lazy at the expense of others.

To summarize, the Christian tradition was most important in the development of our institutions for charity and correction because it furnished a cosmic drama—the story of creation, sin, judgment, and salvation—in which suffering had a meaning and so did efforts to relieve and correct it. Helper and helped could believe that their personal action counted for something in the very structure of the universe.

Of course most Americans in the years 1815–1845 were nominal Christians, rather indifferent if not scornful. Clergymen had to strive mightily to keep their congregations together and increase them. One reason they emphasized individual morality and salvation so much was because this made their message relevant and appealing to their listeners. But if ever the indifferent citizens did have to confront problems of charity and correction, they perforce fell back on Christian attitudes and doctrines—there was no serious alternative—and conscientious people who thought about these matters or tried to take the leadership usually began with religious premises and religious or quasi-religious institutions.

Only gradually in the later nineteenth century did this religious orientation give way to secular views, based on a naturalistic social (sometimes biological) science, in which the sacred drama of Christian orthodoxy would seem irrelevant (and in which it was usually not at all clear how personal suffering or helping counted for much). These secular views were present in the years 1815–1845 in an adaptation of the European theories called *liberalism*. They did not deal primarily with charity and correction—with provision for the dependent, defective, and delinquent—but, rather, with public policy as it affected those who could and did look out for themselves in the marketplace and around the hustings. In any case they tended to support the Protestant ethic. Or, since secular liberalism had its greatest appeal among those who affirmed the Protestant ethic, it might be better to picture the two intellectual movements as growing from a common root.

Chapter

3

Secular Ideas About Social Welfare,

1815–1845

IN SECULAR THOUGHT as in religion the European, specifically English, heritage of the Anglo-Americans was fundamental, but it was much modified by the historic context. Liberalism in England in the years 1815–1845 was a partisan doctrine, associated with a well-defined middle class and open to criticism from both rural squires and urban workers. In America, where class distinctions were informal and vague and where social equality was sought or defended, liberalism received little systematic criticism or even explicit formulation. It merged easily into types of democracy and individualism that were notably different from those of Europe. With regard to social welfare, these differences led to peculiar difficulties in defining community interests and responsibilities and to an unusual emphasis on voluntary agencies in charity and correction.

Thomas Jefferson set forth our general political theory in the Declaration of Independence (1776). He was rephrasing arguments that colonial spokesmen had often used, which went back directly to the *Two Treatises on Civil Government* by John Locke (1690). Like Locke, Jefferson wanted to justify a revolution, to show why the revolutionaries were good moral men and not mere usurpers and criminals, why indeed it was the authorities of the former regime who were bad men getting their just deserts. The theory was simply a statement about the nature and function of government:

> We hold these truths to be self-evident, that all men are created equal, that they are endowed by their Creator with certain unalienable Rights, that among these are Life, Liberty, and the pursuit of Happiness. That to secure these rights, Governments are instituted among Men, deriving their just powers from the consent of the governed, That whenever any Form of Government becomes destructive of these ends, it is the Right of the People to alter or abolish it, and to institute new Government, laying its foundation on such principles and organizing its powers in such form, as to them shall seem most likely to effect their Safety and Happiness. Prudence, indeed, will dictate that Governments long established should not be changed for light and transient causes. . . .

Government is, in this view, essentially a compact among the citizens to defend rights that are given them by their Creator and that exist before society takes form. John Locke had taught that in a "state of nature"—for example, in a wilderness before a government is organized—there is nevertheless a "natural law" according to which a person enjoys his natural rights to his life, liberty, and property. If someone threatens his life, he is morally justified in defending himself, even if he has to injure or kill his assailant. Similarly, if someone tries to enslave him or take his property, he is justified in fighting back. Even though he uses violence, he is not a bad man; he is a good man who is acting like a policeman in enforcing the natural rights that are his under the law of nature. But to have everyone act as his own policeman is a great inconvenience, because the law is unwritten and unclear, and good men who want to abide by it are unorganized and weak. Therefore, as a convenience, they organize governments that clarify, apply, and enforce the natural law.

Once the government is organized, its officials can rightfully take the lives and liberty of citizens—they can imprison criminals and even execute them, draft citizens for military service, and take their property by means of fines and taxes—but only if they act in legal ways. They have great powers for compulsion, but they are limited by the law, and they are justified because the governed give their consent to the law.

This theory asserted a positive notion about social welfare: government exists to protect and enhance the rights of its citizens. In that context "social security" implied not a great social-insurance program but simply the safety of life and property from those who threaten it—the criminal and the tyrant. The rights specified in our federal and state constitutions are limitations on government action: its officers cannot deny the freedom of speech or assembly, for example, or enter a home without a warrant. But the notion of equal rights is expansive, and one way to look at the history of social welfare is to see the government as moving from the mere protection of civil liberties toward the provision of social benefits as a right— toward public education and public assistance, for example.

Locke's theory said nothing about how the law-abiding citizens might organize under the compact or give their consent. He himself thought that the government might best include a hereditary king, a house of lords (also largely hereditary), and a house of commons elected by a relatively few property owners. This arrangement recognized the facts that the practice of ruling took a special degree of preparation and interest, that some people were much more powerful and concerned about it than others, and that the realm as a whole had an interest that was somewhat apart from and greater than the interests of various factions within it. Locke, and the English generally, recognized a need for a governing class that was prepared and able to take a long-run view of the common interest. The Americans became much more democratic than that, however. They came to believe that most officials, except perhaps some judges, should be elected for short terms of office, and that humble citizens, who had little knowledge of public affairs or stake in them, were nevertheless competent to decide whether their elected officials were doing a good job.

Technically, the main organs of American government were the states, the heirs of the original colonies. Practically all legislation touching social welfare—poor relief, health, education, labor, crime, the family—was state legislation. The federal government was like a league formed by the states to manage certain common interests in diplomatic affairs, the public lands, and interstate commerce. (The term *congress* connoted a diplomatic meeting of sovereign states, as in "Congress of Vienna," not a national legislature.) With regard to social welfare, each state government stood on a level with the English Parliament. In England Parliament decided on welfare policy for the whole nation, but in the United States each *state* government could legislate as it chose and policies could vary greatly among the states. This was to prove a great difficulty as welfare problems involved an industrial labor force and markets that extended far beyond state lines. The theory, very pertinent in the early days of the Republic, was that government by consent ought to be close to the people, and state governments were much closer than the federal government.

While the states had the power to legislate, they rarely administered. Their legislatures passed laws about education or poor relief, but they delegated the administration to local communities—the county, township, or municipality. Local officials were generally elected for short terms of office, worked part time, and were compensated, if at all, with fees for the services they performed. If the communities elected competent and honest officials and watched their work, the service was good; if not, they themselves suffered.

In short, a consequence of American political theory was that government officials were inhibited in fact and spirit by the limitations placed upon them, that most domestic legislation was decentralized to the states and most administration decentralized to the communities. Given the relative isolation and self-sufficiency of communities in an agrarian society, this was a reasonable and effective arrangement, often praised by travelers and other observers. Certainly an ideal democracy should rely heavily on participation and control in a local community. But this system made difficulties for long-run and wide-ranging policies and planning, and it could lend itself to intolerance and even tyranny in local public opinion, for example, with regard to the harassment of poor migrants or local minorities.

In its European context political liberalism was an argument against the pretensions of the absolute monarchs. In theory, these kings and dynasties—the Bourbons in France, the Stuarts in England—stood above the contentions of factions and individuals and ruled for the common welfare, somewhat as a patriarch looks after the long-run well-being of his whole family. In fact, the absolute monarchs played the leading part in promoting legislation intended to build up the political and economic power of their nation. They typically believed, for example, that a strong, prosperous country required a favorable balance of trade, that its exports should be worth more than its imports, so that there would be a net inflow of gold and silver. To this end they decreed many laws governing what people should produce and not produce and how they should trade. The American colonies were originally chartered so as to enhance the English economy, and the English government both supported them and regulated their settlement and trade with the general good of Englishmen, both in the colonies and at home, in mind.

This doctrine, that the sovereign should actively direct the economy toward the common welfare or "commonwealth," was later called *mercantilism*. Its spirit applied not only to international trade and colonies but also to local conditions of production—"labor legislation," we would say today—which were regulated so as to establish a fair price for producers and consumers. It even applied to sumptuary legislation, which governed consumption—legislation dealing with matters such as what clothes people could wear. The Americans were hostile toward English regulation of their work and lives, but once they had won their independence the new state legislatures were full of mercantilist schemes to develop the economy. Mostly they offered privileges or legal monopolies to investors who would venture something thought to be in the public interest. Sometimes legislators would grant a subsidy or even pass a state tariff to help a producer. (The interstate commerce clause of the federal Constitution soon forbade these state tariffs and made the national domain a huge common market.)

The practical difficulty with mercantilist legislation was that in the short run it was likely to help one party or faction and hurt another. An absolute monarch was perhaps able to take a long view, to keep a close watch on the privileged so that they did not abuse their advantage, and somehow to compensate the disadvantaged. Representatives in a democratic legislature had to work out a compromise on these points amid many demagogic distractions. They could manage to do it, of course—the success of democratic governments rests on that possibility—but it was often difficult going, and it still is.

So the problem of making wise decisions in the legislature, as well as the remarkable expansion of the economy, led Americans to turn toward *economic liberalism*, which held, contrary to mercantilism, that government should not intervene in the economy except in a minimal way. This doctrine was first elaborated in *An Inquiry into the Nature and Causes of the Wealth of Nations*, by Adam Smith (1776), often called simply *The Wealth of Nations*. Whereas mercantilists were inclined to think that the nature of the wealth of nations was represented by the gold and silver coin in circulation, Smith held that its true nature was the annual produce of its land and labor. Whereas mercantilists were inclined to think the cause of national wealth was a favorable balance of trade, Smith looked for whatever could increase production.

Smith's analysis brought out two crucial factors, one technological, the other psychological. The first was the division of labor: if men specialized in one skill or line of work, they would improve their competence. (Of course they would produce a great surplus over their needs, which they would have to exchange. They would become more dependent on the market, more interdependent, as the total product rose.) The psychological factor was that men worked harder and produced more if they could see a personal advantage in their efforts, if they worked essentially for themselves.

These ideas were timely: the rise of the factory system greatly increased the division of labor and more and more products were sold at market rather than consumed directly, and the Protestant ethic had given a sanction to economic enterprise. Taken together, Smith's arguments defined a clear standard of social welfare that would be increasingly accepted and important: the more we produce, the better we live. It followed that government should seek to increase production. Ironically, Smith argued that the best way to do this was simply to let producers follow their economic interest as they see it. Let men pursue their economic self-interest with a minimum of political restraint or encouragement, he said, and they will, in the long run, make better decisions than mercantilist planners. There is, he argued cogently, a marvelous natural harmony in the marketplace—in the relation of supply, demand, and price, for example—that will guide enterprise and effort into the best channels.

Political liberalism was quite compatible with mercantilism—John Locke was a mercantilist, as were most of the signers of the Declaration of Independence. Political liberalism merely held that the state should be limited and guided by the natural rights or civil liberties of its citizens. On the other hand, *economic* liberalism—*laissez faire*—was compatible with an absolute monarchy or benevolent despot: many kings stimulated free markets. Nevertheless there was an affinity between an absolute monarchy (or any strongly centralized state) and mercantilism: the belief that the community had an interest that was broader and deeper than the sum of the interests of its citizens. This was obvious with regard to maintaining law and order against the criminal or outlaw, but it might go much further in the regulation of economic or, for that matter, religious or social affairs. Similarly, there was an affinity between political liberalism, a decentralized political organization, and economic liberalism.

The main thrust of political liberalism had been to challenge the notion of a wise ruler, a patriarch who would make political decisions for other people; it had emphasized that the ruler's subjects must consent, more or less explicitly, to decisions made about them, and even participate more or less directly in making those decisions ("No taxation without representation," the Americans had argued). The main thrust of economic liberalism was to challenge the notion that there was some wise planning agency, some national board of trade, that could make economic decisions for other people. It was better, Adam Smith and his followers argued, to let the individuals decide for themselves how they wanted to work or invest or trade—better not just for them, but for everyone in the long run. So plausible was Smith's doctrine that modern economic science has been largely a revision and development of that doctrine. Modern socialist thought began as a critique of this liberal school of political economy.

By 1815 the early mercantilist tendencies of American legislatures were weakening. Agrarian interests, particularly in the South, found support in Adam Smith's case for international free trade (low tariffs). Jacksonians referred to Smith's arguments against monopolies (meaning an exclusive grant of privilege by the state to a favored group of investors) and also to his doctrine that the value of a product depended essentially on the labor that went into it. Even Smith's critics in the United States, who stood for a protective tariff and a national bank, regarded their ideas as modifications of a line of thought that was essentially liberal. On the other hand, no one in America before 1845 found much relevance in the gloomy side of English liberalism, the doctrines of Thomas Malthus and David Ricardo, who envisioned a great surplus of population, a great shortage of land, and much consequent suffering. It was the happy theme of unrestrained economic expansion that the Americans liked, because it suited their situation and prospects.

Americans did not have to question or criticize European liberalism because they could appreciate its appropriateness in the everyday growth of their nation. In the West unsettled lands became organized territories and then full and equal states in the Union, much as John Locke had imagined governments to take form. Citizens moved, borrowed, produced, and sold in a common market of a size that European nations did not approximate until the 1950s. Citizens did not need liberal philosophers to help them assert or defend their rights. They could see their own way. Already in the 1830s their ethos was defined by Tocqueville under the name "individualism." By this Tocqueville meant a turning away from public affairs and the traditional athorities of church and state toward the private affairs of one's family, neighborhood, and work. The spirit of individualism was not egoism or rapacious and antisocial greed. It was an attitude of personal responsibility, minding one's own business, looking out for one's affairs, with a good deal of mutual respect and tolerance for neighbors who were likewise looking out for themselves. "Every tub on its own bottom," as the saying went. Ralph Waldo Emerson put the spirit in verse in a preface to his essay on politics (c. 1840):

When the church is social worth,
When the state-house is the hearth,
Then the perfect state is come,
The republican at home.

Emerson, who became recognized in America and throughout the world as an authentic voice of this spirit, did not publish tomes about natural rights or political economy. His perspective was religious. He thought there was a common soul—an oversoul—that all men shared in part, and he felt that one had only to put inherited tradition and convention aside, to trust and rely on oneself, to tap its inspiration. Self-culture, self-realization of one's potential, which was at the same time the potential of all mankind filtering through the individual—such was the nature and proper end of liberty, in his view. Envy and self-pity were denials of one's individual dignity. To Emerson, as to his mentor, the Unitarian clergyman William Ellery Channing, "the elevation of the laboring classes" did not mean higher living standards or better social-security programs but the enhanced dignity that came from forming high moral standards for oneself and trying to live up to them.

This sort of transcendental anarchism was an enthusiasm of Yankee idealists and preachers, perhaps, although it inspired many people across the nation and the world. A more popular and less religious view of individualism was that society was a meritocracy in which individuals were rewarded in proportion to their effort and ability. Such a democratic class structure—where careers are open to talent—was contrasted with a social structure in which occupation, wealth, privilege, and power were ascribed, as, for example, in the hereditary classes of Europe. Franklin in his autobiography tells how when he was a young man he was full of projects for a self-recruiting leadership of society. He thought such leadership might arise in a sort of fraternal order of the "free and easy"—the poised and competent— or a "united party for virtue." Jefferson wanted his country to encourage a "natural aristocracy" of talent, which he contrasted with the artificial aristocracy of birth and family. His famous plan for a comprehensive system of public education—later largely realized—was intended to recruit and train these able individuals.

At a still more concrete and practical level American individualism was embodied in the honor accorded to the "self-made man." Ben Franklin was the model for this type, as were the founders of the Astor and Vanderbilt fortunes in their generations. By 1840 aspiring politicians like Abraham Lincoln had learned to emphasize that they had been born in a humble log cabin and perhaps had as young men split rails to fence in the wilderness. The most vulgar form of this celebration was the literature of "success," books of advice about how to get ahead in the world and stories in which pluck and luck, fortified and circumscribed by the virtues of the Protestant ethic, helped young men rise from rags to respectability and perhaps to fame and fortune. The great commercial vogue of the success literature came in the late nineteenth century, when tales by Horatio Alger, among others, sold by the millions, but the essential view of life and society was well established by the 1830s.

If American individualism in its constructive sense included self-reliance, self-realization, and, more vulgarly, minding one's business and getting ahead in the world, there was also a social side to it, which Tocqueville noticed and praised highly. In Europe, he observed, social action was usually the work of some aristocrat, some lord of church or state, who saw a social problem or need and acted as a patron or authority to meet it, applying his own great resources and rallying those of his powerful associates. In America, social action resulted from a group of ordinary citizens getting together, forming an association, electing leaders, and contributing time and effort to their common cause. Tocqueville had in mind the reform movements of the 1830s—for temperance, Sunday schools, or public edu-

cation, or against slavery, among many others—but the same attitudes and methods went into the founding of churches or projects to
build a bridge or a canal, or—to look on the dark side of it—to form
a vigilante committee or administer a lynching. In this general ethos
the American individualists, more or less equal, turned from minding their own business to managing their common interests by do-it-
yourself social action that depended on responsibility and leadership
arising within a group rather than among the eminences of church
and state. In this view government followed its citizens rather than
led them. It was, as Lincoln said, government "of the people, by the
people, for the people."

At its best the psychology of individualism gave American life a
good deal of zest, dignity, and poignancy. It brought into the focus of
consciousness the choices that individuals made about the management of their affairs. Was a family well off in its style of life and place
of residence? Did the future promise well for it? Or should it look for
something better? If so, what? It was up to the family itself. The aspiration, anxiety, and general self-consciousness of such decisions
could stimulate empathy with the inner lives of other people, sympathy with their particular hopes or fears. Such feelings may have
prompted the amiability, generosity, and sentimental charity that
travelers often remarked in American life. On the other hand, the individualist could feel that he achieved his status largely by his own effort, and he might expect a similar effort from others. There is no
way to measure the incidence of such sentiments, but it is reasonable
to suppose that people in the middle and upper ranks of society felt
them more intensely, because in fact they had more choices and the
consequences of their choices were clearer. Even those who were
well off could feel the insecurity of their situation—disease and accident at the very least—and they might feel guilty about wasted opportunities. Many people believed that there was actually an advantageous discipline in a touch of poverty during childhood. It was
thought that the children of the rich were especially likely to be
spoiled and to dissipate their estate: "Shirtsleeves to shirtsleeves in
three generations," the saying went.

In this general perspective, to try and fail was unfortunate but
understandable. One could always try, try again, the same way or in
some other direction. Every self-made man had handicaps, disap-

pointments, and failures. What was wrong was not to try at all or not to try again, to sink instead into a feckless, helpless dependency. Herein lay the force of the distinction between the deserving and the undeserving poor, which was and still is important in our welfare programs. The deserving poor were those who were trying, despite their handicaps and disappointments, to escape dependency and become self-sufficient. The undeserving were willing to take advantage of others to escape their own responsibility. This notion went back to religious ideas about faith and personal responsiblity, and it was dramatized in the minds of people whose heroes were self-made men on the make.

To summarize, the social and intellectual influences at work in the years 1815–1845 had great significance for the form and development of welfare institutions. There was a remarkable degree of homogeneity among the Anglo-American citizens and a consistency in the religious, political, and economic ideas that helped them rationalize their situation. There were certain notions of social welfare that were positive in the sense that they applied to everyone, not just to the dependent, defective, and delinquent: they pointed toward general goals of social policy. Society was thought to be a collection of individuals, or rather families and breadwinners, since in fact most people lived in small kinship units for which the husband and father provided the support. Each family was trying to make its way in the world (and very important, to provide for its children) as its breadwinner saw fit. Government was a convenient device to assert or defend individual rights—usually, in fact, the rights of the citizen and breadwinner. The economy was a big marketplace where breadwinners sought their own advantage without much collective restraint or guidance. Wealth and social status were supposed to show achievement and to be a consequence of self-discipline and family discipline. There was no sharp formal definition of classes; families were distributed along a continuum of imperceptible degrees between relative wealth and poverty. There was a decided spirit of equality among individuals and families. Social action was largely a voluntary do-it-yourself arrangement among individuals with a common interest.

Such beliefs called forth and sanctioned the initiatives and energies of the nineteenth century. They built the economy and made the nation seem like a country of opportunity and freedom for the ordinary man. They furnished an exciting demonstration of the benefits of liberal capitalism and political democracy.

But what of "the least of these"—the dependent, defective, and delinquent? For them there were charity and correction. At best these might be planned and administered with religious concern and solicitude. In that case there was often more emphasis on the responsibilities of the helpers than on their effects on the helped. At worst they were perfunctory or cruel. It would take two generations to gain support for a scientific philanthropy that would look beyond the personal relationship between helper and helped to the social causes of personal problems and would affirm more critical and less moralistic notions of treatment. The main outlook in this scientific view would be for large-scale public programs aimed at basic circumstances of poverty and deviance, and it would therefore contradict doctrines established in the ascendancy of liberalism. Among these doctrines were the notion that the class structure in America represented a sort of meritocracy; that government and administration were best decentralized to local communities; that it was generally unwise for government to interfere much in the play of market forces; and that voluntary arrangements were likely to have a better spirit and better results than public agencies.

Chapter

4

The Poor Law, 1815–1845

THE STORY OF practical provision for the dependent, defective, and delinquent in the years 1815–1845 is largely a blank. Our main sources are legislation, reports by administrators, and studies by reformers. Legislation tells us what was supposed to be; administrative accounts are typically perfunctory or defensive; and reformers concentrated on exposing faults and advocating causes. Ordinary administrative circumstances and events are left to the imagination. Moreover, both theory and practice rested on contemporary assumptions about the nature of the community and the social duties and rights within the community, and these must be made clear.

As a concrete image and a practical matter, people thought of society and government in terms of the locality in which they lived. State government was remote; it was a body of legislators meeting for a few weeks every second year, passing laws that told local officials to bestir themselves. It is difficult to imagine now how isolated and self-sufficient local communities were. Most families raised their own vegetables, butchered their own meat, and milked their own cow; crossroads stores carried items like salt, sugar, tea, and tobacco. Even a town house often had a sizable garden and a cow in the barn. News consisted of neighborhood gossip, and church affairs were the most frequent occasion for organized social life.

The concept of community that ordered these experiences was still, after two centuries in the new world, the European (specifically English) village, for what alternative was there? Accordingly, it was assumed that neighbors would have the same cultural background; Irish, German, and other immigrants drew off by themselves. Church and government, public and private, would be naturally linked in common life. There would be some sort of patrician leadership; a few unfortunate dependents, crippled, perhaps, or widows; and probably some ne'er-do-wells or rogues.

This traditional picture of the community, which implied a stable population, a well-established culture, and a hierarchical class structure, was often incongruent with the new world, where settlements were relatively fast-changing and formless. After 1815 it seemed more and more archaic. The growing market economy pressed in on local self-sufficiency and directed men's attention to centers of trade. It brought potent influences on state government with regard to transportation, banking, and economic regulation. The organization and reorganization of political parties gave new zest and scope to the competition for votes, in which statewide and even national linkages were advantageous. In building their congregations, evangelists competed with established preachers. Generally and very unevenly, local communities lost their central place in contemporary thought about common problems and resources. On the one hand, individuals became more enterprising; on the other, some larger societal organization began to seem more significant. It is helpful to look at practical arrangements for social welfare in the perspective of these changing features of social life.

The most comprehensive and positive responses to the disorganizing factors just mentioned were the dozens of utopian communities that took form during these years. In general, they illustrated the freedom and opportunity that prevailed in the nation and its reliance on voluntary association. No power forced these people to join together, nor did any stop them, so long as their communal life did not outrage conventional decency (which it sometimes did). In outer form their little societies looked much like rural villages; in this framework they established fellowships that guaranteed cradle-to-grave security as a matter of right and personal solicitude, without relying on the elaborate schemes and bureaucratic administration that have characterized the twentieth century. In some respects their goals were similar to ours, but their means were different, just because of the sentiments that underlay their community rights and duties.

Some of the communitarians, like those who settled in Amana, Iowa, or the Rappites in Indiana, were German sectarians who obviously tried to reconstruct the European village. Others, like the Shakers (the largest and longest lived of these groups), the Perfectionists at Oneida, New York, and the Transcendentalists at Brook Farm, were Anglo-Americans but drew their membership from different regions or classes. Most were united by peculiar, even fanatic, religious doctrines, but some, like Robert Owen's colony at New Harmony or the two score "phalanxes," formed in the model prescribed by the French reformer, Charles Fourier, were aggressively secular. Most failed, but many earned not only security but substantial wealth. Somewhat similar to these groups were the Mormons, who gathered strength in the years before 1845 and brought to the territory of Utah enduring forms of the New England town and its cooperative enterprises.

Unlike twentieth-century welfare programs, which typically meet a specific category of need or problematic behavior, the communitarians went directly to the heart of the matter. They held their property in common, at least in part, so that everyone had a share, as in a family. They also arranged strong indoctrination and social control to ensure that everyone felt a personal and mutual responsibility for the common life. Their discipline demanded the ascetic virtues of the Protestant ethic, excepting its worldly emphasis on competition and "success." These places were much like monasteries, with frequent occasions for confession, criticism, and correction of misbehavior, often by techniques resembling present-day encounter groups.

Obviously these communities realized ideals and offered satisfactions that had deep roots in our culture and have a continuing appeal, and it is not clear why they did not multiply and adapt themselves to changing circumstances. Doubtless the concept of the village commune became increasingly archaic in economic, social, and intellectual terms. Economically, the communitarians did not meet the market demand for large-scale and opportunistic investment and production. They wanted not economic progress but relatively simple and stable modes of work that would enhance their common life. Still, they might have adapted if it were not for the prerequisite of a religious or quasi-religious conviction that separated them from the world of nonbelievers, and the strong self-discipline and social control required by the common life. A sympathetic observer and historian, writing in 1874, thought that many communes did succeed in providing security and comfort. His main criticism was that they were parochial, boring, lacking the stimulation and culture of the urban metropolis.[1] By that time it was apparent that the country's future lay in geat diverse cities, not rural villages, and utopians of the next generation would think of a national revolution, perhaps violent but preferably peaceful, rather than groups of people withdrawing to make themselves an example to others.

In any case the communitarians in the years 1815–1845 gave concrete expression to many notions underlying welfare institutions in the period. They elaborated the tradition that social relations were best ordered in the form of a face-to-face community much like a rural village; that the group was properly united by a common moral authority—usually the Bible and supplementary divine revelations, rightly interpreted—which laid down how people ought to act and respond to others; that within this framework people were more or less equal children of God, stewards of His bounty, sharing in it among the vicissitudes of life.

The communitarians were an extreme. In the rest of the rural democracy, social solidarity and sharing were ideals left mostly to the individual conscience. Here the poor law was a testimonial, more or less respected, to the ancient order of society. It was part of our English and, beyond that, our Christian heritage. If people had been good Christians, no public poor law would have been necessary. Private almsgiving and congregational charity would have done the job. In fact in England poor relief had been left to individuals, churches, and monasteries until the sixteenth century. There was then no public relief, tax supported and administered by government officials. Between 1534 and 1601 there were major changes in this situation. England turned Protestant, and its hierarchy of bishops and priests became responsible to the king rather than the Pope. Furthermore, English monasteries, which inclined toward Rome, were secularized, ending their important work of poor relief. Hence, the king and Parliament began passing legislation to help the local congregations—the parishes of the Church of England—do the job better. Laws gave parish officials who looked after church property the power to tax the congregation if voluntary contributions were not sufficient;

1. Charles Nordoff, *Communistic Societies of the United States; From Personal Visit and Observation* (New York: Hilary House, 1961, first published 1875), pp. 416–18.

other regulations governed the administration of parish relief and eligibility for such relief. These statutes, enacted between 1534 and 1601, were summarized and codified in the second chapter (i.e., act) of the 43rd Parliament of Queen Elizabeth, held in 1601. When Englishmen settled America and felt the need for some similar provision, colonial legislators reenacted versions of the act just as they followed English patterns in their other legislation. In these forms it remained our fundamental provision for the needy until the Great Depression of the 1930s.

What principles laid down in 1601 seemed relevant more than three centuries later, despite the great changes of society and thought in the intervening years? One was *public responsibility*. This meant simply that the law designated officials (called "overseers of the poor") and charged them with a duty. The parish, or whatever local government, had to appoint such officials, and they had to relieve the poor. The central government (acting through the courts) might punish localities that did not carry out its intentions. This was not like the situation in France, nor like that in Quebec and Louisiana, where Frenchmen had settled. There matters were left to private individuals and the church, in the older pattern.

A second principle was *local responsibility*. In England the parish was a geographic area as well as a congregation; every part of the realm was served by a parish church (which might be quite distant in sparsely settled areas), just as, later on, every part of the land would be in a postal district served by a local post office. The parish congregation was held to be responsible for its own poor. It should not push them out on other parishes; if they became needy elsewhere, it should receive them back. This idea was formalized in the settlement law of 1662 (also brought to America), which laid down the conditions by which a newcomer could gain a settlement: renting a substantial property for some stated length of time or paying taxes or serving as a public official of the place. The law supposed that others, looked upon as transients, should return (or be returned) to their own parish for relief. In its assumption that everyone was rooted in his place of settlement and its denial of the fact and desirability of increasing mobility of labor, especially among the poor, it was a backward-looking and cruel feature of relief.

A third principle was *relatives' responsibility*. The parish did not have to provide if there were parents, grandparents, or (adult) children or grandchildren who could do so. Officials of course looked into this possibility.

Finally, the overseers were authorized to put the poor to work. Children were bound out as apprentices or unfree workers; there was a market for this kind of child labor. Adults might be employed at various tasks, in a workhouse or outside. This provision went back to a fundamental notion underlying the poor law, the "work ethic," which held that people ought to support themselves insofar as they were able, that they ought not to live in idleness by begging from those who did work, and that there were degress of responsibility between complete self-sufficiency and complete dependency: dependents ought to help themselves as much as they could, even if it were only a little.

In short, people were expected to look out for themselves and their families. If they got into trouble, they would turn first to their relatives and neighbors, just as we do today. If these resources were inadequate, the community was morally obliged to share with them through the poor law, but on the other hand officials were justified in seeing that individuals or members of the family did not evade their responsibilities. The poor law is sometimes said to have established a right to relief, but in its historical context it long antedated the Lockean notion of individual rights and was originally founded on religious obligations and mutual responsibilities.

In England the poor law was enacted by Parliament, the national legislature; in America, by the several colonies (and later territories and states as they were formed). Consequently poor relief in the United States was seen as a state rather than a federal problem. The state poor laws, like their prototype, made the local communities responsible and delegated administration to them. There was no state agency to supervise localities until 1863 (in Massachusetts), and in fact very little state supervision until the 1920s. The principal check was an occasional investigation of a scandal.

As for practical arrangements, there were in general two types. In New England, and wherever Yankees went as they moved across the country, communities were organized in "towns" or townships—a settlement and the surrounding land. Settlers had a parish church (often Congregational) in the English pattern. Town business was handled by part-time unpaid citizen committees, including the overseers of the poor. Elsewhere the pattern of settlement was more scattered—isolated farms and a crossroads store and church, rather than the compact New England town. In some states the Anglican or Dutch Reformed Church had been established and had tried to maintain a territorial parish organization, but by 1815 the church had long since lost practical importance. Except among Yankees, the county was the center of government for poor relief as for other local services, such as roads or criminal justice. Here the elected county supervisors or commissioners had the authority to help those in need. Often these gentry were elected from separate districts and each handled problems in his district as they arose, referring momentous or expensive decisions to the collective body.

The poor law revision in Pennsylvania was particularly important because it was copied in the law governing the Northwest Territory and in the acts of the great states carved out of it or settled farther to the west. Northern Pennsylvania had been settled largely by Yankees who held to the town system; in the rest of the state the county system was usually favored. The law accommodated both arrangements.

In the cities—seaports or river ports—the town fathers usually delegated authority to a poormaster, and often there were specialized institutions and hospitals for the homeless sick. The big picture is a varied response depending on local problems and traditions, whatever the law.

In the typical case under the poor law as it appeared in the great rural expanses, the breadwinner was incapacitated or the family broken and the ordinary informal sources of support were not available. Of course the general plane of living was very low by today's standards. To be needy was not to lack the means of decent life but to face a threat to survival.

If a needy family had a home and was able to help itself but unable to support itself completely, the overseers might give it an allowance or arrange to pay its bills at the store or its rent. This was called "home relief" or, if the family got food, rent, or medical care rather than money, "relief in kind." If families or individuals were unable to care for themselves or needed supervision (in the case of the mentally disordered, for example), the overseers fitted them into some functioning family unit and paid their host for the service. If there were many such cases, the overseers would seize upon a time when the community was likely to assemble (election day, perhaps) and conduct an auction or "vendue" to dispose of their charges. They would present the cases to the citizens and ask for bids for their care. The low bidder would get the contract and the responsibility. Often bidders would undertake to care for several or all of the cases and in effect operate a private poorhouse on a public subsidy. Sometimes the caretakers were themselves on the margin of dependency, and in effect they were relieved along with their charges by a single grant. Sometimes they hoped to put the paupers to appropriate and useful chores. When the overseers delegated the care of the poor to one or two households, this was called "farming out the poor." This approach was advantageous because it simplified the overseers' work, the budgeting of costs, and also such supervision of the arrangements as the overseers chose to exercise. The overseers also "bound out" (i.e., apprenticed) orphans or the children of those on relief.

As both population and problems increased in some of the little communities, the expedient of farming out the poor became less satisfactory. Here the notion of a public almshouse or poorhouse took hold. Its proponents had several aims. One was humanitarian, to end the humiliating and embarrassing auction of the poor, the mercenary bidding on human misery: much better to have an established place of refuge for these unfortunates, with an official responsible for their care. So in eighteenth-century America religious or ethnic groups sponsored a few private almshouses to look out for their own, and a few public bodies took this step. It was easy to see the possible economy in such a institution: almshouse keepers might devise ways to put inmates to helping one another or perhaps to some elementary work for self-support or profit (oakum picking, for example: pull discarded ropes into fibers used for calking seams in wooden ships). In rural places authorities might buy a "poor farm" where residents helped with chores as they were able (this was a different meaning of "farm" from the delegation or "farming out" of the care of the poor). So much for the impotent or handicapped. With regard to children and the able-bodied poor, it was easy to imagine a program that would realize their potential and train them for the future. This training might be work managed so strictly that it would deter loafers from taking advantage of charity. In the sense of an agency for training and deterrence, the institution was called a "house of industry" or a "workhouse."

These ideas, all familiar in 1815, soon began to take on a new urgency. One growing problem was that of dealing with the people who were lost in the increasing stream of immigration and migration; another, the need for assistance to manufacturers and shippers who had to face new competition from England after the War of 1812 and, later, the Panic of 1819, which affected commerce, especially in the West. A third factor was the experience of England, then in the throes of the industrial revolution, where various schemes for the management of the poor and needy had been tried, studied, and found wanting, and where, in the ascendancy of economic liberalism, the problems of poverty and pauperism were receiving systematic and critical scrutiny.

In the postwar crisis of 1817 in New York, businessmen, physicians, and clergymen—men who could see the problems, felt some patrician and Christian responsibility to face them, and knew what the English were thinking—set up a Society for the Prevention of Pauperism. Similar organizations of concerned citizens appeared in Philadelphia in 1817 and in Baltimore (the third-largest city in the country) in 1820. These voluntary efforts were followed by public commissions to investigate the poor laws in Massachusetts (1821), New York (1824), and the City of Philadelphia (1827). Taken together, these bodies and their reports represented a new approach to new conditions. Whereas eighteenth-century discussion about the needy had been mostly religious—charity sermons to encourage giving, for example—in the nineteenth-century people took a harder look. They asked what were the causes of need, what might be done to prevent it, and what might be done to get dependents back to self-sufficiency. They tried to take a systematic, critical view and to develop their plans in a rational way. They took steps toward a science of social welfare and a profession of social work.

Although these people often spoke of "the poor" and "poverty," the center of their concern was the extreme of indigence: "paupers" and "pauperism," or dependence on public or private charity. Mere poverty was familiar among the "laboring poor," who lived from hand to mouth. Dependency was different and more important because, according to the teaching of liberal economic theory, the money spent on charitable relief had to come from somewhere, and it either reduced the amount that was available for self-sufficient workers to share with their families or—equally serious—reduced the amount that wealthy capitalists would otherwise invest in labor-saving and wealth-producing investments. Although charity was certainly a moral responsibility, it was also, in terms of economic theory, a burden on the self-supporting and productive classes and a drag on economic progress.

Just as liberal economists thought that universal poverty was not an inevitable condition of society, that many people might escape it, that by studying political economy in a rational spirit leaders could learn how a nation could produce more and therefore have more to share, so they believed that, through analysis and wise policy, pauperism or dependency might be much reduced. Given the moral assumptions of the Protestant ethic that guided their own lives, it is not surprising that these early students of pauperism found that many of its causes indicated that the needy one himself was to blame, partly or wholly, for his plight.

In its first report (1818) the New York Society for the Prevention of Pauperism listed nine causes of dependency: ignorance (the pauper did not see the opportunities in his situation or did not know how to take advantage of them); idleness (he preferred to loaf); intemperance in drinking (he could not control himself); "want of economy" (he spent his money foolishly); imprudent and hasty marriage (before the couple was prepared to undertake the responsibilities of family life and parenthood); lotteries (which tempted the poor with the hope of easy gains); pawnbrokers (who encouraged the poor into personal debt at high interest rates); houses of prostitution (a distraction from proper family life and a threat to health); and finally the numerous charitable organizations of the city (which allowed themselves to be exploited by crafty beggars).[2]

The practical proposals of this first report were the following:

1. Divide the city into small districts and appoint district visitors who would acquaint themselves with indigent families "to advise them with respect to their business, the education of their children, the economy of their houses" and "to administer encouragement or admonition, as they may find occasion." This proposal looked backward to the informal, personal social controls of the village.
2. Help the "laboring classes" make the most of their earnings by

2. Society for the Prevention of Pauperism in the City of New York, *First Annual Report* (New York, 1818), reprinted in Ralph E. Pumphrey, and Murial W. Pumphrey, *The Heritage of American Social Work* (New York: Columbia University Press, 1961), pp. 59–62.

promoting savings banks, mutual-benefit societies, and life insurance.

3. Enforce settlement laws more strictly.
4. Prohibit street begging (by which paupers could appeal to the undiscriminating generosity of bypassers).
5. Provide employment in houses of industry or materials for the poor to work on at home, as they ordinarily did in the system of "domestic industry."

These observations about the causes of pauperism and the practical proposals that resulted were plausible enough so that intelligent and well-meaning people would often reiterate them during the century, and much of our story will show how and why they proved to be superficial. For now it is enough to note that these early appeals did not attract much support or have much consequence. In 1823 the New York Society changed from its broad goal to a program of encouraging free education for children and a "house of refuge" for juvenile delinquents, and soon thereafter it expired.

The state commissions in Massachusetts (1821) and New York (1824) had a more specific charge—to study the administration of public charity under the poor law—and came to more specific recommendations. The Massachusetts report discussed the possibility of simply eliminating public relief, as some English theorists had proposed, but it recognized that "the present system of . . . public or compulsory provision for the poor is too deeply riveted in the . . . moral sentiment of our people to be loosened by theories, however plausible. . . ."[3] Instead, it endorsed another English argument that opposed *home relief* and favored *indoor relief* in "Alms Houses having the character of Work Houses or Houses of Industry." Such institutions with their strict regimen would discourage mere loafers from applying for help, it was thought, and would at least employ the poor in partial self-support. Later reports repeated this logic, which supported the ongoing change from "farming out" the poor to building regular public institutions. So, in the 1820s and 1830s, the county poorhouse or township poor farm became part of the American landscape.

---

3. Massachusetts, General Court, Committee on Pauper Laws, *Report* (1821), reprinted in Pumphrey, *Heritage of American Social Work*, pp. 62–6; the quote is from p. 65. Other reports of this period are reprinted in *The Almshouse Experience: Collected Reports* (New York: Arno Press, 1971).

These early proponents of indoor relief had plans that were more radical than they were actually able to effect. They had in mind a general system in which every community would have its poorhouse, and accordingly outdoor relief and farming out the poor would be largely eliminated. The new institutions would be run in a strict, economical, and deterrent fashion under some central supervision. This was the way the English were heading, toward their momentous poor law reform act of 1834, which made the workhouse the instrument to deter pauperism.[4]

Ironically, however, as the English poor law reform, centering on the workhouse, was debated and put into operation in the 1830s, the American movement died out. In America the poorhouse appeared in places where local authorities thought it would be cheaper or decidedly less trouble than home relief or farming out the poor. No central authority supervised its administration. Sometimes it was businesslike, sometimes not. In any case it was more custodial than deliberately deterrent. One reason that poor law reform died out in America was the notable prosperity of the 1830s. Another, of more enduring significance, was the hostility English workingmen expressed toward the workhouse (which they called "the bastille"). Because the English laboring class did not have the vote, the middle class there was able to sustain the reform. In America most white men had the vote and the middle class was much less distinct and militant. Furthermore, English immigrants were often prominent in such labor organizations as took form. In these circumstances neither Whigs nor Democrats would have found much advantage in pursuing the notion of workhouses for deterrence. In any case it was not pursued.

The American situation as of 1837 was summarized by the English traveler Harriet Martineau in her account, *Society in America*. A conscientious observer, she was already a famous advocate and popularizer of English liberalism, in particular its poor law reform. "The pauperism of the United States is, to the observation of a stranger, nothing at all," she said.

> It is confined to the ports, emigrants making their way back into the country, the families of intemperate or disabled men, and unconnected

4. In English usage, soon adopted in America, "indoor relief" meant relief for people who lived in an institution, subject to its discipline; "outdoor relief" meant relief for people who lived outside the institution in their own homes.

women, who depend on their own exertions. The amount altogether is far from commensurate with the charity of the community; and it is to be hoped that the curse of a legal [i.e., public] charity, at least to the able-bodied, will be avoided in a country where it certainly cannot become necessary within any assignable time.[5]

This was the situation in the country at large, but already conditions in "the ports"—Boston, New York, Philadelphia, Baltimore, and New Orleans—foreshadowed much trouble. Meanwhile, however, there were also hopeful signs as men began to distinguish among different kinds of problem people and devise special institutions to deal with them in a more rational and practical way.

5. Harriet Martineau, *Society in America*, 2 vols. (New York, 1837), II, 289.

Chapter

5

The Promise of the Institution,

1815–1845

Reform MOVEMENTS IN the years 1815–1845 created several types of institutions that were later pulled into the field of "charity and correction." In general, they helped relieve overcrowding in the local almhouses and jails and provided more specialized and rational treatment for the unfortunate inmates. Examples of such institutions were state and county penitentiaries; houses of refuge for neglected or delinquent youngsters; schools for the deaf, dumb, and blind; general hospitals; and asylums for lunatics. In the end they disappointed the hopes of their sponsors, as their successors disappoint us today. But it is important to recognize how the historical context led people to see promise in such institutions. Established in a mood of sympathy and hope, they often embodied clear insights into ways of helping or dealing with problem people.

In those days of rural democracy the punishment and "correction" of offenders against the law were the subject of hopeful schemes. Alexis de Tocqueville himself came to study our prisons, and many other foreign travelers compared them favorably with those in Europe. The Americans had a great advantage in penal institutions inasmuch as there was little surplus and often a decided shortage of labor in the expanding nation. In big seaports, of course, there were anonymous transients and plentiful occasion for crime and vice. Near the frontier, where settlement was sparse, there were rootless violent men who formed gangs of rustlers, highwaymen, or river pirates, although that phase soon passed. But most citizens lived in communities in which people could recognize and watch over each other and keep a sharp eye on strangers. Here were more opportunities for work than for crime.

There is no empirical research on rural crime control in this period—on the incidence of various types of crime or on law enforcement. Anecdotes and legislation, however, indicate plainly that crime control, like poor relief, was a part-time, amateur affair. To generalize broadly, there were two teams of lawmen. In sizable villages there was a justice of the peace who tried and sentenced minor offenders and had various powers in civil law (he could conduct marriages, for example). For help he had a constable who caught, guarded, and punished offenders. Of course the justice and the constable relied heavily on their neighbors for assistance. The officials were paid fees or portions of fines, a system that gave them some incentive: the more actions they took, the larger their income. For most offenses in rural life—disorderly conduct, drunkenness, vagrancy, trespass, and petty theft, for example—this team was sufficient.

For more serious cases involving the risk of substantial punishment, civil rights required that there be a more formal process. Hence, there was a backup team of lawmen: the county court, sometimes made up of several justices of the peace acting as a body, and the sheriff. The sheriff was, technically, the executive officer of the county court. He or his deputies guarded prisoners awaiting trial (and material witnesses, if they were held), called the jury, and executed the sentence of the court if the trial led to conviction. The sheriff was also a peace officer, like the constable, and sometimes went after lawbreakers himself, perhaps organizing the neighbors into a posse. This was especially true where settlement was so sparse that there were no village constables. (Under territorial government, where state and county courts were not yet in existence, the executive of the federal court was called a *marshal*, and local constables sometimes had that title.) The sheriff also had many tasks in civil cases (evictions, for example), and he often oversaw arrangements for conducting elections—a strategic job in politics.

So, at the county seat, beside the county courthouse, under the eye of the county sheriff stood that foundation of our penal system, the county jail. For each prisoner each day the sheriff received fees, as he did for his other tasks. Somewhere around the courthouse square there was an inn that made a point of catering to the legal guild and contestants at law when court was in session. It also catered to the occasional inmates of the county jail. Sometimes the innkeeper was also the sheriff or had cozy relations with the sheriff, which helps account for the drunkenness that occurred among prisoners who could afford it.

The county jail appeared early in colonial days, but until the 1790s imprisonment was mostly an incident in the prosecution of crime. Suspects were held pending and during trial (unless they could afford to get out on bail), but when the trial ended so did confinement in jail. The innocent went free (assuming that they could pay their fees to the jailer; otherwise they stayed until they worked out some way of paying or the county picked up the costs). The guilty were clamped in the stocks or pillory for public humiliation; tied to a whipping post and flogged; branded with a red-hot iron; mutilated, as by cropping an ear; or in many cases, for serious crimes such as rustling, arson, or murder, promptly hanged in a public ceremony. During the eighteenth century such terroristic corporal punishments were challenged from two sides. Pietistic religious attitudes, spread widely by both Quakers and revivalists, tended to sympathy with the criminal, although not, of course, with the crime ("I was in prison and ye came unto me"; Jesus had suffered a criminal's death on the cross). Many colonists were in fact transported convicts sent from England to get around its barbarous penal law and also to alleviate the American labor shortage. But many God-fearing Quakers and other good citizens had been thrown in jail and punished for their opinions about religion and war. To this sentimental religious sympathy were added the reflections of European philosophes about the ways in which tyrants abused the criminal law to punish criticism of their tranny—an application of the notion of the rights of man to the rights of suspects. This sentiment found strong support in revolutionary America, where one side's liberty was the other side's subversion.

The enlightenment critique—for example, Cesar Beccaria's influential *Essay on Crimes and Punishments* (1764)—advanced definite beliefs about the administration of justice: crimes should be defined clearly and systematically; the law should be codified so the suspect could better defend himself against unjust accusations. Punishment should fit the crime in an explicit and equalitarian way so that the offender could understand his risk and the judge could not be arbitrary or play favorites in passing sentence. Punishment should look beyond vengeance or retaliation to make the criminal a good citizen. These premises led to the policy: Imprison the guilty for different periods of time, related in a rational way to the seriousness of their offense, and put them to constructive tasks, partly for self-support in the lockup, partly to train them in good habits and some useful skill.

There were differences between the pietistic attitude toward the offender and that of the enlightenment, but in America they were mutually reinforcing. Leadership in prison reform came from the Quakers, still a potent element in Pennsylvania and in Philadelphia, the greatest city of the new nation, and influential too in neighboring New Jersey and New York. They were in close touch with their coreligionists in England and familiar with the enlightenment critique. Accordingly, they set the pattern that was followed elsewhere: first the codification of the criminal law to prescribe fines or imprisonment at hard labor or solitary confinement instead of corporal punishments; then the erection of a state prison, which was designed to employ the long-term convict at hard labor. This was the idea of the Walnut Street Prison in Philadelphia (1790), which was more or less imitated in the state prisons of New York (1797), New Jersey (1797), Virginia (1800), Massachusetts (1804), and later on in most states.

In practice, the new system seems to have relieved the burden on the county sheriff. He no longer had to execute brutal public punishments on convicts, and he got rid of his most troublesome prisoners by sending them off to the state penitentiary. In the process he or his deputy took the offender to the state institution. The trip earned him a fee and afforded him an opportunity for political business, especially if the prison was near the state capital, which was usually the case. Meanwhile, however, relatively harmless petty offenders, locked up for a few days or months, stayed in the county jails, where their presence earned fees for their jailers. As for the inmates of the state penitentiary (as a prison for labor was called), it was expected that they would furnish a convenient labor force for the introduction of manufactures, a point that interested many farsighted merchants. Indeed, during the years when the Embargo and the War of 1812 disturbed U.S. trade with Europe, they did sometimes prosper, along with other "infant industries."

These first penitentiaries were poorly planned for their mission. After 1815 their deficiencies became more obvious, particularly in fast-growing Pennsylvania and New York. On one hand, crime increased, stimulated by all the factors that also made pauperism grow in these years, and prisons became overcrowded; on the other hand, the wartime market for prison manufactures collapsed. Moreover, it appears that by long experience the inmates had worked out their own social organizations, which put cliques of their leaders in virtual control of the prison. Consequently there was much discussion of new prisons and systems of discipline that would better realize the hopes for imprisonment at hard labor as a means of reforming the convict.

Two schools of thought about prison discipline divided these hopes. One, led by the Boston Prison Discipline Society, advocated the practices that developed at Auburn Prison (New York) between 1816 and 1821, known as the "silent system." The other, supported by philanthropists around Philadelphia and favored by many other observers, including Tocqueville and Dorothea Dix, endorsed the plan of the famous prison at Cherry Hill, near Philadelphia, opened in 1831; this was known as the "separate system." Vehement as the disagreement was—for the opposing parties accused each other of stupidity and bad faith in a most intemperate fashion—the two systems had much in common. Both groups recognized that the great problem with the older prisons was that they had allowed too much free association among the inmates, so that the worst could influence the others and could easily organize to exploit them and dominate the institution. To break up these evil associations, the reformers proposed to separate the inmates from one another. At Auburn each convict slept in his own cell at night (in the old jails they had lived together in big rooms, and solitary cells were only for isolation and severe punishment); during the day prisoners worked and ate together, but in strict silence so they could not communicate. When they moved from their cells to the work place or dining room they shuffled along in the "lockstep"—one hand on the shoulder of the man ahead, head facing the guard, eyes downcast. Violations of the rule of silence were chastised by flogging or solitary confinement in a dark cell. At Cherry Hill, under the "separate system," the isolation of the prisoners was, in theory, complete. They lived and worked in their individual cells, which opened on a small exercise yard.

Under either system the offender was supposed to have occasion to reflect on the evil of his ways. Separated from bad associations and the licentious camaraderie of traditional jail life, the terrific boredom and loneliness of these silent tombs would induce him to read— perhaps even learn to read—the Bible that was thoughtfully placed in his cell. Warden, chaplain, and philanthropic visitors would seize this opportunity to teach him that he had a divine soul and an eternal destiny, to urge him toward conviction of his sin, repentance, and the hope of God's merciful forgiveness. In this way the institution would make possible a definite and complete break with his past and offer a definite and constructive redirection. It was an organized inducement of the character change typical of religious conversions, by which even law-abiding and respectable people were brought to see their sinfulness and to enter the strait gate and narrow way that led to salvation. Wardens liked to tell graphic stories in which guilt-ridden desperados tearfully confessed how they went wrong (usually very early in life), resolved to change, and did.

In sum, the functions of the state prisons were to substitute hard labor for corporal punishment, to get dangerous offenders with long sentences out of the county jails, to keep them from bad influences in prison and under a strict discipline, to encourage them to reflect on their evil behavior, to get them to work so as to pay for their own support (including the cost of their jail fees and transportation to the prison), and, it was hoped, to provide a surplus for their future. Given a good warden, a conscientious staff, an adequate physical plant, and a market for the prisoner's manufactures, the operation was at least orderly and low cost. Where the warden and staff were weak, the facilities inadequate (too few cells, for example), and the market for prison products poor, there was ample room for failure and scandal. In any case there was a much more rational system than in earlier institutions, and compared with later years there was considerable agreement on principles: it was supposed that the behavior of offenders followed from their free will but that the environment was also important as either a temptation or a moral inspiration;

prisons should punish in a constructive way by influencing the offender to mend his ways; and the labor of the convicts should pay the
costs of the prison.

Two other innovations in this period also served to remove certain classes of convicts from the local jails. They appeared in the big
seaports and foreshadowed a large number of similar institutions that
accompanied urbanization. The county Bridewell or workhouse took
prisoners with short terms, up to a year, perhaps, whose labor time
would not be worth the trip to the state prison. Mostly these offenders
were sentenced to a few days or months for vagrancy, disorderly conduct, or petty theft. They were not very dangerous, and it might be to
the advantage of local politicians to provide a penitentiary for them
instead of keeping them idle in jail. Usually the sheriff got his take
whether they were in jail or in the workhouse; in the latter they
might be at least partly self-supporting. Often they quarried and
crushed stone used in construction, or they might work on a farm.
There was usually some separation of inmates and discipline in the
fashion of the state prison, but less systematic and strict.

The "house of refuge" or "school of industry" took juveniles.
Some of these were lawbreakers: often juries were unwilling to convict them, especially the younger ones, if it meant that they would go
to jail or prison; so, without a special place to send them, they might
simply go free. Many were not criminals but were separated from
their families and on their own. In rural communities they might be
discovered when a family fell on poor relief. Then the overseers
would bind them out to some local family that wanted a chore boy or
girl or an apprentice. If they committed a misdemeanor they came
before the justice of the peace, who, if their family was unable to
manage them, would bind them out to some family that could. As
cities grew, the number of such children increased and the market for
their services decreased, so for want of a better alternative they were
often sent to the almshouse or jail. The house of refuge was an alternative, intended to remove the youngsters from such unpromising associations and to train them in good attitudes and habits. It appeared
first in New York City in 1825, shortly thereafter in Boston and Philadelphia, then in other sizable cities.

Unlike the almshouse and the jail, the refuge had a program for
the children. They were regulated much as in a penitentiary, with
every activity going by the book and bell. Often there was a rule of

silence. Discipline was strict. The long hours of industrial training or work were cut in half, however, to allow for academic schooling and physical exercise. For guidance there was much didactic moralizing, just as in all schooling of the time. Moreover, masters were supposed to show a sympathetic and constructive spirit toward their charges. Today these places seem grimly regimented, but their general conception was similar to that of the residential boarding schools that educational reformers were envisioning for the sons of the rich. In both cases education was supposed to be more than classroom instruction or learning special skills; it was intended to foster general patterns of habit and character. A rational plan was for a total style of life that would mold and direct the impressionable youth in the right way. Proponents of residential boarding schools wanted to bring forth Christian scholars and gentlemen whereas the refuge masters tried only for ordinary morality and competence, but both assumed the promise of the institution as a rational means to their end. In any case the refuge made more sense than the pernicious associations of the almshouse or the jail; Tocqueville was particularly enthusiastic about the idea and its possibility as a preventive of adult crime.

In two respects the "house of refuge" differed from the state prison or county workhouse. It was a "private" agency, established and maintained by voluntary contributions, and it was modeled on a school. In these ways it was like the schools for the deaf and dumb and for the blind that were also set up in these years. Taken together, these institutions were part of much larger movements of the time: a general concern for humanitarian reform and a more specific effort to rationalize and improve the formal education of young people.

We do not yet have a historical interpretation that links these developments in a definite and clear way. There is no doubt that religion was an important element in the creation of the special schools. It inclined people toward sympathy with suffering and toward a sense of personal responsibility to do something about it. But religion might—and traditionally did—indicate merely that handicapped people and vagrant children had a special license to beg and that the fortunate had a special responsibility to give them alms. Or some rich man or monastic order might provide an institution, but it would be merely custodial. The founders of a school for delinquent or defective children not only felt a responsibility to help but gave their impulse a deliberate and constructive cast that was new. Their religious inspiration was personal—they felt a calling, a yearning to be of service, and one of their objectives was to bring to the scamp or the handicapped the inspiration or consolation of religion—but they often sensed quite shrewdly the impersonal factors, the failures of society, as it were. We have seen that the promise of the institution, like that of the utopian community, was to create a total environment that would furnish wholesome circumstances for change: the institution or utopian community would do the job that the existing community—the family, neighborhood, economy, or polity—was not doing. Together with this philanthropic and altruistic motive there was also a prudential one: rational helping would not only reduce unnecessary suffering but, if it worked, reduce the long-run costs of care and improve the social order.

This combination of philanthropy and prudence extended with particular force to education. Common schools would, it was thought, help the common man get ahead and discipline and train him for his civic responsibility in a democratic society. Academies and colleges would open careers for the uncommon man and train an aristocracy of talent. In this perspective the schools for the delinquent and defective that appeared in 1815–1845 were part of a much larger movement for schools of all sorts. Like the academies and colleges created in such large numbers during these years, they were sponsored by private citizens who saw a need. They were for uncommon youth who needed special help. They represented a creative overlap of the religious and philanthropic impulse with the exciting innovations in formal education taken as a whole.

In short, these years saw both an increased sensitivity to need and an improved prospect of benefit. These trends were especially clear to people in the business and professional class, who were more than ordinarily conscious of social change and eager to direct it. For the rationalization of charities was much less advanced than that of the schools, and both were much less impressive and momentous that the great specialization of economic institutions (as the nation turned more toward market exchange) or of organized religion, with its sectarian institutions, theological schools, publishing programs, and missionary ventures. Certainly humanitarian reform flourished best among New Englanders, whose economic, religious, and educational institutions were more specialized and rationalized than those of other groups in the nation.

Regarding education for the handicapped, attention went first to the deaf ("and dumb"), perhaps because they were a much larger class than the blind. Most of them were infant victims of the terrible fevers that ravaged the populace during these years (scarlet fever was particularly destructive to hearing). Their organs of speech were unimpaired; they were mute because they had not heard enough to learn to talk. There were isolated efforts to help these children before 1811; then a Hartford physician whose daughter was afflicted called upon the Congregational clergy to take a census of deaf children. They discovered 84 and guessed that there were about 400 in New England alone. Accordingly, a special school seemed desirable.

In 1815 a group of philanthropic gentlemen in Hartford formed a society and hired Thomas Gallaudet, a theological student, to go to Europe and acquaint himself with the methods of instruction practiced there, notably in France and Scotland. When he returned he helped raise an initial fund, mostly from individuals but including a large gift from the state legislature, which also granted the society a charter. Known at first as The American Asylum for the Education and Instruction of the Deaf and Dumb, it opened in 1817. It drew its pupils mostly from New England, where state governments arranged to send their deaf children to it, but it professed to be for the whole nation, and in 1819 it received a land grant from Congress to help it along. Meanwhile, however, other schools opened in New York (1818) and Philadelphia (1821), where the plight of deaf children in the almshouses called attention to the problem. In 1823 Kentucky established a school. This was a state venture in which private contributions were small. Because it was expected to take children from the Mississippi valley, it also received a federal land grant. Presently other states in the West and South set up their own institutions.

In 1829, after several years of interest and committee work, the New England Asylum for the Blind was incorporated. Its inspiration was the labor of a Frenchman, Valentin Haüy (1745–1822), who had founded schools in Paris, Berlin, and St. Petersburg. It was an enthusiasm of a number of philanthropists around Boston, notably Thomas H. Perkins, who provided the mansion in which it was housed (it was later called the Perkins Institution in his honor). Its director was

Samuel Gridley Howe, a physician and in many ways a representative of the Yankee reform spirit. Already famous for his service in
the Greek war of liberation against the Turks, he later took a leading
part in movements in behalf of the common schools, the mentally ill
and defective, and Negro slaves, and he became a member of the
State Board of Charities when it was created in 1863. Dr. Howe went
to Europe to pick up ideas but soon made himself a world-famous
authority, especially for his painstaking work with Laura Bridgman
and Oliver Caswell, who were both deaf *and* blind. His school actually began operation in 1832. In the same year a similar institution
opened in New York, where children from the almshouse were the
first students. Philadelphia created the third school in 1833, and
Ohio the fourth in 1837. As in the case of schools for the deaf, the
first ventures were private in origin, with the state making an initial
gift and then paying for the instruction of pauper children. Beginning
with Ohio, and especially in the West and South, institutions were
public, although they sometimes took over private schools.

In establishing these schools the humanitarian motive was
stronger than the prudential one. These reforms were, it seems, particularly fit subjects for the exalted rhetoric of that romantic era.
Deafness is depicted as terribly sad, pitiable, woeful, hopeless, de-
plorable. The deaf live lonely, cheerless lives, unable to take part in
the benefits of civilization or the consolations of religion, living in
the silence of the tomb. The blind are likewise piteous. They live in
the darkness of the tomb, almost helpless, doomed to idleness and
miserable dependence. The schools appear as a "noble charity" that
will deliver these unfortunates from their isolation, offer them the
consolation of religion, and bring them into society, where they can
share their feelings and find a degree of practical independence and
usefulness. The word *miracle* often occurs in descriptions of their service. A very important part of the work of the schools was preparing
the pupils for an "exhibit," a public performance that showed off
their new-learned skills. Often they went on long tours, not only to
state legislatures to win additional support but also to cities and rural
towns. Audiences were large, appreciative, and often shed tears. In
part these exhibitions were an advertisement for students, for the
classes were sometimes very small to begin with. The scores or
hundreds of possible students revealed in the preliminary censuses

were slow to take advantage of the opportunity; someone had to send them or fetch them.

As for the program of these schools, the directors proposed at first simply to get across to their charges certain principles of self-help and the substance of a common-school education, that is, reading, writing, and arithmetic. The deaf learned a sign language, the blind a touch-legible print. In time questions would arise about these early instructional techniques. The deaf, it was said, should really learn lip-reading and vocalized speech rather than sign language. The blind should learn Braille rather than the raised alphabet that Dr. Howe favored. The number of subjects and the period of schooling should increase, as in ordinary day schools. The question of adjustment to the community after the pupil left the residential school would come to the fore. The schools would reject the role of a "noble charity" and take on that of a rightful service. The initial enthusiasm and sense of marvel that fostered them would evaporate in the light of newer and larger technical and social questions, and in later days it would be difficult to realize that the enthusiasm had been generous and the marvel authentic.

As special schools for delinquents and defectives were part of a much larger development of educational institutions, so lunatic asylums were part of more general changes in health care. The basic changes were more scientific views of disease and new roles for the hospital. As it happened, however, the very problems of medical science in this period of growth made the treatment of mental illness seem much more promising in the years 1815–1845 than it has since then.

In fact the great welfare problem of those days was not poverty or crime but terrible epidemics. None equaled the yellow fever that struck Philadelphia in 1793 and killed one-tenth of the residents, but this was the prospect that occasionally caused townsmen to flee their homes as from war or fire. Cholera came and went. In many places malaria was endemic. Doctors simply did not understand the path of these contagions. They were prepared to treat people who were already sick, not to prevent plagues. The best they could advise was to quarantine the victims, to keep them out of town or confined to one part of town. They also thought that a better water supply and a general cleanup would help. This thought stimulated the creation of municipal water works to replace individual wells, and much other sanitary legislation was passed. So public health administration began, without knowing what the enemy was.

Despite the fact that medical science was helpless, the mood was hopeful. Leprosy and bubonic plague, two scourges of earlier centuries, had disappeared, and in the eighteenth century the use of vaccination against smallpox had begun to contain that terror. There was much wise counsel about personal hygiene—cleanliness took its place alongside godliness—and many earnest statistical inquiries attempted to correlate epidemic disease with various factors, material and cultural.

Meanwhile in somatic medicine there was a major breakthrough. Most eighteenth-century physicians thought of disease as a general imbalance of the body's system, specifically of the four humors or fluids that were supposed to determine health and temperament. They diagnosed in terms of general symptoms—fevers and fluxes (discharges)—and tried to treat the symptoms in order to restore balance to the system. Bleeding, blistering, and purging were common therapies. After 1790 this ancient theory of humoralism lost its credibility. Doctors in the great hospitals of Paris began to make increasingly refined observations of patients and the course of their illnesses, which they could readily do in the large, crowded wards. When a patient died (the usual outcome), they performed an autopsy and looked for correlations between symptoms and the specific pathology of organs and tissues. Accordingly, they learned that fever or diarrhea might relate to many different internal conditions, that there was a difference between typhus and typhoid, for example. Moreover, they showed by conclusive "numerical" (statistical) experiments that the traditional treatments, especially bleeding, were actually harmful. To be sure, it was not very encouraging to a patient to learn that he really had typhus instead of typhoid and that the doctor would not shorten his life by bleeding him, but from a scientific point of view—with regard to a better theory and ultimately a better practice of medicine—the promise was great indeed.

In any case the work in Paris set a new standard of clinical training and research and confirmed a new role for the hospital. Clinical observation had always been central to the physician's education, but traditionally it took place in the chance occurrences of an apprenticeship. Some apprentice physicians also attended lectures in university medical schools, but these were remote from the bedside. In the hospital, however, students could see at once examples of a particular disease at different stages, and lecturers could readily illustrate their points. Learning was concentrated. Lecturers could specialize, study, and publish their findings. Of course during these years many fledgling American doctors never got past the apprenticeship stage, but many—the best of them—went to Europe for their training and came back to demand the professional advantages of a hospital in their communities.

This was a new role for the hospital because traditionally it was less a medical institution tham a form of poor relief. Specifically, it helped travelers or others who had no home or family that could care for them when they were sick. In rural England and the colonies there were no hospitals. Sick neighbors, if they needed help outside the family, fell under the poor law. If there were a doctor in the neighborhood, the overseers would pay him to treat the patient at home. If the patient had no home or no friend to sit up with him, he was farmed out to another family. Hospitals appeared where there were a lot of transients without homes or neighborly claims. They became a popular town charity, keeping the sick and dying off the streets. England created twenty-two in the years 1700–1760. Philadelphia founded the first one in the colonies in 1751; New York founded one in 1771, Boston (Massachusetts General Hospital) in 1811. These were all "private," organized, financed, and managed by voluntary action, although the municipality or state offered grants and privileges to help encourage donations. In 1799 the federal government organized its Marine Hospital Service to take care of sailors in large ports. It was financed by a tax on their wages—a primitive form of medical insurance—and administered by the Treasury Department.

As city almshouses grew in size in the early nineteenth century, they provided infirmaries for their inmates, many of whom needed medical care. These often became the nucleus of large city (public) hospitals—"Old Blockley" in Philadelphia and Bellevue in New York, for example. Soon all sizable cities had hospitals of some sort. In general, there were two distinctions between the voluntary charitable hospitals and the almshouse infirmaries. The latter were part of the poor law system, and transients, in particular, were often ineligible for them; furthermore, almshouse patients often needed long-term or custodial care whereas the private hospitals specialized in medical emergencies. But there was no authoritative line of policy or distinction of function in these formative years. Here and there groups of philanthropists, doctors, or public officials would rally themselves to create a service. The point is that there were two dynamics at work: the need for special institutions for the sick poor in larger cities, and the professional interest of doctors in hospitals as a resource for the practice and teaching of medicine.

Both the social need and the professional interest were more urgent in Europe than here. Indeed, American doctors faced peculiar difficulties in advancing their work. European physicians learned by experimenting with multitudes of pauper patients and ultimately by dissecting their corpses. This technical viewpoint went against the religious attitude of people who were taught to believe in the sanctity of the human body—even that of a pauper. The autopsy was ghastly to those who believed in bodily resurrection. European doctors could defy these unenlightened responses because they had the support of the dominant classes—business, professional, and landlord—who generally shared their scientific attitude and aspirations (as we do today). Moreover, in medical practice these doctors could impose their standards through licensing laws, which the dominant social classes also supported.

In America, however, scientific physicians faced much stronger and deeper religious opposition to their ways because the classes that were uneducated or unenlightened from the scientific point of view were politically important. This was particularly true with regard to autopsies. Medical students (or their hired hands) often had to rob new graves to get cadavers merely to study anatomy. Sometimes they tried to buy dead bodies from prisons and almshouses. The managers of Old Blockley were called "the Board of Buzzards" because they were thought to condone this practice. (Philadelphia early became a center of the new medical education.) For the rest, it was impossible to enact strict licensing laws that would standardize training. Who was to tell the sovereign Common Man that charlatans with snake oil or grave "homeopathic physicians" were really unscientific and untrustworthy?

There was also a breakthrough in the treatment of mental illness. At bottom, people came to perceive it with naturalistic rather than religious assumptions. Traditionally men had associated madness with an unseen world of spirits. They believed the Bible tales about how devils entered the body and Jesus cast them out. The witchcraft trials took for granted a theory of demonic possession. It was an everyday fact of religious revivals that when the spirit moved people they spoke in strange tongues, went on all fours, and were otherwise demented. In the new view the problem was not unseen spirits but something gone wrong with the body, specifically the brain. So, for example, people with fevers often raved like maniacs; cure the fever and the mind was also restored.

As a practical matter there were in the colonies (as in England) three ways of handling those unfortunates who were, as the legal phrase went, *non compos mentis*. They might be kept at home, with some degree of restraint or protective custody. A family with a large dwelling could spare a room, often in the attic or the cellar. Other families might build a special shed in the yard. The afflicted could not be watched all the time, so a strong lock and bars were usually necessary, and perhaps chains (they could gnaw through ropes). The whole affair was a great embarrassment to the family and, of course, an aggravation to the lunatic. Suspicion and murderous hostility grew on both sides.

Often there was no family or relatives to provide for a lunatic. Then the unfortunate party fell under the poor law and was farmed out to some other family. If he were tractable, fine; otherwise—the shed and chains. If there was a poor farm or an almshouse, it got the job. Sometimes the lunatic would wander or escape. The woods were full of crazies anyhow; some were pitiful, some dangerous. As vagrants, especially if disposed toward violence, they wound up in jail. In short, as a practical matter insane people were treated like dependents or criminals.

But suppose the relatives were enlightened enough to see that the afflicted one was sick, not accursed, and suppose they were wealthy enough to get help? The number of such families grew in eighteenth-century Europe, and to accommodate them doctors turned their homes into private madhouses. Then they had to work out a program that was suited to people who were neither possessed by demons nor miserable paupers or violent criminals, but only sick gentlefolk. King George III himself was insane off and on for forty years, and many literary celebrities among the early romantics became mentally ill. Obviously, for people of this quality a degree of comfort, dignity, and trust was in order. It was while serving in a private madhouse in France that Dr. Philippe Pinel learned the principles of "moral treatment" that he began to apply when, in 1792, the Revolutionary government put him in charge of the great Paris asylum, the Bicetre. In an act that symbolized the new spirit, he ordered the chains struck off the inmates.

At first the medical view of mental illness had led in a different direction. Dr. Benjamin Rush, a leader in American psychiatry in 1815, a friend of Jefferson and a great man among the Philadelphia doctors, had tried bleeding his insane patients and blistering the scalp (draw off the fluids, reduce the pressure). He invented a "tranquilizer," a chair that bound people like a straitjacket, and another chair in which the patient was spun until calm. Dr. Pinel's *Traitise de la Folie* (1801, translated 1806) rejected that sort of treatment. In his view proper asylum care was not so much physical as "moral" or psychological. It was an environment and an experience in living that led the patient back to health. Quite similar practices were undertaken at the York Retreat in England (founded 1793), where a Quaker family named Tuke, who were not doctors and were even skeptical about medical science, provided a mild and wholesome regime for unstable Friends.

As a medical theory, moral treatment began with the proposition that the material brain was very susceptible and malleable, especially in children. Physical illness might affect it, but so could environmental circumstances or stimuli that were somehow confusing or abnormal. If the problem was pathological conditions or stimuli, the solution was to correct them. This might involve curing somatic disease, but it might require a change in the person's social relations and life style. The brain was malleable toward sickness *or health*. Moreover, doctors thought that the brain was divided into parts (or bumps, as it were) that governed different faculties (or aptitudes) such as memory, understanding, passion, conscience, and so forth. Much anatomical research went into trying to establish where these bumps were. Everyone was born with a hereditary disposition toward his brain shape and activity, just as he had a hereditary disposition toward his physical proportions, but experience would inhibit or stimulate his development. The doctrine of phrenology, which grew very popular after 1834, held that one could judge a person's mental capabilities by studying the shape of his skull (the notion that a bulging forehead indicates unusual intelligence is a vestige of this belief).

In any case the physician's task was to discover the source of the difficulty and to correct it. If the patient was raving in a fever, depressed by loss or calamity, or upset by childbirth, the case was simple enough. If there was a history of peculiar symptoms, the physician made an assessment of the predisposing and aggravating factors and devised a plan to remedy them. He assumed that lunacy was a derangement or imbalance of some particular faculties, while others were sound enough. Mental illness was an exaggeration of ideas or feelings that might in moderation or in unusual circumstances be normal; it related to only part of life. The practical plan was to soothe or reassure in one direction, to encourage or stimulate in another. Usually this involved a separation from the home or other pathological circumstances, in particular from the humiliating and painful sort of confinement that was the lot of most of the afflicted: hence the notion of an asylum or retreat. Here were understanding attendants who *could* watch the patients all the time, so that strict or harsh restraints were minimized. Here was the possibility of a carefully controlled and wholesome environment that would restore the patient's balance or teach him a better one.

Moral treatment was the inspiration of the asylum opened in 1817 by Quakers at Frankford, near Philadelphia; McLean Asylum (opened 1817, part of Massachusetts General Hospital); the Bloomingdale Asylum (opened in 1821 as part of New York hospital); and the Hartford Retreat (opened 1824, thanks in part to the people who had earlier helped form the American Asylum for the Deaf). These were all private hospitals that took mostly pay patients, although the last three did receive public aid and accept some paupers. Meanwhile southern states were founding institutions for the insane. There was one at Williamsburg, Virginia as early as 1773, then one in Kentucky (opened 1824), South Carolina (1828), and Virginia again (1828). These state institutions were madhouses in the older tradition, however; they were intended to relieve the problems of local authorities.

As a practical matter the great problem with moral treatment was its high cost. The director needed a large, able staff of attendants and the means for a variety of diversions and occupations. The ideal retreat was a pleasant rural estate with a relatively few patients who knew the doctor well and might join him at meals. The rich could afford to send their relatives to such private institutions; for others, in public institutions, a degree of regimentation, custody, and restraint, preferably without violence, was a reasonable compromise.

But in the 1830s two statistical generalizations combined to open a new prospect. One pointed to a high incidence of insanity in the United States compared with other nations. This was supposed to reflect the demands inherent in progress—the cost of civilization, as it were—and in particular the tensions and intensity of life in America, which many people (like Tocqueville) thought was the shape of the future. American alienists (as doctors who specialized in mental illness were then called, in the French fashion) were very critical of the sources of alienation in the national life: our bustling changes (remember the tale of Rip Van Winkle), our pursuit of wealth and social status, and the guilt-ridden passions of our religious revivals. A second statistic was the high incidence of cures in American asylums that did practice moral treatment. In 1827 the respected Dr. Eli Todd, director of the Hartford Retreat, published a report that said he had cured 21 of the 23 cases that he had admitted that year, for a recovery rate of over 91 percent. A British traveler who visited the institution and praised it highly publicized this fact the following year; it tended to confirm the sensational claim an English physician had made for his private asylum. Soon other American doctors using moral treatment put forward similar claims.

The new prospect, accordingly, was for *public* care of a *curative* sort. This was the idea of the Worcester (Massachusetts) State Lunatic Asylum (opened 1833) and the Brattleboro (Vermont) Retreat (opened 1836), both run by disciples of Dr. Todd, and also the Boston Asylum (opened 1839), a municipal institution much praised by Charles Dickens during a visit in 1840. By that year there were at least 19 asylums, of which 7 or 8 offered good examples of moral treatment. An enumeration of the insane and feeble-minded by the Census of 1840—itself a reflection of the growing interest in the subject—found 17,457 cases. This figure was low, since it included mostly bizarre examples, especially among the retarded, but it indicated a proportion in the general population of 1 to 997. Only one-seventh of these cases were under medical supervision; the rest were mostly in the attic or the shed, the almshouse or the jail.

Into the gap between promise and performance stepped Dorothea Dix. She had been tutor to the children of William Ellery Channing, the leading Unitarian clergyman in Boston and a famous humanitarian; then she had taught a private school and written a successful textbook on natural science. She received a small inheritance and, suffering from poor health, retired at the age of 39. That winter she taught Sunday School in the East Cambridge jail, and her heart went out to a few lunatics who huddled forlornly in their unheated cells. (It was thought that insane people were insensitive to cold because they often tore off their clothes.) Finally she went to court to get them some heat, and meanwhile she began to visit other places where the mentally ill were held. After two years, in 1843, she presented a "memorial" to the legislature of Massachusetts. A sensational case-by-case record of misery and abuse, it pushed the state into enlarging its asylum at Worcester and became the model for a series of similar reports. In the end Dix was responsible for founding or enlarging 32 mental hospitals in the United States and abroad.

The thrust of Dix's chronicles of horror was that conditions could and certainly should be improved. In general, she stood for three points. One was simply *humane* care instead of isolation, neglect, and cruelty. Second was the idea of a *special state institution* with substantial state financial aid; most of the mentally ill were indigent, and their proper care was financially beyond the reach of private charity or typical local governments, with their little jails, poor farms, and almshouses. Third was medical care: here she advertised the good results promised by moral treatment.

Dix's practical method was to go from county to county, township to township, a progress that was celebrated in the little weekly newspapers that were springing up in the countryside. Usually she was the house guest of a local philanthropist or physician. Then came the visit to the afflicted, carefully noted. Then the descent on the legislature. By that time she knew personally the officers of the state medical society and many distinguished practitioners. Philanthropists were honored by her company. The caretakers of the insane were dignified inasmuch as their tasks, problems, and performance were put in a humanitarian perspective. Probably the doctors were her strongest allies; certainly she worked in their interest. As medical professionals they could not command the authoritative status of their colleagues in Europe. Their efforts in public health and medical research faced peculiar difficulties in a democratic society. On the other hand, they believed that mental-health problems were of special importance in American life, and asylum care, especially moral treatment, offered the prospect of a therapy that would not offend democratic sensibilities—would not require licensing laws or autopsies or strict municipal ordinances, for example. Already in 1844 the asylum superintendents had organized a national association, which later became the American Psychiatric Association, and established a professional journal, the first in the English language on medical care of the insane. This was before the American Medical Association was organized (1848) and before Dix began her crusade. (She was a firm friend of the new association.) At first these medical superintendents had to concentrate on nonmedical problems of construction and administration, which they did with enthusiasm and ability.

In time her hopes were sadly disappointed, but the crusade of Dorothea Dix had constructive aspects. It established the notion that the mentally ill needed medical supervision, with its humane and scientific tradition. It formulated a high standard of care and in fact much improved their accommodations. It elaborated a body of law that standardized and clarified the problems of commitment, responsibility, and personal and property rights. Moral treatment was certainly oversold at the time—the statistics were mistaken, for one thing—but a century later it would return to favor in the advocacy of a "therapeutic milieu" for mental patients.

To summarize the situation in the years 1815–1845, when the rural democracy was the unchallenged norm of American life, the basic idea of social justice was that of classic liberalism. Citizens were supposed to have equal rights (no legally privileged classes), substantially equal dignity of person, and equality of opportunity. Of course there were distinctions between rich and poor and inheritance was a factor, but these were matters of degree without sharp class divisions, and they were supposed to represent, in a rough, general way, differences of ability and effort. The ethical norm might be stated as follows: from each according to his inclination and talents, to each according to his achievements.

In theory, the equality of rights applied to all adults; in fact, it was limited to men who shared European cultural backgrounds and norms of behavior. There were already movements toward a more inclusive definition in favor of equal rights for women, Africans, and Native Americans, but they did not have much support.

The antecedents of modern social-welfare institutions came less from a secular ideal of social justice than from religious humanitarianism. To be sure, most people thought that social justice was a matter of following Christian moral precepts and that true Christianity, notably Protestantism, impelled society toward democratic values and forms (medieval Christianity, represented by Roman Catholicism, supported monarchy and reaction, in this view). In fact American churches were democratic in their structure, dependent on the voluntary support of their members (no legally privileged or supported denomination), and politicians deferred to religious values if not to religious dogma.

For religious humanitarians the emphasis was on sympathy and duty. The unfortunate had a duty to bear up, to try to make the best of their situation. More to the point, the fortunate had a duty to help them. Humanitarian reforms expressed the traditional Christian compassion for suffering and the urge to relieve it in "the least of these, my brethren." To this traditional and sentimental identification was added a belief in progress and a prudential motive that was more secular, scientific, and constructive. Helping the unfortunate was not only a token of divine mercy but might be done so that life was better for everybody in the long run.

So, for example, philanthropists would not just give a pauper alms to relieve his needs; they would try to help him move from the indignity, the humiliation, of begging to the self-respect and independence of self-support. They would protect him from temptation on one hand and give him a chance to do his share on the other. They would protect the convicted criminal from the terrorism and public sadism of corporal punishment and give him a chance to mend his conscience and his ways at constructive labor. They would save dependent, delinquent, or handicapped children from the vagaries of casual charity and the neglect and misery of the almshouse or jail and put them in a more wholesome environment that would deliberately prepare them for more constructive roles in society. Similarly, they would take the lunatic from his brutal or callous keeper and his hopeless, helpless life and put him in an asylum that would make him comfortable if not actually whole again. All these reforms would not only improve the well-being and dignity of the sufferer and eliminate the evil of unnecessary suffering, but might very well cut the cost of helping in the long run. In every case the specialized institution, the separated and protected environment, would afford a degree and kind of control and help that were not available in the family or the neighborhood, let alone the jail or the almshouse.

Historians who have studied these years and movements have often marked in them an ambivalence. Religious humanitarianism and other kinds of benevolence are also seen to be a form of social control. Many reforms—temperance and the public schools, as well as the workhouse and the penitentiary—appear to be intended in part to make a disorderly lower class behave itself and keep to its work (for the profit of the upper class). However this interpretation may apply to the temperance movement and the penitentiary, it does not fit the schools for the handicapped, hospitals, or asylums, which were often promoted by the same sorts of people and arguments. Certainly humanitarian reformers in these years did not emphasize self-interest or class interest. Duty, not interest, was their perpetual theme. They addressed themselves to the conscience of individuals, not the interests of a class. Their enemy was not the lower class but ignorance and apathy in every class. In fact they could reasonably appeal to the individual and disregard the social affiliations of their audiences because their society did have a remarkable homogeneity. Alas, it would soon give way to a more complex order of things and ideas.

Chapter

6

Urban Charities, 1845–1900

SOCIAL HISTORIANS HAVE described at length the transition from a rural and agrarian society to urban and industrial ways of life. The purposes of this chapter are, first, to indicate how these changes affected the groups involved in welfare problems and practices and, second, to describe some responses that were in the traditional spirit of fellow-feeling or religious humanitarianism. The next two chapters will discuss responses that were more secular and scientific and pointed toward twentieth-century developments.

The phrase "industrial revolution" refers to the replacement of the craftsman by the factory, handicraft operations by power-driven machinery, the local market by one that was distant and impersonal. In place of the craftsman in his shop, with his apprentice and journeyman assistants, stood—after some intermediate steps—the capitalist who provided the enterprise, raw materials, and machinery; the mechanic and engineer who put together the technical process and kept it going; the "operative" who tended the machines; and the wholesaler and retailer who marketed the product. The labor force, skilled and unskilled, was paid in wages for the time worked, and therefore swelled a class of "employees" that had formerly been limited mostly to the fields of construction and transportation.

With regard to social welfare, these changes in the structure of the labor force were very important. In the first place, the workers were often deprived of the support of customs that had determined the conditions of their employment in the local market; exposed now to more competition with less regulation, they often suffered. They

71

became increasingly dependent on money wages without even the modicum of self-sufficiency enjoyed by rural workers who had a garden and a cow or a pig. Both the amount of wages and their regularity depended on a state of trade that was beyond personal or even local control. Of course these changes had many beneficial features, not only because they increased production but also because in many cases they made work easier and pleasanter and offered more opportunities. But in terms of security—of being able to count on a livelihood and to exert influence over particular work situations—employees were at a disadvantage. The plight of the operatives in particular was often hapless and grim.

This division of the labor force along lines of technology and market specialization was a common and profound effect of industrialization everywhere in Western Europe. In the United States it was complicated by the changing pattern of immigration. The scale increased: in 1840, 84,000 Europeans came to our shores; in 1850, 369,000; in 1890, 455,000. Even under the best conditions migrants are vulnerable to sickness, accident, and demoralization and likely to need help. But as it happened the host of newcomers included masses who were particularly unprepared and vulnerable. The immigrants of 1850 included refugees from the Irish famine, for example; those of 1900 included Jews escaping persecution in Russia. Moreover, these immigrants were culturally separated from the natives not only by their language and foreign backgrounds but also by their religion and social values. Some, like the Jews, could in time adapt to the notions of the Protestant ethic, but most had difficulty getting the natives' point of view or spirit. Since immigrants ordinarily crowded into the unskilled jobs in construction, transportation, and manufacturing, the labor force was stratified along ethnic and religious as well as functional lines. The natives, who had the better jobs, could ascribe the poverty, pauperism, and misbehavior of the lower classes to their race or culture. This made social reform difficult.

These divisions by occupation and ethnic group were represented in geographic distributions, which were important because legislation and administration were determined by the political representatives of the several districts. So in the expanding cities residential neighborhoods were quickly segregated for different classes and ethnic groups. Already by 1850 the immigrant slum was a common feature

of the big seaports; as the slums spread and multiplied, their association with dependency and delinquency became obvious. But city
governments could not have solved the problem of the slum even if
they had been so disposed. Most social legislation was the business of
state government, and at this level distinctions within the city were
swept together in the much larger one between farmers and the rural
towns that served them, on one hand, and the urban metropolis, on
the other. By 1900 the suburb was also established, with its distinctive representatives and point of view on state policy. On the national
level—which was ultimately the key to an effective response to modern social-welfare problems—it was significant that immigrants and
industry were heavily concentrated in the Northeast but national legislation depended on the assent of the South and West. Moreover,
the correspondence between economic class, ethnic group, geographic area, and political interest was not simple. Many political issues in
welfare were between different elements of the dominant native
groups, and sometimes big-city Catholics and rural Protestants could
get together, for example, to defeat child labor legislation.

Religion made for another important division. Already by 1850
native Protestants were beginning to align themselves as liberal or
evangelical. This distinction corresponded roughly to the urban–rural
division; in any case it made a difference in the way people would
perceive, diagnose, and prescribe for social problems, and ultimately
it brought out the crucial question of personal responsibility for one's
behavior. Immigrants, for their part, tried to reestablish their traditional forms of worship. The general religious divisions that they
enlarged, between Protestant, Catholic, and Jew, were no more bitter
than those that emerged between different denominations of Protestants, Catholics of different national heritage, or orthodox or reform
Jews.

It is characteristic of the modern welfare state that its policies
aim at rather long-range goals and seek to affect broad areas of social
life—education and health as well as income, opportunity as well as
social control. In a democratic state this sort of policy presupposes a
relatively well-informed and rational understanding of personal and
social problems, an inclination to seek consensus, and a good deal of
technical planning. The great divisions that opened up in American
life between 1850 and 1900—between labor and capital, skilled and
unskilled workers, native- and foreign-born, rural and urban dwell-

ers, religious denominations, and Northeast, South, and West—made it difficult to arrive at and implement such policies, and in this respect the United States was at a relative disadvantage compared with other leading industrial nations. When modern ideas began to become politically appealing, in the Progressive period after 1900 and later in the New Deal of the 1930s, it was often said that the nation was a generation behind Europe in its social legislation. Here were spreading industrial slums with their burden of suffering and ugliness, and people who might have done something to improve the situation had either stood by complacently or put a snobbish rationalization on the plight of the unfortunate, blaming the victims, as it were.

Inasmuch as the history of social welfare must deal with social justice and social responsibility, this kind of moralizing is appropriate, and the complacency and snobbery of the powerful are proper targets. On the other hand, a serious effort to reconstruct the history of policies and institutions reveals that the facts and the alternatives were by no means so clear as they later appeared to be. To begin with, our general historical interpretation of these years causes a bias in our perception of them. Recent historical interpretations of the period have emphasized its negative features—social disorganization, social problems, the loss of roots. Obviously reform movements, which are a dynamic of conventional political history and the history of social welfare, were in part a response to these difficulties. Obviously many people who lived through the transition, people even from the classes that found advantage in it, were worried about these negative features.

Nevertheless it is very easy to take for granted now the positive features of the change, which furnished a substantial base for complacency if not snobbery. In international perspective, the distinctive and impressive fact about American life in the years 1850-1900 was not urban slums but unprecedented economic growth; not the lag in labor legislation and social insurance but the high wages of skilled labor and the extent to which lowly immigrants and their children actually exercised their new economic, political, and religious freedoms; not the disorganization of the slum but general instability and change in all institutional systems. Social instability is both demoralizing and an opportunity for creative ventures.

In any case the people who were most directly concerned with welfare programs and administration, whose story we tell, were by 1900 optimistic rather than pessimistic. They thought they had learned a good deal and were well on the way toward solving their problems in everybody's interest. Certainly among the various divisions of American society their interests and way of thinking were links that would in the next fifty years grow more important than even they imagined.

The early institutional responses to urban poverty came from people who had religious interests and motives. There were two broad types. One was native, Protestant, and missionary. It expressed a concern of pious and rather well-established people for those whom they perceived as strangers and outsiders (and of course unchurched). The other type developed among the immigrant groups as forms of mutual aid and solidarity in a threatening environment. The two groups were usually hostile, often bitterly so, but in their religious inclination they shared many assumptions. For one, they looked upon charity as incidental to the grand business of salvation, as essentially a personal relationship between individuals that was good for both parties. The giver, like the Good Samaritan (who was often mentioned), consecrated his time and means. The material relief was important to the recipient, but so was the spiritual consolation and inspiration that accompanied it: caring and sharing on the giver's side encouraged faith and hope on the receiver's.

This religious charity had a quality that was decidedly inward and antiformal. "When thou doest alms," Jesus taught, "let not thy right hand know what they left hand doeth" (Matthew 6:3). This dictum was intended partly to keep the giver from sinful pride in his good deed and partly to spare the recipient from the humiliation of his position. It was contrary in spirit to the later secular and scientific interest in method, system, and deliberate social change for worldly ends. It looked backward to mutual concern, the fellow-feeling of communal life, not forward to rational social planning and formal, responsible bureaucratic agencies.

In short, in 1850 philanthropy, whether native or immigrant, was religious in its inspiration and goals. By 1900 a large and influential number of people, although still a minority, had come to think of philanthropy as "scientific." In interpreting this change it is important to realize that the people who began it did not intend to turn the gospel of salvation into secular humanitarianism. They only wanted to do a religious task better.

Among Protestants the city mission was a specific response to slum conditions. Its proponents were addressing two fundamental features of their religious situation. One was a theological modification that, compared with traditional Calvinism, emphasized God's mercy toward sinners and the importance of a person's effort toward salvation. The world was still thought to be a vale of tears and God was still supposed to shed His grace in a powerful emotional conversion, but the path to perfection was more hopeful for more people and the millennium closer. Such doctrines, preached by Charles Grandison Finney and others, gave sanction and impetus to the great evangelistic revival of the 1820s and 1830s. Hundreds of thousands of people were stirred and became zealous to awaken others. Revival meetings were one result; foreign missions a second; city missions a third. The latter were necessary because the city churches were unable to bring the growing number of townsmen into their congregations. There had always been many unchurched people in the seaports—sailors, for example, and migrants. Often these were runaways of some sort, pitiful or sinister. Now their number grew rapidly. Meanwhile downtown residential neighborhoods changed to accommodate commerce, industry, and immigrants. Good churchgoers moved away. Downtown churches got weaker at a time when they needed to become stronger.

The purpose of the city mission was to bring the truth of revealed religion—the good news of the Bible—to those who did not have it. The first fruit of this spirit was not a special church with a preacher but a "tract society" with a visitor. A tract society was set up by leaders of established denominations working together to print and distribute little pamphlets of religious exhortation that made the Bible message easy to understand and relevant. Sometimes the tracts aimed at groups whose situation was especially risky: sabbath-breakers, tipplers, prostitutes, or children. The distributors—volunteers and laymen—went boldly from door to door and person to person. They handed out literature, explained it, pleaded and prayed with the listener. They went back again and again, visiting regularly with responsive people or families.

Thus they learned about the squalor and dangers of slum life, and in time their efforts focused where need seemed greatest. They learned that people needed help before they could hear the good news. On their rounds they found many occasions to care for the sick, feed the hungry, clothe the ragged, teach the illiterate. Then they learned that those listeners who took heed were reluctant to join a neighborhood congregation. The newcomers dressed too poorly or could not afford the pew rent or found the worship unintelligible or stuffy. Nor were established congregations able—if they were at all willing—to change to accommodate the stranger.

What was needed, it appeared, was not an occasional visitor with a tract but a special kind of church with appropriate leadership and worship and with a wide range of institutionalized helping. As these missions began to appear in the 1850s they foreshadowed many modern social services: besides handouts there might be a restaurant or a lodging house, free or inexpensive; workrooms where poor women could sew (the garments were paid for and given to the poor, usually) or nurseries where working mothers could leave their children; a free dispensary and drugstore; a Sunday school; a school for children too ragged or wayward for ordinary schools (there were hordes of such children); a "shelter" for waifs who were homeless or for Magdalenes; and an employment office (which often placed women or children in farm homes, where they worked as servants or did chores).

The mission churches were "free": they did not demand pew rent or contributions. They provided their services below cost. Consequently they were not self-supporting. Some were missionary stations set up by wealthy congregations; others were funded by city denominational associations that were pleased to delegate their duties in this way. Many sought funds among country churches by the same advertisements and methods that were used to win support for foreign missionaries.

In time these churches were a disappointment. At first the tract societies had hoped to evangelize the world; the city mission was a means to that end. The hope hung on, many souls were saved, but there was no mass conversion of the Irish or Germans, Jews or Italians. Much good was done, many institutions established, but the social services too were awkward. What was originally a charity incidental to the message often came to look like a sectarian bribe. Or it looked like a worthwhile job in itself, regardless of its part in religious conversions, and *that* thought suggested technical questions about just what the job was and how best to do it. Still the missions persisted, persist to this day, long after other social services have dwarfed their efforts; those that listen can hear their message and share their concern.

A brighter future awaited the Young Men's Christian Association. The first local group took form in 1851 in Boston, although there was an English precedent. Soon there were many others and a national confederation to link them (1854). The movement grew apace among young white-color workers during the Panic of 1857. The YMCAs flourished among country boys who had come to the city. They were migrants, but they spoke the language and shared the values of the majority. They were typically poor, aspiring, upward mobile. For them country-style religion was a resource against the temptations of city life. Amid saloon, pool hall, and brothel it offered a guide and inspiration. It helped them to be responsible workers, diligent and enterprising. They could see that religious fellowship was a source of strength and mutual aid. They might have joined the downtown churches, and doubtless many did. But most likely the congregation was too fashionable or the preaching too bland or learned. The first local associations were for prayer meetings and visiting the sick and the stranger. Then came the impressive array of services: places for meeting and recreation—the game room and gymnasium, substitutes for the saloon; the residence hall, inexpensive and clean, and the restaurant; the list of approved rooming houses; help in getting jobs and advice about the problems that young men have in the city; formal education related to self-culture and employment. In these efforts the YMCAs had help from local businessmen—often themselves country boys who had made good—and from revivalist preachers like the great evangelist Dwight Moody, who beginning in 1876 raised thousands of dollars for their work. Presently they had professional staff: the YMCA secretaries trained in the YMCA colleges, Springfield (1885) and George Williams (1890). The YMCA is significant because it confronted most of the problems that newcomers to the city face, but under nearly ideal conditions; its clients were not demoralized but eminently helpable; its resources were large, its spiritual and service sides plainly reciprocal.

In 1880 the Salvation Army came to America. William Booth, a Methodist evangelist, had organized it in England fifteen years before. It was the greatest of the city missions, and at first it often spread under those auspices. It found its special work not in immigrant slums, which were an American phenomenon, but among vagrants and derelicts of a sort very numerous in industrial cities, in America as in England. It developed a showy, sensational mode of evangelizing—uniforms, bands, parades, music hall tunes with pious lyrics, the hallelujah spirit and hallelujah lassies (women played a conspicuous part in its work), the dramatic testimony of the reformed drunkard. Its organization was military, rational, and efficient. It seized effectively on the imagery of a war against Satan in his very strongholds.

At first the Army's material relief was decidedly secondary to evangelistic meetings to save souls. American Salvationists early found a mission to prisoners, after some of the warriors had been thrown in jail for disturbing the peace with unauthorized parades, street preaching, and open-air meetings. (By the 1880s city officials and police were often Irish Catholic, and they and their saloonkeeper friends had different ideas about a war against Satan.) There were a few other ventures into social service until, in 1890, General Booth himself published *In Darkest England, And the Way Out*, an effective description of the misery of slum life and an interesting plan for rehabilitating "the submerged tenth," in part by setting up labor colonies overseas. The plan was not much advocated in the United States, but it left a residue in the form of salvage operations in which the Army employed needy men to collect usable junk and refurbish and sell it or give it away. Meanwhile the Army went into service in a big way, with urban centers where men could get food and lodging free or, more usually, at minimum cost; homes for "fallen women," often prostitutes, and their children; summer outings for children; and nursing and medical help.

In its "rescue" mission the Army was particularly critical of the fundamentals of "scientific charity" as it was taking form—careful investigation of applicants, cautious case conferences, relief appropriate to need and according to plan, the crucial distinction between the deserving and the undeserving. The Army wanted to help the rankest sinner, to catch him and show him that he too was loved, that he had only to respond in kind to escape the clutches of Satan. Knowing the hope that lay in remorse and repentance, it appealed deliberately to the undeserving.

Between Protestant and Catholic perceptions of the task of practical charity there were important differences. Protestants grew up

with the country in the nineteenth century. Members of denominations like the Baptists and Methodists who were poor and struggling
in 1830 were likely to be affluent and powerful in 1900. Conscientious reformers among them worried about their estrangement not
only from immigrant slums but also from the industrial laboring
class. Even so, these reformers could subscribe wholeheartedly to the
traditional Protestant ethic of personal behavior and to the movements for social amelioration that remained alive after the Civil War.
They thought that Progress was not coming fast enough, not that the
idea of progress was itself peculiar.

Catholics were few in 1830 and socially well established. They
were of English descent around Baltimore, French around St. Louis
and New Orleans. After 1845 came the deluge of Irish and German
Catholics, poor and foreign in their ways. After 1880 came the Italians, Czechs, and Poles, who were even less adaptable.

In the crises of migration these newcomers might conveniently
have converted to Protestantism, which had advantages, or drifted
into secular indifference. Many did, but most made the sacrifice
required if they were to retain their traditional faith. Indeed, challenged by the natives and without the traditional social supports of
the old country, religion often became more important in their lives
than it had been in Europe.

With regard to charity, the bishop—and ultimately the flock
who chose to support him—saw it not as meeting a dramatic new
need but as one of a wide range of activities and responsibilities in the
pattern of Europe. The bishop's first priority was to see that the sacra-
ments were available to the faithful. He had to get priests out in the
field, help them organize the parish and build the parish church.
Given mobs of poor strangers, the ethnic and doctrinal antagonisms
that surfaced when they got together, and the active competition of
Protestant missions or merely secular diversions, he had his hands
full. Next he might turn to education, some provision to instruct
children in their religion and a seminary to train clergymen, who
were in very short supply.

In a healthy parish the families could help one another over
many everyday emergencies, and parish acquaintance was the foundation of many mutual-benefit societies like those federated into the
German Central Verein (1855) and the Irish Catholic Benefit Union
(1869). But the resources of parish families and their priest were lim-

ited, and the benefit associations were mostly interested in helping their contributing members. Very soon the bishop had to think about a second, institutional line of defense against need. So were founded a variety of charities, all of them conceived to supplement the home. Hospitals were for the sick poor who could not be treated at home; some were for "incurables," but in any case the treatment was likely to fail, leaving the family without a breadwinner or his wife. Hence the orphanage and the home for the aged.

But why did the bishop (and the flock that supported him) feel that they had to set up a lot of charitable institutions? There were public institutions for which Catholics along with everybody else paid taxes. There were private institutions, many of them nonsectarian and willing to help. Why should the bishop not concentrate on parochial schools and diocesan seminaries and let the charities go?

Often it had to be that anyhow, but the fundamental fact in this situation was not simply that Catholics were needy and helpless but that as Catholics they lived in a hostile environment. To the Catholic hierarchy (and the flock) the Protestant missions were schemes to steal the afflicted one from his heritage at the cost, it was profoundly believed, of his immortal soul. "Nonsectarian" institutions were in fact Protestant. So were the public institutions. (Not until the 1870s would priests begin to share the chaplaincy of almshouses, jails, or asylums, or even get inside them to see their communicants among the inmates.) The spectacular rise of the "American" or "Know-nothing" party in state and national politics in the 1850s revealed the natives' latent suspicion and hatred for the church of the Irish or German Catholic.

While charity was one way that Catholics (and other immigrant churches) could draw together to express their solidarity amid hostile neighbors, this immediate occasion only gave force to the accepted belief that charity was a commandment of God. It was a duty (none more sacred), not an option to pick up or discard. Morever, there was in the heart of the poor Catholic a special consolation about these religious charities, a continuity with his past. He was familiar with hardship and suffering in Europe. He did not share Yankee notions about universal reform in a hurry. When trouble came, as it always had, the church was there. The institutions were staffed mostly by religious orders, usually brought over from Europe by the bishop, good people who had consecrated their lives and crossed the sea in the service of God. They did not bother to elaborate the distinction between the deserving and undeserving poor (although they recognized it). They were more likely to offer a casual acceptance than a censorious inquisition, to pity the poor woman who had to leave her children in an orphanage rather than to examine her resourcefulness.

In 1845 a conference of the Society of St. Vincent de Paul was first organized in the United States, in St. Louis. The Society was an association of laymen established twelve years earlier in Paris. Its first members were university students who joined together to improve by mutual example their practice of Christian life. Their means was to visit the poor, sick, and prisoners, to give them moral support—advice, reassurance, and consolation—and material aid. They also, as they were able, taught children, distributed tracts, and undertook other charitable work. The American bishop stimulated their organization; they were a resource to supplement the chronic shortage of religious vocations for his expanding enterprises. Conferences (i.e., local chapters) spread rapidly during the nativist agitation of the 1850s and in time became a major influence on Catholic charities. The Society's appeal was mostly to urban parishes and to people whose antecedents were in Northern and Western Europe. It never enlisted women, although there were auxiliaries and other groups for charitably disposed women to join. As urban parishes began to follow class and ethnic lines, the "Particular Councils"—citywide conferences of Vincentians—were a means whereby the more fortunate parishes could help the others. Although person-to-person visiting was the core of their service, the Vincentians in time actively encouraged and supported the whole range of schools, refuges, asylums, homes, and other enterprises, and they became particularly interested in efforts to organize Catholic charities.

In the nineteenth century Catholics and Protestants divided most sharply over the question of care of dependent children. Since this was before medical science understood germs and infections, serious disease and accident were often fatal, especially in the poorer sections of the city, leaving many orphans. Even if they were healthy, poor immigrant families had an especially hard time staying together and maintaining discipline, and crises appeared at every age. The most pitiful was the newborn infant abandoned by its mother, left on the doorstep, perhaps, or in an ash can. For these children the almshouses of larger cities reserved a ward, and a private "foundling hospital" was a favorite charity. (Some of these had a revolving cradle where the mother could deposit the child, ring a bell, and leave anonymously. This arrangement was imported from France, where it was favored as offering the poor mother an alternative to the horrid sin of infanticide.) Children who survived infancy might suffer neglect, especially when both parents worked. In any case they faced the temptations and diversions of the street and were likely to drift away from supervision. Some runaways went to orphanages or refuges for delinquents. Most stayed on the street, urban Huckleberry Finns who got along somehow as newsboys, stable boys, shoe-shine boys, pin boys, or delivery boys. For them philanthropists set up special Sabbath schools, ragged schools (an idea imported from England), and houses with lodging, bath, and food available for pennies. Residence in these places involved some supervision and education; the charges were supposed to encourage the child's self-respect. Inasmuch as the orphanage or refuge generally held the children only until age twelve, a supplementary institution, the "industrial school" or "protectory," was devised to give teenagers appropriate discipline and vocational education.

These problems were worst in New York. There the leading authority on the subject was Charles Loring Brace, secretary of the Children's Aid Society from its founding in 1853 until his death in 1890. As a student at Union Theological Seminary in 1849 he had spent his Sundays visiting the city's paupers and prisoners on Blackwell's Island. In 1852 he joined the famous mission at Five Points, which became one of the largest in the city. He undertook to organize religious meetings and schools for vagrant boys, "street arabs" whom he called "the dangerous classes" because of their great potential for adult pauperism, crime, and political villainy. He soon left Five Points to form the Children's Aid Society. It was supported by Protestants of various denominations, whom he reached through a regular canvass of congregations in the city and around the countryside.

Brace's program came to include all sorts of institutions—he opened the first lodging house for boys in 1854—but his great enthusiasm was the "placing-out system." To "place out" meant simply to put a child in a foster home rather than in an institution. It was similar to the traditional binding out of children under the poor law, which was still the practice in rural communities where there was a market for chore boys or girls or simply company. The difference was that the Society placed city children at great distances and retained guardianship over them as a form of protection. Brace also placed many young children. (Sometimes the foster parents adopted the children, but in the nineteenth century adoption ordinarily regularized a relationship with an illegitimate child or a stepchild.)

Placing out became big business—Brace's agency alone placed more than 92,000 children during his secretaryship—and Brace argued plausibly that it was much better for the child than life in the street, the orphanage, or the almshouse. He appealed to every current ideal about family life and the rural home. Placing out was also cheaper, for the foster parents received no compensation for taking or keeping the child. But to Catholics what seemed obvious was that a Congregationalist clergyman was sending Catholic children to farmers in Illinois or Minnesota who would raise them as Protestants. Even if the agency sought to match the child's ancestral religion, few Catholic families were available as foster parents. Catholics who studied the system found many flaws in it: permanently broken families, poor placements, poor follow-up, bad results. They favored the well-run institution, where the discipline was firm, the education religious, and the child restored to his family if better times came. This was the pattern of Europe. (Institution authorities seem to have looked upon their service in many cases as a sort of temporary free boarding home for families in crisis.)

So great was the need that both orphanages and child-placing agencies increased in number and size after the Civil War. To complicate matters, state after state adopted the principle that children should be removed from almshouses and that, if a child was removed to an orphanage, the institution should be of his parents' faith. Often this restriction also applied to the selection of foster homes. This policy made it plain that the private institution was doing a job that was a public responsibility, and hence it enhanced the argument that such agencies were entitled to a public subsidy for their work. For a long time many state and municipal authorities had helped or stimulated private philanthropy by means of grants and concessions—forgiving taxes on real estate, for example. This arrangement was supposed to encourage citizens to undertake voluntarily work that was in the public interest, and to do so at reduced cost to the taxpayer.

Moreover, the philanthropic spirit of these enterprises was supposed to ensure an administration that was more sympathetic and hopeful than that of the public functionary, particularly the lackeys of the spoils system.

At first Protestant philanthropists—Brace, for one—approved of public subsidies, but as time went on it appeared that Catholics would get by far the largest benefit, and there were second thoughts on the subject. By the 1890s studious comparison of expenditures and caseloads in various jurisdictions indicated that in the big-subsidy states (New York, Pennsylvania, Maryland, California, and the District of Columbia) administration was lax. Orphanages were the type of welfare institution that got most subsidies, but the principle pertained also to private correctional institutions, hospitals of all sorts, and—the really big stake—public aid to parochial schools.

Ultimately there was a practical compromise whereby the courts would accept public subsidies to private welfare and health institutions but not to schools, and in the twentieth century child welfare was a subject on which many interests could get together, including to a conspicuous degree the professional workers who ran the agencies, whether they were Catholic or Protestant. But before 1900 these efforts to do good only aroused antagonism.

The history of urban public (as distinct from private) charities between 1850 and 1900 is an example of the well-known failures of city government during those years. Their administrators did not reach out to the problems, as the authorities in charge of schools or public health did. When the almshouse or the jail filled up, they built an addition. As the town grew up around their institution they sold the land (at a high price) and built farther out in the country. The additions usually took the form of specialized institutions—almshouse hospitals for the insane, tuberculous, or maternity cases—but these were essentially custodial. Observers deemed them inferior to comparable state or private institutions, which usually did aspire to a more constructive and professional spirit in their administration. (The almshouse hospital for general medical and surgical practice sometimes became in part a teaching hospital, protected by the rising prestige of the medical profession and critical and advanced in its services.) The number of almshouse paupers in proportion to the population dropped steadily between 1880 and 1903, from 1,320 to 1,014 per million. Meanwhile by 1900 more than half the cities in the country with populations over 200,000, where the need was greatest, gave up public outdoor relief. These included New York, Philadelphia, St. Louis, Baltimore, San Francisco, New Orleans, Washington, Kansas City, and Louisville. Private charity for children and for families in the home increased to meet this need.[1]

Like local services—police, fire, streets, transportation, or utilities—public charities were demoralized by the spoils system. But while the general citizenry could complain about most bad services, only a few philanthropists were concerned to take the part of the pauper or the delinquent. From the viewpoint of the political boss, eager to distribute the spoils of his victory among his supporters, the welfare institutions offered him contracts for construction and supply and institutional jobs, every one of them ticketed, from attendant to superintendent. Contractors might cheat on their work or provision, or there might be outright theft, as when supplies bought for the inmates went instead to officials. The job slots were usually divided among the members of the governing board—the county supervisors or the committee that ran the agency—and used to place political allies or pay political debts. Workers were expected to campaign for their benefactor and to kick back part of their salary. The staff of these institutions was selected for political loyalty and activity rather than competence, and it changed with every election. It exhibited little of the personal or professional concern that was supposed to characterize the workers and executives in private charities. Instead of a nun or a hallelujah lassie, a political hanger-on.

The evils of the boss, the machine, and the spoils system were a native growth. Rural politicians practiced all these tricks, and charity and correction were as vulnerable in the country as in the city. But the size and growth of urban services and the immigrant constituency of the boss made the problem especially conspicuous. Middle-class philanthropists who took the lead in reforming charities and correction were particularly bitter about the failings of the spoils system, and much of their effort to improve matters was directed toward somehow eliminating or controlling it. This theme will be prominent in later chapters.

Meanwhile political scientists and historians are no longer so fa-

1. The facts on almshouse paupers and cities that gave up public outdoor relief are from Amos Warner, *American Charities*, rev. ed. (New York: Crowell, 1908), pp. 204, 236.

vorable to the reformers' point of view as they once were. They can now make out the constructive service that the urban boss and machine performed for their constituents. In this perspective the political organization itself is sometimes characterized as an informal but effective welfare agency.

An early statement of this point of view was an article by Jane Addams about her experiences as a settlement house worker in the Chicago ward of the notorious long-time boss Johnnie Powers. Called "Why the Ward Boss Rules" (1899), it appeared in a revised version as the conclusion of *Democracy and Social Ethics* (1902). The ward boss ruled, she said, because he was in his constituents' eyes a good man. In his personal life he was likely to be conventional, sagacious, and trustworthy. He was an easy touch and generous at the charity bazaar. His organization arranged festive occasions and distributed baskets of groceries and turkeys during holiday seasons. He was loyal and helpful to his friends. He had influence with the police, the judge, the licensing agency, the county almshouse. He might get his supporter a job, either on the public payroll or with some contractor who did business with the city. He was thoughtful, attending marriages and funerals, perhaps helping with a substantial gift. It was his political interest and business to win over the voters through whatever help he could give them. His constituents were not interested in the reforms that appealed to many natives. As for the boss's favoritism in contracts and bribes, this showed that he was powerful and respected or perhaps that he was like Robin Hood, taking from the rich to give to the poor.

This picture of the good boss trading favors and services for votes, rather than the thieving spoilsman, certainly has an element of truth. Undoubtedly the political organization offered a sort of indigenous helping that the immigrant could understand and appreciate. In public institutions the laxness and abuses of administration—with regard to admission and discharge, for example—often helped the constituent's family. Even custodial care was better than being on the street.

Nevertheless from the perspective of technical welfare service this interpretation invites a good deal of correction. Our evidence about it is limited to the insights of people like Addams, who was bound to be sympathetic, and to self-serving statements by the bosses themselves about how they loved the poor and made themselves helpful. It is impossible to check or qualify these statements because there were no records. But it stands to reason that the benefactors exercised a kind of personal discretion that would make a social worker flinch. In the crucial matter of finding jobs, of course there were not enough to go around. The boss and his henchmen gave them to people who served the organization. Julia Lathrop, a friend of Jane Addams and one of the most knowledgeable observers of welfare institutions, reported in 1893 a conversation that puts the relationship between the good boss and his grateful clients in a clearer light:

> I chanced to be standing in the asylum corridor one day just after there had been a revolution of the county wheel [an election], when a stout, aggressive and excited Irish woman, evidently an attendant, bore down upon one of the commissioners present, who was also of foreign birth, and said, "Mr. Blank, I want to see you." To which he replied, with a helpless gesture, "Well, I hope you don't want anything, because I haven't got anything left." —"Aw, don't tell that to me, Mr. Blank! Do you know I live two blocks from your house, and we've got nine men in our house that worked mighty hard for you?" "Well, I can't help it; I haven't got anything left. Can't you see I am busy talking now?" To which the attendant replied more imperatively than ever, "Well, I want to see you alone. Where is Mr. So-and-so?" With which she flounced on, to return later.[2]

As an informal welfare agency the political machine was at best an expression, like the immigrant charities and the Protestant missions, of fellow feeling and solidarity. Even less than those organizations did it have the inclination to clarify and criticize the means and ends of helping. Given the general situation of the immigrant working class, what they really needed was not an easy touch, a generous customer at the bazaar, or a dubious favoritism in administration. In her reflections on the ward boss Addams never meant to approve of his means and ends. Her point was that he and his constituents were manifesting an inclination toward solidarity and helpfulness that was basic and wholesome, and that her middle-class friends and fellow reformers should somehow try to meet those needs in a constructive way. She thought that government should offer real service and concern instead of the cautious hands-off policy that many reformers favored. She herself felt such solidarity very strongly; it led her to start

2. Julia Lathrop, "The Cook County Charities," in *Hull-House Maps and Papers* (New York, 1895), pp. 153f.

her settlement house in the slums. But she was also interested in social science and in rational programs of social amelioration and welfare. In this respect she was very much in tune with many forward-looking projects that critical-minded middle-class philanthropists were proposing or founding.

Chapter

7

Philanthropy and Science, 1850–1900:

State Institutions

$\mathbf{M}$OST SCIENTIFIC IDEAS about American social welfare had their first public hearings in four institutions that took form after 1850. The earliest was the boards of charities and corrections, which had responsibility for state institutions and for state policy toward the almshouses and jails that fed into them. Then came the charity organization societies, which asserted a responsibility for local private charities and their relationship to local public charity. Later the settlement houses appeared in a wave of democratic idealism and social reform. These three agencies differed in their partisans and preoccupations, but they had much in common. This is why, as they came along, they joined the National Conference on Charities and Corrections (1874), later called the National Conference of Social Work (1917) and the National Conference on Social Welfare (1948), which endures today. The common elements were that they were all creatures of the urban business and professional class and represented its aspiration toward and growing enthusiasm for a scientific philanthropy. But their diversity prefigured the confusion and perplexity that would mark their future.

It is important to realize how feeble these beginnings were. The problems—dependency, crime, mental or physical disability—were large, especially when they were concentrated and exacerbated by big-city life. Inquiry after inquiry revealed an obvious and pathetic degree of unmet need (to use a later term). Particular organizations for charity or corrections were often large by the standards of the time, intended to accommodate scores or hundreds of people. If their beneficiaries and budgets were added together, the totals were really awesome. But the philanthropists, humanitarians, or reformers who gathered in occasional conferences were a mere handful of interested people who realized that the problems were much larger and more complicated than most of the citizenry imagined, that the provisions were usually inadequate and often self-defeating, and that a great public interest was neglected.

Potentially, these proto-social workers had powerful allies. They appealed to the conscience of the community, to its religious and political ideals, to its long-run best interest. They were few and without an organized constituency, but what they said was very relevant to the interests of well-organized and potent groups such as churches, political parties, and professional associations. Their strength was that they professed, quite genuinely, to rise above selfish or parochial interests. They carried forward old ideals of humanitarian reform and social justice, of social progress, but increasingly they aspired to be scientific. By this they meant secular, rational, and empirical as opposed to sectarian, sentimental, and dogmatic. It was easy to fault their conclusions but not their spirit. As long as Americans were willing to concede in the abstract that philanthropy (fellow-feeling, good will) was good, and so was a scientific spirit (fact-minded, rational, objective), their general cause was safe. Faults might lie in a particular line of argument or judgment, but in theory at least, the scientific spirit pointed toward self-correction and consensus. Of course in thinking about philanthropy and social justice there would be partisans of religious and political causes, and they would disagree; probably all of them had some insight into the situation, most likely all of them were to some degree fallible. On what better ground could they meet and agree than that of a "scientific philanthropy"?

And yet this spirit, growing in and with the business and professional class, was always vulnerable. In the late nineteenth century many people came to think of science as first of all a challenge to religion rather than an aid to philanthropy. Scientists were saying that the Bible was full of myths and errors, including such fundamentals of Christianity as creation and miracles. Clergymen who recognized the force of these arguments tried to reinterpret the scriptures and the faith. Their audience was mostly in congregations supported by the business and professional class, and they were often leaders in the movement toward a "social gospel" and a rational social service. Sometimes their efforts to adapt the church to the modern world looked like a gloss on secularization, and they and their parishioners drifted away from the discipline and consolation of the ancient religion. In short, the discussion of scientific philanthropy was caught, on its religious side, in the more general warfare of science and theology during those years. In this battle congregations of farmers and workers clung to traditional doctrines, and incidentally they often resented the social advantages and airs of the social gospelers. Their leaders, the evangelist and the bishop, said: Religion first, then philanthropy and social justice; salvation first, then secular reform.

Nor was the going easier in politics. Here the idea of scientific philanthropy was caught up in the larger argument over government and political economy. Regarding public relief and social services, the "scientific" preference was for technical competence and a nonpartisan civil service, against administration by a spoilsman's lackey. But there were many conscientious and reflective people whose reading of social science carried them far beyond civil-service reform and the technical problems of charity and correction to sweeping remedies for general causes. Studies of pauperism, crime, and corruption pointed to the saloon, for example; prohibition was the answer, said many country people (city people too—Jane Addams was a member of the Women's Christian Temperance Union). Other studies brought out the predominance of immigrants in the problems of the city and the working class: patriots favored legislation to sharply restrict immigration, especially by nationalities that seemed troublesome. Many union leaders believed that a law limiting the work day to eight hours would get at the fundamental problem. The followers of Henry George held that a single tax on unearned increments in the value of land would do it. Out west it was thought that the free coinage of silver would foil the gold-bug conspiracy (the election of 1896 was fought on this issue). Orthodox economists held strictly to free trade, opposing the tariff and also labor legislation: this was their route of progress. Others argued that capitalism itself was at fault, that poverty and injustice would disappear or fade under a regime of cooperative ownership, or a genial Christian socialism, or after a proletarian revolution. In short, the handful of philanthropists interested in a scientific kind of charity and correction faced the potent hosts of spoilsmen on one hand and the deep-thinking enthusiasts for some political panacea on the other.

Such, in general terms, were the tensions of the early years of scientific philanthropy, tensions that continue to bother its successors. Its advocates addressed themselves to important technical problems in a scientific spirit that aspired to rationality and efficiency, and in a philanthropic spirit that emphasized a moral responsibility to help those in need and to act in the long-run public interest. But these adovcates were themselves identified with particular groups in American society, not merely the business and professional class but, within it, the part that was interested in liberal religion and more businesslike government. These broad identifications were enough to arouse distrust among the masses who worked on the farms and in the factories, but even within the middle class it was easy to argue that the philanthropists went too far or did not go far enough. The philanthropists themselves expressed these tensions in their feeling that they wanted to be scientific, but not too theoretical or deductive; practical, but also farsighted, looking for the big picture and the long run. In fact the generalizations of social science were not reliable or clear, and their translation into policy and practice was dubious indeed. The history of modern social welfare and social work is, accordingly, filled with obscure realities and questionable enthusiasms.

As it happened, the relationship between social science and welfare administration was plainer in the early years of the state boards than it would ever be again. The first state board created the first national association for social science, but in a few years they went separate ways.

The first state board of charities was created in Massachusetts in 1863. The Bay State was the most industrialized in the nation. Its labor force had been enlarged by refugees from the Irish famine (1846) and by a continuing stream of English workers attracted to the textile mills. Its leadership of Boston Brahmins and Yankee politicians was unusually coherent and farsighted. It is significant that the state was also foremost in provision for health and education, as well as in labor agitation, labor statistics, and labor legislation. Franklin B. Sanborn, who became secretary of the board and a leading authority on social science, was a disciple of Emerson and a long-time editor of the Springfield (western Massachusetts) *Republican.*

At the time the state administered eleven institutions directly and subsidized six others. The governor thought that some central oversight was desirable and consulted the venerable Samuel Gridley Howe. "It began to be seen," Howe said, in the board's second report (1866),

> that if there could be some agency to collect all the valuable facts learned by the observation and experience of the many able and honest men who were acting without concert at various points, and to compare the results in various institutions at home and abroad, valuable knowledge might be obtained which would tend to promote economy, to prevent mistakes, to rectify errors, and, in a word, increase the good results of so much effort by making all pull in one direction toward one common end.

Although the chief motive was economy of administration, research and reform played an important part:

> Above all, it was seen that such an agency might consider carefully the causes which create such great numbers of dependents; might ascertain the social conditions which affect these numbers; and when those conditions are such as can be modified by legislation, appeal to the legislature; when they are such as can be modified only by the people, then appeal to the intelligence and moral sense of the people.[1]

As the board began its work there stood before it the model of the (British) Association for the Promotion of Social Science, established in 1857 by the heirs of the English utilitarians and economists who had sponsored the poor law reform of 1834 and other legislation for education and public health. Already the French had founded a similar organization, and there was a local group in Boston (1862). Shortly after it was constituted, the Massachusetts Board, including Samuel Howe and Franklin Sanborn, issued a call for an American association. Over 300 people attended the first meeting in Boston, October 5, 1865. Their organic act defined their objectives as

> to aid the development of Social Science, and to guide the public mind to the best practical means of promoting the Amendment of Laws, the

---

1. Massachusetts Board of State Charities, *Second Annual Report, 1866*, pp. xii–xiii.

Advancement of Education, the Prevention and Repression of Crime, the Reformation of Criminals, and the progress of Public Morality.

One central challenge to public morality was, of course, the growing volume of dependency, and a special concern of the association was

pauperism and the topics related thereto; including the responsibility of the well-endowed and successful, and the wise and educated, the honest and respectable, for the failures of others.

The hope was to bring together diverse interested parties so that discussion would bring out

the real elements of Truth; by which doubts are removed, conflicting opinions harmonized, and a common ground afforded for treating wisely the great social problems of the day.[2]

To focus their work, the members divided themselves into four sections: education, public health, social economy, and jurisprudence. These sections were addressed to the interests of the whole society, not simply those of the poor and disadvantaged. Education included, among many other topics, public schools, reformatories, and universities. Public health included epidemics, hospital management, and the adulteration of food and drugs. Social economy included all forms of pauperism "and the relation and the responsibilities of the gifted and educated classes toward the weak, the witless, and the ignorant." It also embraced labor legislation and more general economic questions about the national debt, taxes, and monopolies—presumably in their effects on social life. The Department of Jursiprudence included criminology and penology and, especially, the "amendment of laws . . . for when the laws of Education, of Public Health, and of Social Economy, are fully ascertained, the law of the land should recognize and define them all."[3]

From the first there were questions about the inclusiveness of these sections and also about the assumption that "social science" would produce laws that could be translated into wise legislation. (An example of this belief was the supposition that the "law of supply and demand" in economics supported the doctrine of free trade, or more

2. American Social Science Association, *Constitution, Address and List of Members* (Boston, 1866), p. 3.

3. *Ibid.*, pp. 15–16.

generally *laissez faire,* in social legislation.) By 1874 Franklin Sanborn, chairman of the section on social economy, told his friends candidly that he knew no one who could define "what it is we call social science." Whatever it was, it was (in words that would echo down the years)

> neither a science nor an art, but a mingling of the two, or of fifty sciences or arts. . . . Whatever concerns mankind in their social, rather than in their individual relations, belongs to this comprehensive abstraction, and social science shades off easily and imperceptibly into metaphysics [philosophy] on one side, philanthropy on another, political economy on a third, and so round the whole circle of human inquiry.[4]

As he spoke in 1874, the Department of Social Economy was dividing into two parts, one dealing with questions closer to economic theory—trade and finance—and the other with "Social Economy, strictly speaking," which included topics "at first assigned to the Departments of Health, Education and Jursiprudence."[5] Meanwhile Sanborn was getting company in his capacity as executive of the Massachusetts State Board of Charities. New York and Ohio created such boards in 1867; Illinois, Pennsylvania, Rhode Island, and North Carolina in 1869; Wisconsin and Michigan in 1871; and Connecticut and Kansas in 1873. (In general, these were states with big cities or, as in Michigan and Kansas, large groups of New Englanders.) In 1872 and 1873 a few board members in western states had met informally; in 1874 Sanborn invited all the boards to meet as part of the Department of Social Economy. Other semiofficial groups had earlier taken this path: the National Prison Association (1870) and the American Public Health Association (1872).

So the original idea and hope of the Social Science Association began to disintegrate as constituent interests grew large and autonomous enough to shift for themselves. The National Conference of Charities and Corrections, as the assembly of state board officials was called, met with the parent body until 1879, when it began a separate gathering. Many of its members, such as Sanborn, also continued with the older association as it became more academic and speculative. (Sanborn was lecturing on social science in these years,

4. *Journal of Social Science,* no. 6 (1874):36.

5. *Journal of Social Science,* no. 11 (1880):87.

notably at Cornell, where President Andrew White was much interested in instruction that would combine interests that were theoretical and practical, academic and civic.) Then in a few years the academics in the Social Science Association began to separate into their own organizations, following a general pattern among college teachers: part of the American Historical Association (1884), in turn, split off and became the American Political Science Association (1904); part of the American Economic Association (1885) became the American Sociological Association (1905).

Meanwhile the National Conference of Charities and Corrections focused on the practical tasks of dealing with the dependent, defective, and delinquent classes, and its members often regarded theoretical analyses as either irrelevant or farfetched and divisive. When the old Social Science Association finally dissolved, in 1909, its history showed plainly the difficulty of fitting social science to the practicalities of welfare policy and administration.[6]

State boards of charities differed in their organization and functions. To generalize broadly, they had to deal both with local institutions, public and private, and with agencies that the state itself established and funded. With respect to local institutions, the problem differed according to whether the county was rural or urban. In thinly populated places there were likely to be too few inmates for specialized programs, and little leadership. Here the obvious solution was to congregate special classes in an agency under state auspices. Such was one thought behind the early lunatic asylums and schools for the blind and deaf. Urban counties might have groups large enough to justify a separate local institution, but their local services were notorious targets of the spoilsmen, who were more interested in political rewards than in technical competence. Urban reformers consequently looked to state provision as a way around the abuses of local politicians.

This decision was complicated by the problem of funding. The local almshouse and jail were unquestionably a local responsibility, paid for out of the local property tax. This arrangement seemed not only just but also wise, because local taxpayers had the opportunity and interest to see how their elected officials were spending the pub-

6. Luther L. Bernard and Jessie Bernard, *The Origins of American Sociology* (New York: Crowell, 1943), pp. 591–607, 618–23.

lic fisc. Suppose some lunatics or delinquents were sent to a state institution: it was reasonable that the local taxpayer should continue to pay, especially since the state institution would presumably reform or heal its inmate, and this was in the community's long-run interest. The trouble was that a rational program was likely to cost much more, in the short run at least, then perfunctory local custody—perhaps two or three times as much. At that rate rural officials would think twice—many of their constituents lacked the amenities of a well-run asylum or reformatory—and would decline the option. Urban politicians were more willing to spend, but they wanted to spend in their own bailiwick, not give the money to state officials in some distant rural setting.

Well, then, let the state take over and pay all the costs of its own institutions without charging the counties directly. How could the state raise such funds? By levying a property tax, presumably. This meant that rural counties would still pay a higher rate to take care of problem people, most of whom were, after all, heavily concentrated in the big cities, while the high returns from city land, which was disproportionately valuable, would still be siphoned away from city politicians to the state. Conceivably the state might pay a subsidy to local public (or private) agencies, lay down proper standards as a condition of receiving the subsidy, and check up on the actual service. But this was an unprecedented complication and did not answer the needs of thinly settled counties.

In short, state policy was caught between two fundamental political considerations. A program that was proper and promising was likely to cost more than local taxpayers were willing to pay, and taxpayers were unwilling to share funds across jurisdictional lines if such sharing was not plainly to their advantage. Behind these alternatives stood the general antagonism of rural and urban interests, so marked in the period, which often had religious and ethnic dimensions. In these divisions, middle-class reformers in the city often made common cause with their country cousins, and their notion of a scientific approach—technical and nonpolitical—found some support among rural politicians, who had more to gain than to lose from the growth of state agencies as long as the cities paid their own share.

State institutions were supposed to suffer less than county institutions from the spoilsmen because of their administrative organization. Whereas county institutions were usually directly under the elected county supervisors, state institutions ordinarily had an unpaid ("honorary") board of managers or trustees. This was the traditional pattern of private charities, in which board members were often wealthy donors appointed by a self-perpetuating body of trustees. Managers of state institutions were usually appointed by the governor (sometimes by the senate or with the approval of the senate) for long and overlapping terms, a practice that was intended to prevent the appointees of a particular governor from dominating them. In a political sense they were an honor that the governor awarded to his wealthy friends, especially those who already had some reputation for philanthropy—who may have campaigned to establish the institution, for example. Women sometimes served on such boards. The managers appointed an executive, presumably on the basis of professional merit, and the executive a staff. At best, the state institutions were really free of the spoils system. At worst, they had some protection because their employees were responsible to managers who were appointed because of their philanthropy rather than to politicians hungry for spoils.

This peculiarity of state administration began as a consequence of the fact that state governments were not, in the nineteenth century, conceived as administrative agencies. The main organ of government was the legislature, which met for a few weeks every second year. The governor was a caretaker. Some of his really important powers applied to the state militia. He and other high executives—the state treasurer, for example—worked one day a week in the weeks when they worked at all. The state prison and lunatic asylum were the principal continuing expenditures of state government until the rise of the state universities. Some special committee of managers, trustees, or inspectors was necessary if there was to be any one at all prepared to check on the institutional executive.

While this arrangement perhaps diminished the perils of the spoils system for the state institutions, they were not free from politics. As they increased in number there were obvious needs for some degree of coordination and standardization among them. Each new one took form in a number of related decisions: whether to build at a distance or to expand an existing operation; where to locate the institution; whether the program should be different or more of the same; what its design should be in relation to its purposes.

The location and construction of new institutions were the first and largest payoffs connected with them, and they attracted the attention of politicians and contractors. Meanwhile all sorts of vested interests accrued around existing institutions. Insofar as they were autonomous they might enjoy the benefits of continuity in administration. But they might be too conservative, restraining new departures or covering up scandals. If a scandal broke—a common episode during this period—political authorities and the public needed some technical evaluation. Ideally, the state board then stepped in to help with the decisions and advice. Ideally, particular institutions found in it a source of or support for nonpartisan technical advice and support. In fact, of course, they often found a rival and a critic, and preferred to deal directly with the legislators.

What should be the relationship between the state board of charities and the boards of managers of the state institutions? The dominant belief in the nineteenth century was that the state board should be, like the institutional managers, honorary, unpaid except for perhaps for actual expenses, and chosen from prominent people with an interest in philanthropy. It should *supervise* the institutions but not *control* them. To supervise meant to visit them, inspect them, collect facts about them and their problems, and report to the governor, the legislature, and the electorate. To control meant to hire, fire, and let contracts—to exercise political power. This business, it was thought, should be left to institutional officials under their separate boards, not to the central agency. An administrative agency, whether a board of institutional managers or a state board of control, could not be expected to inspect and judge its own work: it would temporize or cover up. A supervisory board would have no administrative interest to protect.

The device of "supervision" recognized two fundamental facts in the situation: (1) the state of knowledge was such that a wide range of institutional autonomy and experimentation was reasonable, and (2) control invited political interference. It also recognized the influence of existing institutional boards and of a class of philanthropists who were so wealthy and concerned that they could undertake the duties of management and supervision. Administrative "boards of control," on the other hand, found favor in Wisconsin and Kansas, western states where there were few established institutions or genteel philanthropists and where citizens were somewhat more inclined to trust elected officials than in the urban East.

In any case the state boards generally turned from research into social problems to the practical problems of institutional management. They were scientific in that they looked for economy and efficiency. Here was food for thought. On one hand, there was some improvement. The boards were close enough to the pre-1850 generation to feel the contrast between the promise of the institution and the older pattern of haphazard and unspecialized care, so obviously indifferent or brutal. They could see much material progress in particular institutions as the plant and grounds were improved. (The rural edifice that seems to us today so orderly and imposing, even beautiful, was for years an uncompleted wing in a mud field.) There were by 1870 professional executives who were able to think comprehensively about plant, staff, and program, with forums in which to speak—the National Conference, for one—and careers to build. This was a new continuity that promised progress. On the other hand, there was a disappointment of the hopes of the 1830s and 1840s. Existing institutions filled up with a residue of difficult cases; in the urban states these were disproportionately immigrant and working-class people easy to dismiss as worthless. Partisan politics confused both policy and administration.

A subtler positive influence was the truly impressive investment Americans were making in public schools, universities, and hospitals. These were not for deviants. They won much broader attention than almshouses and jails could ever attract. We are interested in the continuity of development of welfare intitutions, but our protagonists saw their problems not simply in terms of their halting perplexities but in terms of this wider perspective. When they referred to the model of "the school," "the hospital," "science," "the professional," they had in mind this momentous collateral development of institutions, a circumstance that was absent from the thinking of earlier humanitarian reformers such as Dorothea Dix or Samuel Gridley Howe.

The crime problem appeared to grow along with the cities in the 1850s and to leap up after the Civil War. The statistics were equivocal, but there was certainly a great increase in misdemeanors and minor crimes and a growth in illegal business such as organized prostitution. In the 1870s the "tramp problem" came to the fore, a consequence of the industrial depression and the increasing surplus and mobility of industrial labor. Southern states, which traditionally had a high level of violence, were disorganized by the war and by the emancipation of the slave labor force, which led to new devices for social control.

Certainly the penitentiaries built in the Jacksonian period grew crowded and vulnerable to the spoils system. This was bad for their discipline and also for their program, which was, by the 1860s, pretty much limited to a perfunctory kind of hard labor. Extensive pardoning became necessary simply to reduce the jail population. It was partly justified because of very faulty court procedures and long sentences (imposed by the penal code). There were the beginnings of a systematic parole or aftercare program, but for the most part early release was simply an occasion for political favoritism.

Another way to reduce overcrowding was to build new institutions, an approach that offered the possibility of innovation. Here was the opportunity for the "reformatory," first for men, then for women. Reformatories (or, more generally, "correctional" institutions) were considered a step forward. It was recognized that the older separate or silent systems had been an improvement over the corporal punishments of the eighteenth century inasmuch as the punishments fitted the crime in a more systematic way (the worse the offense, the longer the sentence). They were also more constructive than torture (strict discipline and hard labor were better than physical pain). But whatever the reformatory quality of these prisons (much neglected, everyone agreed), they were still frankly punitive and deterrent. The new reformatory idea, an enthusiasm of the years after 1870, professed to turn away from punishment and deterrence in favor of an effort to prepare the offender to reenter society.

As a practical matter the reformatory idea proposed (1) a marking system, according to which convicts would register their good behavior; (2) a grading system, according to which they would receive rewards for good behavior in the form of privileges and responsibilities; and (3) release from prison when they were reformed rather than when an arbitrary fixed sentence expired. Thus authorities tried to appeal to the convict's good will, not his fear and guilt. The plan implied a much broader institutional program in order to make possible the rewards and responsibilities; an indeterminate sentence (not fixed in advance); and a follow-up to see whether the ex-convict was living up to his promise.

These plausible ideas took form in the new Elmira (N.Y.) Reformatory (1877) under Zebulon Brockway, the most famous warden of the day. As it happened, they also answered the need of the older prisons. Whereas the juvenile reform schools took youngsters who would otherwise go to county jails, the reformatory proper took adult felons (those over 16), first offenders who would otherwise go to state prison. This was a worthwhile classification. While adult prisoners worked at "hard labor" (i.e., whatever drudgery was more or less profitable), the reformatory introduced some academic and technical education to prepare the inmate for his return to the labor market.

This emphasis was interesting because "convict labor" became a political issue in the 1880s. Labor unions, then on the rise, bitterly opposed any arrangement whereby prisoners or prison-made goods competed in the open market with "free labor." The situation was especially bad in the South, where convicts were leased like slave labor to work outside the walls. It was also bad in the North, where contractors would install their factories inside the walls. Everyone agreed that prisoners should work, both for their own sake and to reduce their expense. No one wanted to go back to corporal punishment. In time people agreed that prison production for "state use" was the most acceptable arrangement. The trouble was that the state's needs and purchases were too small to keep the inmates employed.

An irony: unwilling to employ convicts in competition with free labor, reluctant to let them idle, authorities leaned toward the reformatory idea simply to give inmates something to do. Behind the irony, a fundamental change in nineteenth-century America, germane not only to prison management but also to vagrancy, crime, and much pauperism: from a shortage to a surplus of industrial labor.

As the promise of the penitentiary was disappointed, so were the hopes for the asylum. The case that Dorothea Dix dramatized had been conceived in terms much narrower than the real size and complexity of the problem. "Moral treatment" presupposed a small hospital (250 patients) and a therapeutic program. These first asylums were soon overcrowded, and this spoiled the therapy. Increasingly patients were poor immigrants in the urban working class, and class and ethnic snobbery made it difficult to sympathize with them. The first response of asylum doctors to this situation was simply more of the same, and in many states a second state institution took form. But when the state boards of charities were established their members began to get a clearer picture of the number, type, and distribution of patients and the unprecedented costs of a therapeutic provision for them.

In the 1850s it seemed possible that the federal government might grant land to the states to help them finance this service. There was a precedent for this in its assistance to the special schools for the deaf. In 1854, after several years of energetic lobbying, Dix and her allies persuaded Congress to pass a bill with this objective, but President Franklin Pierce vetoed it. He was afraid that if the nation agreed to help provide for the indigent insane the states would try to shift the whole burden to it, and perhaps add the burden of the indigent who were not insane. If the federal government accepted the principle that it was responsible for helping to support the lunatic, it might end as the "universal almoner." Clearly, Pierce thought, this was a task best left to the states. His argument, which put states' responsibilities alongside states' rights, won strong support in Congress, which sustained the veto by a large margin. Inasmuch as the federal government later gave substantial land grants to help states develop railroads and technical education, it is curious that the state boards of charities and the National Conference of Charities never showed further interest in this type of federal support. The situation suggests how deeprooted was the feeling that charity and correction were state and local responsibilities.

By the time the state boards appeared on the scene, the great practical fact was that, despite old and new asylums, large groups of the mentally ill were still in poorhouses and private homes, in the plight that Dix had lamented in the 1840s. Their situation was even more poignant to their keepers because the prospect of some special provision had been partly realized. Because the asylums had not been able to deliver on the promise of therapy, attention turned to the problem of custody. There were three types: miserable and unsupervised at home, likewise in the local almshouse, and somewhat more comfortable and hopeful—and twice as expensive or more—in the state asylums. (There were also a few private asylums, very expensive, which catered to the rich.) It often seemed to state boards that some compromise was possible between the neglect and misery of lunatics in the poorhouse annex and the relatively high cost of those in the state asylum. It also seemed possible to distinguish between patients whose affliction was chronic but mild and those whose sickness was recent and "acute" but more promising.

One solution was to have the state build large custodial institutions that would at least empty the almhouses and provide decent care. This was the thought behind the insane department of the Massachusetts State Almshouse at Tewksbury (1866) and the Willard Asylum (N.Y., 1869). Another solution was to make the state hospitals exclusively therapeutic, for the treatment of recent cases, and to send the chronic cases from them to relatively inexpensive county asylums, perhaps with some state subsidy and supervision. The Wisconsin Board championed this system after 1878. Asylum doctors and friends of the insane generally opposed the idea of separate county institutions to care for chronics, however: it would, they feared, mean negligence and the abuses of the spoils system. They were willing to experiment with separate buildings ("cottages," or barracks for 50 or 100 patients) on a common campus, and even with separate "colonies" at some distance from the main buildings. But they wanted doctors, not poorhouse wardens, in charge of the operation, and state, not county or municipal, sponsorship. In the end they did establish the main trend, marked by the New York "state care" act (1890), but in view of the continued high costs and the vested interests of county officials the progress nationwide was slow. In any case the problem of costs and institutional efficiency preoccupied the asylum doctors and the state boards in the years before 1900.

Meanwhile the asylum doctors were themselves the subject of criticism in the medical profession because, it was said, they were making slower progress than the profession as a whole. Their early claims that insanity was curable were shown to be founded on elementary mistakes. (For example, because records did not properly identify previous patients, those who were admitted and discharged several times were counted as cured at each discharge). The improvement of scientific research in somatic medicine was yielding a much better understanding of bodily organs, functions, and pathology. Most of this advance was in European medical schools, but American students brought it to the United States. In the treatment of mental illness it created a gap between the older type of "alienist," who practiced moral treatment in a madhouse, and the new-style neurologist, who studied the nervous system and its afflictions in the spirit of the physiologist and the pathological laboratory. (American neurology emerged not in the lunatic asylums but in the military hospitals of the Civil War, in wards reserved for injuries to the nervous system).

The general progress of medical science culminated in the 1880s in the identification of germs as agents of disease. The specific etiologies brought out by the germ theory had far-reaching implications for prevention, care, and cure. This momentous breakthrough stimulated the movement, already evident among asylum doctors, toward physiological research and away from the older manner of observing behavior in the wards. In the 1890s forward-looking asylum doctors were asking that the legislatures call their institutions "mental hospitals" and were installing nursing schools and pathological laboratories after the fashion of general hospitals. The business of the pathologist in his lab was to study and dissect the brain of a deceased patient, to try to match its morbid features with bodily conditions and behavioral symptoms. The hope was that such investigation would reveal germs or something that made people crazy.

Another step forward was the classification of various mental problems that had been dumped on the asylums and especially on the poorhouses. These included the alcoholic and the epileptic, for whom a few special institutions were established before 1900. But the largest group was the mentally retarded or "feeble-minded," as they were called in the nineteenth century. Philanthropists began to ask for special institutions for the retarded in the 1840s. In 1847 Samuel Gridley Howe made a report to the Massachusetts legislature on the subject and the next year received some idiots into his school for the deaf and blind. This enterprise grew into the Massachusetts School for Idiotic and Feeble-minded Youth (1851), now called the Walter E. Fernald State School; New York also established a school in 1851.

Like their prototypes for the deaf and blind, these institutions were originally intended for education, not custody. Much thought went into classifying the students according to their capability and into planning what and how to teach them. Soon authorities recognized a low grade ("idiots"), who needed continuous help; a middle grade ("imbeciles"), who could become partly self-sufficient; and a higher grade ("feeble-minded"—also used generically), who by degrees approximated normality and could be trained to live independently. In time the schools filled up with pupils who needed custodial care or a more protected environment than their families could provide. Moreover, it appeared that many of the higher grades were "moral imbeciles," easily tempted if not naturally disposed to sexual or criminal misbehavior. While they could manage independently, society might well be justified in keeping close watch on them.

The significance of these incompetent or barely competent people was brought out in the 1870s by two studies that emphasized hereditary features of crime, pauperism, insanity, and mental defect. In 1875 Richard Dugdale published *The Jukes*, an account of a family in rural New York that had, he said, been an enormous problem and cost to the public over five generations. Dugdale had come to America from England and, despite his youthful inclination to art and a heart condition, had become a successful businessman. But his avocation and main interest in later years was social science. He was a member of the Social Science Association and many similar groups. In 1874 he was the (volunteer) secretary of the New York Prison Association, and at its request he made a tour of county jails; this tour led him to dig out the history of the family he called Jukes.

Although Dugdale emphasized heredity, he did not oversimplify. From Italian criminology he had gotten the idea that a scientific criminology must begin with a painstaking study of individual offenders. From Henry Maudsley's *Physiology and Pathology of the Mind* (1867, the first of many editions of a leading textbook on neurology), he learned about the interdependence of heredity, environment, and psychological development. His investigations confirmed what theory suggested, that heredity much influenced the environment in which children grew, that sickness and social deprivation arrested the development of a physiological structure which was the necessary frame for intelligence and moral aptitudes such as personal responsibility and self-discipline. "The whole question of the educational management of crime, vice, and pauperism rests strictly and fundamentally upon a physiological basis and not upon a sentimental or metaphysical one," he wrote. Because "disease, because unsanitary conditions, because educational neglect . . . arrest . . . cerebral development at some point, the individual fails to meet the exigencies of the civilization of his time and country." This "process of atrophy, physical and social, is to be met by methods that will remove the disabilities which check the required cerebral growth. . . ."[7] The pauper and the "idiot" or "neurotic type"—he used these words generically instead of "feeble-minded" and "insane"—were, he observed, typically "degenerate." He meant "degenerate" in its primary biological sense—that is, deteriorated or thrown back to a less organized state or phase in the evolutionary process and lacking in vitality—although he often implied the connotation of vicious and blameworthy. The criminal, he found, had a better constitution, more strength, intelligence, and courage, but lacked favorable conditions for his moral development. Accordingly, children of disadvantaged parents might grow up paupers, if they inherited a poor constitution or lived in unhealthful conditions, or criminals, if their social development was "arrested," although in the latter case their bad habits and uncontrolled passions might reduce them to pauperism in old age.[8]

Dugdale's immediate interest was correctional discipline, but his "tentative inductions" brought out the relationships between "sanitary conditions" (public health), physical development and health, mental development and health, and social institutions and moral development. He linked heredity and environment, physical and mental health, sickness, pauperism, and crime. The association of "charity and correction" and "the dependent, defective, and delinquent classes"—phrases that came into currency in the 1870s and 1880s—reflected this insight into causal relations as well as the fact of public responsibility.

Meanwhile the New York State Board of Charities was also surveying pauperism and crime. Its findings, published in its tenth annual report (1877), agreed with Dugdale's in emphasizing the licentiousness of paupers and criminals and their unhealthy or bad habits. The Board was particularly interested in the increase in vagrancy, so obvious in the "tramp problem" that came to the fore during the depression of 1873–1879. What struck the Board, particularly Josephine Shaw Lowell, was the plight and danger of vagrant women, who were thrown into jails or almshouses that were likely only to debauch them further and engender in them a particularly troublesome brood.

7. Richard Dugdale, *The Jukes: A Study in Crime, Pauperism, Disease, and Heredity*, 3rd ed. (New York, 1877), pp. 55f.

8. *Ibid.*, pp. 49f, 58f, 86.

"There are," Lowell said in a report to the Board in 1878, "two distinct and separate objects to be arrived at in dealing with these women: to reform them if that be possible, but if that cannot be done, at least to cut off the line of hereditary pauperism, crime, and insanity now transmitted mainly through them." Neither object could possibly be attained, she went on, while these women were left in the county almshouse or jail. So she began a campaign for a state custodial institution for feeble-minded women of childbearing age (16–45) and a women's reformatory. The custodial asylum was authorized as an experiment in that year and legally established in 1885 (when it was called "one of the noblest charities in the state"). The reformatory was authorized in 1881 and opened in 1887.[9]

The thought behind these institutions, which were widely imitated, was to get particular types of human problems into a special state institution where a professional person, a doctor or in the case of correctional institutions a teacher, might develop a wholesome regime and program for them. Dugdale's notion that these unfortunate people were "degenerate," atrophied or deteriorated in a biological or medical sense, gave philanthropists a vision of the difficulty and complexity of their problems. It chimed in with the speculations of European scientists like Cesare Lombroso and Max Nordau, who also wrote of degeneration in famous books. It was an organizing idea of *American Charities*, by Amos Warner (1894), the first and longest-lived survey of the field.[10]

In 1897 Alexander Johnson, who had been secretary of the Indiana State Board and later ran an institution for the feeble-minded there, while serving for several years as secretary of the National Conference of Charities and Corrections, tried to pull his interests and reflections together in his address as president of the National Conference. Looking for a generic concept for the scientific side of scientific philanthropy, he suggested "asthenontology, the science of human weakness." His thought drew not just upon scientific speculation but especially upon the accumulation of experience in the state institutions that had been set up with high hopes of rehabilitating the delinquent, lunatic, feeble-minded, epileptic, and inebriate. It was time, Johnson thought, after twenty-four years of deliberation, that

9. Her report is printed in William R. Stewart, ed., *The Philanthropic Work of Josephine Shaw Lowell* (New York: Macmillan, 1911), pp. 91–121.

10. Amos G. Warner, *American Charities* (New York, 1894), pp. 55–58.

the Conference recognize what the history of these institutions made clear, the "sad fact of incurability, or incorrigibility, of unreformability." It followed that the "mother-state" should care for its "weaker children" in sequestered colonies where they would be comfortable and well provided for but unable to reproduce their kind.[11] All the Conference presidents from 1896 to 1900 voiced this opinion.[12] It seemed that science offered a real possibility that experts might distinguish the congenital criminal and the hereditary pauper, the hereditary lunatic and idiot, from those who could be rehabilitated, and that authorities might provide appropriate institutional care for each kind. Thus biology entered into a line of thought that was formerly dominated by religion and political economy, and custodial institutions were envisioned as a form of prevention.

11. National Conference on Charities and Corrections, *Proceedings*, 1897, pp. 4–7.

12. *Ibid.*, *Proceedings*, 1896, pp. 7, 9; 1898, p. 2; 1899, p. 9; 1900, p. 6.

Chapter

8

Charity Organization and Social

Settlements, 1877–1920

AS THE STATE boards of charities became absorbed in the administration and program development of the great institutions they oversaw, the partisans of charity organization and social settlements began to dominate the National Conference of Charities. There were many more of them, if only because they were city-based and every sizable town was a likely prospect for their attention. Charity organizers and social settlers addressed themselves to different problems and showed different aspects of the philanthropic and scientific spirit, but they had a similar historical development: away from ambitious hopes to organize the community by stimulating its sense of solidarity, and toward more or less specific and professional services. So in their way they paralleled the evolution of the state boards.

In part, the "charity organization society" (COS) gave form to ideas that had been plainly stated by critics of the poor law in the 1820s. The objectives of those early reformers were to end the abuse of charity, especially by professional beggars; to make charity more effective for those who really deserved it; and to mobilize the forces of helpfulness. Their leading spokesmen did not speak of science. Many were clergymen—Thomas Chalmers in Glasgow and Joseph Tuckerman in Boston, for example—and their thinking turned on the antithesis between public poor relief and voluntary, especially religious, charity. Their proposals were to replace public outdoor relief with

111

private charity; to clarify responsibility for the task by dividing the town into districts, with someone in charge of each specific area; to investigate need; and to visit the poor so that personal association and supervision would accompany the alms. As it turned out, these ideas were institutionalized in the United States in the "general relief societies" that appeared after 1840 (often called "associations to improve the condition of the poor" or "provident associations"). These agencies practiced districting, investigating, and visiting, but their initial enthusiasm waned and by the 1870s their work consisted of perfunctory almsgiving.

Partisans of the COS after 1870 shared with these predecessors an ideal of charity as neighborly aid, in which people knew each other and felt a mutual personal responsibility. Chalmers said his purpose was "to assimilate a town to a country parish."[1] He thought there were four "natural" sources of help for the needy. First was the habits and economies of the needy themselves; second, help from relatives; third, help from neighbors; and fourth, help from the rich to the poor (he had in mind the parish gentry and the peasants). To go beyond these to artificial or formal charity, and particularly to public poor relief, was to forgo the natural controls of neighborly helping and to risk "pauperizing" the recipient, making him dependent and demoralized, unwilling to take care of himself.

Today the great fear of pauperization sounds like a rationale for not helping, and it requires some historical imagination to understand it as the conviction of concerned and conscientious people. It rested on the assumption that people are naturally lazy, listless, and self-indulgent, naturally dependent, that they find labor irksome, and that they will work or take responsibility only under pressure. It seems paradoxical that the same people who feared pauperization also celebrated the dignity of labor and believed that self-aggrandizement—getting ahead—was the mainspring of the economy and that a person's vocation was a sort of religious service. But in fact people in our culture still feel a strong tension between the satisfaction of self-indulgence and the higher satisfaction of self-discipline. Effort and achievement are respected just because they are supposed to show self-discipline. They are considered a service because they do contribute to the common good.

1. Thomas Chalmers, *Selected Works* (Edinburgh, 1856), X, 13.

In any case the fear of pauperism and particularly public out-door relief grew in the nineteenth century. It was increased by the report of a parliamentary commission in 1834 that furnished volumi-nous evidence about how unwise generosity in English poor relief had raised costs and demoralized workers. The commission formu-lated the sensible-sounding policy that relief should be less eligible (desirable) than self-support. (This was also called the policy of deter-rence, since its effect was to deter people from going on relief if they had any way to shift for themselves.) Later in the century historians discovered examples of a similar pauperizing generosity in ancient Rome and medieval Europe.[2] Meanwhile economic theorists sup-ported the notion with an argument that there could be no long-run surplus of labor, that people without work or with very poor work had only to bestir themselves to find some more productive opportunity. These fears of pauperization grew with the unhappy fact and struck the United States with particular force after the Civil War, together with the vogue of Herbert Spencer and social Darwinism.

At the same time, there were always influential critics of these views—Charles Dickens, Thomas Carlyle, and John Ruskin, to men-tion three—and circumstances in the United States did in fact in-crease the danger of a pauperizing charity. The growing slums sym-bolized the misery and need of the urban proletariat just when economic progress greatly increased the surplus of wealth and distrib-uted it widely among other urban classes. Some captains of industry who grew fabulously rich felt that they had to justify their great for-tunes by a "gospel of wealth," a new assertion of the ancient doctrine of stewardship. They were the source of the philanthropic founda-tions that will later figure in our story. But similar sentiments charac-terized the local elites, as they had in the past. Both evangelical and liberal Protestantism, in their different ways, stimulated the social conscience. Of great practical importance was the flowering of "soci-ety," enthusiastically chronicled in the newspapers, in which "society ladies" outdid themselves in charitable enterprises, balls, and bazaars. So just as public relief became more and more suspect, a refulgent private charity seemed to bring its own threat of pauperization.

The COS movement was a response to this situation. It first ap-peared in 1869 among wealthy philanthropists in England, where

2. This material is summarized in C[harles] S. Loch, *Charity and Social Life* (London: Mac-millan, 1910), originally published as an article in the *Encyclopedia Britannica*, 1909 ed.

many private charities had been organized to ease the hardships associated with the interruption of trade during the American Civil War. It came to the United States in the wake of the depression and social disorder of the 1870s. Its founder here was the Rev. Stephen Gurteen, an Episcopal clergyman in Buffalo. His lead was followed in a dozen cities in the next two years, notably by the very well-supported and influential Associated Charities of Boston (1879). The Rev. Oscar McCulloch, a liberal Congregationalist from Indianapolis, laid down the COS doctrine at the National Conference of Charities in 1881 (he later became the leader of the State Board of Charities in Indiana). Josephine Shaw Lowell and other members of the state board in New York took the initiative in starting a society in New York City (1882).

Representatives of the old general-relief societies often asked what was so new about charity organization. But in fact there were substantial differences in the new vogue, caught up in the notion of "scientific charity" or "scientific philanthropy." First, the concept of charity was refined by distinguishing it from mere almsgiving or material relief. True charity, it was said, involved a giving (and receiving) of the self, a note of conscientious personal and individual concern. It looked beyond the immediate act to its long-run consequences. Its long-run goal was to restore the recipient of charity to the dignity of as much self-sufficiency and personal responsibility as he could manage. This rational charity was contrasted with an impulsive, casual handout to a beggar or the indiscriminate dole of the bread line or soup kitchen. It was individualized, and the relief had to be adequate to the specific case and purpose. Scientific philanthropists recognized that there was a subjective aspect of dependency, that the cause and certainly the cure lay partly in the character of the recipient, so that his need was "immaterial" as well as "material." In later generations it would seem that they overemphasized the subjective factor in dependency, but at the time their position was contrasted with one that emphasized religious conversion. The older-style charities—the Salvation Army, for example—had viewed the subjective factor as an absence of religious faith, which might properly be remedied by conversion according to some sectarian dogma. The COS decisively separated its help from that sort of proselyting.

Moreover, scientific charity looked beyond this personal situation to the responsibility of the community as a whole. Above all, the partisans of the COS tried to look at the variety of charities as pulling in the same direction and to coordinate their efforts in a systematic way. They tried to collect data about the agencies and about the social causes of individual dependency. They expected that this oversight would inform, direct, and increase the charitable spirit in the community at large.

Finally, the scientific philanthropists for the most part accepted the principles of economic science as then conceived, and the policy of deterrence that followed from them. Just as they were not sectarian in their religion, they were not utopian in their social thought. Most of them believed that they were riding a tide of progress, not confronting a contradiction in society. Their purpose was to go beyond economic science and deterrence to moral support as well as material help for those who needed it, and to the development of community solidarity around a vital part of its ancient religious tradition— charity.

In practice, a COS was simply a group of people who would join to sponsor and finance an office (perhaps a number of district offices) and pay agents to receive and investigate applications for help. (The COS gave subscribers and others tickets, which they, in turn, gave to mendicants to take to the agent.) But this agent gave only minimal emergency relief, if that. His real job was partly to refer the applicant (if he was deserving) to one or more specialized agencies that did give material relief or service (a dispensary, for example). Sooner or later the agent would call a conference to discuss the case. He invited knowledgeable people—society women, clergymen, agency representatives, lawyers, doctors—who could see different sides to the case and different ways to help. They could help a gifted or backward child get special attention, a cripple get a job, a tuberculous mother go to an asylum. Then the agent would ask someone to visit the person or family, not just to follow up in a routine way but to try to establish an enduring friendship.

Inasmuch as the agent provided a common capability for investigation, a directory of charities, a registration of families being helped, and administrative leadership, charity was organized. But the best part of the work, it was thought, lay in the case conferences and friendly visiting. Conferences brought out vividly the problems, needs, and possibilities, not just for the case, but for the community. They were, together with the collection of facts, the foundation of social advance. Friendly visiting made concrete and constructive the duty of charity, and it brought the classes together. It addressed itself to the crucial individual and subjective elements in the situation.

However moral and rational their appeal, the charity organizers ran into indifference and hostility. Their critical spirit made them likely to provoke both givers and receivers. Givers were told that their works were halfhearted and self-defeating. Receivers learned that they had to do something about themselves as well as about the obvious problems that beset them. The idea of friendly visiting made sense in circumstances where rich and poor grew up together (the original idea of districting had presupposed local acquaintance). It was very uncomfortable when the visitor came from a different section of a large town where the neighborhoods were separated along class lines. The notion of scientific fact-collecting for social advance was easy to conceive but hard to carry out. It was in Boston, where the program worked out better than anywhere else, that John Boyle O'Reilly, the poet of the Irish, wrote his mocking lines about

> The organized charity, scrimped and iced,
> In the name of a cautious, statistical Christ.[3]

The depressions of 1883 and 1893 repeated the cycle of the 1870s: a jolt to the concern and conscience of the community, many new ventures in helping, a residue of experiences and associations to organize. COSs appeared in many cities of the industrial belt, but often these were more form than substance. The main fact about the functioning of a COS was that it depended entirely on voluntary co-operation. To make it effective, givers had to use it. But of course most charity went along in the conventional way. Mendicants continued to solicit on the street, at the door, or by a begging letter, and people continued to help them as they saw fit. Relief societies and church congregations continued to raise funds and do good according to their own lights, ignoring the worthies of the COS. Charitable promoters continued to seek and win support for their causes without attention to duplication and coordination. Public relief continued to be perfunctory or political (public *outdoor* relief was eliminated in some cities, however).

3. John Boyle O'Reilly, "In Bohemia" (1886), quoted in Jane Addams et al., *Philanthropy and Social Progress* (New York, 1893), p. 135.

Within this congeries of voluntary activities scattering apace around the growing city, the COS might offer a nucleus for organization. Some individuals, relief societies, and churches might use it more or less faithfully. Often these users included well-established, wealthy, prestigious people or associations, and articulate spokesmen, and the movement grew around them. But there was no coercive interest, no hard push. Amiable voluntarism was the rule, a growing consensus the goal: tighten up here, add on there.

After 1900 the forces favoring charity organization became decisively stronger. The basic trend was toward the dominance of urban culture and of the business and professional class that were its leaders. Businessmen joined together in the local chamber of commerce, which gave direction to their common interests. Their wives and daughters increasingly associated in clubs that paid much attention not only to charity but also to social problems. Professional people supported associations and schools that offered authoritative opinions on what was wrong and what to do. Charity workers themselves were taking a much more professional stance. In the background was a general political enthusiasm for reform and social justice—the progressive movement—and a more critical-minded social science, spread through colleges and middle-class magazines, that cast doubt on many assumptions of conservative individualism.

In the early COS movement the larger contributors were likely to be wealthy members of old families who felt some patrician duty. The concentration of businessmen downtown gave solicitors a new target, vulnerable to criticism and even pressure if they were not generous to every worthy cause that came along. Moreover, these businessmen or their wives often sought whatever status there was in serving as managers or directors or weighty volunteers of local charities, for the society page celebrated their efforts. As taxpayers they were skeptical about public charities that were run by political hangers-on. They expected better administration in private agencies, where the trustees—men like themselves—could hire and fire an executive who had some professional competence.

Businessmen were especially prominent in the Jewish community, where need was very great among the hosts of recent immigrants and where antisemitism had strengthened group solidarity. They pushed Jewish charities along businesslike lines and then, because they were also asked for contributions to general community agencies, confronted the financial problem directly. One idea was to create a financial federation that would consolidate the solicitations for various Jewish agencies. Such federations appeared in Boston (1895) and Cincinnati (1896). They raised more funds with less expense, less bother, and more dignity. The device spread to Jewish communities in other cities.

In Cleveland, which became one of the leaders in organized charity, the Chamber of Commerce set up a committee on benevolent associations that gave strong support to the COS of that city (although its interests went beyond that agency). The committee, which continued to function effectively for years under a Jewish chairman, expressed concern about the difficulty and expense of fund raising. In 1907 it sponsored a careful study of all the major agencies (61) that depended on public solicitation for support. The study showed that less than 1 percent of the population contributed at all and that 74 people gave over half of all that was collected. It appeared that five out of six contributors either were members of the Chamber of Commerce or belonged to the families of members. It noted that many valuable and efficient agencies were neglected while others received unwarranted support: funds were both hard to raise and poorly allocated. Similar reports in the next few years led the Chamber to propose financial federation: this would, the committee thought, reduce waste, increase income, and improve allocation and administration. (John D. Rockefeller was a strong supporter of this idea.) In 1913 the Cleveland Federation for Charity and Philanthropy became an actuality.[4]

The Cleveland example was followed slowly in other cities, but it showed the forces at work. Big givers were organizing to take a long-run view of means and ends. If they could set up a financial federation, they could demand cooperation and good administration as the price of endorsement or admission to the federation. Their position was much stronger than that of the founders of the COS, who could only appeal as individuals to the good will of their peers. Particular agency executives and their board members might not like what the organized givers had to say, but they were becoming accountable in a new way. In any case both agency board members and

4. Florence T. Waite, A Warm Friend for the Spirit (Cleveland: Family Service Association of Cleveland, 1960), pp. 102–5; William J. Norton, The Cooperative Movement in Social Work (New York: Macmillan, 1927), pp. 69–82.

organized givers looked for experts to advise and manage. Here was a demand that the nascent profession of social work would fill.

In 1899 the U.S. Department of Labor published a study of the discussion of "social economics" in over 1200 women's clubs.[5] Well over half had programs on the subject, which corresponded generally to philanthropy, and the tide would rise rapidly in the next decade. Their interest was less in administrative efficiency and rationality than in the substance and spirit of the service. Issues and agencies as they touched on women, children, the family: these were favored subjects for club programs and committees.

As speakers the women's clubs sought qualified experts. They were pleased and intrigued that more and more qualified experts were themselves female. Before 1890 women had been mostly patrons or volunteers in charitable enterprise, and for a long time they liked to compare the volunteer, who gave willingly of herself, with the more perfunctory effort and vested interest of the paid agent. But as female paid agents increased in number and authority, beginning as clerks, perhaps, then becoming district agents or executives, the prospect of a new professional dignity caught the imagination. Women grew interested not just because the social problems so often involved their poorer sisters but because the fact of employment seemed promising. It is significant that the predecessor of the professional association of social workers was the Intercollegiate Bureau of Occupations, set up in 1911 in New York City to help graduates of elite women's colleges find work. In 1917 one department became the National Social Worker's Exchange, interested not just in jobs but in standards of professional preparation and qualification.[6]

Meanwhile the philanthropists, and among them especially the full-time paid workers, were also organizing themselves. Before 1900 their usual way of getting together was around particular local agencies. (The COS was the broadest of these inasmuch as it undertook to coordinate the others.) Beyond that was the National Conference of Charities and Correction, which met annually for a few days in some

5. "The Attitude of Women's Clubs and Associations Toward Social Economics," U.S. Department of Labor *Bulletin*, no. 23 (July 1899). For the interest of women in practical work, see Anne B. Richardson, "Women in Philanthropy," National Conference of Charities and Correction, *Proceedings*, 1892, pp. 216–23.

6. Roy Lubove, *The Professional Altruist: The Emergence of Social Work as a Career, 1880–1930* (Cambridge, Mass.: Harvard University Press, 1965), p. 130.

city and sold its proceedings to interested readers. There were occasional state conferences of local public officials and in 1882 a more general state meeting, like that of the National Conference, in Wisconsin. By 1900 there were ten state conferences, and in that year five more were organized, in New York, Virgina, Kansas, Missouri, and California. (The New York conference was late in coming because people there already had many associations; the others were signs of growing local interest and strength.)[7]

Even more significant was the appearance of periodicals that gave focus and direction to common interests. The magazine *Lend-A-Hand* (1886–1897) circulated among do-gooders in Boston and its environs. In 1891 the New York City COS began to publish *Charities Review* for its consitutency. In 1896 the Chicago Commons began to publish *The Commons*, which soon became an organ for the settlement house movement. In 1905 *Charities and the Commons* brought all these readers together; the next year it added those of *Jewish Charity*, a New York publication that followed Jews around the country.

Meanwhile the leaders of the New York COS had risen to the occasion by setting up a National Publications Committee for advice, and in 1909 they reorganized all these ventures into *The Survey* magazine, with strong financial support from the Russell Sage Foundation and an able young editor, Paul Kellogg. Kellogg conceived of a publication reaching a national elite of professional and lay leaders and workers in philanthropy and—in the spirit of the progressive years—"social advance." The sequence of events shows the development, increasingly self-conscious and directed, of a national community of charity workers, philanthropists, and reformers. (The initial readership of *The Survey* was about 10,000.)[8]

As the improving organization of a philanthropic community provided a firmer base for agency executives, there were many second thoughts among them. This was particularly true of the big-city charity organization societies, because they undertook, on one hand, to

7. Jeffrey Brackett, *Supervision and Education in Charity* (New York: Macmillan, 1903), pp. 113–19, mentions these conferences and their importance.

8. Clarke A. Chambers, *Paul U. Kellogg and the Survey* (Minneapolis: University of Minnesota Press, 1971), p. 40.

oversee, coordinate, and develop the whole of the community's charitable effort and, on the other hand, to investigate applicants and either visit with them or supervise and advise friendly visitors. To get a COS going, to use it to put order, efficiency, and accountability into the scatter of local agencies: this interested contributors and community leaders. To understand the problems of applicants and to help: this was the ultimate purpose and value of the enterprise. To summarize and analyze the results of investigation and experience, to refine it and pass it on, to improve the philanthropic effort: this was the business of experts, collected perhaps in some professional body, with a shared background, purpose, and standard of work.

At first this critical spirit was addressed mostly toward people who were just learning about social agencies or going to work in them. There ought to be books they could read, classes to take, educational visits to make. In 1887 Amos Warner, a Ph.D. candidate in economics at Johns Hopkins University, became executive of the Baltimore COS. In 1891 he moved to a bigger job, superintendent of public charities in Washington, D.C. Meanwhile he taught "philanthropology"—his name for scientific charity—at Hopkins and later at the University of Wisconsin and at Stanford University. In 1894 he published *American Charities*, which, in several revisions, was for a generation an authoritative survey. Warner died young, but others also saw the need: Charles Henderson, for one, a clergyman and charity administrator who became professor of sociology at the new University of Chicago, and Edward Devine, a Ph.D. in economics from the University of Pennsylvania who became executive of the New York COS (1896) and wrote cogent books on *The Principles of Relief* (1904) and *Misery and Its Causes* (1909).

The most notable of these executives was Mary Richmond (1861–1928). No Ph.D., she had advanced from a clerical job in the Baltimore COS to become its head (1891), had done a fine job, and had moved to Philadelphia (1900), where she had revitalized that city's sprawling, blundering COS and had become a leader in the reform of child labor and municipal corruption. She had begun early to arrange formal instruction for friendly visitors and district agents in her agencies. In 1897 she read a paper at the National Conference, "The Need of a Training School in Applied Philanthropy," in which she pointed to the obvious stumbling and fumbling in charitable

work and said, "We can never acquire a professional standard"—
already this was her goal—"until we have [a] school."[9] The New
York COS brought her in to teach courses at its new Summer School
of Applied Philanthropy (1898–1904), and when it set up *Charities
and the Commons* it asked her to edit, in addition to her duties in
Philadelphia, a "field department" in the journal, which was supposed to facilitate the exchange of good ideas among COS agencies
around the country and to help new ones get started.

In 1907 the Russell Sage Foundation decided, as one of its first
projects, to encourage the extension of charity organization, and in
1909 the Field Department moved from the journal to the foundation, with Richmond in charge full time. She began a series of
publications based on careful inquiry into what superior agencies and
workers were doing. She gave a famous series of summer institutes
that brought together and drew out the experience of skilled workers
from all over the country, and she continued to give courses and
publish.

From the first she was interested in "friendly visiting." Her contribution was to transform it into the notion of deliberate and constructive casework. The earliest investigation of applicants was supposed to test the fact of financial need. In the early COS this was
done by the district agent. But COS theory looked beyond material
need and relief to the "immaterial" or moral factors of dependency.
These might be faults of character, but they were most likely com-
pounded by ignorance, confusion, friendlessness, despair. Hence the
visitor: "Not alms, but a friend" was a slogan of many societies.

Surely immaterial factors and moral support were important, but
it was not enough, from an executive's view, to tell a visitor, "Don't
be insensitive or snobbish! Be tactful, knowledgeable, supportive, rational! Help people see their responsibilities and opportunities, find
their own way!" But now, here are the visitor and the client (Richmond used the term *client*; it suggested that the visitor had a responsibility like a lawyer's): How does the visitor go about doing these
good things? What does she do next? And so blossomed the professional social worker's preoccupation with method.

First, Richmond said, seek to define the situation very carefully.
Collect evidence in a systematic, imaginative search. Put it together

9. Mary Richmond, *The Long View*, Joanna C. Colcord and Ruth Z. S. Mann, eds. (New
York: Russell Sage Foundation, 1930), p. 100.

in a clear, consistent picture so that particular problems appear in their broader context. This process she called *Social Diagnosis*, the title of her major book (1917). In it she went at length into all kinds of evidence, how to find, weigh, and use it. She looked not only at the experience of friendly visitors but at new work in clinical psychology—the study of child development that Lightner Witmer had set up at the University of Pennsylvania, and the clinic that the psychiatrist William Healy had founded to study delinquents at the Juvenile Court in Chicago. Richmond was very interested in medical social service, in which caseworkers helped with the mental state and the home environment of patients under treatment. Everywhere she looked she saw the dynamic balance between the individual and the people around him, between material and social and personal factors. The purpose of the diagnosis was to indicate limits and possibilities in a systematic way, to point toward a reasoned plan of action.

Two synthesizing ideas kept recurring to her, ideas that rescued social diagnosis from a suggestion of mechanical calculation. These were *personality* and *family*. The objective of the diagnosis and action was to improve their functioning. "Social case work," Richmond said in a famous definition, "consists of those processes which develop personality through adjustments consciously effected, individual by individual, between men and their social environment." [10] By *personality* she meant biological individuality plus a growing, changing relatedness to others, a "wider self." Life was, she thought, a tension between the particular person's urge toward self-expression—human diversity—and interdependence. In this tension the most critical element and resource was the home and family: there were learned the "first lessons in individuality and sociality." [11] Any effort to effect adjustments had to take into account both the individual and those closest to him.

A second theme that preoccupied Richmond was the relation between casework, which aimed to improve the situation and prospects of particular individuals, and the broader aims and methods of social reform. She was sensitive about the charge, made so often during the progressive years, that charity work was superficial, that true betterment or progress lay in general legislative schemes. She thought

10. Mary Richmond, *What Is Social Case Work?* (New York: Russell Sage Foundation, 1922), pp. 98f.

11. *Ibid.*, pp. 188f.

that charity and social legislation were reciprocal, and described them with the metaphor—rather inaccurate—of wholesale and retail methods of reform. The most effective reform, she said, began with the problems of particular people, led in time to the proposal and agitation of social legislation, if that seemed called for, and then followed through on the administration and amendment of the law to see that it achieved its expected results in practice. So the social worker's interest in reform was anchored in a concern about individuals, not just their relief but the development of their personality and the quality of their social environment. The adjustment might well be in the individual, but it would certainly involve the social environment, perhaps to the point of a legislative reform. She contrasted this inductive and empirical approach with the ill-founded and short-lived enthusiasms of doctrinaires, of which she had many examples. Her attitude toward social reform was like her attitude toward charity: she wanted to discipline and realize the impulse by means of deliberate diagnosis and follow-through.[12]

While Richmond thought about friendly visiting and casework, her Field Department was developing the idea of community organization. Its original purpose was simply to exchange ideas and issue pamphlets. To help her she brought in Francis McLean, then (1905) superindendent of the Brooklyn Bureau of Charities (COS). McLean, who had independent means, had done graduate work in history and social science at Johns Hopkins, Columbia, and the University of Pennsylvania before going into charity work in Brooklyn in 1898. He later held executive positions in Montreal and Chicago. His task was to answer letters to the Field Department, which was at that time part of the journal *Charities and the Commons*. The response was so strong that in 1907 leading agencies and the Russell Sage Foundation got together to hire McLean as a full-time organizer, with a budget that allowed him to travel as well as write to where help was wanted. Then, in 1911, 62 charity organization societies joined in a national association and took over the work. McLean served as its executive, with a staff of two or three. The number of member agencies grew to 102 in 1913 and over 200 in 1919.[13]

12. Richmond, *Long View*, pp. 214–21; Mary Richmond, *Social Diagnosis* (New York: Russell Sage Foundation, 1917), pp. 365–70; Richmond, *What Is Social Case Work?*, pp. 225f.

13. My account of McLean's work follows Ralph Ormsby, *A Man of Vision: Francis H. McLean, 1869–1945* (New York: Family Service Association of America, 1970).

McLean was an artist in organization, empirical and inductive like Richmond but without her scholarly bent. There was a similarity in their thinking. A person who wanted to organize the charities of a community had first of all to collect facts on which to plan. McLean's device for this was the "social survey." He had served on the team that did the Pittsburgh Survey, a community study of unprecedented breadth and depth that the Russell Sage Foundation had underwritten in 1907–1909. His part was to examine the charitable organizations in the city. He made the survey for the specific purpose of charity organization a regular part of his work. One of its objectives was to bring out the individual character and dynamics of particular communities. Then to work: McLean pioneered the modern notion of a field service; it was not, as he observed, like organizing a mission church or a lodge. He worked with community leaders, agency executives, and staff members on their substantial problems of finance, administration, personnel, and service. Good decisions depended on what people in a particular community thought, felt, and wanted.

McLean learned that the nineteenth-century notion of charity organization did not fit the facts of the twentieth century. Charity organization societies *did* give relief; they were increasingly preoccupied with the kind of long-term family casework that Richmond was so eager to improve. This useful function was in conflict with the other function of the agency as a clearinghouse that would do investigation and friendly visiting but direct clients to special agencies for relief and service. Meanwhile the specialized agencies now often had a capability for casework: hospitals, clinics, schools, courts, "humane societies" (for child protection and foster home placement), relief agencies, and even industry—all employed people for something like casework. (Richmond had thought of casework as generic, applicable with variations to all these settings.) Jewish and Catholic agencies were overcoming their suspicion of scientific charity and helping families through casework.

Already in his survey of Pittsburgh charities McLean had seen the need for a new coordinating device, a "council of social agencies." This was a body of delegates from agencies that cooperated with the Associated Charities (COS) of that city, and it functioned alongside the board of trustees of the Associated Charities. Its purpose was to bring the community agencies together for regular meetings, not around case conferences to help individuals but for a collective review and planning of community needs and services. It recognized the professional expertise and vision of the agencies, their willingness to look up from their immediate tasks and work together, the necessity and even advantage of their voluntary participation in developing the network of services.

So the businessman's notion of federated finance as a device to make agencies accountable and cooperative found a counterpart among agency executives in the "council of social agencies," which would collect the wisdom of professionals and steer by that light. There were obviously differences of ends and means between the businessmen's federation and the professionals' council, but they addressed the same basic problem—charity organization—and looked in the same direction—improved service under private and voluntary direction.

Meanwhile in 1918 McLean asked the member agencies of the American Association for Organizing Charity "whether the family or the community should be the peculiar unit of charity organization." The members set up a committee on "future scope and policy." Its answer was bold and recognized the facts of the agencies' historical development. Their own interest and special competence, they said, was casework with "disorganized families." Often these families would need financial aid, but some would not, and financial need in itself did not determine whether the agency should take the case. Other agencies might be more appropriate to give financial aid, special services, or both. It was best that these other agencies handle the investigation and casework for their own clients if possible. Thinking thus, members voted to change their name to American Association for Organizing Family Social Work (*not* charity), and later to the Family Welfare Association (1930). With regard to the function of coordinating agencies and planning, they would take their place as only one agency in a "council of social agencies." They would *not* be both a service agency and an organization that coordinated other service agencies. With regard to social reform, they would bear witness to its need and practical results as they saw them in their own work, according to the principle of the "retail method."

So, over forty years, the charity organization society became the agency for family social work and a member of a community of agencies that were linked, it was hoped, by a professional ideal of service;

investigation and friendly visiting developed into social casework; and the hope of directing and amplifying the community's spirit of charity became a secular commitment to service and reform.

Like the COS, the settlement house was an English idea. In essence it was simply a residence for university men in a city slum. The specific university was Oxford, which had historic ties to the elite and to the established church. Students there were inspired by John Ruskin, T. H. Green, and other professors and clergymen who had criticized the excesses of economic and social individualism and the materialistic emphasis on economic gain. These critics looked forward to a society that encouraged people's social responsibility, not self-interest, to create a life that was kindly, dignified, and beautiful as well as progressive and prosperous. Some of these thinkers rejected capitalism in favor of an idealized medieval community. Others tended toward Marxist notions of class conflict and a reorganization of power. Most wanted only to modify liberalism and individualism to correspond to Christian social ideals: the world as the subject of redemption, the ever-coming kingdom of God on earth—such were their themes. Residence in a university settlement was a way that their fortunate and soon-to-be-powerful students could begin to carry out their personal duty to the poor and even to contribute to scientific thought about what was best to do in the circumstances. Assuming, as many of them did, that the organization of the working class was a central problem, they could stimulate such organization partly by helping the unions and partly by extending the benefits of education to the workers.

Toynbee Hall, the first English settlement, opened in 1884 under the direction of the Rev. Samuel Barnett. Barnett was an Episcopal priest who had asked for a very poor parish. He had responsibility and means, not only his living and parish facilities but the warm support of influential Oxford professors and students. It is curious that his plan, so definitely linked to Tory paternalism, elite universities, and a well-developed labor movement, should find such a great response in the United States, where there were only shadows or foreshadowings of these English phenomena.

There were two important American types to whom the settlement idea appealed. One was, as in England, the social-minded clergy. Their point of departure was not Tory paternalism but a

problem of American Protestantism. The city mission, the early response of the churches, was failing. Its militant Protestantism was increasingly alien to the immigrant masses. Its revivalistic theology and
spirit were offensive to the more hopeful and rational mood of
wealthier congregations. Among these people the influence of
science and social science gained force; if they were pious, they were
likely to be moved by beautiful rituals or perhaps even by the momentous historical researches of German scholars into the early
church. In short, American Protestantism seemed irrelevant to both
the lower class and the best-educated upper class in the city. In general, the social gospel was an attempt to redefine its relevance for
these groups, and the settlement was a practical instrument of this
spirit. Stanton Coit, who established the first American settlement
(Neighborhood Guild, New York, 1886, later called University Settlement), was a graduate of Amherst College, a sometime hotbed of
missionary zeal. He also had a Ph.D. from the University of Berlin
and was an associate of Dr. Felix Adler, the founder of the Ethical
Culture movement, which practiced a purely ethical and strongly
social religion. His coworker, Charles Stover, a graduate of Union
Theological Seminary (New York), had been a city missionary. Robert Woods, founder of Andover House (Boston, 1891, later called
South End House) acted in behalf of students and faculty of Andover
Theological Seminary. Graham Taylor, a professor at Chicago Theological Seminary, established Chicago Commons (1894) as a means
to advance his interest in "Christian sociology." Union Settlement
(1895) was begun by graduates of Union Theological Seminary.

The second type of supporter—unheard of in England—was the
college woman. In 1887 Vida Scudder, recently back from a year at
Oxford, met with some of her classmates from Smith ('84) and proposed a "college settlement for women." Soon acquaintances from
Vassar, Wellesley, Bryn Mawr, and Radcliffe joined them in a College Settlements Association. In 1889 they opened College Settlement in New York; in 1892, sister houses in Philadelphia and Boston. Two weeks after the New York venture began, Jane Addams and
Ellen Starr opened Hull House in Chicago. The midwesterners did
not know about the College Settlements Association, but they knew
what bothered them and they too saw in Toynbee Hall a sort of answer to their problem. In its third report (1893) the College Settlements Association noted that eighty young women had applied for

residence in its New York house.[14] In time women—mostly college women—made up 70 percent of settlement residents.[15] Alongside these two types of residents were an interesting miscellany of business and professional people and a large number of volunteers who helped out but lived elsewhere.

What motives drew these people together? In a classic statement (1893) Jane Addams summed them up under three heads. First was the desire that American society move beyond formal political democracy—equal rights and manhood suffrage—to actual social democracy. This meant acting together in a common life, not divided by snobbish distinctions of class, race, and religion. (One of her examples of snobbery was "the woman who constantly invites to her receptions those alone who bring her an equal social return"; in a social democracy she would "share her beautiful surroundings," just as the settlers did.) Second was the desire to "share the race life." This notion went beyond criticism of class differences to willingness to experience the great common interests and problems of human existence. As matters stood, Addams thought, the lower class still suffered from "the starvation struggle which for so long made up the life of the [human] race," but the upper class was now largely protected from this mass privation and suffering. Its young people enjoyed the stimulation of the finer things in life and culture, but they also felt separated from their fellow men and somehow useless and bored. The settlements gave them a chance to experience the life of the masses and to put their advantages to good use. Finally, Addams testified to "a certain *renaissance* of Christianity, a movement toward its early humanitarian aspects." The settlers would "express the spirit of Christ" by approaching "the true democracy of the early church." They resented the "assumption that Christianity is a set of ideas which belongs to the religious consciousness, . . . a thing to be proclaimed and instituted apart from the social life of the community."[16]

Here, then, was an exciting opportunity for service for idealistic young people of means and education who did not know what they

14. College Settlements Association, *Third Annual Report 1891–1892*, p. 41.

15. Robert A. Woods and Albert J. Kennedy, *The Settlement Horizon: A National Estimate* (New York: Russell Sage Foundation, 1922), p. 430n.

16. Jane Addams, "The Subjective Necessity for Social Settlements," in et al., *Philanthropy and Social Progress*, pp. 2f, 10, 15, 17, 19.

wanted to do or, in the case of college women, did not have many opportunities for living outside the restrictive roles of daughter, wife and mother, or maiden aunt. Nor can one doubt their protestations that they were really sharing, not just giving, that there was a deep reciprocal and liberating gain for them. "Living among those very poor people," Vida Scudder recalled, "my sense of values changed curiously":

> I was used to hard self-respecting New England, insensibly dominated by the fundamental duty of paying one's debts, after which, if one had a fairly safe bank balance, the luxury of charity might be enjoyed. I found, half a mile away, a different psychological make-up. The patience of the poor! Their amiability, crowded as they were into those mean tenements! Their extraordinary hospitality! I thought how carefully we planned our guests for our one dainty guestroom, and how often my mother and aunt and I would tacitly agree to give ourselves a rest from company. Here, with matter-of-fact readiness, in time of need, one more child, a derelict friend out of work, any neighbor in distress, would be added to cramped quarters. Calculation of resources? Nary a bit. Lavish expenditure on funerals, on fur coats, even—silk stockings had not yet come in—horrifying to my careful spirit, trained never to spend five cents on a horse-car if I could possibly walk. Untidiness, of course. Smells, hitherto unknown. What did it matter? [17]

So the settlements caught on: six in 1891, 44 in 1896, nearly 400 by 1911, when they organized the National Federation of Settlements. They housed a galaxy of finders, makers, and pioneers. Visitors thought that Hull House was "the best club in Chicago." Jane Addams became the most famous and honored woman in America, but she was only foremost among many notables.

Once the model was there, it was easy to start a settlement. A few young people of means would rent a roomy house in the slums, fix it up, and open their door to the neighbors. Low capital investment, low labor costs (a housekeeper), big market. Market for what? Just friendship and helpfulness, according to the residents' interests and abilities. Are the neighbors Italian? Invite them to share slides of Italian art; perhaps they will appreciate George Eliot's novel *Romola*, read in Italian (so Hull House began). Twenty or fifty neighbors come to see the beautiful pictures, the elegant sideboard, the finer things. Then a hundred a day, a thousand, several thousand. By 1907 Hull House had expanded from a roomy mansion to thirteen

17. Vida P. Scudder, *On Journey* (New York: Dutton, 1937), p. 147.

buildings sprawled over a large city block. It had become, willy-nilly, an institution with a program. Such was the general fate of settlements.

This was ironic, because the early settlers had rejected the idea of an institution. It contradicted their ideal of neighborly informality and reciprocity, the spontaneous spirit of Christ in human affairs. How could their leaders guide and criticize this development? Since they needed now to appeal for funds, to expand and maintain the plant and to compensate some residents for indispensable services, how could they explain and justify their work?

In 1896 settlement leaders appeared for the first time in a program at the National Conference of Charity and Correction to say what "their work stood for" and what they were "doing in various fields."[18] From this and many other presentations it appears that they expected to make a contribution in three areas. One of these areas was research. As the preface to the 1896 proceedings said, "No student of social science can now afford to ignore what the various settlements throughout the country are doing . . . The scientific information gathered by their residents can nowhere else be duplicated." In her introductory remarks Julia Lathrop, a resident of Hull House, spoke of "that union of brotherly zeal for humanity and scientific ardor for truth which should characterize every settlement."[19] The settlers' first model for research was the epochal study by Charles Booth in England, *Life and Labor of the People of London* (17 volumes, 1889–1903), applied on a small scale to the American immigrant neighborhood. The substantial results included *Hull-House Maps and Papers* (1895) and the studies by residents of Robert Wood's South End House in Boston, *The City Wilderness* (1898) and *Americans in Process* (1902).

At first there was an enthusiastic empirical spirit about this research and the expectation that university sociology departments, which were just taking form, would use the settlements as laboratories and experiment stations.[20] But these efforts petered out. Serious scientific research takes much time and effort; it requires

18. National Conference of Charities and Correction, *Proceedings*, 1896, p. 106.

19. *Ibid.*, pp. iii, 107.

20. F. A. Perrine, "Scientific Aspects of the University Settlement Movement," *Science*, 21 (1893): 91–92; H. Hegner, "The Scientific Value of Social Settlements," *American Journal of Sociology*, 3 (September 1897): 171–82; R. Woods, "University Settlements: Their Point and Drift," *Quarterly Journal of Economics*, 14 (November 1899): 80–83.

money and skill. Standards of research rose rapidly after 1900 in the universities and in public agencies. But settlements did not become research agencies. Residents appeared as advisers or helpers in research rather than initiators. Robert Woods was a key adviser in the Pittsburgh Survey, and settlers were leaders in pushing for the United States Children's Bureau (1912), an effective public research agency (Julia Lathrop became its first chief). But Woods barely mentioned scientific research in *Settlement Horizon* (1922), his extensive review of the movement.

A second broad area of settlement contribution was social reform. Many of the papers at the 1896 conference sounded this theme, in relation to education, labor legislation, municipal reform, and child welfare. It would grow in importance during the progressive years. The basic historical situation was that, in comparison with the demands of modern urban life, our institutions were in a rudimentary state. Educators, for example, ignored the special problems of preschool children and immigrants, as well as recreation, vocational education, and adult education. Physicians paid little attention to public health (prevention of TB and VD, for example), constructive personal hygiene, home nursing, industrial medicine, or mental illness and hygiene. Lawyers ignored the special problems of juveniles and families, small-claims procedures, and legal aid to the poor. Businessmen and economists paid little attention to labor conditions, labor morale, and the arbitration of labor disputes. In all these situations and many others, settlement residents were in a strategic position to see the need, to publicize it, and to rally interested parties to fill it. (Much of their social investigation consisted of collecting facts to show up this abuse or that problem.) They were in a good position to act as mediators between capital and labor or among antagonistic ethnic or religious groups.

But in their deep tendency toward rationality and efficiency in their work settlement residents began to find these reforms awkward and distracting. The big institution that served thousands of neighbors a week needed large funds; a rash committee or action might and often did alienate wealthy supporters. Or perhaps the reform succeeded and the city itself opened a bathhouse, playground, night school, or clinic. Fine, in theory; the settlement would move on to something else, always a new conscience looking for a new cause. Meanwhile, however, many residents had found a job to do and wanted to get about the business of doing it better.

The job—the third and enduring area of settlement interest—was club work or, more generally, informal education and recreation. Children were the first visitors to the new settlement, the most persistent, the most winning, the avenue to meeting neighborhood families. Soon there were boys' and girls' clubs for children of different ages and interests. Often these gave direction to associations (or gangs) first formed on the street. There were clubs for adolescents, some of them in school, many already employed, and for the "young manhood" of the neighborhood. The gymnasium (hitherto a luxury of college men) and the playground were usually the first large investments apart from the settlement residence. There were important clubs for working girls and housewives: before the settlements came these groups had had almost no formal association that could clarify and focus their interests.

At first the clubs were haphazard—what neighbors wanted or residents could do. Presently, however, it became possible to take a more systematic view of unmet needs and to recruit volunteer group leaders who could respond. Of course the volunteers needed some advice, support, and training. There were many difficulties with clubs and volunteers; many volunteers left town for the summer, for example, just when the children's need was greatest. A large summer camp and program was another expensive addition to the settlement enterprise. There were also great gains. Modern notions of child-centered education got a warm reception (John Dewey was on the board of Hull House, which tried out many of his ideas about education). The original inclination to share the beauties of traditional culture, in the fashion of middle-class women's clubs, soon gave way to groups that practiced handicrafts, painting, music, or drama. The performances tapped a great talent and enthusiasm, but of course space, tools, instruments, and auditoriums all cost money.

Over the years group leaders picked up a good deal of lore about types of people, groups, interests, and problems of organization. The director of club work was second only to the head resident in importance, the nucleus of a growing number of salaried workers. For the most part the lore remained at an empirical and practical level. Robert Woods, who was the dominant figure in the National Federation of Settlements and thought more about the technical side of the work than anyone else, noted the change from the first type of club director, characterized by "physical strength, personal magnetism, and . . . ready understanding and sympathy" to "the educator in . . .

social work" able to apply the lessons of "modern psychologic research and experiment" to "group work for all ages, and to train staff assistants . . . who will carry out his program."[21]

Woods did not go on to develop a technique of group work, however. His reflections were about the role of the clubs in the settlement and the role of the settlement in the neighborhood. He realized that the club was not only a means to draw out the latent potential of its members; it was also a way to develop very concretely a process of working together and mutual understanding, and ultimately a sense of democratic participation and civic responsibility. At the heart of the disorganization of neighborhood life, which he saw so plainly, was a fundamental weakness of group identification. The humble process of associating in the group, organizing, sharing with other groups in the settlement facilities might help form a person with a positive temperament and inclination, the "cooperative man" who would be prepared to help manage not only the immediate social affairs of the neighborhood but also the larger "demands and opportunities of a better industrial order." Woods thought of this as a step in the "Fabian principle of applying democratic methods by successive experiments to industry."[22]

There were, Woods thought, three stages in the "interaction of settlement and neighborhood." The first was simply informal hospitality: residents were hosts, neighbors were guests. In the second, as the settlement added to its plant, program, and staff—that is, as the institution grew—the residents took initiatives to encourage sociability and the neighbors began to share responsibility and decisions around the organization (they set standards of behavior and assessed dues in their clubs and, with representatives of other clubs, made decisions about priorities in the use of facilities). The third stage— still in the future—would be a "new synthesis of locality." In that stage the neighborhood would progress toward a kind of autonomy, loyalty, and public spirit, institutionalized perhaps in a neighborhood improvement society.[23]

The founders of the COS had hoped by districting and friendly visiting to restore a degree of neighborly interest and control. The founders of the settlement went beyond this to the idea of actually residing there and sharing the neighborhood life in all ways, not sim-

---

21. Woods, *Settlement Horizon*, p. 86; see also p. 344.   22. *Ibid.*, pp. 208, 221.
23. *Ibid.*, pp. 341–61.

ply as agents of charity. Woods (and of course many other residents) arrived at a much more complicated notion of neighborhood disorganization and a process that might counteract it. In any case his ideas were in tune with the aspiration of younger workers. "The chief need," he wrote in 1922, "is for trained persons willing to devote themselves, through personal and professional service," to the "new leadership in recreation and education, the new democracy itself." [24]

Many residents, he recognized, favored the informal hospitality of the first period.[25] Many, like Vida Scudder, lost interest as the settlements became professionalized.

> The process was inevitable, I knew [she wrote]. Trained ability became on every line more obviously essential. Also, the old volunteer devotion ran up sharply against another force, which commanded my warm sympathy—the economic emancipation of women. No longer "ladies in waiting," girls now sought paid careers just as their brothers did. Gone were the days when . . . [a headworker] refused for some time to waive her scruples at being paid for being a good neighbor. Almost everybody was paid now. The gain in efficiency was plain, nor need paid workers, thank God, be lacking in devotion. But I may be pardoned if I persist in feeling that there was loss of a certain aroma . . . the crusading spirit of the early years.[26]

In the transformation of a spirit of philanthropy into an institution for social welfare, the sponsors of the COS had a great advantage over the settlement houses. They set themselves a more specific problem: to minimize pauperism (dependency) by restoring paupers to self-sufficiency or preventing their decline. They could get down to cases, agencies, and procedures. They believed in charity and wanted to expand it, but they were not afraid of organization and rational techniques. On the other hand, their focus on pauperism was too narrow, as they themselves realized when they began to explore the idea of prevention. As for the settlements, it was hard for them to escape their "besetting sin of sentimentality and vagueness," [27] but they did look toward the general quality of life, away from pauperism and relief and toward poverty and deprivation, and in that way they were important in redirecting thought from nineteenth-century "charity and correction" to twentieth-century "social welfare."

24. *Ibid.*, p. 351.   25. *Ibid.*, p. 343.   26. Scudder, *On Journey*, pp. 164f.

27. The phrase is by Albert J. Kennedy, a distinguished leader of the settlement house movement in the 1920s, in his biographical notice of his colleague and mentor Robert Woods, in *The Dictionary of American Biography*, Dumes Malone, ed., 20 vols. (New York: Scribner's, 1928–1934), XX, 504.

Chapter

9

The Progressive Years,

1900–1919

IN THE NINETEENTH century there were two lines of thought about social welfare: the doctrine of charity, associated with traditional religion, and that of secular liberalism, associated particularly with political economy and ethical individualism. In the progressive years their differing implications about social justice came together in the first version of the welfare state.

There had always been some contradiction between Christian charity and liberalism. The religious view supposed that personality was touched with the divine and responsive to conscience and duty as laid down in holy writ. It rested upon sentiments of fellow-feeling and human solidarity. It conceived of society as organic, structured perhaps in some communal or familial arrangement, such as the primitive church or a monastery, or perhaps in mutually responsible classes, as in the idealization of the feudal order. Owners of private property were stewards of God's bounty. On the other hand, secular liberalism conceived of individuals as hedonistic and self-seeking. It emphasized their particular rights, notably that of accumulating property or "estate," which was supposed to be a great incentive to effort that they would not make otherwise. Liberals conceived of society as an association or compact of such individuals, contracting with others in what they thought was some mutual advantage, whose pursuit of self-interest, operating in a free economy, contributed in a wonderful way to a natural harmony of interests.

Despite these inherent contradictions, the two traditions seemed to be mutually reinforcing during the nineteenth century. People who set up sectarian charities, state boards of charities, charity organization societies, or social settlements usually had a religious motivation. They accepted liberal political economy as the right idea (the scientific idea) about social policy, but added to it the notion that the affluent had a moral responsibility or duty to help the unfortunate. Those who were scientific in spirit questioned the means and ends of helping, not the liberal idea of social policy. Their various innovations were conceived as better ways of helping people who needed help.

By the 1890s both these lines of thought—religious and secular—were challenged from within. Liberalism as a social theory was a product of the eighteenth century, much influenced in its scientific assumptions by Newtonian physics. Liberals thought there were "natural laws" of the polity and economy, such as the "law of supply and demand," and the intellectual problem was to identify them and act accordingly. In the late nineteenth century social Darwinists, who pushed the individualist and competitive elements of liberalism to an extreme, thought that evolution by the survival of the fittest was such a law, and that it applied to the marketplace as well as to the jungle. But a later type of evolutionary thought emphasized that ideas were not approximations of universal reality but weapons or instruments for dealing with human problems. This insight encouraged a more empirical and practical spirit, evident in the pragmatism of William James and especially in the instrumentalism of John Dewey.

James and Dewey and their associates were particularly critical of the psychological assumptions of eighteenth-century liberalism, that individuals naturally pursued pleasure and avoided work except when bribed by the lure of acquisition. They recognized that people's interests and motives were very broad and shaped by their associations, that one could not deduce a system of social policy from speculations about human nature, as the political economists did. Nor could one deduce the principles of politics from suppositions about a state of nature. Researches in history, anthropology, psychology, and social psychology all brought out that nineteenth-century liberalism and individualism were a cultural peculiarity. Most American scholars—for most of these researchers were academics of a new sort—rejected the socialist collectivism that was sometimes advanced as a systematic alternative to liberalism. They accepted the values of liberal individualism but recognized that many reforms were feasible and advisable. They became a source of ideas for social and political interests that looked toward betterment.

Meanwhile the religious tradition of charitable concern was also modified. The new "social gospel" generally turned away from the agony of personal faith and the salvation of the believer to the influence of religion in advancing the kingdom of God, conceived of as a more wholesome and just society. When the Federal Council of Churches of Christ was organized in 1908, this view became, on paper at least, the policy of the well-established Protestant churches. As for those who were actually engaged in scientific charity, the notion of casework directed attention toward the "social environment" in the case, as Mary Richmond put it, and to the reciprocal influences of heredity and environment on human behavior and problems. In studying the case, or in devising a rational program for a class of cases, the notion of technical competence and service came increasingly to the fore, taking their place beside the older notions of duty and the impulse to help.

So the main tendency after 1890 was toward a more critical social science in the universities and a more critical practice in social agencies. Of course there was a great deal of confusion and divergence. Influences on the course of events came mostly by way of the interest of the business and professional class. Rural people—still very much a dominant group in 1900—were not much interested in the problems of the industrial labor class or urban life. The industrial labor class itself was divided along ethnic, religious, and class lines. Skilled workers, about one-fifth of the labor force, were able to organize the unions that combined into the American Federation of Labor, but as it happened their leaders put their faith in collective bargaining—that is, power—rather than in scientific social policy or philanthropy. It proved impossible to organize the unskilled around a class interest, so that much reform had to be undertaken by others in their behalf.

One change that brought political economy and philanthropic charity into a closer relationship was a converging interest in the subject of poverty. Nineteenth-century philanthropists had thought mostly about *pauperism*, the extreme of poverty at which people are dependent on public or private charity. Political economists had thought mostly about the fact that charity, whether public or private, was subtracted from an economic surplus that might otherwise be spent for productive machinery or higher wages. It was recognized that paupers were only the poorest of the poor and that particularly in the urban proletariat there were many workers on the verge of pauperism. But there was not much empirical knowledge about how many paupers there were, and how many poor, and how poor they were. As the century passed, the increasing productivity of the factory system seemed to promise great abundance, and the standard of living did rise for many people. Against this promise the persistence of need and suffering among large classes of people seemed wrong, and many thinkers puzzled over the paradox of progress and poverty. Thomas Malthus, Karl Marx, and Henry George were the most famous of these thinkers. They were in the deductive tradition of political economy. For them empirical facts about pauperism and poverty were merely evidence for their general argument.

Empirical study of poverty began in 1885, when Charles Booth, a wealthy English businessman, undertook a task of decades, the painstaking description of the working class of London. "The *a priori* reasoning of political economy, orthodox and unorthodox alike, fails from want of reality," he said when he began to present his findings. "At its base are a series of assumptions very imperfectly connected with the observed facts of life."[1] Booth began as a liberal individualist in outspoken opposition to collectivists. In time he changed his beliefs, although he remained rather conservative. His main contribution was to invent the concept of a *poverty line* and to give it an empirical content in the form of a definite standard of living. He based his standard on systematic observation in which he distinguished eight classes ranging from A ("the lowest class . . . semi-occasional labourers . . . of low character") to H (the upper middle class, "the servant-keeping class"). He took as his *normal standard* class E, the bulk of families, whose breadwinners were regularly employed at weekly wages of 22 to 30 shillings. Below them were four classes of people who suffered increasing degrees of deprivation. After much careful work Booth (and his team of helpers) found that, relative to his normal standard, 30.7 percent of London families lived in poverty and 69.3 percent in comfort.[2]

Booth's survey made a great difference in how philanthropists perceived pauperism. As Amos Warner observed in *American Chari-*

1. Quoted in T[homas] S. Simey, and M. B. Simey, *Charles Booth, Social Scientist* (London: Oxford University Press, 1960), p. 68.

2. *Ibid.*, pp. 115f., 184, 275–79.

ties (1894), the COS leaders, when they tried to understand causes, studied the paupers who came to them for help, so they tended to see the personal characteristics of the needy. Booth, however, drew attention to the much larger group of people who were living in *poverty*, that is, deprived relative to a normal standard of living, and he emphasized the circumstances that forced them lower on the scale. Warner, who appreciated Booth's contribution, was particularly interested in the social factors of physical weakness (or "degeneration")—industrial disease or accidents, bad sanitation in homes or at work—but Booth himself had emphasized unemployment.[3] In general, Booth's type of analysis brought out environmental as distinct from personal causes of dependency, and it suggested the promise of environmental reforms.

The notions of a normal standard of living and a poverty line were also significant for economists. In 1890 the Cambridge University economist Alfred Marshall, in the first edition of a textbook that would dominate a generation, stated the normal standard in terms of "the necessaries for the efficiency of an ordinary agricultural or of an unskilled town labourer and his family"; food, shelter, clothing, or amenities below this standard would threaten the efficiency of the worker's performance. Marshall realized that the normal standard was to some extent subjective, that it changed over time, but he believed it was reasonably definite at any particular time.[4] Philanthropists, for their part, found the normal standard a help in defining the amount of need and the adequacy of relief. By 1904 Edward Devine, who had a Ph.D. in economics and was general secretary of the Charity Organization Society of New York, conceived his book *Principles of Relief* around "the formulation and general acceptance of the idea of a normal standard of living, and the rigid adoption of either disciplinary or charitable measures, as may be found appropriate . . . for those families and individuals whose income and expenditure do not conform to such standard."[5]

In the same year, 1904, Robert Hunter, the head worker at University Settlement (New York), published his book *Poverty*, which

3. Amos G. Warner, *American Charities* (New York, 1894), pp. 23–29, 95–117; Simey, *Charles Booth*, p. 95.

4. Alfred Marshall, *Principles of Economics* (London, 1890), I, 122–23.

5. Edward Devine, *Principles of Relief* (New York: Macmillan, 1904), p. 19.

made a sensational and influential statement of the new view of poverty as deprivation relative to a standard of normal living that was necessary for industrial efficiency. He put together statistics that indicated that 10 million (out of 82 million) Americans lived below this standard. Four million of these were actually paupers (that is, dependent on charity). The others were struggling against deprivations that very much threatened their ability to remain self-sufficient. The practical point of Hunter's analysis was the need for "preventive" reforms that would help the already deprived from falling further into dependency. These reforms, he said, "contemplate mainly such legislative action as may enforce upon the entire country certain minimum standards of working and of living conditions."[6] Specifically, he thought the government should establish and enforce minimum standards to

> make all tenements and factories safe
> regulate hours of work, especially for women and children
> regulate and supervise dangerous trades
> eradicate "unnecessary disease" (such as tuberculosis)
> prohibit child labor
> provide educational and recreational institutions
> compensate labor for involuntary idleness due to sickness, old age, or unemployment
> restrict immigration[7]

This was an early statement of some of the social goals of the progressive period, what might be called the first version of the welfare state in America. Most of these ideas had been around for some time, but now they fell together in a cogent argument: look beyond pauperism to the more fundamental problem of poverty; define a poverty line related to physical efficiency (and, more subjectively, to minimal decency); enforce the minimum by positive action of the state (a rejection of dogmatic *laissez-faire* liberalism). Such reforms would not destroy incentive (as the partisans of deterrence had argued); they would increase it by equalizing opportunity and improving the morale of the poor.[8]

These ideas were refined in the next few years. In 1906 Father John Ryan published his doctoral dissertation, *A Living Wage*, which

6. Robert Hunter, *Poverty* (New York: Macmillan, 1904), pp. 5–11, 337f.

7. *Ibid.*, pp. 338f.   8. *Ibid.*, pp. 7f., 339.

elaborated the ethical argument that labor was not a mere commodity in the marketplace, that workers were human beings who ought to receive a wage that would allow them a degree of self-respect and spiritual culture. Ryan soon became the foremost advocate of stating the living wage as a legal minimum wage. He thought that industries that could not meet such a standard were parasitical and better done away with.[9] In 1906 the New York State Conference of Charities authorized an investigation of actual standards of living in New York City by Robert Chapin, a doctoral student at Columbia, where Devine had recently been appointed professor of "social economics." Chapin's study went beyond a few earlier official studies of workingmen's family budgets—it was more analytical and reflective—and by the time the Russell Sage Foundation published it in 1909 it had become the model for several such investigations, notably Margaret Byington's admirable study of the steelworkers' families in the Pittsburgh Survey.[10]

That year—1909—the National Conference on Charities and Corrections appointed a "committee on occupational standards" that was chaired by Paul Kellogg, editor of the *Survey* magazine and recently director of the Pittsburgh Survey. The formulation and advocacy of minimum standards were his kind of social work, and all of the Pittsburgh Survey was pertinent to this theme. In 1910 the committee broadened its subject to "standards of living and labor," and in 1912 it formulated a rather specific list, including the following: a living wage in industry; minimum wage commissions in each state; an eight-hour day and a six-day week; factory safety legislation and inspection; legal standards for housing, especially tenements; prohibition of manufacture in the home, that is, sweatshops; legal standards for camps for migratory workers; no wage labor for children under 16; proper accommodation for "the unemployable" in labor colonies and industrial training for those who could use it; and compensation or insurance for industrial accidents and disease, old-age retirement, and unemployment.[11]

9. John A. Ryan, *Social Doctrine in Action, A Personal History* (New York: Harpers, 1941), pp. 80f., 88–92.

10. Robert C. Chapin, *The Standard of Living Among Workingmen's Families in New York City* (New York: Charities Publication Committee, 1909); Margaret F. Byington, *Homestead: The Households of a Mill Town* (New York: Charities Publication Committee, 1910).

11. National Conference of Charities and Correction, *Proceedings*, 1912, pp. 388–94.

The National Conference committee submitted these standards to the Republican National Committee, which was then forming its platform for the election of 1912. They were rebuffed, but they found a warmer hearing at the founding of the Progressive party under the leadership of the popular former President Theodore Roosevelt. The Progressives wrote the standards into their platform as one way to conserve human resources.[12] Meanwhile the platform of the Socialist party, then rising under Eugene Debs to the peak of its popularity, adopted similar planks. Together these parties won more than one-third of the vote in the election of 1912 (Democrats, 6.3 million votes; Republicans, 3.5 million; Progressives, 4.1 million; Socialists, .9 million).

The Progressive party campaign attracted enthusiastic support from many social workers. Jane Addams, who seconded Roosevelt's nomination, thought that some of the convention's committee meetings were like a "session of the National Conference of Charities and Corrections" or perhaps a learned society such as she attended, and she thrilled to the religious enthusiasm of the meetings.[13] In time it became clear, however, that the Progressive party was a faction within the dominant Republican party. Insofar as its partisans supported the platform plank of minimum standards, they were seeking to help certain depressed groups—immigrants in household industries and southern textile workers, and generally women and child workers—who had no organization of their own, did not vote Progressive, and were often indifferent or even hostile to the reforms offered in their behalf. Moreover, the actual drafting of standards for work, housing, sanitation, and social insurance proved to be full of technical and political difficulties that would endure long after the initial enthusiasm had passed.

To the extent that the affirmation of minimum standards in 1912 was a passing fancy, it was part of a much larger enthusiasm for social reform and social justice that seems to have been inspired by the success of the "muckraking" magazines among the middle classes in the years 1900–1912. The heroes (and readers) of the muckrakers were solid citizens who were portrayed as victims of a corrupt alliance

12. Allen F. Davis, *Spearheads for Reform: The Social Settlements and the Progressive Movement, 1890–1914* (New York: Oxford University Press, 1967), pp. 194–201.

13. Jane Addams, *The Second Twenty Years at Hull House* (New York: Macmillan, 1930), pp. 28–32.

between political "bosses" and big businessmen. The main message was that the government ought to serve and protect the people, especially taxpayers and consumers. In this righteous indignation there were also more philanthropic strains, evident in the charity organization societies, the social gospel, and the settlement houses. Middle-class people who learned that they were the victims of corrupt politicians, trusts, stock market manipulators, and packers of tainted meat (to name a few muckraker targets) could sympathize with the plight of those whose labor was treated as a mere commodity and whose circumstances were below decent American standards.

Whatever the practical perplexities, by 1912 the nineteenth-century concern about paupers, criminals, and institutions for their relief or correction was somewhat eclipsed by a bold new notion of "social welfare" that addressed itself to impersonal causes of poverty and injustice and looked toward a more equal and just society. So philanthropy and social policy were brought closer together.

In the 1890s interest in the welfare of children began to change significantly and to become more central in social work and social reform. Nineteenth-century "child-saving" had sought out the child who was practically separated from his family (the Huckleberry Finn type, especially in the big cities). Its main dynamic was the rivalry of religious groups to save the children's souls. In this work correct religious indoctrination was fundamental; for the rest, there were angry debates about which was better, the orphanage (favored especially by Catholics) or the foster home (favored by some Protestants). A third option, keeping children in the general almshouse, along with their older relatives, perhaps, was rejected by both sides. After the Civil War several states passed laws to get children out of the almshouses. Religious groups favored such removal, and religious orphanages grew because of it, especially where they could collect a subsidy for the care of the child. As it happened, there was not much imagination in the program of these institutions, which was rigid and repressive in the manner of nineteenth-century schools, so that informed opinion tended to favor foster care (or "placing out").

Foster care depended on the usefulness of children around the house and farm ("Little Orphant Annie's come to our house to stay, /To wash the cups and saucers up, and an' brush the crumbs away

. . .").[14] As critics observed, such children were vulnerable to exploitation or abuse, which is why many of them ran away. Prospective parents were reluctant to take children too young to work. But good administration could solve these problems. The Massachusetts State Board of Charities, which led in this work, along with the State Board of Michigan, arranged for agents to supervise its foster children (1869) and also for the "boarding out" of younger children (1882). Boarding out meant that the state paid foster parents to take care of ("board") the child who was too young to pay his way by helping.

In Massachusetts this policy applied only to dependent children who were *state* charges, however, and many remained the responsibility of local officials. Most of these were in Boston, where a private agency, the Children's Aid Society, stepped in to take care of them. Like the State Board, it favored placing out. To this agency came, in 1886, Charles Birtwell, who did much to advance a professional standard in work with children. Birtwell was a recent graduate of Harvard, where, like many other young men entering the field—Robert Woods for one—he had found inspiration in the famous "social ethics" course of Francis Peabody. (Peabody, a learned Unitarian clergyman, was part of the galaxy of philanthropists who made Boston's charities the envy of other communities.) Birtwell's job was to place and supervise children and to help young probationers. There in Boston, where agencies were so numerous and well supported, he better than anyone else could see a range of options for helping children in the home or removing them to some particular institution or foster home. Given the range of options, the problem was to define them more clearly, especially the qualities of various foster parents. Birtwell worked out a systematic way of studying and selecting foster homes, but his chief contribution was a point of view: "The aim will be in each instance to suit the action to the real need—heeding the teachings of experience, still to study the conditions with a freedom from assumptions, and a directness and freshness of view, as complete as though the case stood absolutely alone."[15]

14. James Whitcomb Riley, "Little Orphant Annie," in *Complete Poetical Works* (Garden City, N.Y.: Garden City Publishing Co., 1941), p. 370.

15. Quoted in Henry W. Thurston, *The Dependent Child* (New York: Columbia University Press, 1930), pp. 185f.

So the *real need* of the particular child became the focus of thought, along with a deliberate definition of and search for a variety of dispositions. Of course there were generalizations—kinds of children, kinds of foster homes—but they became much more refined and individualized. The prospect of maintaining or restoring ties to the natural family also offered an option. Boston was a leader in charity organization and friendly visiting, and Birtwell could assimilate to the general improvement in casework his interest in studying dependent and delinquent children and in foster-home placement.

Birtwell had a young friend, Homer Folks (1867–1963), also a graduate of Harvard and of Peabody's course, who became an important agent for spreading Boston notions about child welfare. In 1890 he was appointed general agent of the Children's Aid Society of Pennsylvania, in Philadelphia, where he introduced Birtwell's ideas about thorough investigation and supervision of children and foster homes, as well as the use of boarding homes. He developed a program, which attracted national attention, for placing delinquent children in foster homes. In 1893 the State Charities Aid Association of New York, the leading vehicle of charity reform in that state, which wanted to promote placing out and boarding-home care, hired him as its executive, a position he filled with great distinction until 1947. The better methods and discrimination urged by Birtwell and Folks did much to mollify the opponents of foster care. By 1898 Catholics in New York had organized their own home placement society and J. M. Mulry, a New York lawyer who was president of the St. Vincent de Paul Society, had brought many Catholics around to the idea.[16]

Meanwhile the idea of home instead of institutional care was being extended to delinquent (as well as dependent) children in the form of probation and the juvenile court. The first juvenile court was established in Chicago in 1899. Its moving spirit was the Chicago Women's Club, which beginning in 1883 had done much to improve the decency of police stations and the jail, especially for

16. On Folks, I follow the excellent biography by Walter Trattner, *Homer Folks* (New York: Columbia University Press, 1968), pp. 12–30. On the change in Catholic opinion, see National Conference of Charities and Correction, *Proceedings*, 1899, pp. 167f.; John O'Grady, *Catholic Charities in the United States* (Washington, D.C.: National Conference of Catholic Charities, 1930), pp. 435f.

women and children. The women were also concerned about the miscarriage of justice that occurred when judges let children off without penalty because the penalties—imprisonment or fine—were so inappropriate for poverty-stricken youngsters. The idea was that a special juvenile court and judge would not only separate young from older offenders at this early stage of the legal process but also provide wiser justice. Technically the proceedings were a marked departure from ordinary criminal courts, which emphasized legal formalities and guilt. The new court was a chancery or noncriminal court of equity, in which the judge acted as a wise parent might. In theory he was supposed to fit his dispositions to the particular needs of the child, and in general the court was an example of this new focus in child welfare.

Under this system the favored disposition was a suspended sentence in which the offender would go back to his parents—not to an institution—but under the supervision of a probation officer. There had been precedents for such probation in Massachusetts (1869) and Michigan (1873). Clearly much depended on the character of the probation officers. In the Chicago court this important work was deliberately left to private citizens in order to keep it out of the hands of political spoilsmen. The women who sponsored the juvenile court and got it through the state legislature set up a Juvenile Court Committee under Julia Lathrop that raised money for salaries, carefully chose the probation officers, and helped them in their work. Other courts often followed this pattern.[17]

This type of court spread very rapidly, but its performance was uneven, depending on local interest and support. In New York Homer Folks, who had previously worked for state supervision and standardization of agencies that arranged foster home placement, now, in 1905, became the leading figure in the efforts of state authorities to encourage a more professional type of probation: requirements about records, civil-service exams and procedures, and other features of a rational social-service bureaucracy.

"We learn to deal more and more wisely with those [children] who are in distress, but the forces which produce poverty, neglect,

17. Julia Lathrop, "Background of the Juvenile Court in Illinois," and J. Brown, "Early Days of the Juvenile Court," in Jane Addams et al., *The Child, the Clinic and the Court* (New York: New Republic, 1925), pp. 290–302.

and crime seem to be beyond our reach," Folks wrote in concluding a famous survey of child welfare in 1902.[18] But in fact the plight of child labor would prove central in the progressives' war against poverty. The leader here was Florence Kelley (1859–1932). The daughter of a powerful Pennsylvania congressman (whose partisanship for the tariff had earned him the name "Pig-Iron Kelley"), the translator of Friedrich Engels, a divorcee with three children, she was one of the most brilliant of the group that gathered in Hull House, luminous in her deep compassion and righteous indignation. In 1889 she presented an incisive criticism of child labor statistics at a meeting of state labor bureaus. She impressed Carroll Wright, the federal commissioner of labor, and in 1892 Wright put her in charge of an investigation of Chicago slums. In 1893 the Illinois Bureau of Labor asked her to investigate the sweating system of home manufacture; part of the result was published in *Hull-House Maps and Papers* (1895), and meanwhile she had become chief factory inspector for Illinois under a new factory act.

As a factory inspector Kelley became a foremost authority on the actual conditions of labor in industry. She paid special attention to women and children. Children ordinarily worked around the home and the farm in the nineteenth century, often very hard. What Kelley's investigations revealed was something more, a literally horrifying abuse of many young workers, such that if they survived at all they were likely to be sickly or injured in body and mind and certainly unprepared for responsible adult life. What struck her was not just the suffering of the youngsters but the terrible social cost in later sickness, disability, pauperism, and crime. What infuriated her was not just the foolish rationalizations of employers and the connivance of parents (including the citizens around Alton, Illinois, who took in foster children from the almshouses in surrounding countries to work under harrowing conditions in the glass works), but the general ignorant complacency, the unwillingness of district attorneys to enforce the law and of boards of education to compel attendance at school, and the fatuity of the courts that insisted on a wildly irrelevant "freedom of contract."

A new governor fired Kelley in 1897. She became a librarian and often spoke on labor problems. In 1899 she was chosen to head a

18. Homer Folks, *The Care of Destitute, Neglected, and Delinquent Children* (New York: Macmillan, 1902), p. 246.

new organization, the National Consumers League, which was a combination of several local leagues, the earliest of which had been formed in New York in 1891 under the sponsorship of Josephine Shaw Lowell. The idea was to organize the ladies who shopped in department stores in order to win better working conditions for the salesgirls and children who worked there. In 1898 the New York League investigated a strike in the ladies' tailoring industry and found that even fine garments were often finished in tenements where contagious disease was likely to be present. So the League went behind the labor conditions of store clerks to those of manufacturers. The notion of a consumers league spread nationwide among middle-class women, especially on college campuses, partly in response to the rousing message of Florence Kelley. As for program, Kelley developed the label of approval, analogous to a union label in its certification of standards. In effect she became a private factory and store inspector for conscientious consumers, and the League's membership, small but prestigious and articulate, became leading advocates of protective labor legislation.

Prohibition of child labor was a basic standard for the Consumers League label, and Kelley became chairman of committees on the subject in the National Women's Suffrage Association, the National Congress of Mothers, and the General Federation of Women's Clubs. When she arrived in New York she lived at the Henry Street Settlement, and in 1902 she and Lillian Wald, the head worker there, got the New York settlements to appoint a child labor committee with Robert Hunter as its chairman. The committee collected and published information about working children, especially information on the problems of documenting proof of age. In 1906 the New York committee founded a National Committee on Child Labor that was aimed especially at the employment of children in southern textile mills. This group won considerable support, not only from northern textile manufacturers, who were already prohibited from employing children, but also from southern philanthropists, many of them in women's organizations. The attention to child and female labor gave specificity to the rising demand for minimum wage and maximum hour laws. It was recognized that these workers were unlikely to organize unions, so that a paternal state intervention was necessary, and of course low wages were the reason that parents often connived at breaking the law to keep their children at gainful work.

Meanwhile the increasing attention to the ramifications of poverty (as opposed to pauperism) was causing new reflections about foster care. If home care was better than institutional care, and if it was worthwhile to pay foster parents for the board of children, and if children were sometimes removed from their parents simply because the parents could not support them—why not in that case pay the parents the subsidy that otherwise might go to a boarding home? The question was particularly appropriate in the case of the widow left with several children, who might have to surrender some or all of them so she could get a job to support the others or simply herself. Much of the most successful casework in charity organization societies was with such widows. Agents found sources of material assistance for them, or appropriate employment, and gave them moral support and helpful advice. The conviction grew that a child should not be separated from its home for reasons of poverty alone.

In 1908 James West, a Washington lawyer and a friend of President Theodore Roosevelt who would later become head of the Boy Scouts, asked the President to call a national conference on the subject of dependent children. He had been impressed by the recent enthusiasm for the juvenile court for delinquents, and he wanted to stir up help for dependent children who went into asylums or foster care. The President, who from his days in New York knew and respected Homer Folks, asked that Folks approve the idea and later made him presiding officer of a Conference on the Care of Dependent Children (1909), which became the first of a series of decennial "White House Conferences." The participants, very much an elite of child welfare, took as the keynote of their report the thought that "home life is the highest and finest product of civilization"; that "children should not be deprived of it except for urgent and compelling reasons"; and that, except in unusual circumstances, "the home should not be broken up for reasons of poverty." [19]

The conference sidestepped the important question, however, whether aid to the threatened family should be under private or public auspices. The notion of public pensions for deserving widows with children gained ground and was hotly debated at the National Conference on Charities in 1912. The opposition to public pensions came from experts associated with the older charity organization societies, who thought that such a "widows' pension" (or mothers' pen-

19. Trattner, *Homer Folks*, pp. 104–7.

sion or fund for parents) was a misleading name for a new kind of public outdoor relief, open to all the dangers of fraud and political corruption or, at best, perfunctory administration, that they had found in outdoor relief. Most families that were separated had many problems besides poverty, they argued—sickness or inability to manage, for example—and needed casework. As for financial aid, people in the community should feel a personal responsibility to help and the recipients should feel a reciprocal responsibility to help themselves as much as they could; that was what organized charity was about. Other criticisms of public pensions were that it would be better to invest public money in measures for health and safety that would diminish the risk of widowhood (the campaign against TB, for example) or in insurance programs that would rationalize the costs of accident or illness as part of the cost of industrial production.

The 1912 debate turned on the experience of the first operative program, begun in 1911 in Chicago. Merritt Pinckney, who administered it as part of his work as judge of the Juvenile Court, admitted that there were many problems. The program had been publicized in a misleading way, and he was swamped with applicants. He called on the private relief societies of Chicago to provide experienced workers, at private expense, to review the claims; they rejected two-thirds. Because the Cook County fathers had appropriated very scanty funds, the "pensions" granted were far below adequate levels (averaging $6.33 per child per month). But, he said, a public agency could in principle develop good administrative practices, as evidenced by the notable improvement going forward in public services for foster home placement and juvenile probation. Moreover, while public grants were not adequate, neither were those of private relief agencies. There was much doubt as to whether private charity could finance this sort of relief. Homer Folks, who was present at the debate, preferred that widows' aid come from private sources but recognized that if private charity could not secure sufficient funds public agencies would step in. Neither he nor Julia Lathrop, who also commented, expressed any doubt that public administration could be as conscientious and professional as that of private agencies.

What was ignored in this particular discussion of public or private administration was the point that the advocacy of mothers' pensions rested in part, as Edward Devine said in 1913, on popular "opposition to, and prejudice against, private charity, and especially against what is known as organized charity, distinguished by investigation, the keeping of records, discrimination in relief, and insistence upon full use of personal resources . . ." and that this difference of opinion rested "less upon evidence than upon . . . social philosophy . . ."[20] By this time twenty states had widows' pensions, and by 1921 forty states had them. The principle was accepted of a public relief fund for widows with dependent children, separate from ordinary outdoor relief and with a different standard of adequacy and administration. The details of the laws differed greatly as to whether they were optional or mandatory upon local authorities, how grants were determined, financed, and administered, and by what agency of government. And despite the popular prejudice against charity organization principles, the long-run pressure was toward a discriminating sort of investigation and service.[21]

So the interest in child welfare led in many directions—better casework and supervision in foster home placement, juvenile courts and probation, child labor legislation, and widows' pensions, not to mention the hopes for the public schools in those days when John Dewey's ideas about child-centered education and democracy were spreading across the land—and in 1912 it issued in a major departure in the federal government: the United States Children's Bureau. As early as 1900 Florence Kelley had proposed a national commission that would collect, analyze, and interpret facts about children, pulling together, for example, information that was then lying scattered in the federal bureaus of education, labor, and the census. Among likely subjects she mentioned infant mortality, birth registration, orphanage, child labor, desertion, illegitimacy, and degeneracy. The Henry Street Settlement, where she lived, had pioneered a program of public health nursing, and Lillian Wald, its head worker, was especially interested in health statistics. In 1903 the two women proposed such an agency to Edward Devine, who publicized their thoughts in *Charities* and brought them to the attention of President Theodore Roosevelt. Roosevelt took up the idea and asked Wald to come to Washington to discuss it. "On that day," she recalled, "the Secretary of Agriculture was departing . . . to find out what danger

20. Quoted in Robert Bremner et al., *Children and Youth in America: A Documentary History*, 3 vols. in 5 (Cambridge, Mass.: Harvard University Press, 1970–1974), II, 377f.

21. See, e.g., Edith Abbott, "The Experimental Period of Widows Pension Legislation," in National Conference of Charities and Correction, *Proceedings*, 1917, pp. 154–65.

to the community lurked in the appearance of the boll weevil. That brought home . . . the fact that nothing that would have happened to the children would have called forth such official action." [22]

The National Child Labor Committee undertook to draft the legislation, with careful consultation among existing agencies of statistical and child welfare work. Introduced in 1906, it was identified with the agitation to prohibit child labor and opposed mostly by southerners who raised the questions whether such an agency was constitutional, whether its proposed work was not better done by existing bureaus, and whether it was not in any case an attack on the rights of parents. These arguments were doubtless a rationalization of economic interests, but they reflected popular skepticism about restricting child labor. In 1909 the White House Conference on Dependent Children asked for a Children's Bureau and President Roosevelt sent a special message to Congress in its favor. After long delay the bill was signed into law by President William Howard Taft in April 1912 as events were pointing toward the climactic presidential election of that year.

As chief of the new bureau Taft appointed Julia Lathrop, a resident of Hull House who had distinguished herself through her work on the Illinois State Board of Charities and the Chicago Juvenile Court Committee. Her purpose, she said, was "to serve all children [not just the poor], to try to work out the standards of care and protection which shall give to every child his fair chance in the world." [23] With a tiny initial appropriation ($25,000) and staff (15), she wanted somehow to establish a reputation for scientific disinterestedness and accuracy. Her first investigation was a brilliant stroke. She avoided the politically controversial subject of child labor and set out to discover what proportion of babies died and why. This was a mystery because, among other problems, birth registration was so poor that no one knew how many were born. Lathrop projected a series of studies of representative places, beginning with the industrial town of Johnstown, Pennsylvania. She reversed the usual procedure by beginning with records of birth rather than death and following the babies through their first year. She worked with health authorities, newspapers, women's clubs, and clergy. Her investigation focused on

22. Quoted in Josephine Goldmark, *Impatient Crusader: Florence Kelley's Life Story* (Urbana: University of Illinois Press, 1953), pp. 94–96.

23. U.S. Children's Bureau, *First Annual Report*, 1913, p. 6.

the social and economic conditions of maternal and infant care. The study brought out "a coincidence of underpaid fathers, overworked and ignorant mothers, and those hazards to the life of offspring which individual parents can neither avoid nor control." It pointed to "the imperative need for ascertaining a standard of life for the American family." [24] A later series of studies of deaths of mothers in childbirth likewise brought out the fact that easily remediable conditions—good prenatal care, sanitary arrangements, licensing of midwives—could much reduce the mortality rate. In 1914 the Bureau published the first edition of *Infant Care*, a booklet of commonsense advice about hygiene and care that, through many editions, became the government's best seller. [25]

These first investigations publicized and clarified the sensational fact that infant and maternal mortality in the United States was much higher than in most European nations (about one baby in eight died in its first year). In a few years Lathrop was pleased to report that between 1915 and 1921 there had been a great improvement in birth registration statistics and a substantial drop in infant mortality (24 percent), for which her office could take some credit. In 1914 the Bureau expanded its staff of field agents and research assistants. (Two hundred and twenty-five people took the civil-service exams for these positions; 110 passed, 85 women and 25 men; 23 women and 4 men were finally hired.) [26] By that time its research capability for library and field investigation was well founded, and it was issuing valuable publications that analyzed legislation, described agency operations, and studied problems in all fields of child welfare—health, dependency, delinquency, mental retardation, illegitimacy, recreation—with attention not only to urban but also to rural children, whose situation was in many ways worse than that of city children but whose plight had been largely ignored in the development of child welfare, led as it was from New York and Boston.

These publications, technical and popular, provided impressive support for the scientific ideal in social welfare, which Lathrop

24. *Ibid.*, p. 7; *Second Annual Report*, 1914, p. 8.

25. U.S. Children's Bureau, *Fourth Annual Report*, 1916, pp. 7–9; Dorothy E. Bradbury, *Five Decades of Action for Children: A History of the Children's Bureau, U.S. Children's Bureau Publication no. 358* (Washington, D.C.: Government Printing Office, 1962), pp. 9–10.

26. Bradbury, *Five Decades*, pp. 8–9; U.S. Children's Bureau, *Third Annual Report*, 1915, p. 7.

always proclaimed; but equally important were the Bureau's service functions. Lathrop knew who her political friends were and knew from long experience how to get their help in her work. Every community study depended on local cooperation. The effort to improve birth registration depended largely on volunteer help from women's clubs. In 1915 the Bureau, working with the General Federation of Women's clubs, organized a National Baby Week patterned after one celebrated in Chicago two years earlier. In more than 2,000 localities people got together to arrange meetings, exhibits, health examinations, "a few days . . . for studying the needs of their babies and asking themselves whether they were giving every baby his fair chance, or what common action was needed in order to protect all their youngest and most helpless citizens."[27] A second Baby Week in 1917 was even better organized and more successful, despite the nation's recent entry into the World War, and during that year the English joined in, despite their absorption in the war.

So as the settlement houses were turning toward special sorts of group work and recreation, the ideals of research and community organization that early animated them were realized, in a way, at the national level in the Children's Bureau. For Julia Lathrop, like Florence Kelley, was at the heart of the Hull House group; like Jane Addams, she was a leader among those Chicago ladies who learned all about public apathy and political corruption and the vagaries of scientific philanthropy and still were not discouraged, who never thought to indulge in alienation.

The outbreak of war was, in the thinking of social workers, a threat to social progress. The progressives' effort to establish minimums had aimed mostly at state legislation or local ordinances. As the movement rose to its peak in 1910–1913, many states passed or improved laws about factory safety, workmen's compensation, minimum wage, maximum hours, and industrial-welfare commissions to administer labor laws; there was also much legislation for child welfare, especially supervision of foster care and orphanages, child labor acts, and widows' pensions; tenement house commissions to consider or enforce housing regulation; and many laws and agencies for health and sanitation. This great body of state and local legislation had to be

27. U.S. Children's Bureau, *Fourth Annual Report*, 1916, pp. 12–13.

implemented, tested, improved, and expanded. In addition, an economic slump in 1913–1914 brought unemployment to the fore. In the face of these demanding tasks the international crisis after 1914 seemed like a distraction at least. At worst it brought on violence and destruction, a nationalism and militarism that were opposed to the rationality, peaceful cooperation, and cosmopolitan good will that moved many philanthropists.

No social workers favored "Prussian autocracy" or its allies, but a division arose between those who favored England and France and those who favored strict neutrality. Social workers and their friends were more divided along these lines than most people. Many of them thought that Germany was a leader in industrial-welfare legislation, and they feared the rise of American militarism. Jane Addams, an admirer of Tolstoy, was a leading pacifist. So were most Hull House residents and those who gathered around Lillian Wald in New York. In 1916 many social workers moved away from Theodore Roosevelt, who was decidedly interventionist, and toward Woodrow Wilson, who sounded more neutral. They opposed American "preparedness." As late as February 1917, when Paul Kellogg published a neutralist editorial in the *Survey*, the mail response was about equally pro and con.[28]

On the other hand, charity organization and settlement houses and the religious and social traditions that underlay them were English, and the English "Fabian socialists"—George Bernard Shaw and the Webbs, for example—were more influential among American liberals than were German professors. In the event, President Wilson led the country into war as a sort of altruistic crusade "to make the world safe for democracy," as he said, and the war aims—the fourteen points—rallied the middle classes—the politically significant classes—as to a great cause.

Social workers learned then, to their surprise, that there was still a warm hearing for their notions of social reform. The war required an unprecedented mobilization of the nation. Social justice became important because it was a key to good morale and patriotism. Conservation of national resources was important, and laborers, children, youth, and mothers were plainly national resources. In the

---

28. Clarke A. Chambers, *Paul U. Kellogg and the Survey* (Minneapolis: University of Minnesota Press, 1971), pp. 58f.

emergency, businessmen who had thought that politicians were likely to be either crooks or demagogues sprang into public service; in the labor shortage, they were interested in many schemes for industrial welfare that would attract and keep workers.

So in 1918 the National War Labor Board, which passed judgment on wartime wage disputes, affirmed "the right of all workers, including common laborers, to a living wage . . . In fixing wages, minimum rates of pay shall . . . insure the subsistence of the worker and his family in health and reasonable comfort." Its determinations rested upon new and extensive cost-of-living and budgetary surveys.[29] A federal law prohibiting child labor on goods in interstate commerce, passed in 1916, was declared unconstitutional in 1918, but the standard was promptly made part of government defense contracts and Congress soon passed another law that would, it was hoped, bypass the constitutional obstacle. The government built new housing for war workers, carefully following standards drawn by Lawrence Veiller, the leading tenement house reformer.[30]

In the great national mobilization women's groups received full recognition. The Council of National Defense, which directed the whole effort, carried on its work through two channels: "state councils of defense" and a "women's committee" that served as its contact with women's organizations. Apart from recruiting women for war work and helping them, the women were active in programs for food conservation, bond drives, health, and various kinds of relief.[31] One of their most successful ventures was a "Children's Year" beginning in April 1918, worked out with Julia Lathrop and the Children's Bureau. This event emphasized four points: public protection of maternity and infancy; mother's care for older children; enforcement of child labor and education laws; and recreation for children and youth that was "abundant, decent, protected from any kind of exploitation." Thus the Baby Weeks of 1916 and 1917 were writ very large. The Children's Year ended with an important international conference, intended, as President Wilson said in authorizing it, to "set up cer-

29. W[illiam] Jett Lauck, *The New Industrial Revolution and Wages* (New York: Funk & Wagnalls, 1929), pp. 43–45, 47–50.

30. Davis, *Spearheads for Reform*, p. 223.

31. "The War Relief Work of the Council of National Defense," American Academy of Political and Social Science, *Annals*, 79 (September 1918): 229–232 and passim.

tain irreducible minimum standards for the health, education, and work of the American child." The activities reached some 17,000 committees and 11 million women.[32]

Even more impressive than these civilian activities were the welfare programs for military personnel. There were in general two types, war risk insurance and training-camp programs. War risk insurance was a major venture into social insurance. It began simply as the work of a federal bureau in 1914 to offer insurance on ships and cargoes that private carriers could not afford because of the risks of submarine warfare. In 1917 this protection was extended to ships' crews and later to all members of the armed services. The act offered servicemen an opportunity to make an allotment of part of their pay—not more than half—to their dependents, with the agreement that the government would match or exceed it. It provided that if a serviceman was disabled on account of injury or disease in the line of duty the government would pay him and his dependents a monthly compensation varying according to the size of his family. It provided vocational rehabilitation for those who could use it. If a serviceman died, the government would pay monthly compensation to his unremarried widow, children under 18, and dependent parents. The act offered the serviceman additional protection against disability or death at very low rates. No other nation was so liberal. In a few months the Bureau developed the greatest insurance business in the world.[33]

Commissions on training-camp activities had their origins in the demoralization experienced by American soldiers campaigning along the Mexican border in 1916. Raymond Fosdick, sent by the Secretary of War to look over the situation, noted that "there was nowhere to go and get away even for a short time from the monotony of drill. . . . There were the small border towns with saloons and redlight districts for their sole attractions, and from lack of decent diversion the men gravitated there in their off time. . . . It is no wonder that an appallingly large percentage of the troops there were . . . disabled

32. J. Peixotto, "The Children's Year and the Woman's Committee," American Academy of Political and Social Science, Annals, 79 (September 1918): 257–262; Bradbury, Five Decades, p. 116; U.S. Children's Bureau, Standards of Child Welfare (Pub. no. 60, 1919) gives an account of the Conference.

33. S. M. Lindsay, "Purpose and Scope of War Risk Insurance," American Academy of Political and Social Science, Annals, 79 (September 1918): 52–68.

though personal immorality." In the mobilization of 1917 the President and the Secretary of War resolved to make the environment of the camps wholesome and attractive. For years settlement house workers had talked about the importance of proper recreation in forestalling demoralization and delinquency. Now their message was relevant to the hordes of uprooted young people in the service. The objective, Fosdick said, was "a vast positive program . . . to compete with the twin evils of alcohol and prostitution" and to reduce the need for "the suppressive work" aimed at vice. Actually much of the work in the "cantonments" was done by the YMCA, which, like the settlements, had increasingly focused on athletics and recreation for young people of Protestant persuasion; the Catholics and Jews had similar programs. For the rest, the American Library Association undertook to see that there was "always a good book within reach of the fighting man." There was an educational program, necessary in the case of immigrants and hillbillies who proved unable to read or write, optional for others. The Young Women's Christian Association helped solve "one of the biggest problems . . . women visitors to camp," by establishing "hostess houses." There were also well-organized social programs in the camps and in the surrounding communities.[34]

More than any other organization the American Red Cross was the symbol and vehicle of the wartime spirit of social service. Based on a Swiss model, it was organized in the United States in 1881 by Clara Barton, a famous Civil War nurse, who for decades led its relief columns to flood and fire. It was a volunteer agency made up of local chapters, with a tiny staff at national headquarters. Its function was to raise funds, collect goods, and channel them to the needy in time of disaster. In 1905 it was reorganized under a charter from Congress that gave it a special responsiblity to help servicemen. Its leader then and for decades thereafter was Mabel Boardman, a society lady who had a knack for enlisting wealthy and prestigious people in its work—William Howard Taft was a strong supporter. The 1905 reorganization brought in Ernest Bicknell, former secretary of the Indiana State Board of Charities and the Chicago Bureau of Charities (COS). He arranged that leading charity organization societies act as

34. R. Fosdick, "The War and Navy Department's Commission on Training Camp Activities," American Academy of Political and Social Science, Annals, 79 (September 1918): 130, 135.

standby staff for the Red Cross's disaster work, a great improvement. When the European war broke out in 1914, the American Red Cross began to help the victims. In 1915 there were 145 chapters and 22,000 members.

The Red Cross served the military in the Mexican Campaign in 1916, but as war approached President Wilson set aside the society ladies and established a War Council of bankers and businessmen led by Henry Davison, a Morgan partner who had long been active in its work. The Council's first task was to enlist new members and contributions. It hoped to raise the budget from $5 million to $50 million. Davison had more confidence; he set the goal at $100 million. The campaign, in June 1917, followed the first Liberty Loan (bond) drive and used the same devices. These arrangements, which had been worked out originally in fund-raising drives for the YMCA, included a comprehensive division into areas and quotas, responsible local committees in charge, and concentrated publicity and solicitation. The drive was oversubscribed by $14 million, and two later fund drives were successful beyond expectations. During the war the Red Cross raised over $400 million, and its membership rose to 21 million in a total population of 106 million. Here was concrete evidence of the potential appeal of service. These funds went for four kinds of helping: traditional disaster relief for civilian victims of war in Europe; canteens and clubs for servicemen; nonmedical services in military hospitals; and "home service" with families of servicemen.

"Home service" was new. It was intended to apply the principles of social casework with disorganized families to help servicemen and their families cope with the emergencies of wartime separation. Its purpose was to maintain morale on both sides of the separation. Part of its work was to give information and technical help, for example, with regard to dependency allotments, emergency furloughs, or simply mistaken addresses. But it also dealt with emotional problems of separation and the whole range of family management and discipline. Mary Richmond, who had just finished *Social Diagnosis*, coined the name "home service," wrote the admirable manuals, and planned the institutes to train volunteers for this work. There were nowhere near enough trained social workers to give family service so extensively—every local Red Cross chapter was supposed to have such a unit—so volunteers were essential. Richmond planned institutes that lasted six weeks, full time, and taught volunteers how to approach families, aid them in defining their problems, and go about helping. The institutes included field work with a family agency. The courses included basic information about family and child welfare, including interviewing, health, home economics, ethnic factors, personal factors, community resources, and laws. The service was available upon request by the serviceman or his family.

Red Cross home service gave a powerful stimulus to the development of social work in the United States. Hitherto family and child welfare had been associated with economic dependency and charity; it was hard for people to accept help—or give it—without feeling awkward about the fact of pauperism. The serviceman's family was not primarily or essentially dependent, however; it was above the poverty line, usually, and had a rightful claim that the social worker was glad to recognize and build on in helping. It was therefore easier to construe helping as a technical service analogous to that of a lawyer or doctor. Moreover, the viewpoint and ideal of the technical service were introduced to rural places or small towns that had formerly been entirely amateur or moralistic in their attitudes.[35]

In sum, experience gained during the World War took ideas about reform and social service—particularly the positive state, minimum standards of living related to personal (and now national) efficiency and morale, the importance of family and child welfare, recreation and community organization—and gave them a new cogency and sanction. It also gave their advocates and practitioners a new and unexpected status and a vision of new opportunities. Moreover, the war brought a near approach to three major reforms that had long been advocated and promised to change the fundamental circumstances of poverty and disorganization. One of these reforms was a restriction on immigration, a literacy test (1917) that would, it was hoped, reduce the competition at the bottom of the labor force. Second was the prohibition of the manufacture and sale of intoxicating

---

35. On home service, see Mary E. Richmond, *The Long View: Papers and Addresses,* Joanna C. Colcord and Ruth Z. S. Mann, eds. (New York: Russell Sage Foundation, 1930), pp. 417–19. The Red Cross might have developed "home service" in the 1920s but instead went into home nursing: see Phyllis Watts, "Casework Above the Poverty Line: The Influence of Home Service in World War I on Social Work," *Social Service Review,* 38 (September 1964): 303–15.

beverages (1920), which would end the personal and political corruption that were identified with drunkenness and saloons. Finally, women were granted suffrage by constitutional amendment (1920), and it was expected that this would much improve the quality of politics in the decade to come.

Chapter

10

The 1920s: Constructive Ideas

IN THE PERSPECTIVE of political history the 1920s appear as a conservative interlude, a frustration of the hopes of the progressives and a seedtime of New Deal reforms. This view focuses on the defeat of legislation intended to limit the exploitation of working people and to improve their bargaining power, along with that of poor farmers and consumers, and on the troubles of ethnic minorities. But with regard to social welfare it ignores several constructive ideas that would, in the long run, have important consequences. One was the notion of industrial welfare or personnel management, which granted in theory many claims of the worker and acknowledged a responsibility in the employer. Another was improvement in the rationale and organization of social services in both private and public agencies. A third was more critical attention to a professional spirit and technical competence in the delivery of services.

In part, the conservatism of the 1920s reflected disillusion with political solutions to social problems. President Wilson had brought America into the World War in the spirit of a progressive crusade, to "make the world safe for democracy." His Fourteen Points—the American war aims—proposed valuable reforms but did not reckon on European hatreds and cynicism. Dissatisfied by the Versailles Treaty, Congress refused to join the League of Nations. Meanwhile European nations refused to pay their war debts. Instead of a world safe for democracy there was the threat of a communist revolution spreading from the new Bolshevik stronghold in the Soviet Union, which created a Red Scare even in the United States. In the opposite

163

camp was the rise of fascism in Eastern Europe and Italy. In short, some sort of totalitarianism, rather than an individualist capitalist democracy in the American style, seemed to be the result of the war: not what Americans expected or wanted.

On the domestic scene the reforms of the progressive years were a disappointment. Many attempts to improve the electoral system, to minimize boss control and political corruption, proved unavailing. Labor and social legislation, passed with high hopes, was easy to circumvent and difficult to enforce. Woman suffrage did not effect the moral improvements that were anticipated. New immigration laws introducing a quota system were intended to discriminate against people from southern and eastern Europe—Italians, Greeks, Slavs, Poles, Jews—and stirred their resentment as well as the doubts of others who opposed such racist thinking. (The restriction was supposed to help labor by reducing competition among the least-advantaged groups of workers.)

Perhaps the most important disillusion was that the prohibition of the manufacture and sale of alcoholic beverages, the Eighteenth Amendment to the Constitution, proved to be more trouble than benefit. Two generations of earnest reformers, including many social workers, had pointed to the relationship between the saloon and pauperism, sickness, crime, vice, political corruption, and the demoralization of the working class. It was hoped that Prohibition, a "noble experiment," in the phrase of President Herbert Hoover, would strike at a root or cause of these problems. Whatever the good results, they were more than balanced by the widespread disobedience of the law and the patronage of bootleggers and speakeasies. The noble experiment became associated with a repressive "puritanism," an attack on personal liberty by fuddy-duddies who might also take the most restrictive view of sexual relations, who might get together to challenge the teaching of the theory of evolution or even join the Ku Klux Klan, a quasi-political organization that regarded itself as a defender of the traditional virtues.

So various circumstances and events in the 1920s fostered disillusion about political solutions. It touched all classes of society: sophisticated elite, solid nativist, humble immigrant. Not only the particular reforms but also the high-minded moralizing of the progressives was challenged, even the profound ideal of social democracy and social justice that had animated Jane Addams and many settlement house workers. Disillusion was especially marked in the business and professional class. Young people of this class, who once rallied to the settlement houses, now affirmed a more personal and individual spirit of rebellion and liberation. Or, if they were political, they might move much beyond the pragmatic reforms of the progressives to an extreme position, rejecting liberal capitalism in favor of some traditional religious or agrarian order or, more likely, a socialist revolution.

Alongside many proclamations of skepticism and aspiration, which had in part the frivolous quality of the Jazz Age, was a constructive movement of thought that was very significant for the idea of scientific philanthropy and social welfare. It drew strength from two undeniable and momentous facts: the success of the unprecedented wartime mobilization—the power and prosperity manifest in it—and then the even more remarkable peacetime prosperity of the 1920s. Underlying these impressive events was the steady technical progress of American agriculture, manufacturing, and commerce to undoubted supremacy in the world.

This growth of economic power and prosperity—this rise in the standard of living—in no way depended on the ideas of scientific philanthropy or social welfare, considered as provision for the dependent, defective, and delinquent classes. It had a great deal to do with social welfare in its more general sense as defined in the progressive years, that is, the effort to minimize poverty and to spread opportunity and wealth in society. From this point of view the interesting question in the 1920s was neither how Americans should take care of the unfortunate and dangerous nor what new social legislation might help distribute security and opportunity. For it was pretty clear that the fabulous advances did not depend on such legislation but on something much deeper in society. The interesting question was, What are the features of American society that have made it more productive and prosperous than other nations?

This question had been asked first about the economic advance in Europe during the eighteenth and nineteenth centuries, and the answer then was the doctrine that a liberal capitalist political economy stimulated and rewarded hard work, enterprise, and productive innovation. This answer seemed particularly true of the United States, where the market and the entrepreneurial spirit were more free even than in Europe. But during the twentieth century—and flowering in the 1920s—there was a new emphasis among the managers, merchants, and bankers who directed the economy: not just traditional hard work, enterprise, and gadgetry but a self-conscious rational technology, something one could develop and teach and learn in a school of agriculture, engineering, or business administration. For, just as there was a science in extracting or processing materials, there was a science of organization and marketing and investment. This belief in rational technology, which also appeared in the schools of medicine and education, ran very deep in American thinking. Thorstein Veblen, a profound and original student of the American political economy, thought that the hopeful radical element was the engineers, not the proletariat. John Dewey, the philosopher of democracy, expected that political questions could be resolved by a technique of rational inquiry and experimentation deliberately borrowed from science. Both men had their greatest influence in the 1920s.

No one represented the American confidence in liberal capitalism and rational technology better than Herbert Hoover. Orphaned and poor, he nevertheless made his way through the first class at Stanford University ('95) in geology, and he quickly rose to become the foremost mining engineer of his generation (in 1913 he wrote a textbook that would be preeminent for many years). Already very wealthy, he turned to public service and in 1921 became Secretary of Commerce. Looking to reduce waste and increase productivity, he devoted much effort to organizing producers to standardize parts and in other ways cooperate along technical lines, and his department helped them collect the information they needed for marketing and planning.

As Hoover recognized, the prosperity of the 1920s rested largely on technical progress, which increased productivity and stimulated investment while prices held steady, and therefore made possible high profits and wages. Much of the prosperity was in newly developing industries, notably automobiles and everything that went into them, but also electric appliances, the radio, the movies, and food processing, to name only a few. These enterprises created a strong demand for the engineer, the technician, and the professional as well as for the assembly line worker and clerk. And because they sold on enormous mass markets they created a demand for the middleman and the advertiser.

Among the many new-style engineers and professionals were the experts in "scientific management" and the part of it that dealt with "industrial relations" or "personnel management" or "industrial welfare work." Scientific management, as first expounded by Frederick Taylor and his followers, undertook to replace rule-of-thumb practicality with very thorough and careful analysis of the workers' tasks, leading to a plan deliberately to increase their productivity. This might have meant simply the speed-up, the more efficient exploitation of the workers' time, but the professionals often took a more long-run view. Worker incentives and fatigue figured in their calculations. Personnel management began as a special office to handle hiring and pay. It was necessitated by the increasing size, complexity, and impersonal character of the labor force in large-scale establishments, where the manager could no longer keep an eye on workers or even foremen, and something more than a line of job-seekers at the gate seemed called for. In a rational view the company needed the right man intent on doing the right job; it needed to recruit and promote him, perhaps to train and retire him.

These efforts to be rational and scientific about tasks and organizations resulted from two fundamental facts about modern business administration. A large, complex organization is vulnerable to failure or sabotage anywhere along the line, and it was obvious that workers might take advantage of the situation to organize unions that would be adversaries, rather than servants, of management. These insights led employers not only to strenuous "open-shop" (antiunion) campaigns but also, in a more positive way, to the development of "industrial-welfare work" in their plants or stores.

In 1919 the U.S. Bureau of Labor Statistics published a major study of this work in 400 establishments. Among the efforts, which were voluntary in the sense that they were not required by the necessity of production or by law or custom, were medical service, rest or recreation rooms, libraries, night classes, family service, disability funds, and various kinds of mutual-benefit organizations for insurance or pensions.[1] Much of this work was in the tradition of paternalism, but by 1920 Ordway Tead and Henry Metcalf published *Personnel Administration*, which summed up for many years the more scientific view, "the direction and coordination of the human rela-

1. "Welfare Work for Employees in Industrial Establishments in the United States," U.S. Bureau of Labor Statistics, *Bulletin*, no. 250 (February 1919).

tions of any organization with a view to getting the maximum . . . production with a minimum of effort and friction, and with a proper regard for the genuine well-being of the workers."[2] This idea spread among employers during the prosperity decade. Workers' councils (company unions), profit sharing (advantageous stock purchase), and more elaborate insurance were often part of the program.[3]

Moreover, on the basic issue of wages many business leaders came to recognize that mass production presupposed mass consumption and mass consumption presupposed high wages. The prewar notion of a "minimum wage" set in relation to family budgets and cost of living gave way to a more expansive notion of a "living" wage (or "cultural" or "social" wage) that was both more ample in its standards and *linked to the rising productivity of the worker.*[4] In fact this view seems to have been a rationalization of the marked increase in money wages and purchasing power between 1917 and 1926, but at least it reflected a change in employers' attitudes toward the production and division of wealth.[5]

Not all employers in the 1920s held these conciliatory views of labor-management relations or wage levels, but a large number of prominent leaders did. They followed the reasoning of experts who intended to be scientific about personnel administration and labor economics. They gave voice to businessmen who wished to mute the theme of exploitation and class conflict, to recognize the claims and aspirations of workers, to enlist them in a common interest, to assert in a positive way the social responsibility and leadership of the business community, which had been much defamed by the muckrakers.

These enlightened attitudes, as well as the facts of high employment, high wages, and high profits, encouraged Herbert Hoover, to say in his successful campaign for President in 1928, "We . . . are nearer to the final triumph over poverty than ever before . . . We

2. Ordway Tead and Henry Metcalf, *Personnel Administration: Its Principles and Practice* (New York: McGraw-Hill, 1920), p. 2.

3. There are good contemporary statements and bibliography in Amos G. Warner, Stuart A. Queen, and Ernest B. Harper, *American Charities and Social Work*, 4th ed. (New York: Crowell, 1930), pp. 375–95, 590f., and in the *Encyclopedia of the Social Sciences* (New York: Macmillan, 1930–1935), articles on "personnel management" and "welfare work, industrial."

4. W[illiam] Jett Lauck, *The New Industrial Revolution and Wages* (New York: Funk & Wagnalls, 1929), chap. 7, 8.

5. George Soule, *Prosperity Decade* (New York: Rinehart, 1947), pp. 218–20.

shall soon be in sight of the day when poverty will be banished from this nation."[6] So one dream of the progressives, an end to poverty, seemed within reach. The progressives had put their faith in political solutions, legislation to establish minimum standards. Hoover, who had supported the Progressive party, went behind this notion or beyond it to a faith in fundamental improvements in economic technology and attitudes. He embodied these notions and saw them on all sides. He felt that they had little to do with the intervention of the state. Such beliefs, held by many managers of industry and commerce, and by the economists who served them, were a hopeful balance to the general disillusion with political solutions and social legislation.

With regard to more traditional charity and correction, the business and professional class gave active support to three promising trends. One was the marked increase in philanthropic foundations, which had a remarkable creative potential. Second was a multiplication of businessmen's luncheon or "service clubs," which, like the older sort of fraternal order, often focused helpfully on service needs. Third was the community chest, which carried forward earlier ideas of charity organization.

Philanthrophic foundations or, in the ancient phrase, "charitable trusts" were the memorial of very rich individuals. They were already known in 1601, when a famous Elizabethan Statute of Charitable Trusts and Uses codified the law about them. In those days the gift was often in the form of land and provided an endowment for a church, school, or hospital. In practice the property was transfered from the donor to a self-perpetuating board of trustees who would manage it as the owner intended. The gift had to be in the public interest as broadly defined by statute, and it was spared the taxes that fell on property used for profit. In effect it allowed rich philanthropists to fund large-scale activities that were more or less like the charitable work of the church or government, but without the obstruction or red tape of sectarianism or politics.

When millionaires and multimillionaires began to appear on the American scene, they gave philanthropy a new scale. Andrew Carnegie's article "Wealth," in the *North American Review* for June

6. Herbert Hoover, *The New Day: Campaign Speeches* (Stanford, Calif.: Stanford University Press, 1928), p. 16.

1889, argued that the riches of these captains of industry and commerce were a public trust to administer in the public interest. He gave about $350 million in foundations. John D. Rockefeller, who gave some $530 million, was also much interested in putting large-scale philanthropy on a business basis.

These ventures had imitators in the progressive years, but they encountered much doubt. Great fortunes, it was said, were a result not of managerial acumen but of the exploitation of workers and consumers. Large-scale philanthropy, in this view, was merely an effort to win public approval of ill-gotten gains or tainted money, or perhaps to subvert the righteous opposition. Such criticisms were made at length in hearings on industrial relations in the U.S. Senate, published in 1916.[7]

The improving reputation of businessmen during and after the war and the host of new millionaires increased the number of philanthropic foundations on one authoritative list from 102 in 1920 to over 350 in 1931.[8] (By this time the federal income tax law was offering an incentive to such philanthropy.)

Most foundations addressed themselves to education or health; only a few concerned themselves specifically with charity, correction, and social work. Among these the Russell Sage Foundation (1907) was preeminent. In the 1920s the Commonwealth Fund (1918) demonstrated many possibilities of the mental hygiene clinic, among other ventures in child welfare and health, and Julius Rosenwald gave support to the University of Chicago School of Social Service Administration, among his many philanthropies for education. Taken together, the foundations spent only a tiny fraction of the American philanthropic dollar (most of which was given by individuals to religious causes), but foundation dollars were likely to go into research, education, or demonstration at some carefully chosen and promising point. They brought out the relationship, later to become so familiar, between health, education, and welfare, and they were an important force for scientific rationality. They were useful in test-

7. U.S. Commission on Industrial Relations, *Final Report*, U.S. Senate Document 415, 64 Cong., Sess., 11 Vols. (Washington, D.C.: Government Printing Office, 1916), VIII, 7427–8013; IX, 8015–8480.

8. President's Research Committee on Social Trends, *Recent Social Trends in the United States* (New York: McGraw-Hill, 1933, pp. 1202f.

ing new ideas and in supporting notions that were more meritorious than popular.

Foundations were the fancy of very wealthy families. "Service clubs," as they came to be called, drew on leading business and professional men in every community. Rotary International, the earliest, began as a federation of sixteen local clubs in 1910. The Kiwanis took form in 1916 and the Lions in 1917. There were others, but these three were much the largest. By 1929 they had a combined total of 6,839 local organizations and well over 300,000 members. Rotarians were especially interested in work with boys and crippled children. Kiwanis helped underprivileged children and Lions aided the blind. These were national emphases; local clubs could be mobilized for various local causes. The same class of people furnished much support for the American Legion as it rose to prominence in the 1920s. The Legion developed a program of services for veterans and their families and became especially interested in the problem of juvenile delinquency. Besides these service clubs—but much earlier in origin—were the fraternal orders, which helped their brothers in need but sometimes looked beyond their own membership. The Masons, Odd Fellows, and Loyal Order of Moose were well known for their institutions; the Eagles were among the most influential partisans of old-age pensions; and most of the orders arranged some mutual insurance against various risks. Much of the work of service clubs and fraternal organizations was amateur and shortsighted, but much was not. In any case these clubs were a large new factor that stood beside the women's clubs as a resource for social workers interested in community organization.[9]

The community chest was primarily a device to help the local elite of merchants, manufacturers, and professional people carry out their responsibility for philanthropy and service. Usually merchants took the lead. Often the enterprise was part of the general civic interest of the Chamber of Commerce. Business and professional organizations had furnished leadership in many aspects of the wartime mobilization, particularly fund raising. In addition to the very successful campaigns to sell war bonds and support the Red Cross, there

9. *Ibid.*, p. 936f; C. W. Areson, "Significance of Social Service Activities of Noonday and Fraternal Groups in Relation to Community Organization," National Conference of Social Work, *Proceedings* 1927, pp. 434–41.

was in 1918 a national drive for a "war chest" for seven national voluntary agencies that attended to the needs and morale of servicemen and their families (YMCA, YWCA, Salvation Army, National Catholic War Council, Jewish Welfare Board, Playground and Recreation Association, and American Library Association). As it happened, leaders could not carry this wartime enthusiasm directly to postwar local community concerns, but the idea of local mobilization took hold in the form of the community chests: their number increased from 12 in 1919 to 363 in 1930.[10]

From the businessman's point of view, he was continually being asked to help individuals, groups, and institutions. Various motives encouraged him to respond. Many businessmen felt fortunate and pious, and aspired, along with their wives, to a good name and the accolades of the society page. Others recognized a self-interest: philanthropy, like advertising, was part of good business. Others saw that voluntary charities were an alternative to public agencies and the spoils system, which still dominated local affairs. They preferred to give donations rather than pay taxes. A few may have agreed with radicals that agencies and services were ways to palliate social injustice and divert good will from fundamental protest.[11]

Whatever motives led businessmen to support "private" welfare organizations, they had to make decisions about giving: to whom, when, and how much. As a start they could work with a federation of established local agencies, but that made it necessary to arrive at some fundraising goal. To set the goal, a committee of businessmen had to review requests for funds, approving this, changing that. Often the committee had to look behind the request to the organization and functioning of the agency. It had to review applications for membership in the federation: Did the community need such an operation? How would it fit the existing pattern? Did its program seem well conceived or effective? How did its claim compare with other claims? Often the fund raisers were led to take a broader view: What were community needs, what were duplications or gaps in services, how might the agencies pull together better? Obviously such judgments were very debatable, but the questions pointed to factual evidence of

10. President's Research Committee, *Recent Social Trends*, p. 1205.

11. Morell Heald, *The Social Responsibilities of Business: Company and Community, 1900–1960* (Cleveland: Case Western Reserve Press, 1970), pp. 83–147.

a sort that interested businessmen: general features of organization, accounting, and budget-making, for example.

When to give was a problem because before the chests were set up solicitors came any week, day, and hour, a persistent bother. The essential idea of the community chest in the 1920s was federated finance, one big fund drive instead of a lot of separate ones. The big drive would be well organized and advertised in the fashion of the wartime campaigns. A systematic canvass also raised community consciousness and put pressure on dubious givers. Usually it increased the giving. In 1919, 12 chests raised $14 million; in 1930, 363 raised $75 million.[12] Where campaigns failed, they made people think about their commitments.

Many social workers had doubts about the chests. Executives of welfare agencies did not like to justify their work to a committee of businessmen. They doubted the wisdom of budget committee decisions. Some thought they might do better on their own; strong agencies and particular agencies with a national base, such as the Tuberculosis Society or the Salvation Army, were reluctant to join. Some preferred to rely on their own initiative and on the commitment of donors or volunteers to their own work; budgeting and fund raising through the chest was relatively impersonal and unsentimental. On the other hand, social workers were glad to get the businessmen's financial and technical support, and they were pleased to learn that many businessmen respected their professional expertise. They recognized a geat new potential for community organization. Certainly the professional spirit in social work advanced fastest in the private agencies and under the patronage of the chests.

While they were reorganizing private charities under the community chest, businessmen and their allies in the professions were also looking at public agencies in a new light. In the nineteenth century people who thought about government services had thought mostly about the evils of the spoils system and how to limit them. In that view agencies for charity and correction were best separated from politics by the institution of a "lay board of managers," an unpaid or "honorary" board that would make policy and approve decisions to hire or buy. This administrative pattern was like that of

12. President's Research Committee, *Recent Social Trends*, p. 1205.

private charities, which were also governed by boards. The "state boards of charities," when they appeared on the scene, were supposed to put more system into the state institutions through "supervision" rather than outright "control," that is, by checking up on the several institution boards and advising them, rather than issuing orders to them. Control invited spoilsmen and corruption; unpaid supervisory boards attracted conscientious philanthropists: this was the doctrine.

The emphasis on supervision applied mostly to state institutions. County and municipal agencies were more helpless targets of local politicians. They increased in size and number along with other municipal services—roads, water, garbage collection, streetcars, schools—and with many municipal regulatory or licensing bodies. By 1900 the states also had moved from their initial work with defectives and delinquents to many other sorts of activity. In years to come, for example, the state highway system would be a major concern. This administrative machinery for charity, correction, and other services grew rapidly during the progressive years. The progressive belief in the positive state—that government could and should help in common interests and problems—encouraged the vision that government activities were really public utilities, that they were in some ways like so-called "private utilities" or businesses. Accordingly, principles of scientific management and business administration that were being applied in profit-making concerns might also apply to public services.

A theoretical base for the new view was *Politics and Administration*, by Frank Goodnow (1900), a political scientist at Columbia University. The business of politicians, he thought, was to win popular support for their platforms and to negotiate compromises: they determined policy, the objectives and rationale of state action. To implement policy was a technical problem best handled by a competent team. Goodnow knew about the improvement of administration in European nations, and he carried forward the older idea of civil service reform—eliminate the spoils system—to a more constructive notion of administrative efficiency.

As it happened, the systematic study of public administration in the United States began with a venerable charity, the Association to Improve the Condition of the Poor (AICP) in New York City. The chairman of its board, R. Fulton Cutting, a leading banker, was also head of the Citizens' Union, a group of reformers organized in 1897 to challenge Tammany Hall. The AICP grew critical of how the city government managed its charities. In 1901, for example, its director offered to manage a public bathhouse for $7,500 less per year than the city department was spending. In 1903 William Allen became executive of the AICP. He had a Ph.D. in economics from the University of Pennsylvania and had been secretary of the State Charities Aid Association of New Jersey, a private organization that visited and reported on public institutions. This association's original purpose was humanitarian—to protect and help the inmates—but Allen was an enthusiast for scientific management and saw great possibilities in good records that would help compare costs with results. In 1905 he persuaded Cutting to fund a Bureau of City Betterment to study the efficiency of municipal services. He was joined in this effort by Henry Bruere, a young lawyer who had been in charge of the philanthropies of the McCormick family in Chicago. They found much evidence of incompetence, if not corruption, and meanwhile Dr. Herman Biggs, the distinguished leader of the city's health department, asked them to collect data that would help justify his agency's work and requests for its expansion.[13]

Impressed, Cutting got his friends John Rockefeller, Andrew Carnegie, and Edward Harriman, the railroad magnate, to fund a Bureau of Municipal Research (1907). The Bureau began a famous series of investigations and surveys, first in New York, later in other cities and states, and it furnished a model and some leaders for the Economy and Efficiency Commissions that studied the federal government (1911) and many state governments, notably that of New York (1915). In 1911 the Bureau began a training school for experts in public administration. In 1922, much expanded, it took the name National Institute of Public Administration.[14] In 1920 there were 25 such agencies, which organized themselves into the Governmental Research Association. By 1930 there were 62, and an authoritative survey concluded that the 1920s were "above all, a decade of administrative improvement, perhaps the most effective and promising in the history of the United States."[15]

From the start the Bureau emphasized fact-minded inquiry, empirical and objective. It developed a "survey team" and systematic

13. Jane S. Dahlberg, *The New York Bureau of Municipal Research, Pioneer in Government Administration* (New York: New York University Press, 1966), pp. 5–14, 28.

14. *Ibid.*, pp. 15–26.

15. President's Research Committee, *Recent Social Trends*, pp. 1421f, 1429.

methods of investigation. It devised financial accounts so that executives could see where and how money was spent and compare the costs and results of various functions or agencies. It developed the budget as a rational justification and plan of an agency's work. Its purpose was not simply or even primarily to reduce expenditures but to get better value for the money spent. Very soon its experts shifted from a preoccupation with dishonesty or incompetence to an emphasis on capability in management, from inhibiting the spoilsman to helping the executive. They believed that the legislature (or council in cities or counties) properly made the policy; the executive administered. Give the executive the power to act, they said, like the executive of a private corporation, but hold him responsible through the devices of carefully worked out accounting and budgeting. The dynamic idea here was the expert manager, hired to be efficient, recruiting and developing his team of subordinates like a business executive. The best example was the appointed city manager working for the elected city council, but the same idea applied to governors and Presidents.

As for welfare administration, the new experts characteristically thought that various agencies and services should pull together in a common department under a professionally competent administrator who would be appointed by and report to a chief executive. This idea of executive control and responsibility clashed with the older idea of supervision by unpaid boards. It was very important to the new experts that the welfare administrator see the big picture of the services he managed and that the chief executive see the bigger picture of all governmental services, among which charity and correction were only part. This vision implied centralization of responsibility and power, and standardization where possible, in order to make operations comparable and to provide central coordination, planning, and development.[16]

Along with the new administrative emphasis the name changed from "public charities" or "charities and correction" to "public welfare" or "social welfare." The new name was intended to suggest a more constructive policy in the progressive spirit—prevention and rehabilitation—and beyond that an effort or "provide scientific and practical ways of attacking problems of inequality." So thought How-

16. Sophonisba Breckinridge, *Public Welfare Administration*, rev. ed. (Chicago: University of Chicago Press, 1938), pt. III.

ard Odum, a leading academic sociologist and student of public welfare, in a review in 1932. "There was need," he remarked,

> for scientific study and broader application of the social sciences to social organization and to the practical workings of government. The problem of inequality involved, on the one hand, the large number of individuals whose deficiencies, physical, mental, social, and economic, grow out of natural inequalities, and, on the other, a large and varying group whose deficiencies and inequalities emerge from economic maladjustment.[17]

This change from "charity and correction" to "public welfare" or "social welfare" was a heritage of the progressive period. It did not fade away in the 1920s but took practical form in new executive departments. The new name appeared first in city government (Chicago, St. Louis, Cincinnati, and Cleveland used it by 1915) and then in states (Illinois, 1917; Massachusetts, 1919). By 1929 all the larger, more important states, at least twenty-three of them, and many cities had reorganized their welfare institutions and agencies into executive departments, usually as part of the general reorganization of administrative machinery, and usually after a survey by specialists in public administration.[18]

Social workers and philanthropists were divided about the doctrines and practice of the new public administration. On one hand, a notion of "efficiency" that applied readily to street maintenance, sewage disposal, or automobile licensing did not apply so well to probation, foster-home placement, or care of the mentally retarded. It was (and is) difficult to measure the "product," the quality or value of social services. Moreover, agency executives could plausibly argue that the way to efficiency was to give them a free hand, not burden them with a lot of regulations, directives, and accounts from a distant central office that was all too often staffed by outsiders or academic theorists. Or, worst of all, the whole scheme of the efficient manager rallying his team to deliver services better or cheaper might be a sham, a cover-up for the old spoils system of rewarding political friends or servants.[19]

On the other hand, the science of public administration made

17. President's Research Committee, *Recent Social Trends*, pp. 1227f., 1230.

18. *Ibid.*, pp. 1229, 1234, 1251f.

19. Breckinridge, *Public Welfare Administration*, pp. 557–61, 606–9.

sense (as did its sibling, business administration), and there was certainly much to improve in public-welfare administration. The states and big-city counties had institutions housing hundreds or thousands of people; their executives had common problems: construction, maintenance, sanitation, fire protection, personnel, purchasing, medical service, and recreation, to mention a few. The inmates were a large and potentially valuable labor force, often already employed on farms or in shops. These were rich resources for planners and engineers. Prisoners might make automobile license plates and road signs for the highway department, for example, and various institutional farms might supply many inmate needs; a knitting industry might provide underwear and other garments not only for inmates but also for foster children in public programs. The central office might offer trouble-shooters and services that were very useful to executives. Increasingly agency staff were career people, and later the 1920s and 1930s would seem to them like golden years when the self-sufficient institution or system of institutions was a subject of much attention and constructive thought.[20]

As for outdoor relief and extramural services for offenders and mental patients, the experts were disposed here, as elsewhere, to consult authorities in those particular fields. Usually they found them in professional associations or schools of social work, and what they heard, of course, was the need for trained and qualified staff and the practices worked out in agencies that the professionals thought were most advanced.[21] These ideas were then digested and conveyed to the politicians with the stamp of sound public administration. It was a slow progress, however. Politicians retained their ancient affection for the spoils system, and they were not pleased when it turned out that sound public administration and economy and efficiency were likely to cost more in the short run, especially in social services, while long-run benefits were speculative. Nevertheless the main drift was toward a professional form or quality of casework, "an extension or

20. James Leiby, *Charity and Correction in New Jersey, A History of State Welfare Institutions* (New Brunswick, N.J.: Rutgers University Press, 1976), chaps. 12–16, discusses problems of administration and coordination in and among various state institutions.

21. Frank Bane, *Public Administration and Public Welfare*, typewritten transcript of tape-recorded interviews conducted in 1965 by James Leiby for the Regional Oral History Office, Bancroft Library, University of California, Berkeley, pp. 86–90, 95f.

development of the techniques and methods of private social work," as Professor Odum put it.[22]

But in the 1920s most professional social workers continued to be more doubtful than hopeful about public agencies, by contrast with the private agencies, which were flourishing in the enthusiasm for community chests and mental hygiene. In the National Conference of Social Work, the largest forum for professionals and their allies, public welfare was not prominent. "It always had the back room," recalled Frank Bane, one of the rising men in state administration, who had reorganized Virginia's welfare institutions in 1926. In 1929 he and his friends among state and municipal executives decided they needed a stronger organization; the next year they got a substantial commitment from the Laura Spelman Rockefeller Fund to establish the American Public Welfare Association, with Bane as its director and Marietta Stevenson, a Ph.D. in political science who had served with the Children's Bureau, as his assistant. The Association would stand for scientific public administration in public welfare, and when it opened its office in September 1931 its officers and members were moving very rapidly to center stage in the crisis of the Depression.[23]

Industrial-welfare work, organized philanthropy in the foundations and service clubs, the community chest, the new public welfare—all these movements, advancing in the 1920s, encouraged social workers who wanted to improve the technical competence and professional quality of their efforts. Doing a job right, it seemed, required a rational bureaucracy and a qualified expert. If the job was helping ("service" or "welfare"), the appropriate expert was the social worker.

The main drift to bureaucracy and expertise spread wide in American life. It centered in business and government, but it also infused medical services and education. By the standards of the hospital, school, or agricultural extension service, bureaucracy and professionalism had not advanced very far in the field of charity and correction, and the way to improvement seemed plain enough. In

22. President's Research Committee, *Recent Social Trends*, p. 1226.

23. Bane, *Public Administration and Public Welfare*, pp. 94, 112–22.

1929 Porter Lee, a leader in social-work education and that year president of the National Conference of Social Work, summed up the historic trend as he saw it. Contrasting the enthusiasms of the progressive years with the concerns of the 1920s, he made a distinction between social work as *cause* and *function*.

A *cause*, he said, is an effort to get rid of some evil or to establish some good—some program or institution, for example. Once it achieves its objective, it is likely to lose momentum. "The slow methodical organized effort needed to make [the result] enduring . . . calls for different motives, different skill, different machinery." What is needed then is "an administrative unit whose responsibility becomes a function of well-organized community life."[24]

> Since cause and function are both carried on by human agents, they make use of the same human characteristics. Nevertheless, their emphases are different and their demands in the long run require different combinations of human qualities. Zeal is perhaps the most conspicuous trait in adherents to the cause, while intelligence is perhaps most essential in those who administer a function. The emblazoned banner and the shibboleth for the cause, the program and the manual for the function; devoted sacrifice and the flaming spirit for the cause, fidelity, standards, and methods for the function; an embattled host for the cause, an efficient personnel for the function.[25]

As functionaries, social workers had to have more intellectual conviction than sentiment; they had to account for their work not only to enthusiasts for the cause but to the larger public that had to support the function. They had to justify their work and develop it not only as good in itself but in comparison with other goods that the community also wanted. Hence the need for research to assess the problems, allocate the resources, and measure the results.[26]

Of course Lee granted that both cause and function were parts of social work. His purpose was to clarify and dignify the technical and professional side. Moreover, his emphasis was on the external conditions of accountability, as it were—the institutional framework and the broader public support—and he did not in that address mention

---

24. Porter R. Lee, *Social Work as Cause and Function, and Other Papers* (New York: Columbia University Press, 1937), p. 4.

25. *Ibid.*, p. 5.   26. *Ibid.*, *pp.* 8, 12f., 18f.

changes in the actual practice of social work that also inclined in the same direction.

For one of the main historic facts about charity and philanthropy, as matters struck the rising generation of the 1920s, was that it had been a vehicle of class distinction. It represented the moral responsibility of people who were well-to-do and fortunate for those who were poor and unfortunate. The hope for a science of charity or philanthropy did not in itself challenge this fundamental class relationship, but it did introduce a critical note: it brought out the impersonal and social factors of human distress, and therefore it cast suspicion on the social arrangements that made some people well-to-do and others miserable. This suspicion suggested that helping was not, after all, merely the personal generosity of the fortunate patrons, which moralists might praise. It was, rather, the responsibility of the community, for which the representatives of the community might be held accountable.

In the 1880s the founders of charity organization had hoped that their effort would increase as well as direct the spirit of charity—of concern and responsibility—in the community. It did, but meanwhile the whole idea of charity began to take on a patronizing, undemocratic quality. (The residents of settlement houses had hoped, in their way, to show a more democratic spirit, sharing with the poor rather than doing good for or to them, receiving as well as giving.) During the rise of scientific charity and the trained or professional charity agent, it was supposed that the professional would work mostly with the lay people who put up the money, served on the boards, and acted as "friendly visitors." Scientific charity at first asked that the volunteer patron give of himself as well as his money, his friendship as well as his alms; the trained agent was an assistant, an organizer of these charitable acts.

When Mary Richmond and others developed a method of investigation, diagnosis, and tactful helping, they laid down standards of procedure and responsibility that few volunteer visitors were prepared to uphold. The supply of volunteer visitors was drying up anyhow because the candidates themselves felt awkward and undemocratic. From this point of view professionalism in social work was a welcome substitute for snobbish patronizing. As the fourth edition of Amos Warner's *American Charities* (1930) put it, in a deliberate contrast of "the humanitarian approach" of the 1890s (when Warner wrote) and "the professional approach" of the 1920s, the latter implied

> skilled service in place of or in addition to good intentions and sympathy; making knowledge and skill available to persons who wish to use them rather than setting out to reform people regardless of their wishes in the matter; sporting interest in a difficult task rather than smug satisfaction with "doing good"; and expectation of reasonable compensation rather than a spirit of self-sacrifice . . . See how inappropriate for this are such labels as charity, uplift, reform.[27]

The author noted that

> some of the older generation . . . lament the "loss of idealism" among the younger workers. But while the quiet, objective social worker of today may not be so spectacular as the enthusiastic reformer of a generation ago, there is good reason to believe that he is doing a much more effective job.[28]

Social casework enjoyed the most exciting development in social-work practice. It had taken form around the belief that when people asked for charity an investigation was in order. The idea was to make sure that the applicant was deserving and that the help was appropriate and specific to his problems. Often several kinds of assistance were called for, not just money or food but medical care, job opportunity, or a business loan. Often the problem involved the attitudes or personality of the applicant or his family, who might need "moral uplift" (emotional support), advice, the active concern of a friendly visitor. But the presenting problem (as social workers would later call it) was economic dependency. After 1900, however, other social institutions began to employ people in casework. These were hospitals (for the nonmedical problems of illness); mental hospitals (for social study and extramural work); schools (truant officers and visiting teachers); courts, especially juvenile courts (probation officers); and correctional institutions (parole officers). Often the clients of these institutions needed money, but this was not the core of their problems; rather, they needed help in managing their personal affairs.

Then, during the World War and after, the "home service" of the Red Cross affirmed the usefulness of casework "above the poverty

---

27. Warner, *American Charities and Social Work*, pp. 25f.   28. *Ibid.*, p. 26.

line," and the spreading popular interest in "child guidance" and "mental hygiene" also brought out a large and appealing group of clients whose problems were personal and emotional rather than financial.

It seemed to social workers interested in improving service that these varieties of casework had much in common and that it should be possible to distinguish generic features that would make it easier to teach, criticize, and improve the work. This interest centered in eastern cities where local agencies set up training schools: New York (1898), Boston (1904), and Philadelphia (1908). The New York School was the leader, partly because of the large agencies there, including the main offices of national associations, and partly because it had a substantial endowment from the philanthropist John S. Kennedy.

Mary Richmond, a luminary on the New York scene who sometimes taught at the school, had thought mostly about the first stage of casework: how to collect facts, record them in an orderly way, and sort out problems and resources. She promised a book on "treatment" but did not deliver. Meanwhile thought on the whole subject took a more "psychological" turn. In part the new interest followed the invention of the intelligence test, introduced into the United States in 1909, rapidly developed, and given in institutions, in schools, and—in a massive program—to soldiers in the war. Thus began the testing that occupied "clinical psychology" and made possible more refined analysis and comparison of individual qualities. The study of child development and the work of child guidance involved giving and interpreting tests. Meanwhile some psychiatrists turned from the search for germs that caused insanity to "mental hygiene": the name suggested a preventive program aimed at bad habits or influences that might lead to breakdown. Children were a likely target for mental hygiene as for psychological tests, especially if they were troublesome or delinquent.

In 1909 the psychiatrist William Healy organized the Juvenile Psychopathic Institute to study offenders brought to the juvenile court in Chicago. In 1915 he published *The Individual Delinquent*, a lengthy, thoughtful, and influential account of his findings. The next year he established the Judge Baker Clinic in Boston. Many of his advisers and supporters also appeared on the National Committee for Mental Hygiene (1909), which began as an effort to help patients in mental hospitals but presently took up preventive aspects. In 1918 it sponsored a course for "psychiatric social workers" at Smith College, the beginning of the distinguished school of social work there. Military psychiatry was a focus that year, but in 1919 Mary Jarrett, the social worker who managed the Smith program, gave the National Conference of Social Work a prophetic paper on "The Psychiatric Thread Running Through All Social Case Work," and interest in mental hyiene dominated the conference.

In 1921 the National Committee and the New York School of Social Work persuaded the Commonwealth Fund to establish a few demonstration clinics for child guidance. At that time there were perhaps 7 such clinics; by 1927 there were 102. Most influential was the Bureau of Child Guidance, set up under the aegis of the New York School and the direction of Porter Lee and the psychiatrist Marion Kenworthy. Kenworthy was a Freudian, and Jessie Taft and Virginia Robinson, leaders at the Philadelphia school, were also teaching from a psychoanalytic viewpoint.

Of course in this movement there were large gaps between leaders and followers, theory and practice, but Robinson's dissertation, A Changing Psychology in Social Case Work, published in 1930, summed up an unmistakable trend. Mary Richmond had written about "the influence of mind on mind" and the "development of personality" in the "adjustment . . . between men and their social environment," but her main interest was objective facts about the client that would individualize his particular situation.[29] The new psychology was much more subjective in the sense that the worker tried to see things as they appeared to the client. Obviously individuals responded differently to situations that were objectively much the same. Something about their inner life—hope, fear, doubt— seemed to account for the differences. Moreover, the inner life depended intimately on the needs, circumstances, and crises of personality development, on fundamental attitudes that might go back to infancy. Developmental psychology and particularly Freudian theory gave workers a framework for analyzing inner needs and behavioral symptoms.

So old ideas—investigation, social study, social diagnosis, friendly visiting, treatment—took on an intriguing new dimension.

29. Mary Richmond, What is Social Casework? (New York: Russell Sage Foundation, 1922), pp. 98f.; National Conference of Social Work, Proceedings, 1917, p. 112.

The generic feature that united the varieties of social casework expanded from an orderly way to collect and sort out facts to a way of understanding them in the framework of developmental psychology and mental hygiene. The "influence of mind on mind" and "friendly visiting" were transformed into a therapeutic relationship. The psychiatric social worker in the child guidance clinic became a model for the profession.

In later years it would seem easy to dismiss this enthusiasm—the psychologies were confused, the therapies ineffective, the viewpoint politically conservative—but at the time it was liberating. If behavior was symptomatic, founded in attitudes that were determined early in life, a response to common human needs and problems—this insight discounted moralizing and opened the way to constructive sympathy; one might try to deal with the emotional situation that prompted the symptomatic behavior. The "cases" that shuffled forlornly through the literature of charity and social work shone in a new light, no longer objects of pity or bad examples but people struggling toward some sort of growth, security, and autonomy. In a larger historical perspective the sympathetic probing of the intimate family relations of these troubled people was part of a new candor about human motives and especially sex, a relief from the illusions of Victorian ideals of love and the family. Many partisans of psychiatric social work were themselves psychoanalyzed and helped by that self-knowledge.

In fields other than casework the professional image and skill were less well defined. In time professionals would formulate methods analogous to casework for "group work" and "community organization," but in the 1920s these forms of practice were empirical and confused. The main arenas were settlement houses or "community centers," YMCAs, YWCAs, the Scouts, and more vaguely, recreation and adult education. Whatever theory these practitioners had came rather indirectly from John Dewey and the ethos of progressive education. Its drift was curiously similar to that of the new casework. Dewey rejected an older notion that education was essentially an academic discipline imposed in catechisms or textbooks. He regarded it as an aspect of general growth and development, and tried to build schooling around the natural interests and curiosity of the child. Child-centered education was somewhat analogous to client-centered casework. In any case Dewey's doctrine was congenial to settlement house workers, whose program was to bring people together in clubs and who recognized that the coming together, the medium of group participation, was as valuable as the specific group objectives.

Moreover, Dewey's ideas about education had a social and political side that appealed to the group or community workers. He was foremost among the liberal thinkers who tried to rescue nineteenth-century individualism from its narrow vision of the egoist pursuing his private economic or legal interest. The individual was part of the community, Dewey felt; the community was part of the individual; and socialization and participation were the modes of this relationship.

In this desire to bring together the individual and the collective, the first influential statement was *The New State: Group Organization the Solution of Popular Government* (1918), by Mary Parker Follett (1868–1933). An heiress who had done graduate work in political science, Follett distinguished herself by her effort to turn the public schools of Boston into after-hours community centers. She was a sharp critic of the progressive faith in politics:

> The ballot-box! How completely that has failed men, how completely it will fail women. Direct government as at present understood is a mere phantom of democracy. Democracy is not a sum in addition. Democracy is not brute numbers; it is a genuine union of true individuals. The question before the American people today is—How is that genuine union to be attained, how is the true individual to be discovered? . . . We find the true man only through group organization. The potentialities of the individual . . . are released by group life.[30]

Participation in a community, rather than "representative government" in which political parties rallied "crowds": this idea gave dignity to the clubs and neighborhood associations of the settlements. Robert Woods expressed somewhat similar thoughts in *Settlement Horizons* (1922) and *Neighborhood in Nation Building* (1922). But the chief philosopher of group work and community organization in these years was Eduard Lindeman. A farm boy of Danish extraction, Lindeman became an outstanding student at Michigan State University, edited a farm newspaper that promoted cooperatives, organized the forerunner of the 4-H clubs in Michigan, worked in recreation

---

30. Mary Parker Follett, *The New State: Group Organization the Solution of Popular Government* (New York: Longmans, Green, 1918), pp. 5f.

during the war, and taught at a YMCA college. Intelligent and practical, he asked himself how experts could help people in groups and communities organize to realize their common interests. In 1920 he gave a paper at the National Conference of Social Work on "Organization and Technique for Rural Recreation," and the next year he published *The Community*. His thinking impressed Follett, who introduced him to influential philanthropists in New York. He worked with her for the next few years and also with John Dewey, then teaching at Columbia. In 1924 Lindeman joined the faculty of the New York School. But in the end his interest was more in social philosophy than in social work practice methods in group work or community organization.[31] By 1930 "community organization" had the connotation of organizing givers and agencies in the community chest, rather than citizens in communal living.[32]

Meanwhile the professional image took a different form in Chicago. Specialized training there began in 1903 as an extension course of the University of Chicago organized by Graham Taylor, a clergyman who had taught Christian sociology in theological schools and was head worker of Chicago Commons, a large settlement house. In 1907 he got a grant from the Russell Sage Foundation to foster research. Encouraged, he incorporated the Chicago School of Civics and Philanthropy (1908), which had on its board not only the do-gooders of Chicago but also representatives of the state universities of Michigan, Wisconsin, Minnesota, Illinois, Iowa, Indiana, Nebraska, and Kansas.

To direct the research, Taylor hired Julia Lathrop. Lathrop engaged as her assistant Sophonisba Breckinridge, a lawyer with a Ph.D. in political science from Chicago, who was then a dean of women there. Breckinridge brought in Edith Abbott, who had a Ph.D. from Chicago in economics and had done postgraduate work at the London School of Economics, and who was teaching at Wellesley College. Neither Breckinridge nor Abbott had been interested in conventional charity and correction or philanthrophy. Their interests were in woman suffrage and labor economics, and they were recent residents of Hull House. They proved to be excellent re-

31. Gisela Knopka, *Eduard C. Lindemann and Social Work Philosophy* (Minneapolis: University of Minnesota Press, 1958), pp. 18–35, 107f., 170f.

32. Roy Lubove, *The Professional Altruist: The Emergence of Social Work as a Career, 1880–1930*, (Cambridge, Mass.: Harvard University Press, 1965), pp. 175–80.

searchers and later brought Abbott's younger sister Grace to Chicago; Grace Abbott, also a political scientist, became an expert on the problems of immigrants and executive of the Immigrants Protective League (1908–1917).

The teaching at the school was, as in other schools, unstructured and haphazard. Helen Wright, who came there as a student in 1912 and later became dean, thought it was "far below [that] of a recognized college. The lectures were usually informative . . . but . . . all too often . . . sounded as if they were given with hasty preparation or no preparation at all." An exception was "the research department" under Breckinridge and Edith Abbott, where there was "real teaching." Steadily the pair worked for higher standards for courses, admissions, teachers, and curriculum planning. In 1920 the University of Chicago accepted the school with full graduate status as the School of Social Service Administration.[33]

Until that time proponents of professional education had usually favored "independent" schools, separate from universities and set up to respond to agency needs and interests. When John S. Kennedy endowed the New York School (1904), he favored this policy "in analogy to training schools for nurses which are connected with hospitals rather than any separate university department," and a 1912 decision affirmed that view. The agencies had something to teach, something they wanted their employees to know; social science courses seemed too theoretical and impractical.[34]

Accordingly, professional schools, such as they were, were associated with practice, especially practice in the advanced—professionalized—private agencies in big cities. By contrast, and quite apart from the academic inclinations of its leaders, the Chicago School was perforce interested in the public-welfare agencies that dominated the scene in the Midwest. Its ties were especially strong with the Children's Bureau, perhaps the most prestigious social agency in the nation, where Julia Lathrop was chief from 1912 to 1920 and Grace Abbott from 1920 to 1934. The Children's Bureau did research on preventive, protective, and developmental programs and their ad-

33. H. R. Wright, "Three Against Time," *Social Service Review*, 28 (March 1954): 42–44, 49–51; Louise Wade, *Graham Taylor, Pioneer for Social Justice, 1851–1938* (Chicago: University of Chicago Press, 1964), pp. 180–183.

34. Elizabeth G. Meier, *A History of the New York School of Social Work* (New York: Columbia University Press, 1954), pp. 21, 40.

ministration; it promoted county welfare boards to coordinate public services; and for a time it administered a federal child labor statute and a program of aid for maternity and infancy.

So while schools in New York, Boston, and Philadelphia were looking for a generic method among the varieties of social casework, Breckinridge and Abbott wanted to create an expert in social welfare, someone who was prepared not just to deal with clients but to conduct research on problems and programs; to understand the legal and administrative features of social welfare, particularly its public forms; and to understand the history of and current proposals for social experimentation. They wanted preparation in broad principles as well as practice methods. They often invoked the example of legal or medical schools, which felt a responsibility to advance legal scholarship and medical science and to imbue their students with that spirit. So it should be in social work, they thought.[35] They published weighty tomes on public-welfare administration and immigration, and established a doctoral program and a scholarly journal, *The Social Service Review* (1927). They did not comment on the distinction between social work as cause and function, but in fact they blended the two in a broad notion of research, policy formulation, planning, and administration.

The effort to improve the quality of social work in the 1920s was part of a much larger movement toward specialization and rationalization in American institutions. People who provided funds, whether for public or private agencies, caught the vision of the expert toward which the practioners aspired. For the rest, advanced thought in the 1920s carried forward three themes of the progressive years. One was the shift of attention from pauperism (dependency) to poverty (living conditions below a certain minimum). The progressives had thought that state labor legislation was the way to define and establish the minimums—working conditions, wages, health, housing, and so forth. In the prosperity of the 1920s many philanthropists, economists, and business leaders argued that an end to poverty was much in the interest of employees and investors, and that the best way to it was to have business leaders voluntarily apply the doctrines of scientific management and welfare capitalism. Second, this sense

---

35. Edith Abbott, *Social Welfare and Professional Education*, rev. ed. (Chicago: University of Chicago Press, 1942), pp. 13–17, 48–56.

of social responsibility and leadership in the business community extended to the administration and finance of private philanthropy and to the encouragement of scientific public administration, which were both seen as alternatives to the spoils system and demagoguery. Third, the spread of scientific psychologies among well-educated people, and particularly among social workers, gave a new breadth, depth, and sympathy to casework.

There was much promise in these ideas, but in the event they were somewhat discredited by the confusion, suffering, and despair of the Depression years that began in 1929. In that context thought turned toward the responsibility of the government to provide economic security, and ideas about social insurance and public assistance came to the fore.

Chapter
11

Social Insurance and Pensions

Before 1930

$\mathbf{T}$HE 1930S ARE a turning point in this history
because the federal government began to act in new ways. The
changes involved new ideas about the proper role of government in
social life, a realignment of political interests, and new views in political and economic theory. The main practical consequences were the
labor legislation of the New Deal and the Social Security Act of
1935, which was intended to establish a framework of economic security and brought social insurance and public assistance to the
center of welfare policy. This chapter will describe the disappointing
progress of social-security legislation before 1930. Chapter 12 will put
the New Deal legislation into this context.

"Insurance" was a promising device to people who thought
about social welfare because it seemed to be an alternative—an advantageous alternative—to charity. Traditionally the theory and practice of charity had been founded on a sense of religious obligation,
the commandment to help the needy and unfortunate. Scientific
charity began with that obligation and only tried to carry it out in a
more farsighted and effective way. Most social reformers thought of
their efforts as primarily altruistic or philanthropic—a kind of public-
spirited helpfulness. (Of course many of them acknowledged a secondary prudential motive, that philanthropy and reform would minimize discontent and encourage social stability, but they thought of
themselves as first of all doing good and being helpful.) Insurance, on
the other hand, in its modern technical form, was based not on char-

191

ity or sympathy but on mutual self-interest. Its founders and advocates were not benevolent altruists but prudent businessmen. They were investors and entrepreneurs. They took risks—economic risks—and learned to rationalize some of them by insurance.

Modern insurance was first devised in the fourteenth century to protect merchants against the risk of loss of cargo at sea. In the beginning each insurance contract had a different set of underwriters. The merchant would agree with other merchants that if his cargo was lost they would share the loss, whereas if it was profitable they would share the profit. In England the business developed at Lloyd's of London (1769), a coffee house where merchants met. In the eighteenth century merchants and bankers organized themselves into "companies" just for the purpose of underwriting insurance on a regular, large-scale basis. This way of acting was more convenient and safer than negotiating each contract among a different set of individuals. The business of insuring cargos is now called maritime insurance. The general idea was later extended to related risks—that the cargo might burn on the dock or in the warehouse, for example, or that the manufactory and its stock might burn. (This was fire insurance.) Presently other sorts of accidents in the process of producing and exchanging goods became insurable under the general name of casualty insurance.

Life insurance was a later development. It was not on goods in shipment but on the life of the insured. It did not benefit him directly but protected his family against the risk of the loss of his earning power if he died. It was first devised for sea captains and supercargos, who might go down along with the ship. Later on, merchants and professional people bought it. Aristocrats and landlords did not need life insurance; their economic security was their landed estate, which passed to their family. But a merchant, lawyer, or physician earned money by his skill. If he died, his family lost its source of income. Life insurance was especially convenient because the insured could take out a policy in relatively small amounts—a multiple of $1,000 in America—whereas a landed estate would cost much more and would be a problem to manage. The insured got protection at once in amounts he could afford.

Science entered the insurance business through the officers of insurance companies, who became or hired "actuaries." They would systematically compile statistics about the number, frequency, and financial loss of fires, for example, and by applying the mathematical curve of probability they would calculate the chance of loss. On this basis they could classify risks and charge accordingly. They could issue more or less standard policies in which there was a rational relationship between the premium they charged and the benefit they paid. Of course they did not know whether they would win or lose on any particular policy, but they estimated that in the long run the odds were that the income from premiums would much exceed the benefit payments plus the cost of administration. The customers, for their part, were able to plan on the expense for fire insurance as a more or less fixed charge of doing business. They—the customers—did not know whether they would win or lose on the contract, but they were willing to substitute a small fixed loss (the premium) for the chance of a disaster that might wipe them out. So *actuarial science* enabled them to *rationalize risk:* a group of people—in this case businessmen in a particular risk category—shared their risk through the medium of an insurance company. Because insurance companies were profitable they attracted investors; competition drove down the rates and improved the service, especially as government stepped in to regulate the business and improve its statistical base.

Premiums in life insurance were based on "mortality tables" derived from records of births and deaths. Actuaries studied these to learn how long people might, on an average, be expected to live. Knowing this, they could set a premium that would, on the average, cover the company's expected payments, administrative costs, and profits. The same mortality tables made it possible to devise a retirement insurance, called an *annuity,* such that if the insured person stopped earning money at a certain age the company would pay him a definite income for the rest of his life. This was, in effect, a lengthy savings program (small premiums paid over the years) that would assure the payee a lifetime income.

The casualty and life insurance business grew rapidly in the nineteenth century along with the great expansion of trade, industry, and a middle class that relied for economic security on its skill rather than on a landed estate. It was both a protection for property and family and an attractive investment in the days before the savings bank and stock market had appeared to absorb the economic surplus of the well-to-do. It enabled the middle class to recognize and confront economic insecurities in a rational way.

Early in the nineteenth century a second group of people developed another form of insurance. These were artisan-shopkeepers—butchers, bakers, all kinds of wrights and smiths, men who made or did things in their own shops. Traditionally they had been organized in guilds for the purpose of controlling prices and working conditions in the local market. Others—a growing number—were skilled employees in the iron works, mines, and shipyards. As the factory system spread, particularly in England, these people became interested in "friendly societies" that were part labor union, part secret society. Some were small and limited to a particular trade and area, much like a local union. Others had a broader base. Much of their appeal was social: members got a sense of belonging, reinforced by rituals, secrets, and perhaps degrees of secret knowledge, in the fashion of the Masonic Order. These features were a diversion in the years before modern commercial recreation.

Beside social life, mutual aid was an important function. In time of need, brothers (members) helped one another. Most common was a death benefit: when a brother died other members attended the funeral and assessed themselves a small amount for a gift for the family. If a brother got sick, other members were supposed to visit him, and sometimes they assessed themselves a little to help out the family. Or the society might retain a physician or a pharmacist to serve ailing members at reduced cost. If the brother was out of work, other members might assess themselves for an out-of-work benefit (in effect, this might be a strike fund). Members might visit or actually provide a residence for aged brothers who needed help.

Taken together, the overlapping array of unions, friendly societies, and fraternal orders was a resource for the upper ranks of the working class and increasingly for people in clerical or white-collar vocations. It offered social life, recreation of a sort, and a small degree of protection against some risks of loss of income. The more broad-based orders had a great vogue in England and America. They began as local lodges, then combined in national associations. Bigger associations had many advantages. Their size made them more stable—there were more members to contribute and share—and members could transfer benefits, as it were, if they moved to another town. Perhaps the largest such association was the Independent Order of Odd Fellows (Manchester, England, 1810; United States, 1819). Other large American orders were the United Ancient Order of

Druids (1830), the Ancient Order of Foresters (1832), and the Improved Order of Red Men (1834). Later the Eagles, Moose, and Elks came to the fore.

At first the friendly societies and fraternals did not apply actuarial science to their benefits; they did not calculate risks and costs. Their efforts were like an organized passing of the hat in an emergency. But as the societies grew, the benefit features became more prominent, particularly the death benefit (life insurance). The officers learned actuarial science and began to figure the premium for the various benefits, particularly the death benefit, as part of the regular dues. They devised a new form of funding or capitalization, the "mutual company." "Mutual" meant, roughly, cooperative: the insurers and the insured were the same people; they joined a club to insure one another. By and large the club dues were sufficient to pay out the benefits, with only a small contingency fund for bad years. There was some risk to the members: in a really bad year, if the contingency fund was not sufficient for the benefits, they might be assessed an extra amount. On the other hand, they might also share the profits in the form of dividends. In general, the fraternals and later the mutual companies offered low-cost life insurance that was very popular in the United States. In time they became like the commercial (profit-making) life insurance companies, using actuarial science, accumulating reserves, and subject to government regulation.

There was a significant difference between the commercial life insurance companies and the fraternal or mutual insurance companies in the size of their policies. The older companies appealed to rather well-to-do people who wanted rather substantial protection for their survivors. The friendly societies simply provided a fund to pay for burial and ease the immediate crisis the family, although in time the size of their policies grew. Meanwhile some commercial companies developed a special line of insurance for low-paid industrial workers. Called industrial insurance, it was suited to the market in two ways. First, it was sold in very low denominations—multiples of $50. It was a burial policy, important as such for many poor working-class families, and very cheap, a few pennies a week or month. Second, it was sold by aggressive salesmen who solicited door to door, then came around regularly to collect the premiums. It had high costs of administration (the salesman), but it was profitable because of the huge mass market and the high lapse rate among its buyers. The

Prudential (1875) and the Metropolitan (1879) were the first great American companies to sell this sort of insurance.

So by 1900 the insurance business had grown large in the United States. Marine and casualty companies served business; old-line and mutual life insurance companies were popular with the business and professional class; and many skilled laborers had substantial coverage. Industrial insurance companies had devised special policies and sales techniques to suit the low-paid labor class. The emphasis in personal insurance was on life insurance; the death benefit ranged from a sum for burial expenses to an estate that would provide for the widow and children. Insurance against other risks—sickness, accident, retirement—was much less developed, but the principle and the actuarial science were available and respectable. Already the government was helping the insurance business and regulating it; it was quite conceivable that the principle might be much elaborated, especially for the working class, whose risks were so high in the industrial order. This concept was the foundation of "social insurance."

At first social insurance was called workingmen's insurance, and it was supposed to meet the special needs of the urban industrial worker. Peasant or yeoman farmers were largely self-sufficient on their land, and family and neighbors could help out in emergencies. The urban worker had no garden, and his family and neighbors were usually less reliable. He was vulnerable to any interruption in pay, in which case he was likely to fall on charity. Already by 1880 it was possible to identify the main risks to steady pay. The breadwinner could not work if (1) he was sick or (2) he had an accident (on the job, most likely); (3) if there was a slack demand for labor (high unemployment); (4) if he grew too old or feeble to work; or (5) if he died. Moreover, it was possible to conceive of some sort of insurance that would secure him and his family without recourse to charity— something like what the unions and friendly societies were already providing but much more comprehensive and adequate. Insurance would be better than charity because the worker would retain a degree of self-sufficiency. When trouble came he could put in a rightful claim instead of begging for help. He could plan in advance to meet adversity. Insurance would also, of course, be better for the charitable, whether private donors or public taxpayers. It would reduce the burden on them and allow them to direct their energies toward the needier cases.

In short, the case for insurance was strong, as shown by the growth of the business in the nineteenth century, and the case for special insurance for urban wage earners seemed very strong indeed. One might have expected that workers would rush to get it. This did not happen, partly for specific historical reasons that will soon appear but partly also because of two general facts about the psychology and practice of insurance. (1) Psychologically, most people simply were not prudent or farsighted enough to provide adequately by rational standards. This was true even of middle-class families that prided themselves on their self-sufficiency; working-class people were even more likely to trust to luck, kin, and neighbors. (2) Technically, the calculation of insurance involved complex actuarial considerations. A plan for retirement in old age, for example, did not mature for thirty or forty years after it began. These difficulties were evident early in the story, and in one sense social insurance was a special type devised to overcome them.

Essentially, then, social insurance was conceived as government-sponsored or assisted insurance for urban industrial workers. The government stepped in to help in a job that was difficult for ordinary commercial insurance. The government made insurance compulsory for certain risks and classes, which were generally very large. Workers and their employers got it whether they wanted it or not. It became a sort of fixed cost on production that employers could not dodge. This helped in planning. It gave actuaries a much better base for prediction. Moreover, the government might closely regulate the insurance business—if, as often happened, existing benefit plans were expanded—or it might administer the program itself. This ensured sound (responsible) practice and continuity in administration. Finally, the government might improve the benefits to the worker. The government could set the share that employers and employees would contribute, and it could add money itself out of general tax revenues. In any case the worker got out more than he contributed directly to the insurance fund.

As it happened, social insurance first took hold in the 1880s in Germany. Germany was, like the United States, industrializing very rapidly, a generation after England, but the historical context was different. The German government was dominated by a landed aristocracy led by the Hohenzollerns. This aristocracy was a proud ruling class, authoritarian but paternalistic, pious and public-spirited. It wanted modern industry, the basis of national wealth and imperialist power ("a place in the sun," the Kaiser said). Its leaders were displeased by the disorganization, exploitation, and misery of the English proletariat, however, and contemptuous of the English philosophy of liberalism and *laissez-faire* economics that seemed to justify it. Hence, German leaders were willing to help industrialists by a tariff, public transportation and communication, and an impressive educational system, culminating in a revolutionary association of higher education and scientific research. At the same time, they expected employers to take decent care of workers. This collectivist and nationalist spirit was forcefully rationalized by German economists, notably Gustav Schmoller and Adolph Wagner, who rejected English economic analysis in favor of a line of thought that was much more historical and moralistic. Disregarding the abstract "economic man" of English theory, they asked how real historical people and societies managed; in place of the English question, what was good for production, they asked what was good for people and especially for Germans. In 1872 they organized the "Verein fuer Sozialpolitik," which for decades gave authoritative scholarly attention to social problems and, among other enthusiasms, encouraged social insurance.

While German social scientists cultivated a degree of state socialism, by the 1870s German workers had formed a revolutionary socialist movement that was much opposed to private property, nationalism (it favored labor class unity across national boundaries), and traditional Christianity. It was anathema to the German leaders and to Prince Otto von Bismarck, the prime minister, who in 1877 put through sternly repressive antisocialist legislation. But Bismarck was sensitive to workers' grievances, not at all beholden to business interests that favored English-style *laissez-faire*, and in fact willing to pacify the workers through constructive measures for their welfare. In 1881 he introduced in the Reichstag a legislative program that ultimately created national health insurance (1883), accident insurance (1884), and disability and retirement insurance (1889). So Germany became the acknowledged leader in the movement for social insurance as it spread over Europe and to the United States. In a way this was an embarrassment to friends of the movement; one connotation of social insurance was German collectivism, militarism, and imperialism, all dramatized in the events leading to World War I. Yes, German workers got compulsory social insurance; they also got compulsory military service. Was it all part of the same package?

A collectivist spirit, a governing class based on land rather than industry and commerce, a class-conscious labor movement: these were feeble or absent in the United states.

In the 1870s the Knights of Labor provided workers with a national organization. Part union, part fraternal order, part secret society, the Knights agitated the "labor problem" and gave expression to labor solidarity. The main hope of their leaders was somehow to establish a cooperative form of industry that would erase the divisions between capital and labor, employer and employed. They were also given to political enthusiasms. Some thought that legislation limiting the work day to eight hours was a route toward cooperation; others favored laws about money and banking that would raise prices and make credit more available. By 1900 the Knights were defunct and the American Federation of Labor was ascendant. Federation leaders accepted private property and capitalism. They were not interested in a cooperative organization of industry, and they thought that socialist agitation was a futile diversion. They learned to take advantage of the situation. They organized the organizable—skilled trades, mostly native-born or second-generation workers, often with an imported tradition of unionism. The unions increased their membership during the progressive years, but in 1917 they rallied only one-fifth of the wage earners.

In their own view union leaders were merely realistic. They thought in terms of power. Power meant the ability to win a favorable labor contract from an employer, by a strike if necessary. They did not wish to leave the mass of unskilled and foreign-born workers unorganized; those workers were in fact unlikely to have the resources and discipline necessary for a successful strike. As for government, union leaders favored legislation to protect women and child workers (who could not organize) and good conditions for craftsmen employed by government, and they were much interested in local building ordinances and police actions during strikes. But they knew from experience that employers were likely to dominate politicians, lawmakers, administrators, and courts. They did not trust paternalistic government any more than they trusted paternalistic employers. They trusted each other—the union—to win them a good job and a high wage. Given that security, they could look out for themselves. And in fact the situation of skilled and organized labor in the United States was better than in Europe.

With such inclinations, union leaders were not likely to favor social insurance, and the impetus for the idea in the United States came from the business and professional class. In 1891 Carroll Wright, the U.S. Commissioner of Labor, who had a national reputation for his fact-minded and "ethical" approach to the labor problem, engaged John Graham Brooks to prepare a report on "Compulsory Insurance in Germany." "What will strike one most forcibly, in perusing this report," Wright said, "is the fact that the compulsory insurance system of Germany aims at securing all (and more) that had been aimed at under various systems of charity, and that the ethical side of the system was most potent in securing its establishment."[1] Brooks, a Unitarian clergyman, was also interested in the "ethical side." The point of his account was the historical root of insurance in associations for mutual aid among German laborers and the growing sense of the "duty of the state to the working classes." He traced this duty to the philosopher Fichte's doctrine (1800) that the "state . . . is . . . to be filled with Christian concern for the weaker members . . . The conceptions of property and contract are such as compel such intervention of the superior authority in order to realize the ends of justice and equality among men."[2]

> The principle of insurance is distinctly ethical [Brooks concluded]. It assumes such redistribution of burdens and misfortunes as far more nearly to satisfy our sense of social justice. The only question is the practical one. Can the state manage this ethical principle so as really to help the weaker classes, or will the machinery prove so expensive that the cost of living among such classes will not be lessened?[3]

In 1898 William Willoughby, an official of the federal Department of Labor, published another description of European systems, *Workingmen's Insurance*, and in 1911 the Commissioner of Labor issued at two-volume account of *Workmen's Insurance and Compen-*

1. U.S. Commissioner of Labor, *Fourth Special Report, 1893. Compulsory Insurance in Germany*, prepared by John Graham Brooks (Washington, D.C., 1893), pp. 10f.

2. *Ibid.*, pp. 20f.   3. *Ibid.*, p. 286.

sation Systems in Europe. Popular support for the idea came from the people gathered into the National Conference of Charities and Correction and a new group, mostly professors of "labor economics" or "social economics" or others who were somehow interested in "labor law" and its administration, who called themselves The American Association for Labor Legislation (1906). In 1901, the National Conference appointed a committee on workingmen's insurance led by Charles Henderson, a Baptist clergyman become professor of sociology at the University of Chicago. Its report (1906) pointed to the spread of the idea of insurance in the United States, its potential as an alternative to charity for workingmen, and the accomplishments of various programs already operating on a voluntary basis. "Workingmen's insurance should be fostered by state legislation," the committee said, cautiously adding that it did "not necessarily mean insurance at the cost of government and by means of state administration."[4]

Conference members soon took a more positive stance. In 1911 Louis Brandeis, speaking for the committee on standards of living and labor, argued for a comprehensive system of workingmen's insurance for protection in case of accident, sickness, unemployment, old age, and death. It would make workers more independent and hence more free, he said, but his main point was that it would increase "social efficiency." There was much human wastage in industry, he said, and the costs of insurance would be so high—perhaps 25 percent of payrolls—that when they were rationalized as an insurance premium, a fixed charge against production, people would realize how serious the problems were and institute preventive measures. He made an analogy with fire insurance, in which rates had fallen 90 percent in fifty years.[5] In 1912 the conference made "compensation or insurance" part of its minimum standards to reduce poverty and conserve human resources. These standards became part of the Progressive party's platform in that year.

The American Association for Labor Legislation (AALL) began as a section of the International Association for Labor Legislation. Its membership was small (200 in 1908) but prestigious. It had an overlap with social work. Samuel Lindsay, one of its founders, a professor

4. National Conference of Charities and Correction, *Proceedings*, 1906, p. 456.

5. National Conference of Charities and Correction, *Proceedings*, 1911, pp. 156–62.

at Columbia, became head of the New York School of Social Work, and Henry Seager, another founder and also a Columbia professor, wrote *Social Insurance*, the first more or less popular book on the subject, as the Kennedy Lectures at the New York School in 1910. (He attacked an unreflective American "individualism" and favored a more "collectivist" sense of responsibility. He also favored withdrawing "the lowest grade of workers" from "competitive industry" to "farm and industrial colonies.")[6] The AALL frequently found a wide audience for its message in *Survey* magazine. Its main work was to study labor legislation critically so as to improve it, and particularly to draw up model bills that friendly legislators might introduce. It then rallied authoritative testimony for such measures. Of course these bills were for state legislation—this was where responsibility lay—and in that forum the struggle for social security took shape.

Protection against the loss to workers from industrial accidents was the first mode of social insurance enacted in the United States. It came early because it had some appeal to employers and was similar to the commercial casualty insurance that they already held. It is interesting because its history shows the transition from commercial to social insurance, the technical and legal difficulties of formulating a program, and some confusion about the goals of insurance. Moreover, its progress, or lack of it, influenced later proposals for other kinds of insurance.

Danger was always a condition of work. Farmers and craftsmen, herdsmen and sailors used dangerous tools in dangerous jobs. English custom recognized this fact and formulated it in a principle of common law. Farmers and craftsmen were responsible for their own safety, of course. But if they hired someone to help, paying him wages and expecting to profit from his work, they were also responsible for his safety. If he was hurt or killed because of some fault of the employer, some failure to take precautions, he or his heirs could sue for damages. The employer was responsible and liable if he neglected his responsibility.

This doctrine was conceived when enterprise was small and master and men worked together. It had to stretch when progress transformed the weaver and his apprentice into the textile factory, or

6. Henry Seager, *Social Insurance: A Program of Social Reform* (New York: Macmillan, 1910), pp. 19f.

the carter and raftsman into the railroad. What stretched was the notion of some intervening factor between the employer and the employed. In a suit for damages the employer was assumed to be innocent until proved guilty. His lawyers could elaborate three defenses, all of which put the responsibility elsewhere. (1) The employee knowingly *assumed the risk* when he took the job. No one made him work under that condition. (2) A *fellow servant* was the negligent one. If the telegrapher fell asleep and workers were maimed in a train wreck, was the company responsible? (3) The worker may have *contributed to his own injury*—he may have come to work tired or drunk. These were powerful defenses, and in any case it was difficult for laborers to go to court and to get others to testify against their common employer. Often the plaintiff settled out of court for a pittance. The lesson was, Avoid accidents, because the employer is not going to help much.

Legally, technically, the defenses might be proper and the employer not personally responsible, but it seemed wrong that poor workers should bear so much of the risk and loss. As labor organization grew in England and later in America, its leaders looked for legal relief. For example, the law could spell out employer responsibility in factory (or other) safety acts, backed up by inspection. Employers who violated the law would lose their defenses in a suit for damages. The slow business of passing and improving this legislation and administering it, which took place during the 1880s and 1890s, was the first response to the problem of industrial accidents, and labor leaders were interested in other ways of minimizing the employers' defense against liability.

As wage workers grew in number, filling the cities, and as doubt spread about soulless corporations and the increasing division into rich and poor, a new prospect opened. A new type of lawyer appeared, the "ambulance chaser" who specialized in representing accident cases. He knew how to pick jurors (also poor) and to play on their sympathy and class feeling. He worked for a "contingency fee"—half of what he could win in damages. Often juries were exceedingly generous. The employer might appeal to a higher court and win at least a reduction of the amount of damages, but appealing was expensive and troublesome.

Here was a cost of production somewhat like a fire. Commercial insurance companies handling casualty insurance stepped forward.

For a regular premium they would take this worry off the employer's hands; they would make the settlement or take the case to court. Technically the policy did not protect the employee against loss but protected the employer against losing a suit for damages. That is, if the case went to court and the employer lost, the insurance company would pay the judgment.

Meanwhile a second strategy was to minimize the ideas of "responsibility" and "liability." In this line of thought industrial accidents were part of the cost of production and the problem was to rationalize them in terms of a schedule of compensation. There was no suit for damages, no trial. If a worker suffered a certain injury, he would, under normal circumstances and according to law, receive a certain compensation from his employer. The notion of "workmen's compensation" bypassed the legal arguments about who was guilty and responsible, and focused instead on the real problem, the worker's loss.

Workmen's compensation did not in itself imply insurance. It held that the employer had to pay certain benefits, but he might pay them out of his pocket. On the other hand, a workmen's-compensation law made it much easier to insure against loss as a result of industrial accidents. The law defined covered industries and benefits, so it was easier for actuaries to compute the risk and premium; losses by compensation were much more predictable than losses by damage suits. Usually private companies could handle this business, but the law might set up a state insurance company to insure employers, either exclusively or in competition with them.

So the notion of workmen's compensation was usually linked to an insurance program in which employers in a certain risk category shared their loss through the medium of an insurance company instead of paying it out of pocket. This arrangement was supposed to have four other advantages: (1) It minimized the hostility that was engendered when workers had to take an employer to court. (2) It increased the portion of the payment that went to workers instead of to lawyers. (3) It held out the possibility of reducing accidents, inasmuch as employers with good safety records could reasonably ask for lower premiums. A form of merit rating would give employers an incentive to promote safety. (4) Inasmuch as employers would ordinarily add the cost of the insurance to their price and pass it on to consumers, it would put the cost of industrial accidents where it belonged. As it was, if the worker and his family did not receive adequate compensation the cost of their care fell on private charity or on public poor relief, which was financed mostly out of the property tax. A charge on the industry and the consumer was more just as well as better for the injured one.

The first compensation law was enacted in Maryland in 1902 (declared unconstitutional in 1904). In 1908 the federal government passed a law to protect its own employees. In 1910 Crystal Eastman published *Work-Accidents and the Law*, a volume of the Pittsburgh Survey, a careful study that was an indictment of the old system of employer liability. The National Association of Manufacturers endorsed workmen's compensation in 1911. Between 1910 and 1913, 22 states enacted some compensation legislation. The number increased to 39 by 1917 and 43 by 1920. These were busy days for the AALL and seemed to open the way for other forms of social insurance. Instead, events were a lesson in the complications and difficulties of the subject.

Every legislature had to decide, for example, which workers and industries were covered. Agriculture and domestic service were exempted, but how about an exemption for employers with only a few employees or a lot of part-time workers or workers who were out of the plant, on the road? Were "industrial illnesses" covered as well as "accidents"? How long before compensation began—two days or two weeks? Compensation should include the cost of medical care, the cost of living for the family while the worker was disabled (sick pay, as it were), and the cost of prosthetic devices and rehabilitation. This could add up to a large sum. What arrangements might be made for medical help? Would there be a company doctor and hospital or a choice of care? What fraction of wage loss would the employer pay— one-half or two-thirds? Would there be any maximum limit on the weekly amount or on the total amount? For example, two-thirds of weekly pay up to $20 per week, for no more than 52 weeks, or a total liability for medical and part-pay of perhaps $2,000 or $5,000? Often the disability compensation was (and still is) set in fixed payments that had no relationship to need or rehabilitation: $100 for loss of a finger, $1,000 for loss of hand or eye.

In each of these respects there was in each state law a struggle to set and improve the standard. The basic question was the level of benefit. Was it in fact high enough to compensate the worker for his loss? If not, the program was a failure. States differed greatly. In 1934, on the eve of the Social Security Act, the most generous state program, New York's, covered perhaps four-fifths of the worker's loss; others were much less generous. Low benefit levels were not lost on labor leaders, who felt confirmed in their belief that workers ought to rely on themselves rather than on government. They retained an interest in the older pattern of a suit for damages with the hope of a big judgment. Meanwhile, however, the AALL leaders continued to emphasize merit rating and prevention in their discussion of the subject. Insurance should not merely compensate the victim, they believed; it should and did give businessmen an interest in promoting safety. Sure enough, the National Council for Industrial Safety (now the National Safety Council) began its work in 1913, supported by employers and insurance companies. This notion that the goal of insurance was not just compensation but also prevention would especially appeal to Americans.

Workmen's compensation covered the risk from industrial accidents and illness. Breadwinners had health problems that were not job related, of course, and so did their families. "Health insurance" was intended to meet these broader needs. Bismarck had put it first (1883), as befitted its importance. (He called it sickness insurance; the emphasis on health came from Lloyd George, the prime minister who led the campaign for the English program [1911].) In 1915 the AALL and its social-reformer allies had a conference and decided that it was, in a slogan that became famous, "the next step in social progress." They influenced many national organizations to encourage discussion—social workers, doctors, manufacturers, labor unions, and women's clubs, among others. Several states appointed commissions to consider legislation. It looked as if the sudden success of workmen's compensation might be repeated.[7]

A committee representing all the interests involved carefully drew up a model bill. It proposed compulsory health insurance to cover all wage workers in the state, excepting domestic and casual workers and salaried employees who made more than $100 a month. It paid the physician, the surgeon, and the nurse, and provided medical supplies. It included the whole family. It paid benefits for moth-

7. I[saac] M. Rubinow, *The Quest for Security* (New York: Holt, 1934), pp. 207–9.

erhood and funerals. It provided two-thirds of the wage loss of the breadwinner. Such coverage was expected to cost about 4 percent of payrolls, to be contributed 40 percent by the worker, 40 percent by the employer, and 20 percent by the state government. In general, it followed the German pattern.[8]

Discussion was supposed to help the cause, but it seemed to have the opposite effect. Businessmen had supported workmen's compensation largely because it seemed better than old-fashioned employer's liability. Now, as they were beginning to pay its cost, came an expensive new proposal. Some labor leaders supported health insurance, but most opposed it, including Samuel Gompers, head of the American Federation of Labor. (It was suspected that employers might introduce physical examinations with attention to the dread "disease of unionism.")[9] Commercial insurance companies had managed to get much of the compensation business, but they were to be excluded from health insurance, and the death benefit was in direct competition with "industrial insurance." Taxpayers' associations opposed the new burden of providing the state's 20 percent.

Leading the opposition were doctors and their allies. Some professors in prestigious medical schools and public health officials were favorable, but the great majority of practitioners, represented by their professional association, were bitterly opposed. Their hostility is a little puzzling, because the program had advantages for them: they could serve patients without worrying about ability to pay. But in fact the doctors saw only a mistaken attempt to reorganize the practice of medicine. Under the proposal local associations would handle the insurance. These authorities would have a choice of three ways to engage physicians: (1) salaried district physicians without any choice; (2) a salaried local staff with freedom of choice among its members; (3) a "panel" of approved physicians who would treat patients and collect from authorities. The last option was closest to conventional practice, but in any case a "third party" appeared between the doctor and the patient. The third party would fix the relationship, set the fee, and approve the service. It would interfere with the autonomy and confidence of the relationship. It would be like "contract medicine" and "lodge medicine"—both associated with inferior treatment

8. *American Labor Legislation Review*, 6 (June 1916): 155.

9. "Proceedings of the Conference on Social Insurance," U.S. Bureau of Labor Statistics, *Bulletin*, 212 (1917): 563, 568.

by physicians who were unsuccessful in conventional private practice. It might even be "political medicine," part of the spoils system. As doctors well knew, the scientific advance in medicine had come largely in charity hospitals that were professionally managed, where doctors donated their time.

Given this widespread opposition, the constitutional problem became serious. Like workmen's compensation and most social legislation, health insurance was justified under the "police power," the authority of the state government to protect the health, safety, and morals of the people. Because the proposal was for compulsory—enforced—contributions, contributors might object that the state was taking their property (tax or premium contributions) without constitutional justification. Workmen's compensation had the stimulus of a common-law liability on employers, but health insurance was a novelty. No one believed that employers were responsible for an employee's child's illness, for example; why should they be compelled to pay? Could the state compel those who were not covered to pay for benefits for covered wage earners?

California, a leader in progressive causes, faced the issue directly. In 1918 advocates of health insurance submitted a constitutional amendment to clear the way. After a hard-fought campaign the voters decisively defeated it, 358,000 to 134,000. In New York, another progressive-minded state, partisans tried to pass health insurance legislation in 1919. They had the advantage of support from the leaders of the State Federation of Labor and the popular governor, Al Smith. They made concessions to the vested interests of doctors, employers, and commercial insurance companies. Still they lost. In both states opponents confused the issue by resorting to demagoguery, linking health insurance to German imperialists on one hand (building on the wartime propaganda) and Russian Bolsheviks on the other. The basic fact was that there was little popular support for health insurance. Reformers had hoped that "the working masses" would see the advantage of the proposal, as a foremost advocate said later, but they "did not see and they certainly did not demand." Ironically, the opposition was rallied and organized so that it became "strong enough to kill the agitation, the very thought of it, for years to come." [10]

10. Rubinow, *Quest for Security*, pp. 214, 209.

The defeat of health insurance and the conservative mood of the 1920s—doubt about government coupled with confidence in business leadership—shaped the campaign for unemployment insurance. Some labor unions had paid out-of-work benefits, but compulsory insurance against unemployment was first enacted in England in 1911. William Beveridge, its chief proponent, thought that unemployment was essentially a problem of the organization of the labor market. He thought, that is, that there were for the most part enough jobs but that they were not well matched to the workers. Each employer, each industry tended to accumulate a reserve of workers who were sometimes needed and sometimes not. To rationalize the labor market, he thought, one should set up a nationwide network of labor exchanges on which employers could draw as they needed. For its part, casual labor—labor employed in good times but laid off in bad—could easily move where demand was brisk. Of course some people would still be occasionally unemployed, and for them Beveridge proposed compulsory insurance. Every payday the worker, the employer, and the government would contribute a small amount to a central fund, and when he was unemployed the worker would draw specific benefits. The act of 1911 was intended to be actuarially sound. Benefits were based on payments, not need: they did not take dependents into account, for example, and they were limited to fifteen weeks a year. Beveridge also recognized that there were other kinds of unemployment that did not arise simply from a mismatch of men and jobs— cyclical and technological unemployment, for example—and for these he recommended appropriate measures. But the heart of his program was to rationalize the labor market and "decasualize" the labor reserve. As it happened, the situation was favorable between 1913, when the act went into effect, and the end of the war.

In America the AALL generally accepted Beveridge's ideas, but it chose to emphasize the notion of insurance as a device to prevent unemployment. In 1921 it advanced an "American plan" for "unemployment compensation." The solution to unemployment, it said, was to stabilize—or decasualize—the labor force. The trick was to give employers an incentive to keep workers on the payroll, a penalty for laying them off. Unemployment insurance would do this if employers paid its costs in proportion to their unemployment record. There was an analogy with workmen's compensation: just as "merit rating" gave an employer incentive to promote safety and reduce the cost of his insurance, so merit rating in unemployment insurance would encourage him to reduce layoffs. In 1931 the AALL went beyond this position to propose that each employer be required to set aside reserves to subsidize his own workers for a time after he laid them off, just as he set aside reserves in good times to pay dividends to stockholders even when the firm made no profit. This "unemployment reserves" plan, it argued, would provide even more incentive to employers than merit rating and insurance. The plan had many critics, but it was enacted in Wisconsin in 1932 and endorsed by the Governors Interstate Commission that year. In it the function of income maintenance and the device of shared risk—shared among employers—was subordinated to the policy of prevention.

While the AALL and its reform-minded friends expounded everybody's long-run interest in social insurance, another type of program appeared that was in part a rival and rallied more popular support: the pension. In Europe a pension was a gratuity granted by the king (representing the state) to someone who had served him well. Sometimes the king rewarded outstanding writers, artists, or courtesans, but especially the grants went to soldiers. Public officials felt obliged to care for disabled veterans, and also for those who retired after long service. Americans too had provided military pensions after their wars, and after the Civil War the political strength of the Grand Army of the Republic, an organization of Union veterans, made the provision especially generous. The laws were intended to compensate for disability, but eligibility became easier and a corps of "claims agents" appeared to advocate particular cases, using "private bills"— that is, special acts outside the ordinary pension law—if necessary. At their boldest, veterans wanted "service pensions"—stipends simply for service, not for disability or incapacity. In 1890 a federal law authorized pensions for veterans who were unable to work as a result of any disability, service connected or not, except those caused by personal vice. A generous administration allowed many veterans unable to work because of old age to qualify. Wives and dependent children received benefits. In 1907 Congress passed a general service pension—most veterans and their widows were aged by this time—and in the next few years payments rose to their high point.[11]

11. William Glasson, *Federal Military Pensions in the United States* (New York: Oxford University Press, 1918), pp. 234, 250–53.

Expenditures on military pensions were enormous. As Isaac Rubinow, a leading authority, pointed out in *Social Insurance* (1913), they cost more than three times as much per year as the British old-age pension system.[12] Moreover, they were tinged with scandal, not only the gross fraud in making claims and in administration but the well-known fact that congressional friends of the pensioners were often also advocates of a high tariff who needed some big government spending program to reduce the surplus that a high tariff was piling up on the federal treasury. (Beneficiaries of high tariff protection were also in their way receiving a government subsidy.).[13] The veterans' excesses had forestalled pensions for federal civil servants. "In Washington there was no less popular cause," Rubinow commented, "than a civil pension list." The effort was more successful among municipal employees—policemen, firemen, teachers; Rubinow thought this was because of the "close connection between 'government jobs' (city 'jobs' especially) and political influence or graft."

> A policeman or foreman receives his appointment because of a service rendered to the "organization" [Rubinow continued]. It is, therefore, a privileged position to which the ordinary principles of a wage contract do not apply. His wage is usually much larger than what he commands in ordinary life, his emoluments are higher. The pension fund is simply one of the many privileges of the city "job." [14]

Rubinow was trying to explain why the thirst for pensions had not spread to workingmen in private industry, "the industrial army as a whole." Already in 1909 a Pennsylvania congressman had introduced a bill to establish an "old-age home guard" of the U.S. Army, to include any citizen who was at least 65 and had been a resident of the country for at least 25 years; each beneficiary would draw "pay" of up to $120 a year, depending on his (or her) property and income. The American Federation of Labor approved this bill in 1909. In 1911 Victor Berger, a socialist member of Congress, introduced a bill for old-age pensions of up to $208 per year, again fluctuating with need. Many large employers—the railroads, for ex-

---

12. I[saac] M. Rubinow, *Social Insurance; With Special Reference to American Conditions* (New York: Holt, 1913), p. 404.

13. Mary Dearing, *Veterans in Politics: The Story of the G.A.R.* (Baton Rouge: Louisiana State University Press, 1952), pp. 364f., 434, 438.

14. Rubinow, *Social Insurance*, pp. 402, 400.

ample—followed the advice of experts in personnel management, who favored a company pension as a device for stabilizing the work force and retiring older and less efficient employees with a degree of dignity. [15]

Pensions were, like social insurance, a device to provide ("maintain") income in the absence of wages. What made them popular was that they were not actuarially related to benefits, as in social insurance. They simply represented the policy that the public (or the employer) would take care of people who served. Pensions for military and civil servants were supposed to be a compensation for the fact that these people gave up the opportunity for aggrandizement in private industry, a chance of great wealth. In return they would receive a measure of security. When pensions spread to private business it was held that they were a sort of deferred pay or a kind of sinking fund put aside against the obsolesence of human labor, like the fund businessmen accumulated to replace their obsolescent plant and equipment.

Then the idea was stretched from a reward for employment to a special kind of charity for an especially deserving client. This was the "widow's pension" or "mother's pension." The movement began with the first White House Children's Conference (1909), where the delegates agreed that homes should not be broken for reasons of poverty alone. They had in mind the situation in which a widow could not both support herself and care for her children. In that case it was better to give the widow a subsidy and let her mind the children than to force her to put the children in an institution while she worked.

In fact much family welfare was with widows and orphans, or families in which the father had deserted or been sent to an institution. What was new about widow's pensions was the idea that these women were performing a service to society by raising their children and that for this service they deserved a reward. Child welfare agencies increasingly favored "foster home placement" over institutional care, and increasingly they were willing to pay foster parents a subsidy; why not pay the subsidy to the child's own mother instead? (Of course there would be some check to make sure that the mother kept a good home.) This would not be ordinary outdoor poor relief be-

15. Lee Squier, *Old Age Dependency in the United States* (New York: Macmillan, 1912), is a contemporary survey.

cause the widows were being compensated for a public service. It would be set apart from ordinary poor relief because it would be administered separately, perhaps by the juvenile court, another enthusiasm of its sponsors. The "pension" would be better defined and more generous than ordinary poor relief, which was left to the discretion of the poor law authorities. The state might share the cost, and as a condition it might set standards and exercise a degree of supervision.

Such was the general thought behind the Illinois act of 1911 and those that followed it in a rush, in Colorado and Iowa in 1912 and in sixteen more states in 1913. Women's clubs were the main support of the movement; organized labor was favorable. Social workers often found themselves in opposition, at least those in the East who were under the influence of Edward Devine of the New York COS and Mary Richmond of the Russell Sage Foundation. These critics made three points: (1) Mother's pensions were in fact a form of outdoor relief and were liable to its abuses, as suggested also by the example of military pensions. (2) Advocates of widow's pensions assumed that the only problem was money and that a fixed grant, without individualized planning and casework, would solve it. Richmond had just completed a careful study of widows and thought she could see many other complexities. (3) Widow's pensions were likely to be an expensive digression from the main problem, which was the causes of widowhood (especially TB and industrial accidents) and a comprehensive program of social insurance for workers.[16]

These critics were brushed aside as defenders of an outdated notion of charity and a vested interest in casework. They were mollified when the administration of "public aid to mothers with dependent children," as the U.S Children's Bureau called it, did recognize the ideal of a professional family welfare agency, particularly in rural areas that had no private agencies anyhow. (Gertrude Vaile, a friend of Mary Richmond and head of the Denver agency, was a leader in this movement. She became president of the National Conference of Social Work [1926] and a professor at the University of Minnesota

16. Mary Richmond, "Pensions and the Social Worker," *Survey*, February 15, 1913, and "Motherhood and Pensions," *Survey*, March 1, 1913, reprinted in Mary E. Richmond, *The Long View*, Joanna Colcord, ed. (New York: Russell Sage Foundation, 1930), pp. 346–64; Edward Devine, "Pensions for Mothers," *American Labor Legislation Review*, (June 1913): 193–99.

School of Social Work.) By 1930 most states had such a law. Funding was likely to be low and the quality of administration depended on local interest, but at that point the future was hopeful.

Mother's pensions were an American innovation, but noncontributory old-age pensions had been discussed for a long time in Europe. Denmark established them in 1891, England and Australia in 1908. In the English context, very important in America, they were explicitly considered as an alternative to old-fashioned punitive poor relief on one hand and social insurance on the other. They were a special kind of outdoor relief, more generous and decent than the traditional kind, and English conservatives said that they would lead to moral decay. People would not take care of themselves or their families, it was said, but would shift the responsibility to the state. Conservatives favored thrift, self-help, and voluntary mutual aid, perhaps through insurance. Some people favored social insurance for retirement such as Germany and France had enacted. English labor leaders favored pensions. They thought of pensions as a proper reward for a lifetime of work, more so than the poor law, which they hated. They thought pensions would not pauperize but would be a foundation for independence.

In America the English debate was reflected in an influential report of the Massachusetts Commission on Old Age Pensions (1910). Afraid that public pensions might demoralize character and that a program in Massachusetts might put the state's businesses at a disadvantage in comparison with other states, and hopeful about the prospect of voluntary pensions by employers for their workers, the commissioners sided with the English conservatives and decisively opposed public pensions. They pointed particularly to the large costs of the English program, two or three times what had been expected.

But America had its Australia too, out beyond the Mississippi. Those states were full of men without families—cowboys, miners, lumbermen. They had opened the country. They were "veterans of settlement." Was the state to ignore them now? So the first old-age pension law was passed not in urban Massachusetts or New York but in Arizona (1914; declared unconstitutional the next year) and in Alaska (1915).

During the war the cause languished; then it revived. Pennsylvania, Montana, and Nevada passed old-age pension laws in 1923, Wisconsin in 1924, Kentucky in 1926, Maryland and Colorado in

1927. Some of these acts were unconstitutional, others ineffective. The main political support for this legislation came from the Fraternal Order of Eagles. The AALL helped the Eagles draw up a bill, which they sponsored in various states. The main opposition came from businessmen and taxpayers, well organized now, who were interested in voluntary (employer-sponsored) pension schemes and afraid of a big political pension grab. But reality was against them. Reality was the growing number and proportion of the aged and the growing economic dependency among them, which became clearer as the Depression fell. Nineteen states acted between 1929 and 1934.

Before 1930 the blind too were in some states or communities, set apart from other disabled people on poor relief and, as in the case of widowed mothers and the aged, given a form of aid often called a pension. In 1898 Ohio authorized county poor law officials to grant up to $100 a year to poor and worthy blind. Illinois followed in 1903, Wisconsin in 1907. Many states acted after 1915. The blind themselves and their friends in schools and institutions were effective leaders in this cause. The cost was small. The idea of a reward for service, which colored other pensions, was absent here. What persisted was a search for a mode of income maintenance that was somewhere between the stigma and often punitive spirit of traditional public charity, on one hand, and the complexities of social insurance, on the other.

The slow progress of social-security legislation before 1930, compared with that enacted by European states, was a result of American conditions. Americans lacked the class spirit that encouraged European conservatives and working-class radicals to think in collectivist terms. Our form of democracy was individualistic and pluralistic: people looked out for themselves or organized groups to help each other. The history of the spoils system and of pressure politics—the alliance between high-tariff protectionists and Union veterans, for example—did not encourage confidence in government. The fact that social legislation was state legislation, and might put employers at a disadvantage compared with competitors in other states, was a practical obstacle. The courts were solicitous about property rights and freedom of contract, and it proved impossible to win constitutional amendments that would redirect them.

Moreover, there were many positive features in the 1920s. The growth of large-scale organization, both in business and in government, with its corps of specialists, technicians, and professionals, opened paths of opportunity. Organized (skilled) labor was well paid. A flourishing mass culture—music, sports, movies, radio—gave zest to life. Businessmen and philanthropists thought they were solving problems of poverty, social disorganization, and personal deviation by means of voluntary efforts, self-help and mutual aid as opposed to the compulsion and red tape of some political bureaucrat.

Meanwhile in the years after the war Europe looked sick. Strange, unhealthy-sounding ideas spread about art and politics. Germany suffered a terrible inflation, England a prolonged depression. English unemployment insurance, which had worked well before 1920, was stretched by political pressure to pay benefits outside any conventional insurance rationale. It became an expensive form of poor relief ("the dole") thought to be bad for business, bad for workers, bad for everybody. No wonder the AALL emphasized the "American plan" of unemployment compensation.

So optimism mixed with complacency in the decade before the Depression.

Chapter

12

Relief and Social Security,

1930–1946

$\mathbf{T}$HE SOCIAL SECURITY ACT of 1935 is the most important single law in this history. To understand it one must see it in relation to the problems and ideas of the Great Depression of 1929–1941, and also in the perspective of alternatives that were unrealized.

When Herbert Hoover became President in March 1929, a few people recognized that there were depressed areas and other problems in the economy, but the general feeling, which the President shared, was optimistic. A thorough survey by the critical-minded National Bureau of Economic Research had said (1927) that prosperity rested firmly on technological and social progress.[1] When the stock market crash came, in November 1929, it was widely interpreted as a special punishment for excessive speculation in securities, not a sign of fundamental sickness in the economy. Hence, authorities hoped that the decline in business would quickly reverse itself, and they were inclined to be complacent about unemployment. A nightmarish counterpoint developed between their reassuring statements and the alarms that sounded louder and louder, and in the end proved correct.

As the need to act became more urgent, authorities distinguished three policy objectives: recovery, relief, and reform. Recovery meant turning the course of business back toward prosperity.

1. National Bureau of Economic Research, *Recent Economic Changes in the United States* (New York: McGraw-Hill, 1929), II, 862–68.

217

Relief meant to help the unemployed, the most obvious and piteous victims of the situation. Reform meant to improve whatever underlying conditions had brought matters to a crisis. Authorities disagreed about facts and recommendations. Many of them, including President Hoover, were afraid that what was good for relief was not good for recovery and that what seemed helpful in the short run worked against long-run reform, if not the foundations of the democratic way of life.

President Hoover was conspicuously well qualified to lead in the crisis. In 1921, as Secretary of Commerce, he had convened a conference on unemployment to deal with the problems of the short-lived postwar depression, and he was abreast of advanced thought on that subject as well as general economic theory. Even his critics conceded that he was a man of principle, integrity, and intelligence, and those qualities characterized his response to the depression.

Like his economic advisers, Hoover perceived the Depression as a phase of the business cycle. By "business cycle" they understood a fluctuation in aggregate economic activity (producing and selling goods). The cycle—or fluctuation—had two phases, increase or "expansion" and decrease or "contraction." During the expansion, demand was brisk and prices were likely to rise (inflation); during the contraction, prices were likely to decline (deflation). A "depression" was a contraction phase. It was easy for common sense to tell good times from bad, but in the 1920s economists began to analyze this commonsense impression carefully. It happened that the great expansion after 1900 of business, regulation, and taxation had engendered a mass of statistics, and economists could use these to measure the cycle more exactly and to distinguish its components, for there were cycles within cycles; some activities grew as others declined; and there were long-term or secular trends.

The development in the 1920s of the theory of business cycles was of great importance because it turned the attention of economists from hypothetical models of behavior in the marketplace to certain empirical facts about that behavior, and to a more developmental or historical view of the economy. In general, the statistical picture confirmed common sense: for a century there had been a succession of cycles as boom led to bust, then to recovery and a new boom. The long-run trend, however, was decisively upward. In perspective the contractions appeared to be a good thing: they pushed investors to redirect their capital into more profitable or productive kinds of enterprise, and they pushed workers toward jobs or communities that had a better future. The subject was interesting because it led economists to hope that they could recognize particular influences working toward boom or bust and recommend policies that would modify them. Granted that business activity would normally rise and fall, they thought, investors or the government might take some action to make the rise and fall less extreme, the redirection of the economy less painful. This process was called "stabilizing the business cycle," that is, keeping the ups and downs closer to an equilibrium, or full employment of capital and labor.

So history and theory both told Hoover that depression would sooner or later lead to recovery. Moreover, there was reason to think that the Depression might be brief. The last serious and prolonged depression in the United States had been in 1893–1897; later contractions, in 1907, 1913, and 1919, had been short. Hoover's main focus, therefore, was on recovery, on encouraging expansion in business. He recognized that there was a psychological aspect to a "depression" (which is suggested by the use of the word to name a psychological symptom, the opposite of elation). If investors are pessimistic, they will not invest; if employers are pessimistic, they will not hire. The stock market crash—the abrupt fall of the prices of stocks traded on the New York Exchange by an average of 40 percent—was of course very depressing to investors. They did not usually suffer physical deprivation as unemployed workers did, but they lost paper fortunes and a number of them committed suicide. Nevertheless, as the President observed, the economy was fundamentally sound: the real productive forces, the farms, mines, and factories, the energetic and skilled labor force, were there, waiting to be rallied. To help restore confidence, Hoover emphasized the positive indications; looking for signs of recovery, he found them. Later his hopeful statements would seem merely complacent, not courageous.

Meanwhile Hoover thought that falling prices were one cause of pessimism—businessmen would not buy materials or hire labor if they might get them more cheaply later on—and he tried to keep prices from falling. He called in industrialists and asked them to keep their prices and wages steady. He arranged for the government to make credit available to farmers so that they would not have to sell their crops at panic prices, and to bankers so that depositors would not have to sell off the collateral for their loans at panic prices; he made it easy for businessmen to borrow to get their operations going again; he favored a tariff that would protect workers from low-wage competition abroad. As time went on and the Depression deepened, he put more emphasis on its international character and tried to act with foreign nations to improve international credit and trade.

Hoover also encouraged public works, that is, federal, state, and local construction of buildings, highways, or other facilities. He recognized that this government investment would increase demand for material and labor and act as a stimulant to the economy. On the other hand, like officials at the state and local levels, he believed that there were rather narrow limits on this use of public works. Public works cost money, which governments raised by taxation or by selling bonds. But bonds had to be redeemed later by taxation, and higher taxes and borrowing were generally discouraging to investors and businessmen. The notion of stimulating the economy by public works therefore contradicted the notion that the government should hold taxes down and balance the budget. It happened that many states and cities had borrowed heavily to build institutions and highways in the 1920s. Their taxes were already relatively high in 1930.

While the Hoover administration worked on recovery, encouraging an upturn in business, the problem of relief grew steadily worse. Everyone recognized that unemployment relief was considerably different from ordinary poor relief as that was practiced in the 1920s. Poor relief had typically helped a relatively few misfits, very often in the form of private charity. It was part of the business of social workers. The fourth edition of Warner's *American Charities and Social Work* (1930), the leading textbook on the subject, discussed relief in a few pages of a chapter on family welfare. The social workers' enthusiasm was to individualize the case; relate the problem to personal, family, or social disorganization; and arrange a kind of help that would be rational and specific. They recognized the factor of impersonal or social causes of individual distress and advocated social reforms, but that was not central. Obviously the mass unemployment of a great depression brought a much different caseload— people who were ordinarily quite self-sufficient. Typically these people had some resources of their own, some credit with their friends and relatives, but when this informal help failed they fell on charity.

They appeared on the agenda of public policy as a great increase in outdoor relief.

Just as Hoover thought of the Depression as a temporary emergency, pending recovery, so he thought that unemployment relief was properly a temporary emergency that called for a special organization. It was like a flood, famine, or war. Hoover was disposed to think in these terms because he had made his first great public reputation in the World War and its aftermath as an administrator of war relief, and in 1927, as Secretary of Commerce, he had masterfully organized a major flood relief effort in the Mississippi Valley. He had a wide acquaintance and following among philanthropists and social workers of the sort that turned up in the American Red Cross, which mobilized resources for disasters, and community chests, which furnished a nucleus of professional staff for local disaster relief. As for administrative organization, he thought it should be largely volunteer and local. Of course outside help was necessary, but it should be channeled through a makeshift arrangement of local people. It should help local people help each other, drawing extensively on their firsthand knowledge of the situation and the resources available.

Accordingly, in October 1930, as the Depression entered its second winter, Hoover appointed the President's Emergency Committee for Employment. Its objective was to be a clearinghouse for local efforts to provide jobs and relief; it was to stimulate and guide local and especially voluntary effort, to help people define the problem and take responsible action. In August 1931, as the demand grew for something more, Hoover replaced it with the President's Organization for Unemployment Relief, which helped arrange a great nationwide fund-raising drive for local community chests and urged that state governments help municipalities that were foundering.

But opinion grew among people nearest the unemployed that these efforts were not enough. When the National Conference of Social Work met in 1932, most delegates believed that (1) aid should be public rather than private and (2) the federal government should go beyond merely advising and provide funds to the needy. Hoover resisted these ideas. There was a constitutional problem—Presidents Pierce and Cleveland had said very explicitly that the federal government had no power to become a national almoner, and most court decisions agreed—but Hoover's objections were mainly practical. If the federal government stepped in with a lot of money and a big organization, private individuals, municipalities, and states would find it easy to shrug off their responsibility. The political drive for more and more federal money, directed by organizations of beneficiaries and bureaucrats, could pauperize the community, unbalance the federal budget and the credit of the government, and ultimately subvert the system. The old suspicion of public outdoor relief was increased by the experience with the Civil War pension grab and the English dole of the 1920s, which was thought to have pauperized English workers and contributed to the terrible and prolonged English depression.

In fact, no one knew what the situation was. The relevant empirical observations—the number of unemployed, the resources of various communities—were simply not available. Hoover's organization was hearing from governors and mayors that the problem was in hand and that they could manage. The Children's Bureau had begun to collect statistics on some cities, and these indicated that both the proportion of relief given by public (rather than private) agencies and the number of unemployed were much larger than the authorities thought; these figures supported the case for national action. Congressional committees in 1931 and 1932 brought out much testimony about how bad things were, but in 1933, when better statistics became available, it appeared that more than half the unemployed were concentrated in eight states and more than one-third in four (New York, Pennsylvania, Ohio, and Illinois), all of them rich.[2]

Whatever the local capability for public assistance, it was plain that (1) the general property tax, which funded it, was inflexible and inadequate—property values fell sharply during the Depression and many owners were tax delinquent—and (2) many communities had borrowed all they could according to their charters, so that involved legal amendments would have been necessary. By March 1932 seven states had passed emergency relief legislation that authorized them to sell bonds and channel the proceeds to needy cities and counties (these states included the four most afflicted plus New Jersey, Maryland, and Rhode Island).[3] In July 1932 President Hoover reluctantly signed the federal Emergency Relief and Construction Act, which

2. Searle F. Charles, *Minister of Relief: Harry Hopkins and the Depression* (Syracuse, N.Y.: Syracuse University Press, 1963), p. 26; James T. Patterson, *The New Deal and the States* (Princeton, N.J.: Princeton University Press, 1969), pp. 30f.

3. Josephine C. Brown, *Public Relief, 1929–1939* (New York: Holt, 1940), p. 96.

authorized the Reconstruction Finance Corporation to advance money to states for relief. The Reconstruction Finance Corporation had been set up originally as a loan office for businessmen; its loans were well secured and were not expected to cost the federal government anything in the long run. Its managers were careful that the advances they made to states were for self-liquidating construction projects; they were loans, not gifts. But by 1932 the states and the federal government had begun to help communities pay for outdoor relief.

Hoover had not been prepared to comprehend the depth of the emerging crisis or to take very drastic action; a hostile Congress after 1930 added to his difficulties. Franklin Roosevelt, who became President in March 1933, was in a much better situation. He was a relative and admirer of former President Theodore Roosevelt and had served President Woodrow Wilson as Assistant Secretary of the Navy. He was a self-conscious heir to the social-justice theme in progressivism. He had a politician's temperament, good humored and self-confident. He had begun his political career as an upstate patrician foe of the Tammany machine in New York City. He was at that time an ally of middle-class reformers and social workers; his wife Eleanor was a favorite among them. Perhaps he learned about humility and courage from a cruel attack of infantile paralysis, which crippled him permanently in 1921 and seemed to put an end to his promising political career. It did not, and meanwhile he had learned much from Tammany, appreciating in his genial way the good will and responsiveness of its pols. Equally important, Tammany could learn, and it helped forge the coalition of urban boss, middle-class reformer, social worker, and organized labor that made New York a leading state in welfare and labor legislation and administration. Al Smith was their big success, a ward politician who became a great legislator and governor, the "Happy Warrior," as Roosevelt called him when he nominated Smith for the Presidency in 1928. Smith lost to Hoover, but Roosevelt became governor and inherited the New York State administration and its spirit. He was in a good place to see problems and to act.

In principle FDR was rather conservative—he favored *laissez-faire*, minimum government, local responsibility, and balanced budgets—but like the Tammany pols he was not afraid of government action and he was more concerned about the suffering of the unemployed than about the risk of pauperization. In 1931 he pushed through a $10 million state bond issue for unemployment relief and set up a Temporary Emergency Relief Administration to give money to local governments, which then gave it to the needy. This was the first such state agency. Meanwhile he called other governors into conference to explore other actions.

Roosevelt came into national office with a pledge for retrenchment and economy, but it was plain that he was going to spend federal funds for unemployment relief. There was no doubt about the depth of the crisis by this time, and he had a favorable Congress. In May 1933 it passed the Federal Emergency Relief Act, and during those first hundred days Roosevelt got many other bold measures for recovery and reform.

As for recovery, FDR went beyond Hoover's efforts for voluntary price maintenance to an effort to compel "fair competition." This was radical inasmuch as it sharply limited competition, but it had two precedents: first, the progressive effort to legislate minimum wage, maximum hours, and other conditions of labor, and second, the spirit of welfare capitalism, which encouraged employers to be more solicitous about labor conditions. The codes of fair competition were drawn up by representatives of employers, labor, and consumers—mostly employers, in fact—industry by industry. They were published and enforced by the National Recovery Administration (NRA).

Roosevelt also went beyond Hoover's program for public works to stimulate the economy. Hoover had opposed such works if they required that the government borrow money or unbalance the budget. Roosevelt was more willing to spend. The Public Works Administration (PWA), which handled these funds, did not itself do any construction. It provided loans or grants to states or municipalities. It expected them to submit proposals, which it examined carefully, and it expected them to put up 70 percent of the costs themselves. It provided some stimulus, but not much.

Meanwhile in May 1933 Congress authorized almost $500 million for relief and set up a Federal Emergency Relief Administration (FERA) to get it to the states and people who needed it. To manage this work Roosevelt brought in Harry Hopkins, who had run his state relief operation in New York, Hopkins (1890–1946) was an Iowa college boy when he came to New York in 1911 to work in a settlement house, and he rose as an administrator in private welfare agencies. He was an excellent leader because he could focus clearly on objectives and pursue them in an energetic, resourceful, and even inspiring way. Now his objective was to relieve the unemployed, to put the federal government in the business of poor relief. The law gave him wide discretion.

His first important decision was that federal funds should be spent by public agencies. In many localities officials had arranged that charity organization or family welfare societies investigate applicants for relief and decide on their eligibility and the amount of the grant, and the emergency agencies were often voluntary, at least in part. Hopkins thought that relief should be a matter of right, not dependent on anybody's voluntary generosity, and that the people who administered it should be responsible employees, paid for their service and held to account. So the makeshift arrangements that had taken form were put into a common framework. At first this meant simply that the local agents were hired by the local poor relief agency. They sent requests for funds to a state emergency relief agency, which, in turn, dealt with Hopkins' national administration.

Presumably, then, existing state and local public-assistance officials—the people who had been handing out public poor relief— would simply take on an enlarged role and add to their caseload the needy unemployed. They would assist these people largely out of federal funds, and of course the FERA would send them directives governing the administration of its aid. This simple idea was soon complicated. Many states did not have welfare departments that were constitutionally empowered or administratively able to work with the FERA; local poor law officials often worked part time or were incompetent to handle a big problem. In any case existing public agencies were preoccupied with their ordinary caseload, which also had to be helped. Accordingly, the FERA tended to favor a new or separate state organization (State Emergency Relief Administration, or SERA), parallel to the state and local welfare departments but concerned only with the unemployed.

There was a good deal of similarity and overlap in the work of the welfare and relief agencies, but they differed in their character. The SERAs had strong central direction from Washington, a sense of mission (emergency help to the unemployed), and rather sophisticated, standardized administrative procedures; the existing poor relief agencies, particularly at the local level, were as various as the communities that sponsored them, to which they were responsible. Traditional agencies often handed out grocery orders or coal in a capricious way; SERA offices had higher standards and paid cash relief. Hopkins of course drew on the insights of experts in the science of public-welfare administration as it had developed in advanced agencies of the 1920s, and his operation was closer to this ideal than were the servants of local traditions.

Hopkins increasingly wanted to go beyond *direct relief* for the unemployed to *work relief* for them. Ironically, work relief had been associated in the poor law tradition with deterrence; often applicants for help faced a work test such as sawing wood to show that they were not too lazy to work. But in the 1930s work relief had more positive aspects. To the reliefer it meant that his grant was not charity but a sort of compensation. Often the eligibility worker would figure out his relief budget and then assign him to a work project, where he would work for his grant, as it were, at so much per hour (technically this was called work-for-relief). The community got the value of the work; it seemed reasonable that able-bodied unemployed men on relief might occupy their idleness to improve its facilities. Hopkins went beyond work-for-relief, however, to the notion of a public job for the unemployed. The unemployed, he believed, were mostly good people who wanted jobs; it was not their fault if private business could not hire them. A job meant more than mere income; it meant a feeling of usefulness, a degree of dignity, a sense of competence and even service. Unemployment relief should not mean mere income but a real job. Roosevelt agreed.

Conceivably, then, the best form of relief was to take the money from the FERA and transfer it to the PWA, the Public Works Administration already set up to stimulate jobs. But Harold Ickes, the administrator of the PWA, had a conventional view of public works, that they were important public improvements carefully planned and approved. What Hopkins wanted was a crash program to put a lot of people to work. This took form in the Civil Works Administration (CWA), which he set up in November 1933; it soon employed four million workers in quickly extemporized public-works projects. When it ended, in the spring of 1934, many of its projects and workers were transferred to the FERA, which increasingly favored work relief.

In January 1935 Roosevelt proposed a bold new program. The government would get out of "this business of relief," meaning *emergency direct relief to the unemployed*. It would disband the FERA. It would replace the "emergency program" with a "permanent program." The central idea of the permanent program was to distinguish unemployment relief from other types of relief that had fallen under the poor law—relief to broken families, the aged, and the disabled. It would return these traditional sorts of poor relief cases to the states and communities, where they had always been. It would not abandon them altogether but would provide a federal subsidy for certain categories of cases. As for the needy unemployed—the great mass of the Depression caseload—the federal government itself would take responsibility for them. It would provide them with jobs in a great new work relief program. For the longer range, it would introduce measures for social insurance that would prevent or minimize such calamities in the future. The permanent program, in short, was to be the Works Progress Administration (WPA) plus the public-assistance and social-insurance features of the Social Security Act of 1935.

From the start there were doubts about work relief. It was similar to ordinary public works, but those projects were incidental to governing. Work relief was intended less to get something necessary done than to employ the worker. Accordingly, the projects had to be suited to the needy one's skills and, usually, located where he happened to be. On the other hand, the projects could not be mere make-work, intended to fill the time: that would negate the feelings of worth, usefulness, and service that were supposed to dignify the task.

The most successful programs were designed for young people: the Civilian Conservation Corps (CCC) and the National Youth Administration (NYA). The CCC was set up in March 1933 to employ men aged 18 to 25 whose families were on relief. They were sent to camp and paid $30 a month, of which they had to send $25 home to their family. The Army ran the camps, and the Department of Interior or Agriculture helped plan the projects and supervised them. The NYA was a special program for school-age youth. It arranged with schools to give them part-time paid work, which was supposed to enable them to stay in school or college. It also had a program for young people not in school, somewhat like ordinary work relief but including more part-time jobs and with some training objectives.

These programs were relatively small, although the CCC got up to 600,000 enrollees in 1935. The major program was the WPA, the Works Progress Administration (called Work Projects Administration after 1939). Between 1935 and 1943, when it phased out, it spent $11.4 billion, and at its peak, in 1938, it employed over 3.3 million people. It was, therefore, much the biggest "firm" in America—in the world—and its administrative decisions were the responsibility of one man—Harry Hopkins, until he left to become Secretary of Commerce in 1938.

Consider a few decisions: How much money would go to which states? Within the states, which project would be approved? How much should the sponsors contribute? Who would staff the agency? What applicants would be eligible for work relief? What wage would the public work pay? It was hard to imagine that all that money and all those jobs would not somehow become the means of partisan politics. Certainly they were a focus of everyone's suspicion. In retrospect it appears that the administration was, as Hopkins undoubtedly wished, honored by its professional and nonpartisan service. There were inevitably mistakes of management and judgment in so big and extemporized an operation, but serious political abuse was an exception.

The real problems with the WPA lay in its conception. It was easy to say, as Roosevelt and Hopkins did, that policy should distinguish between the employable and the unemployable, that the federal government should furnish work relief and the states and municipalities direct relief. But in fact, as many experts on social work and public welfare pointed out, the "employables" included an indefinite but large number who were only marginally in the labor force; the WPA never provided enough jobs for the employable, and the leftovers fell mostly on "general relief"—old-fashioned outdoor poor relief; most localities were unlikely to provide adequately for their ordinary direct-relief cases, let alone the marginal or leftover employables. In fact most employables lived in families whose needs differed and whose members might be eligible for special forms of relief. There was much duplication in eligibility determination and service needs for work relief and direct relief, and there was a need to coordinate or integrate them. Furthermore, it was very difficult for state and local authorities to plan and develop their work because Congress thriftily cut back WPA appropriations when the economy seemed to be improving.

A rational policy, these critics argued, would improve the FERA pattern. It would have the federal government channel predictable funds for both work and direct relief through the states according to some reasonable formula, with proper guidelines and supervision. The states would contribute money, guidelines, and supervision to the municipalities or counties, which would also contribute a share and actually administer the program. There would be a federal subsidy for all direct relief and an integration of the administration of work relief and direct relief.

The basic idea of the WPA was that the problem of the Depression was unemployment; unemployment was a national problem and was appropriately met by a federal program; it was better met by work relief than by direct relief. Critics of the WPA argued that the problem was not just unemployment but the whole heritage of the poor law and local (rather than national) responsibility; the solution was *shared* responsibility for good public welfare *and* social services.

A second line of criticism of the WPA was economic: the program combined two objectives—doing public work and giving relief—and the combination, it was said, was inherently inefficient. The main purpose of relief was to meet need, but WPA workers were typically employed on the basis of their usefulness to the project rather than the degree of their need. Relief came in the form of a "security wage" that was higher than direct relief but presumably not so high as private employment. It had no relationship to family needs and might be too much for some, not enough for others; on the whole it was likely to be much more expensive than direct relief. As work, as a return on the taxpayer's investment, however, it was not very productive. Ordinarily public works other than routine maintenance were carefully considered and their specifications set; private contractors bid for the work, and inspectors held them to the specifications. This arrangement put a premium on the efficiency of the contractor and his workers. Work relief projects were not designed for economic efficiency, and the most efficient workers were likely to leave—expected to leave—to take advantage of better wages in the private job market. This was hardly a good work environment.

Hopkins himself thought that the main argument against work

relief was that direct relief was cheaper. He believed, however, that people have a right to a share in the national income, that "the human being should come first, and the serviceability of the economic system in which he functions should be estimated by the number of persons who share in its rewards." He thought that "with few exceptions" human beings "have found no substitute for useful work to keep themselves sound of body and mind . . . Work conserves them as a national asset."[4] He was also justly proud of the improvements that his workers made. Behind his—and Roosevelt's—view was a politically momentous fact: a public-opinion poll in May 1939 showed that 89 percent of the respondents thought work relief was the better form of assistance.[5] Soon thereafter the defense boom began to take hold, and during the war years there was a shortage, not a surplus, of labor.

The distinction between the employable and the unemployable was also central in the conception of the Social Security Act of 1935. For people who needed relief and were "unemployable" (out of the labor market), the Act provided a federal subsidy to build up existing state and local programs. These subsidies were made available only to specific categories of reliefers—namely, the aged, dependent children, and the blind—and only when the state programs met certain standards. For those who were employable (in the labor market) and employed, the Act offered social insurance against two important risks of dependency: unemployment and old age. A person in covered employment would accumulate credit so that if he was laid off he would receive a fraction of the amount of his wage for a certain number of weeks. (The benefits were limited, and when they ran out he would, according to the plan, go on work relief or direct relief.) Over the years he spent working he would accumulate credit that would yield him benefits when he retired.

There was no great political pressure for the act; President Roosevelt pushed and carried it as a viable compromise between proposals that were much more conservative or radical. Conservatism, in this context, was the old deterrent or punitive idea of poor relief,

4. Harry Hopkins, *Spending to Save: The Complete Story of Relief* (New York: Norton 1936), pp. 197f., 183f.

5. Reported in *Public Opinion Quarterly*, 3 (October 1939): 590.

which continued to have many supporters, including powerful congressmen, even in the depth of the Depression. The more radical proposals envisioned a large redistribution of income. The most potent of these were home growths, far from the communist or socialist machinations of big-city intellectuals. The most powerful by far were the Townsend clubs, which spread among the old folks in 1934. Dr. Francis Townsend, an Iowa physician who had retired to sell real estate in California, argued that the way to end the Depression was to give everyone over 60 a pension of $200 a month, provided that they spent it within the month. He would raise the money by means of a national sales tax, and he thought that when the old folks spent it they would bring back prosperity. This simple-minded panacea attracted incredible support, especially among elements that were usually identified with the Republican party. It raised the bogey of the pension-hunting pressure group.

Less popular, but potentially more dangerous, was the Share Our Wealth movement led by Senator Huey Long of Louisiana. A poor boy from the hill country, he dominated his state and appealed by flamboyant oratory to people who were usually identified with the Democratic party. His program was an attack on "plutocracy" and a sort of guaranteed income for every family, financed by confiscatory taxes on great wealth. (He was assassinated in 1935, but the Long machine and family carried on in Louisiana.)

Between the extremes of punitive deterrence and demagogic redistribution, the notion of social insurance recommended itself for prudence and justice, as it had for three decades to students of the subject. President Roosevelt was of this mind, and so was his Secretary of Labor, Frances Perkins. In 1934 he saw the opportunity for a comprehensive measure that would be both a resolution of the problem of relief—a "permanent program"—and a monument to his administration. He had visions then of a comprehensive "cradle-to-grave" social insurance, but he realized that it would have to have broad political support. He forestalled a number of legislative proposals that his friends had advanced and appointed a cabinet committee to consider them and put them together. This Committee on Economic Security, which Perkins chaired, included the Secretaries of Treasury and Agriculture, the Attorney General, and Harry Hopkins. The committee made policy decisions based on advice from a technical committee and staff and various advisory committees of outside experts. Arthur Altmeyer, who had moved from secretary of the Wisconsin Industrial Commission to become Assistant Secretary of Labor, became chairman of the technical committee; Edwin Witte, an economist who had specialized in labor legislation, also came from Wisconsin to serve as executive director of the staff. This organization worked for six months to prepare the act the President presented to Congress in January 1935.

In fact the President, with Perkins and Hopkins, had decided the general character of the act, and the committee made policy in that framework. Still, its decisions were many and controversial. In economic jargon public assistance and social insurance are called *transfer programs*. The name refers to the fact that they take income from some people and give it to others. The controversies in staff and committee were over technical details of the proposals. These were important because they determined exactly who paid, how much, who handled the funds, who received them, and under what conditions. Of course after the President proposed the legislation committees of the Senate and House reviewed much of the evidence and all the debated decisions.

There was not much debate about the categorical assistance programs. The mechanism—a "grant-in-aid" from the federal government to the states—was well known and proved constitutional. In practice it helped states relieve certain needy classes of people, but it had conditions whereby Congress tried to make sure that federal funds were well spent, and often these conditions pushed state officials in ways they did not like. The stipulations aimed at just and efficient administration. Each state had to have a definite plan in the charge of a single state agency. The plan had to operate in every part of the state. Payment had to be in money, and agencies had to arrange for fair hearings. The state government had to contribute to the grant. Cost-sharing arrangements differed: In Old Age Assistance (OAA) and Aid to the Blind (AB), the federal government matched the state dollar for dollar for the first $15 per month. In Aid to Dependent Children (ADC), the grant was based on the fact that families of servicemen who had lost their lives in the World War received $18 for the first child and $12 for each additional child. ADC grants were funded up to that level, with the federal government contributing a third of the sum. (This arrangement overlooked the fact that a veteran's widow also got $30 a month, in addition to the grants for the children. Witte and Perkins pointed out this error to the congressional committee, but the committee was interested in helping the aged, not dependent children, and was willing to let aid to the latter begin at a low level.)[6]

The most significant controversy about public assistance was over the proposed condition that the reliefer be enabled to have a "reasonable subsistence compatible with health and decency." This provision implied that the federal government would have the power to establish a national minimum standard as a condition of its subsidy. A second controversial requirement was that the states establish a merit system for those administering the program. Congressmen from the South and rural sections generally were sure that no one from Washington was going to tell their constituents how much relief they had to give or whom they should hire to give it, so those items were struck out.

Debate over the social insurances was colored by the facts that these programs would not help anybody right away, that experts disagreed about them, and that they seemed complicated and burdensome. There were two general areas of disagreement: (1) the objective of the insurance and (2) the political, as distinct from technical, merit of the proposal.

Roosevelt and his advisers regarded social insurance in a traditional light, as a device for individual workers to protect themselves against the risk of loss of income. They wanted the worker to have the dignity of providing through this medium for himself, collecting his benefits as an insurance claim. They were afraid that pension hunters would raid the treasury, so they wanted the insurance programs to be self-supporting just as private insurance plans were self-supporting (benefits were paid out of premiums plus interest on reserves). They hoped that insurance would gradually replace assistance, to everybody's advantage.

Many conservatives favored insurance but thought it ought to be voluntary, provided by the worker or his employer. They resisted the notion of compulsory social insurance. Other conservatives—a growing number—thought that social insurance was a roundabout way of getting at the underlying problem of need. They thought the govern-

6. Edwin E. Witte, *Development of the Social Security Act* (Madison: University of Wisconsin Press, 1962), pp. 162–65.

ment should stick to the old poor relief system but improve its standards and administration. These people typically favored direct relief over work relief. They thought that it ought to be made obvious who was paying and who was receiving, and that costs ought to be held down in every way.

Liberals, on the other hand, wanted to use the insurance mechanism to effect some redistribution of income. They realized that benefits based on contributions of workers and employers would not be adequate for many recipients, especially those who needed help most, who were working part time or received very low pay. They wanted to juggle the benefit formula so that low-paid workers would receive much more than they were entitled to by strict actuarial reckoning. They wanted the government to increase the benefit by contributions raised by means of progressive income taxes on the middle class.

Both conservatives and liberals could agree that there was a bad fit between the benefits of social insurance, as Roosevelt and his advisers conceived it, and the needs of the poor. Conservatives wanted to reject compulsory insurance for poor relief, which history suggested would probably be deterrent and punitive: not much political appeal there during the Depression. Liberals favored devices that would expand social insurance to do part of the job of relief and reform by more aggressive redistribution of wealth: not much political appeal there, to Congress. Roosevelt's proposed Social Security Act offered some federal aid for public assistance at once and the hope of a self-supporting contributory social-insurance program for the future.

The political merit of the proposal lay partly in its moderate stance—beyond poor relief but short of radical redistribution—but the framers of the legislation worried as much about the opinion of the Supreme Court as about that of Congress. Historically social insurance had been state legislation, and it was dubious whether it fell under the limited powers of Congress. Judges were traditionally solicitous about property rights and taxation, and of course they could void the actions of the President and Congress. There was much scheming to invent devices that would present a national social-insurance program as if the state were sponsoring it. This did not work in old-age insurance —actuaries said that state laws would be impractical, so *that* part of the act was justified under the power of Congress to tax and spend for the general welfare.

Unemployment insurance, however, was authorized in the form of separate state programs. The states were induced to act by a federal tax on payrolls, which the federal government would return to the states if they enacted approved legislation. This device was partly to meet constitutional objections to a single federal program but partly too because experts disagreed on the objectives of unemployment insurance. Many favored the "American plan," which would go beyond giving the unemployed help and give employers a motive to reduce unemployment. Their costs would be lower if they kept their unemployment rate low. An increasing number of experts rejected this notion as ineffective and in any case a distraction from the basic job of supporting the worker. In addition to this controversy there was the problem of setting the level of benefits. Plainly a single national level would be too high in some places and too low in others. This problem might have been solved by defining regional standards, but they would have been difficult to work out in Congress. Leaving the problem to the states made it much easier to win the assent of dubious congressmen.

For the rest, the act left out health and disability insurance—a large gap, but the American Medical Association and its allies were strongly opposed and the bill's sponsors did not want to challenge them. (Work-related accidents and illness were provided for by the existing workmen's compensation programs, at the state level.) The act did include substantial federal aid for state public health tasks, especially for maternal and child health and for crippled children. It included grants for public child welfare services and for vocational education. These health and welfare services were supposed to be preventive and to enhance the long-range character of the legislation.

A major amendment in 1939 added Survivors Insurance (SI). This provided that if a worker enrolled in Old Age Insurance died prematurely, his surviving dependents would receive benefits. In effect it added to the program a very important "life insurance" feature that was supposed, in the long run, to help keep widows and children off ADC.

In sum, the "permanent program" of 1935 reorganized the haphazard arrangements for relief that had developed over thirty years and particularly during the Depression. It used the power and resources of the federal government to put more system and substance into them, and added a large component of social insurance. As amended in 1939, the system provided for three important risks. For unemployment it offered work relief (WPA), and for the longer run unemployment insurance (UI). For old age or retirement it offered Old Age Assistance (OAA), and in the long run Old Age Insurance (OAI). For widows and dependent children it offered Aid to Dependent Children (ADC), and in the long run Survivors Insurance (SI). It gave considerable support to public services for health and welfare. There was strong political support in 1935 for work relief and for helping the old folks, but there was no strong political support for, or even interest in, the other parts of the package. Sponsors of the Social Security Act, particularly Witte, were genuinely afraid it would never get through the committees. In the end it passed with a large majority and the courts approved it. It was thought conservative inasmuch as it built on existing administrative structures where it could and it did not define a standard of health and decency for either public assistance or unemployment insurance. Benefits for social insurance would be rather low, and many workers were not covered. As it turned out, the notion of work relief would fade, but the framework of programs established by the Social Security Act would endure and improve.

As Congress worked over the Social Security Act in 1935, the NRA, the New Deal's recovery program, failed. It had rested on the belief that business, labor, and consumers could get together to make and support codes of fair competition. It was kin to the ideas about trade associations and welfare capitalism that Hoover had encouraged in the 1920s, but he and many others thought that, because of its compulsory feature, it verged on the "corporate state" of fascist theory. Businessmen had dominated the code making and got the most benefits, but they could not agree and came to resent this example of planning. There were few regrets when in May 1935 the Supreme Court declared it an unconstitutional regulation of commerce. In the same month the U.S. Chamber of Commerce denounced the New Deal.

Roosevelt's response was to move closer to the urban and labor elements in the Democratic party. In the summer of 1935 he asked for, and got, laws establishing the WPA (big spending, mostly for unemployed industrial workers); a new tax law that was harder on high incomes and undistributed corporate profits; a law increasing federal control over banks and one breaking up holding companies, part of a tougher antitrust policy; and the National Labor Relations (Wagner) Act, which continued and much expanded certain prounion policies of the NRA. The general thought behind these measures was that business had become too concentrated and that there needed to be some countervailing power—competition or labor unions or government regulation. It was a change from the earlier policy of cooperation, and it was clothed in a rhetoric that contrasted "economic royalists" with "one-third of a nation, ill-housed, ill-clad, ill-nourished."[7]

Such acts and statements tended to polarize American politics along the lines of rich versus poor and reform versus reaction. Perhaps the most important practical result was the rapid unionization of many mass production industries by the Committee for Industrial Organization (CIO), which gave form and coherence to the economic and political interests of unskilled workers. The American Federation of Labor also greatly expanded its membership and its political interests. Many of the newly unionized workers were immigrant or second generation, hitherto guided in their political interests by the big-city political machine or the pronouncements of the church. This major new force was much closer to the Democratic party than the pre-1930 unions had been. Roosevelt also won the heartfelt support of ethnic groups that had usually voted Republican, notably Italians and blacks. While he rallied the working class, he also appealed to a growing number of college-educated white-collar workers—professional people and technicians in the bureaucracies of business and government who were humanitarian or progressive in spirit but had mostly voted Republican in the past (social workers, for example).

These broad political identifications gave Roosevelt a great personal triumph in the presidential election of 1936 and very much strengthened the liberal element in the Democratic party. They did not end the Depression, however. For a time, in 1936 and 1937, the

7. These famous phrases are from President Roosevelt's "Acceptance of the Renomination for the Presidency," June 26, 1936, in *Public Papers and Addresses of Franklin D. Roosevelt*, vol. V (New York: Random House, 1938), p. 324, and his "Second Inaugrual Address," in *Ibid.*, vol. VI (New York: Russell and Russell, 1941), p. 5.

economy improved, but then came a severe and discouraging recession. This event brought out a sharp division over policy. Both conservatives and liberals agreed that the short-lived recovery was related to spending on the WPA and that the recession came when the WPA was sharply cut back. Conservatives argued that events had shown that the prosperity was artificial and self-defeating: it was based on deficit spending (the government financed the WPA by selling bonds) and left the government with a huge and discouraging debt to pay off. This argument supported the traditional goal of a balanced budget and a probusiness policy to encourage private investment.

But a growing faction of economists thought that the recession showed that the spending had been too little or cut back too soon. They wanted *more* borrowing and spending. Supporting this position were the ideas of the English economist John Maynard Keynes, summarized in *The General Theory of Employment, Interest, and Money* (1936). Keynes upset traditional economic thought by showing in theory that the business cycle did not have to return to equilibrium at full employment, that it might level off at a low level of investment and employment. This, he believed, had happened in the Great Depression. In this case the government could and should stimulate investment by deficit financing: a balanced budget was a mistaken policy. The notion that spending money on public works might stimulate recovery was familiar to the early New Dealers as "pump priming." The Keynesians went beyond it to favor continuous management of the economy by deliberate and forceful use of the federal power to tax, spend, and borrow: not an occasional timid shove but willful and potent direction.

Out of the polarization of politics and the advance of Keynesianism appeared the outlines of a new policy combining recovery and reform. Recovery was thought of as high or full employment, reform as modest redistribution of power and income. The President, who represented all the people as distinct from the special interests that surfaced in Congress, would take the lead, and the federal government would take the responsibility to manage the economy. It would support relief and other policies (subsidized public housing, for example) to help the poor. It would police business in the public interest (through conservation, banking regulation, and the like) and support competitive or countervailing interests in the economy (labor unions and farmer cooperatives, for example).

These outlines were slow to crystallize—Roosevelt was dubious about his Keynesian advisers—but the conservative opposition was not. It formed in Congress in 1937 and 1938 and forestalled any important new reform legislation. It was rooted in the rural sections and particularly in the southern wing of the Democratic party, which gave it skillful leadership. Rural poverty had early been recognized as a key to the problem, and the New Deal had given much thought to it. Ironically, its main policy, the Agricultural Adjustment Act, had the consequence of helping the larger and more market-oriented farmers, who were also benefiting from the scientific research and activity centered in the state agricultural colleges and extension movements. For the most part these benefits did not help poor farmers; nor were there agencies like urban charities and philanthropies and social workers to take up their cause. The successful farmers were very effective politically, and while they had their own agrarian interests they became more business- and employer-minded in their thinking.

Add to this temper the conventional suspicions of rural people, especially in the South, and resurgent conservatism took a definite form: against the President and in favor of Congress; against the national government and in favor of decentralization to the states and communities; against union labor (southerners particularly wanted to attract investment to their region and opposed national labor legislation that would tend to keep it where it was); against spending and borrowing and in favor of low taxes and balanced budgets. Of course this corresponded to the thinking of many urban (or suburban) Republicans, not just the rich but many in small business and white-collar jobs. These people, like their rural allies, were predominately white Anglo-Saxon Protestants (or "WASPS," in the derogatory term of later years), whereas the liberal Democrats carried on the ethos of urban cosmopolitanism.

The polarization, social and ideological, never became pervasive. There were many moderates on both sides and many factions of all sorts. Conservatives suffered from a negative program and the lack of an inspiring leader, but they were able to hold their own in Congress and especially in the states, where much of the very important implementation of welfare policies went on.

World War II, coming in 1941, broke the stalemate. It gave policy a definite goal—victory—and gave people a common cause to rally around. The international situation leading up to it brought out many contrasts between a totalitarian police state on one side and the heritage of liberal democracy on the other. It ended inhibitions about government management of the economy and spending, and showed plainly both the possibilities and the limitations of government planning. It ended the Depression and unemployment while maintaining a democratic form and spirit. On the other hand, it introduced regimentation and rationing that would have been intolerable except in such an emergency. But most people could see a reasonable middle ground: much more active national policies for prosperity and social welfare than had been acceptable in the 1930s, but still a large degree of decentralized and private decision making about economic and social affairs. The programs of public assistance and social insurance—left pretty much to themselves during the war years—would furnish a basic security, along with expanded social services for the young, the old, the disabled, and the unemployed. The federal government, through public works or other devices, would intervene actively to stimulate high employment and guide the business cycle. This feeling and thought went into the Employment Act of 1946, which gave the President and Congress a mandate to make such policy and a means—the Council of Economic Advisers—to consider the proper course. The lessons of the Depression and the war were to that extent learned, and so leaders turned their attention to the postwar depression that they expected but that never came.

Events of the Depression and the war affected both the market for professional social work and thinking about its political status.

In 1930 professional social work was a scatter of agency personnel, mostly in private organizations in big cities. Its leadership was in national bodies that promoted good standards of work, such as the Family Service Association, the Child Welfare League of America, the National Probation and Parole Association, and a few big-city professional schools. A few public agencies had succeeded in developing their service along lines suggested by such experts; they were forming the American Public Welfare Association.

Private-agency workers were the cadre of the emergency relief organizations. Sometimes they appeared in leadership roles, notably Harry Hopkins and his chief assistant, Aubrey Williams; more often they were supervisors, either on the field staff or over the line workers.

By 1940 the social security act had created three huge new bureaucracies. One administered the federal social-insurance program (OASI), which began to pay benefits that year. A second administered unemployment insurance, together with the employment service; these were state agencies, varied in their character and function, vaguely linked here to labor departments and there to the WPA or to public assistance. Finally there was the public assistance agency, the state and county or municipal public-welfare department. In 1935 these were rudimentary in most states; in the next two years they were organized in a systematic way in the 3,000 counties in the United States in order to take advantage of federal grants-in-aid. These three bureaucracies had much in common, but they developed differently because of their sponsors. OASI and UI were new, they embodied the notion of insurance, in which clients had vested rights, and they had central direction. The county and state welfare departments, on the other hand, carried on the historic work of poor relief; they had to contend with the historic attitudes toward reliefers as expressed by the county or state politicians who were their masters.

Most of the people who worked in public assistance determined or reviewed the eligibility of applicants. This was largely a routine clerical task, and those who carried it out needed mainly an accurate knowledge of rules and enough arithmetic to figure budgets. But it was never simply that. Rules were often complicated and allowed a degree of discretion. Applicants were likely to be ashamed, defensive, uncooperative or even hostile, pitiable, or offensive. It took a degree of patience, tact, insight, and skillful interviewing to bring out the facts and put them together so they could be understood or accepted. There were always problems besides the financial ones, trouble to shoot. Professional social workers were supposed to have the necessary skills, and when family service or child welfare agencies had handed out aid they had used them to individualize the help. It was out of the question that professionals hold the line jobs—they were too few and too expensive—but they took a place as supervisors or administrators, and as such they tried to infuse their values into the organization. They appeared in big-city and state departments, and especially in the federal Bureau of Public Assistance, which took charge of this function for the Social Security Board and sent its field representatives across the land. Its leader was Jane Hoey. Forty-four when she came to Washington, she had had a career in child welfare, in the Red Cross and health agencies, and for ten years as an executive of the New York Welfare Council. She had many friends there, especially among Catholics, a firm commitment to professional standards, and an unyielding self-confidence with temper to match.

State and local departments also got federal grants for child welfare. These came through the U.S. Children's Bureau, which had earlier been the center of professional social work in the federal government and had pioneered a field service. Other programs that hired social workers as a result of the Social Security Act were public health and vocational rehabilitation, and a few worked for the Farm Resettlement Administration and the Bureau of Indian Affairs, then undergoing a rebirth.

An amendment to the Social Security Act in 1939 that required a merit system was a help; so, indirectly was the war, which shook up the staff and caseload. In the postwar world they would settle down in situations where careers in public welfare enjoyed more security and clearer direction than before.

While more public jobs became available, private agencies managed, rather precariously, to hold their own. The community chests that supported them had formerly based their appeals on material need. They continued to offer aid, mostly temporary or supplemental, but as public agencies took over that function they had to shift to services. Voluntary givers continued to support the family service and child welfare agencies that offered casework to unstable or broken families, and the group work agencies that worked with leisure activities and especially youth (there was lots of leisure time during the Depression). The war increased the need for service to families and children and added large new programs, private and military, for the armed forces. Like the public services, private agencies faced much confusion, uncertainty, and change during the emergencies of depression and war, but the main drift was toward more jobs and broader public support for professional aspirations.

As social workers became involved in depression programs of a scale, complexity, and importance that were entirely new, there were reflections about the nature and role of the profession. Traditionally the social worker had been an agent of middle-class or religious philanthropy, often in fact a volunteer or at least altruistic in spirit. He was identified with sponsors, not recipients; even if he took up a cause, it was for some organization or legislation, some particular and specific reform. The aspiration was professional, partly for better service, partly for better status; the relationship of the professional to the agency had been much considered, mostly with regard to how it might encourage professionalism. The emergency relief agencies, and later the public-assistance agencies, attracted a host of workers who saw themselves mainly—and correctly—as line workers in a bureaucracy. They were interested in better working conditions and job security; they felt close to the clients and their woes.

In 1931 an organization arose spontaneously among these instant social workers in New York, Chicago, Philadelphia, and Boston. In the next few years it gathered strength as the "rank-and-file" movement. The name was intended to distinguish the members from the supervisors or executives, the leaders in the profession who gathered together in the American Association of Social Workers. The rank-and-file movement developed a union mentality in an adversary relationship to the bosses and identified with the revitalized labor movement and beyond that with the struggle of the masses. Marxism had a strong appeal to many members, as it did generally among union activists in the 1930s. From 1934 to 1941 activists published a lively journal, *Social Work Today*, a left-wing competitor of *The Survey*. The movement lost its enthusiasm in the war but persisted in efforts to organize social workers by the American Federation of State, County and Municipal Employees (AFL) and the United Office and Professional Workers and United Public Workers of America (CIO).

For their part, the people at the top of the hierarchy were also interested in personnel, administration, and policy. They saw that many of the professional social workers who were recruited to lead the new agencies were unprepared for "spending large sums of money, managing big staffs, coordinating and assuring the effectiveness of several different, highly specialized programs, for planning, interpretation, and public relations," and they "failed to meet the crucial test of successful administrative performance."[8] Clearly, from this point of view, the emphasis of professional education on social casework was mistaken or at best partial; it touched only one function in an enterprise that had many functions. This was the vision of professional education that had caught Edith Abbott and

8. Brown, *Public Relief*, pp. 274f.

Sophonisba Breckinridge of the Chicago School of Social Service Administration and Grace Abbott of the Children's Bureau. Several social workers served on the Committee on Long-Range Work and Relief Policies of the National Resources Planning Board and on the technical staff under Dr. Eveline Burns, whose report, *Security, Work, and Relief Policies,* was transmitted to Congress by President Roosevelt in 1943. The report was an excellent summary of the experience of the 1930s, with thoughtful proposals for the future. Burns, an economist trained in England, gave the report the unmistakable stamp of her deft style and cogent analysis. She went on to teach policy at the Columbia (formerly New York) School of Social Work and by her publications and teaching to encourage those who thought that the changing professional function ought to tend toward a statesmanship of reform rather than toward radical politics.

Chapter

13

Income Maintenance,

1935–1960

IN THE 1920S poor relief was not interesting to experts on social welfare. Their enthusiasm was to make real the ideal of professional service and method that was taking form in private agencies and professional schools, especially around casework with children and families and the mentally disordered and delinquent, but also in agencies serving groups and neighborhoods and the community chest. In the U.S. Children's Bureau one found a broader view that included social legislation and administration and the research necessary for well-founded judgments on such matters, but the Bureau focused on child welfare. When, during the Depression, the federal government elaborated great programs of emergency and work relief, public assistance, and social insurance, it created organizations and problems of a scope that was outside the tradition of professional social work, concentrated as it was in big-city private agencies. In Washington and the state capitals executives planned hundreds of offices, employed thousands of workers, and in one way or another gave millions of dollars to a large part of the population. The Depression-born system was roughly equivalent in size and cost to schools and health services, but it did not have the tradition of citizen and professional concern and involvement that characterized the older institutions.

Who would come forward to define and guide these instant, massive, expensive programs? As it happened, many leaders were trained in economics, particularly "labor economics," familiar with "labor legislation" and administration, and prepared to analyze costs, benefits, and taxes. Executives in public assistance and their helpers gathered into the American Public Welfare Association, with ties to the disciplines of public administration and political science. Social workers generally remained preoccupied with the agencies and services in which most of them were employed, which offered a hopeful prospect for improved methods of helping, but in addition their broader historic commitment to "social welfare" and social reform led them to speculate about their role in the Depressionborn programs and more generally in social policy and administration. In time they came to distinguish between "income maintenance"—huge programs for public assistance and social insurance, which were plainly linked to their traditional concern with poverty and social justice—and "direct services," in which there was an important personal relationship between helper and helped. Obviously there was much overlap between the two. Some people who needed financial support also needed some sort of casework or group work, and getting help to them efficiently ("service delivery," as it came to be called) required planning and special arrangements of a sort familiar to experts in "community organization." Moreover, in their history professional social workers had been led from their original concern with individuals in danger or trouble to underlying problems of poverty and injustice, to the advocacy of minimums of security and opportunity, and to a concern for the dignity and self-respect of those who were aided. They felt that these professional interests, in clients and in social justice, gave them a different perspective from experts or executives whose competence was primarily in economic analysis or bureaucratic efficiency.

This chapter will trace the development of social insurance, of the astonishing system of private insurance that grew up to supplement it, and of the public-assistance programs. The next chapter will lay out historical influences and issues in the direct services.

Arthur Altmeyer believed that "the origin . . . of what we now call social security will be found more largely in our labor legislation than in our poor relief laws. This is in sharp contrast to Great Britain where the development of social security was influenced largely by dissatisfaction with the Poor Law." [1] To him, and to Edwin Witte,

1. Arthur J. Altmeyer, *The Formative Years of Social Security* (Madison: University of Wisconsin Press, 1966), p. vii.

the labor economist he called from the University of Wisconsin to head the staff that actually worked up the Social Security Act, the core of the Act, its long-run significance, was social insurance. These men did not think of themselves as social workers dealing in a broad way with the problems of paupers—that is, with poor relief legislation—but, in a Wisconsin tradition, as experts working with capital and labor to devise a program that was conceived, like workmen's compensation, as being in the interest of both employer and employed, and as a rationalization of the economic system. They looked upon themselves not as utopians who wished to change the system but as practical men dealing with practical men, negotiating and compromising among substantial interests, paying expert attention to the relationship between policy and its administration.

President Roosevelt also wanted social insurance to be central in the new program; he told his planners that he envisioned that a child might at birth receive an insurance policy that would "protect him against all the major economic misfortunes that might befall him during his lifetime."[2] Social insurance was the norm; public assistance—the heir of poor relief or public charity—was a supplement for cases that would fall outside the norm; services—for maternal and child welfare, rehabilitation, employment, and so forth—were ancillary to the main job of income maintenance.

Except for the President and the experts, the vision of cradle-to-grave social insurance did not have much support, and the Act of 1935 provided only two kinds of insurance, against loss of income in old age and retirement and—a very limited program—against unemployment. (Workmen's compensation for loss from industrial accidents was already provided to some extent under state programs.) Even with regard to these risks, coverage was limited to individuals regularly employed for wages or salaries; it did not include domestic workers, farm labor, farmers, or the self-employed. These types of workers were difficult to include because jobs and pay were not standardized, because employment was irregular—workers might have several part-time jobs, for example—and because those concerned did not keep records.

Apart from the problem of who should or could be covered by social insurance were grave problems of the adequacy and equity of

2. *Ibid.*, p. 2.

the benefits. *Adequacy* referred to the amount of the benefit; presumably it would be enough so that the recipient and his family could live decently without falling on poor relief. Since Roosevelt and his experts wanted the system to be self-sustaining without contributions from the public, such benefits had to be paid for by worker and employer contributions. To figure out how much people would have to put in, on an average, in order to draw out enough, on an average, was the business of actuaries, but someone had to decide what they should aim at, how much was enough. *Equity* referred to the fairness between what one contributed and what one got out in protection and benefits. The simplest arrangement was to have everyone pay in the same amount and get the same benefits. The trouble with this scheme was that the wages of many workers were so low that they could not afford to pay much in, and therefore their benefits would have to be very low. The alternative was to have workers contribute a sum that varied with their pay; then the higher-paid workers could get better benefits, as they had gotten better wages and paid larger contributions.

To complicate these problems of adequacy and equity, many people would join the system late in life, only a few years before retirement, and many, particularly women, would work irregularly, in and out of covered employment. These people would have great difficulty contributing enough to earn themselves a claim to adequate benefits. Or, if the benefits were planned so that these marginal workers received, on an average, much more than they contributed, the arrangement would seem unfair to the regular contributors.

As it happened, federal officials were able to evade these problems in unemployment insurance. The federal government simply laid a 3 percent tax on payrolls in covered industries and agreed to return practically all of it to the states if they would set up a state program. Of course the states responded—otherwise their employers would pay a tax but not get any advantage. This scheme had the great merit of being constitutional—there was no doubt that *state* governments could establish social insurance, as they had for industrial accidents. It also left the decisions about coverage, adequacy, and equity to the state legislatures, which decided when to begin benefits, under what conditions, how much they should be, and how long they should continue. Moreover, leaving these decisions to the states bypassed the important disagreement over the "American plan."

In Old Age Insurance (OAI) it was impossible to leave these decisions to the states. Unemployment Insurance paid benefits for a short period—13 to 26 weeks—and in ordinary circumstances these were easily financed by the 3 percent tax; the programs did not need a very large accumulated reserve. OAI, on the other hand, proposed long-term payments (about twelve years after age 65, on an average) based on a detailed earning history for each member, who might have worked forty or fifty years for many different employers in different places. Actuarial considerations required that it be a federal program available everywhere, like the Post Office. Apart from whether a big federal insurance program was constitutional (a doubt not resolved until 1937), there were difficult actuarial problems in the financing of the program. At first it was decided that workers in covered employment would contribute 1 percent of their pay; employers would deduct that amount, add another 1 percent, and send it to a fund in the U.S. Treasury in a lump sum every three months. The Treasury would accumulate a reserve and begin to pay retirement benefits in 1942. For a long time contributions would much exceed payments as young workers contributed. In forty years or so they would retire and the system would mature; then the contributions, plus interest on the accumulated reserves, would balance the claims for benefits. If it did not, there would be ample reserves to make up the difference. The goal would be achieved. Most employees, by making relatively small contributions during their working lives and accumulating compound interest on them, would establish a rightful claim to a modest income in their old age; individual differences in length of life would be accommodated by the sharing of risk. The system would be self-supporting; it would largely, although not entirely, take the place of private and public charity for the aged.

Such was the general idea. As for the problem of workers who joined the system late in life or whose work history was irregular, the system would accommodate them by fixing the benefit formula so that they would get more protection and benefits than they paid for under the principle of strict equity. Young and prosperous workers would pay in a little more so that these marginal members would benefit a little more. This deviation from strict equity increased in 1939, when Congress made many changes in the law. On one hand, it denied benefits to many contributors who were not "fully insured"—who had paid contributions for some time but not long enough. On the other hand, it changed the benefit formula so that workers who entered the system late in life would get even more "unearned benefits," and it added a very important new program: Survivors' Insurance (SI). If a worker died before retirement, SI provided that his dependent wife and children would receive benefits. (A wife was dependent while she had to look after children and when she herself reached retirement age; children were dependent until they were 18 years old if they were not employed sooner.) These benefits were only a fraction of what the breadwinner himself was entitled to, but even so they were in effect a life insurance policy for workers with dependents, and an enormous new claim against the fund. Workers without wives and children paid the same contribution but did not need this protection, although their aged and dependent *parents* might qualify. Finally, Congress ordered that benefit payments begin in 1940, rather than 1942, and postponed an increase in the contribution rate. So the claims against the system were very much increased, but the income was not. As a practical matter, the Treasury could easily pay out these benefits because so many more workers were contributing than were receiving. In effect the projected reserve fund was being paid out for current benefits. But some time in the future an increased burden would fall on the contributors.

To the administrators of the system and to most experts, these problems of coverage, finance, equity, and adequacy seemed to be rather incidental pecularities of getting the system started. The programs themselves—Old Age Insurance and Unemployment Insurance—seemed to be a first approximation of an enterprise that would in time cover many other workers and risks and pay more adequate benefits. It was a vision affirmed by the influential Beveridge Report in England (1942) and by the report of the National Resources Planning Board (1943), and it was elaborated in the annual reports of the Social Security Board and Administration in the next few years. In a way it was realized in the amendments of 1950 and 1954, when coverage was extended to include farm workers, the self-employed, and most others who had originally been left out; when benefits were raised, along with contributions; and when Disability Insurance (DI) was added in 1956 to provide benefits for workers who in effect had to retire early because they were invalids.

Nevertheless there was always a good deal of misunderstanding and doubt about the whole idea of social insurance. Until 1954, Arthur Altmeyer thought, the "paramount question" was, "Would we have a contributory system with both benefits and contributions related to past wages or would we have a uniform old age pension financed either by a general tax of some sort or perhaps simply out of general revenues?"[3] In general, the support for bigger and better social security came from liberals with urban constituencies, but a significant number of them thought the benefits were much too skimpy, while others thought the very notion of "insurance" was too limiting. In general, conservatives favored a contributory and self-supporting system, which would minimize the burden on the general taxpayer, but some of them doubted whether the OASDI program, at least, was really insurance or whether it was appropriate to the need. Ironically, it was the conservatives who, in 1949–1950, seemed about to rally a popular movement against the program. Among them were Robert Taft, leader of the conservative Senate Republicans; Carl T. Curtis, chairman of a subcommittee of the House Ways and Means Committee that studied the programs; and Lewis Meriam, an eminent political scientist associated with the Brookings Institution.

To simplify and generalize, such conservatives held to a conventional notion of insurance and did not approve the deviations from equity that were permitted in social insurance. Nor did they approve the accumulation of a huge reserve fund that would be invested in, and be a market for, government bonds and, hence, would be a temptation to government indebtedness. While they favored insurance, they thought it might best be left to private individuals and commercial companies (the insurance lobby supported this line). The real problem, they thought, was not to set up a dubious compulsory insurance program that matured in forty years but to relieve a lot of needy people here and now.

The matter was really a political question, they thought: Who would get how much, under what conditions, and who would pay, how. This line of argument might lead to a niggardly program and punitive administration in the tradition of the poor law, but that conclusion did not necessarily follow and in the Depression and the 1940s there was a potent political force for a generous program and

3. *Ibid.*, p. 259.

administration: the Townsend movement and a number of similar enthusiasms. These had in common the notion of a fixed pension available to everyone over a certain age. Townsend's followers wanted $200 a month for everyone over 60; others wanted "$30 every Thursday" or some other formula. Townsendites proposed to finance the benefits through a sort of national sales tax, but others thought that the special payroll tax that raised contributions for Old Age and Survivors' Insurance could handily be redirected toward the new objective. Indeed, public-opinion polls indicated that many workers thought that their social-security contributions were for such a program rather than for future "insurance" benefits.[4]

One objection to such proposals was the cost. Edwin Witte estimated in 1940 that carrying out the Townsend program would cost twice as much as *all* taxes collected that year.[5] Even a more realistic "baby Townsend program" paying $40 or $50 a month would benefit many people who did not need help but would be insufficient for many others, and therefore it would require some supplementary program. But the long-run objection was that "pension politics" would lend themselves to political abuse and scandal, whereas a contributory insurance program could be conducted in a more responsible and businesslike way. It would make plain to workers the relationship between benefits and contributions.

Liberal critics, on the other hand, looked upon social insurance as a means to some larger objective rather than as an end in itself. Some Keynesian economists argued that income maintenance programs ought to be a device to stabilize the business cycle, like other government spending and taxing policies. They were not interested in the rationale of social insurance, let alone the refinements of equity and adequacy, but in timely spending and saving. Other liberals looked upon the social insurances as devices for a social reform, the redistribution of income. They wanted government to tax the wealthy, in addition to the wage earners and employers, and to use the proceeds to subsidize the social insurances so that benefits could

4. Michael Schlitz, *Public Attitudes Toward Social Security, 1935–1965*, U.S. *Department of Health, Education, and Welfare, Social Security Administration, Research Report no. 33* (Washington, D.C.: Government Printing Office, 1970), pp. 85–87.

5. Edwin E. Witte, "Is the Continued Drive for Universal Pensions a Social Menace?" in *Social Security Perspectives*, Robert J. Lampman, ed. (Madison: University of Wisconsin Press, 1962), p. 155.

be much larger than the amounts workers could provide by their own contributions. Altmeyer, Witte, and most experts recognized that it was desirable to stabilize the business cycle and to redistribute income, but as practical men they recognized too the great political difficulty in defining and realizing such proposals. They stuck with a relatively noncontroversial concept of social insurance: it was intended to replace a substantial part of the wages or salaries workers lost when they encountered certain risks. They wanted the benefits to be work-related, wage-related, and related to contributions. Workers should pay their way so that the more they put in the more they got out, according to a rational and definite formula. They would have a *right* to their benefits because they had *earned* them. The argument fended off demagogic political fears or hopes by emphasizing ancient American beliefs about work and merit. It said yes to more security for workers but no to what Witte scornfully called the "Santa Claus" theory.[6]

Meanwhile history played tricks on the argument about social security. When it was formulated in the 1930s people had no idea of the prosperity the war would bring; during the war they had no idea that they were on the eve of a thirty-year boom. The political balance changed as a conservative coalition of southern Democrats and Republicans controlled Congress; the very popular President Eisenhower (1953–1961), whose politics were at first unknown, proved to be a conservative. These leaders were primarily interested in economic progress as seen by the business community, and they were dubious about "welfare state" measures that might be a drag on business. More generally, they were caught up in the rise of the cold war and the disillusion over Stalinist socialism; high expenditures for defense tended to hold down spending on social welfare, while revelations about Stalinism tarnished and divided the liberal cause.

While the political mood shifted away from the concerns of the New Deal and the Fair Deal, the prosperity that came after 1940 affected the argument about social security in two ways. First, it became less urgent, a lower priority among public issues. Second, inflation undermined the structure of contributions and benefits. Congress had originally defined the contribution base as 1 percent of the first $3,000 of wages, with the employer also contributing 1 per-

6. Witte, *Social Security Perspectives*, pp. 49f., 98, 107.

cent. In 1935 few workers earned as much as $3,000, and a schedule of benefits reckoned on that base was adequate, especially because the law said the tax rate would rise to 1.5 percent in 1939 and higher later on. As it turned out, Congress delayed the tax increase until 1950, so that collections fell much below what was expected. Meanwhile the early benefits, beginning in 1940 and continuing through the decade, were skimpy despite a favorable benefit formula, and they became especially skimpy as wartime and postwar inflation raised the wages of workers and the cost of living. Obviously the OASI program would fail if it had to operate in the 1950s on a scale of contributions and benefits conceived in the 1930s.

The solution to this problem was to raise the contribution base to correspond to the rising wage level and in that way raise the rate of taxes or contributions. Accordingly, the wage base was increased to $3,600 in 1951 and to $4,800 in 1959, and the contribution rate to 1.5 percent in 1950 and 2.5 percent in 1959. The idea of keeping full reserves, as private insurance companies did, changed. Private companies needed full reserves to protect policyholders in the event that the company went out of business, but the social insurances were not going out of business; those in covered occupations had to join, so actuaries could tell from population figures what the income and liability probably would be. They could require contributions that would cover the disbursements. So OASDI went over to a pay-as-you-go arrangement in which present workers made contributions that were paid out to the retired, disabled, or survivors in the expectation that when their own need arose, then current workers would take care of them. There was much doubt about this change, which weakened the analogy with private insurance; it became ever clearer that the worker's assurance of benefits was a changeable statute rather than an ironclad legal contract. Of course the changeable statutory character was intended to benefit the contributors, and the workers, at least the unions, accepted it as such. Their plea in the late 1940s and 1950s was for bigger and better social security, not greater legal security. They were as disappointed as the expert partisans by the reluctant actions of conservatives in Congress and the White House. They were even more displeased by the progress of unemployment insurance because they had less influence in most state capitals than in Washington. But as it happened they did not have to rely on legislation or social insurance. In the 1940s a new prospect opened to them for a private welfare state, and they were quick to realize its potential.

Employers who provided "industrial welfare" in the 1920s did not regard themselves as philanthropists or paternalists. They were interested in profit, but they felt able to take a somewhat long-run view of it. Enlightened personnel management was supposed to be an advantage to their organization. Their most ambitious benefit schemes—for retirement pensions, extended sick pay, payment for medical costs, and compensation for unemployment—were, as it turned out, very costly and not well conceived. They promised a lot but did not provide adequate funding. They depended mostly on continued prosperity and good company earnings. When the Depression came, demands rose as income fell; managers had to cut costs, and employee benefits were expendable.

Railroads, for example, had in the 1920s the most elaborate pensions of any industry. Management was stable and farsighted, the unions established and powerful. It was plainly in everyone's interest to retire employees before their infirmities became dangerous. The Depression much reduced rail traffic and earnings, however. Between 1929 and 1933, 800,000 workers were laid off. Seniority rules required that they be more recent and younger employees. The roads might have retired older workers sooner, but because their pension plans were not funded properly they deliberately kept workers on past retirement age to keep their costs down. In 1934 Congress stepped in to establish an industry-wide retirement plan (the earlier plans had been for individual companies). The Supreme Court declared the law unconstitutional (a decision that worried the people who were then devising the Social Security Act). Congress tried again, and in time it succeeded. The Railroad Retirement Act provided for a tax on employee and employer, paid into the federal treasury, which agreed to pay annuities and other benefits to retired workers. Railroad workers were excluded from the Social Security Act because of this preexisting arrangement.[7]

Advocates of social insurance expected that the Social Security Act would in time do the job of private pensions or insurances, which had proved so costly and hard to plan or administer on the

7. Charles Dearing, *Industrial Pensions* (Washington, D.C.: Brookings Institution, 1954), pp. 23–26.

scale of a company or even an industry. For their part, the leaders who organized the big unions in the late 1930s took a militant antimanagement stand and echoed the traditional skepticism of unions about industrial welfare.

War changed the views of both management and labor. Welcome as it was, wartime prosperity brought with it a heavy burden of planning and regimentation. Millions of workers were drafted into the armed services. Businessmen were restricted by national objectives and controls in their access to raw materials and in their pricing policies. Workers in private employment were restricted in their movements, unions in their wage demands and right to strike. National policy was to control prices, not only of materials but also of labor. This was frustrating all around. Management needed workers and wanted to hire, but it could not offer higher wages, the ordinary inducement. Unions were in a position of potentially great strength, but they could not take advantage of this position to demand higher wages. The War Labor Board, the controlling agency, recognized the problem and the need to keep up labor morale. It compromised: no increase in wage rates, but authorization for nonwage or "fringe" benefits.

In this form industrial welfare came back, sought by both sides. Many of the benefits were familiar: shift premiums, paid holidays and vacations, paid sick leave, severance pay. But there was a new interest, Depression-born, in insurance: life insurance to protect survivors, retirement pensions for old age, insurance against hospital bills or other medical expenses. The employer might arrange with an insurance company to provide these at low cost, and he might subsidize the payment or even pay the bill himself. Meanwhile in 1942, as taxes on business rose sharply, Congress gave private pensions a tax break. Management could deduct their cost as a business expense, and the employee could delay paying taxes on the retirement benefit. Between 1942 and 1944 the number of private pension plans rose from 1,360 to 4,208.[8]

When controls went off after the war, most union leaders returned to wage bargaining, but the United Mine Workers under John L. Lewis gave a new dimension to the notion of fringe benefits. Lewis had not expressed much interest in the subject before 1945,

8. *Ibid.*, pp. 36f.

but in negotiations then he set out two lines of thought that would dominate the next few years. One was impatience with the Social Security Act. It did not offer much security, he thought. It did not cover important risks, notably the cost of medical care and disability, and its benefits were low. They did not begin to approach what the Bureau of Labor Statistics estimated as a modest budget. Second was the argument that workers got used up in production, just like machines, and that management had a responsibility to provide for disabled and retired workers much as it accumulated a fund to repair and replace its machines. Government could not or would not adequately meet this responsibility or make management meet it, but now the union was strong enough to force the issue. In 1946, after a strike that threatened the postwar economic adjustment, Lewis won an employer-financed industry-wide health and welfare fund paid for by a royalty of 5¢ on every ton of coal his union members mined. Benefits included substantial pensions and complete hospital care. Management protested that the royalty would not begin to cover the costs. They were right: it rose to 30¢ in 1950 and 40¢ in 1952.[9]

Meanwhile in 1946 the Inland Steel Company began to enforce a policy of compulsory retirement at age 65 for beneficiaries of its pension fund. The United Steelworkers filed a grievance because the company had not negotiated on the action, which involved a worker's losing his job. The company argued that the separation was incidental to its operation of the pension and that the pension was a management prerogative on which it was not required to bargain. The Labor Relations Act of 1935 had said that employers had to negotiate on "wages, hours, and other terms and conditions of employment," but it was not clear whether employee benefits were included as a condition of employment. Traditionally management had conceived them as an employer initiative, part of its personnel policy. The National Labor Relations Board decided for the union, and on appeal the Supreme Court agreed with the Board (1949). This meant that employers had a duty to negotiate with union representatives about employee benefits, including company-sponsored pensions and insurance. It gave unions a new interest and power in the matter.

Led by the Steelworkers and the United Automobile Workers, the big CIO unions began to press for elaborate employer-financed

9. Raymond Munts, *Bargaining for Health: Labor Unions, Health Insurance, and Medical Care* (Madison: University of Wisconsin Press, 1967), pp. 30–35.

fringe benefits that would supplement the Social Security Act. Like Lewis, they thought that benefits under the social insurances were much too low and that conservatives had frustrated the hope of enlarging them. "We fought for a noncontributory pension plan in industry," Walter Reuther, the UAW chief, told a congressional committee in 1950,

> because we knew that was the key to getting action at the federal government level. We said "If we can fight to establish pension plans . . . on the principle that the employer must pay the total cost of such . . . plans, then the employer will have an incentive to go down to Washington and fight with us to get the Government to meet this problem because in a Federal program the employee pays part of the cost.[10]

Sure enough, the Social Security Act was expanded and strengthened in 1950 and expanded and improved under the Eisenhower administration. Its social-insurance benefits (and contributions) remained low, however, and meanwhile fringe benefits improved steadily. Union leaders were expected to deliver a better package, and employers were acommodating, at least in the industries that the CIO had organized. In these businesses competition was typically keen but monopolistic. A strong union could settle with one major producer and the others would fall in line; all producers would raise prices to cover the new costs and pass them on to the consumers. Sometimes management and labor would set up a trust fund and handle the investments and claims; sometimes the unions themselves would handle the arrangements, as the miners did, and the needle trades. Often the firm or the industry would make arrangements with an insurance company or several companies; underwriters competed vigorously to land these group insurance contracts, which much reduced their costs of sale and administration. This was true of life insurance and disability insurance, and especially of insurance against the costs of illness—hospital bills, surgery, general medical expenses, major medical expenses. Blue Cross (hospitalization) and Blue Shield (surgery) grew rapidly under this patronage. Sometimes the unions supported direct service rather than payments: the miners built hospitals, the needle trades clinics, and unions gave strong sup-

10. U.S. Senate, Committee on Finance, *Social Security Revision, Hearings*, 81st Cong., 2d sess., 1950, pt. 3, p. 1980.

port to "prepaid group practice" such as the Permanente (Kaiser) Medical Group on the West Coast.

So the employee benefits sketched out in the 1940s were fleshed out in the 1950s. In the most common programs—life insurance, retirement, and medical insurance—the number of workers and dependents covered doubled; by 1960 the percentages of workers in private industry who received these benefits were 58 for life insurance, 42 for retirement, 69 for hospitalization, and 66 for surgery.[11]

In general, this development, which was unanticipated in 1935, testified that workers wanted a degree of income security much beyond that which the Social Security Act offered. It also testified to the vitality of a pluralist society, in which unions, management, and insurance companies, encouraged by the tax policies of the government, in their several ways found a common interest. In theory, as Witte came to see it at least, the employee benefit plans were a second layer of security offering a more generous provision than the minimal benefits that the Social Security Act was intended to offer.[12] In fact, the situation was very confused. There were several thousand separate plans, which differed in whether they covered one employer or many in an industry, whether they were sponsored and managed by employers or unions or both together in some way, whether workers contributed or employers paid all expenses, and whether they were self-insured or negotiated with a commercial carrier.

Both unions and management moved to establish standards amid this multiplicity, but there was much to learn and there were many opportunities for abuse, for collusion between trustees and insurance companies, for example, or in the investment of pension funds. In time Congress made stricter rules about funding and administration as a condition of approval for tax deductions; in 1958 it passed the Welfare and Pension Plan Disclosure Act to require reports, and in 1959 it demanded that certain fund officials be bonded. There was also a doubt about how much workers would benefit from the plans. The argument for a federal OAI program had been that workers would move from job to job and place to place; the assumption of the private plans was that they would stay with a single em-

---

11. Harry Gersh, ed., *Employee Benefits Factbook* (New York: Segal, 1970), pp. 376–80.

12. Witte, *Social Security Perspectives*, pp. 77f.

ployer (or in a few cases a single industry). What proportion of workers would actually stay around to collect the benefits that were being put aside for them? Or would workers hesitate to move because they would lose their benefits? What about workers in companies that failed or were merged? One solution to this problem was proper funding of the benefits and giving workers a vested right—a fixed legal claim to future benefits. This was a great complication, however, and both labor and management saw an advantage in a policy that would allow more discretion in the allocation of benefits, that would, for example, allow higher payments to workers near retirement.[13]

In a larger view, the great question about the private welfare programs was that they exaggerated an inequality in the working class. Unions supported them as a supplement to OASDI, which was admittedly inadequate; if the public social insurances did become adequate, the private arrangements were supposed to furnish an extra measure of security over the public programs. But in fact there were three levels of income maintenance: public assistance, social insurance, and private provision. The social insurances were broad in coverage, but even so they were selective, job- and wage-related in their benefits. The employee benefits were even more selective—not just job- and wage-related but related to the policy and power of particular unions or companies. So it was a new version of the old story: if you had a good job and a good union or company, you did well, but if you were marginally in the labor force, hard to organize, or employed by people who could not or would not provide benefits, then your economic security was poor. Poorest of all, and most controversial, were those on the far margin of the labor market, the old, the disabled, families without a breadwinner, and people who for various reasons found it difficult to get or keep a job. These were the caseload of public assistance, which also grew in ways unexpected in 1935.

The labor economists who presided over the writing and administration of the Social Security Act believed that the central problem was the loss of income to wage earners, that public assistance and social insurance were alternative ways of maintaining income, and that social insurance was the preferred way. For fifty years the cause of social insurance had gained force in all industrial nations; now the United States was coming abreast of this historic movement.

13. Dearing, *Industrial Pensions*, pp. 217–22.

As the coverage of social insurance expanded and its benefits improved, the need for public assistance would diminish.

Meanwhile the "categorical relief" or "special public assistance" programs were still very important, especially for the aged. Old folks were in great need but would not be covered by a social-insurance program. Together with their adult children, who would ordinarily have to help support them, they made up a great political interest. Moreover their enthusiasm for "pensions" was a threat to social insurance. From this angle it was important to the partisans of the Social Security Act to keep a clear distinction between social insurance and public assistance. Old Age Assistance, for example, was intended to offer a federal subsidy to state programs for "aged needy individuals," in the language of the law. In the thinking of the act's administrators, "need," in all the categorical programs, had to be determined case by case through an investigation or means test. Presumably the relieving agency would have a standard budget that set forth the necessaries of life and their cost; an eligibility worker would collect facts about the applicant's income and resources, and if they amounted to less than the budgeted need—if there was a "budgetary deficiency"—the grant would make it up. Of course this case-by-case determination involved an inquiry into the applicant's private affairs, not just his income and resources but, more vaguely, his individual situation and his ability to manage for himself. It was quite different from the notion of the advocates of old-age pensions that applicants should simply give proof of their age and collect a periodic grant, the same amount whether they were rich or poor, needy or not, competent or not. In emphasizing that the categorical relief programs were to be based on need, federal administrators were not only protecting the treasury against a pension grab but also protecting the idea of social insurance from schemes that would subvert it.[14]

As for the congressmen who debated and passed the act, they were willing, even glad, to get a federal grant-in-aid to support their home-state relief effort, but they rejected the proposal that the federal government dictate a minimum level of aid as a condition. This position appealed particularly to Southern congressmen, partly because of their traditional support of states' rights, partly because of their peculiar problems. By every economic indicator the ex-Confederate states

14. Jack Parsons, "The Origins of the Income and Resources Amendment to the Social Security Act," *Social Service Review*, 36 (March 1962): 60f.

were much poorer than other sections of the country. Although poverty was great, southern state legislatures had neither the inclination nor the tax resources to provide much help. As Howard Smith, a powerful congressman from Virginia, remarked, if his state were required by federal legislation to meet the needs of old folks up to $30 a month—if that were defined as a level of health and decency for his state—and if the federal government gave a grant-in-aid for half that amount, or $15, Virginia still would probably have to double its total tax collection just to pay its share for that single program. This argument appealed to all poor states. The South had the further problem that its black citizens were much poorer even than its white citizens, and that an important part of its labor cost depended on that differential. A minimum level of support conceived in national terms would seem like a great deal to these extremely deprived people. It might increase pauperism among them and disturb race relations, and it would certainly put a large, unwelcome expense on the state legislatures.[15]

In short, the federal grant-in-aid for categorical public assistance would help the states, but state legislatures would make crucial decisions about the level of need to meet and also about many specifics of eligibility. Federal legislation laid down conditions for the grant, but except for the requirement that aid be based on need, these conditions dealt mostly with formalities of administration. Initiatives for policy change came mostly from the administrative agency, the Social Security Board (called the Social Security Administration after 1946), and particularly its Bureau of Public Assistance. As it happened, the congressional committees that reviewed and passed on policy were those handling appropriations—Ways and Means in the House, Finance in the Senate. This was because the social insurances involved federal taxes. Public-assistance legislation might conceivably have passed through other committees, but in fact it remained tied to social insurance for the purpose of congressional deliberation. This meant that the fiscal side of the program—the ability of states to contribute, the cost sharing between states and the federal government—received the closest attention, more so than the

15. Smith's testimony, *Economic Security Act, Hearings*, U.S. House of Representatives, Committee on Ways and Means, 74th Cong., 1st sess., 1935, pp. 297f.; see also Edwin E. Witte, *The Development of the Social Security Act* (Madison: University of Wisconsin Press, 1962), pp. 143f.

social or welfare objectives of the policy, which were mostly left to the states.

Nevertheless Congress did attach conditions to the grant-in-aid, and it was up to the Bureau of Public Assistance to enforce them. To get the grant, the state department of public welfare had to forward to the Bureau all legislation and administrative rulings pertinent to the aided programs, with supporting documents, and the Bureau had to pass on whether they conformed to federal conditions. If not, the Social Security Board would seek change and might withhold the grant. Since the conditions were mostly administrative formalities that were manifestly directed toward making the states accountable to Congress, they did not appear very formidable. The Bureau had regional representatives in more or less continuous touch with state officials in their region; they were supposed to advise the states and cooperate with them so as to avoid issues of conformity if possible.

Federal supervision might, accordingly, have taken the form of a perfunctory audit in which examiners checked cases to see whether the grants were correct according to the rules that the Social Security Administration had approved. The case-by-case audit was always part of federal supervision, but by 1940 it was put into the framework of a general administrative review of the state and local agencies in which the formalities of administration were carefully examined with regard to their implications for the goals of adequacy, equity, and efficiency. The social workers who interested themselves in this task had a different historical perspective from the labor economists. The main line of historical development, in their thinking, was not the rise of social insurance but something much more general and long range: the assertion of public responsibility, that is, community responsibility; of aid as a democratic right available to citizens who needed it; and of casework in addition to money. This was the message from the University of Chicago's School of Social Service Administration, where Sophonisba Breckinridge published *Public Welfare Administration* (1927, revised in 1938) and Edith Abbott *Public Assistance* (1940).

In this view the first step had been the Elizabethan poor law, appropriate for its time but tied to circumstances—local finance and administration, the settlement law, relatives' responsibility—that proved increasingly archaic. The main line of reform in the nineteenth century had been to withdraw certain groups—the insane, the handicapped, dependent children—from the local almshouse to some state-sponsored and financed or supervised institution. In the twentieth century the reform had been to promote the special kinds of assistance—aid to mothers of dependent children, to the aged and the blind—separating these categories from the general local relief load and giving them the benefit of better grants and administration through the participation, financial and administrative, of the state government. The depression of the 1930s laid bare the inadequacy and archaic character of the poor law, brought increased aid from state and federal governments to the selected categories, and brought the prospect of stretching and improving them so that help would be available *as a right* to the whole population on the basis of need, not just for particular selected kinds of need. Unfortunately, Edith Abbott remarked, the founders of scientific social work had been persuaded by the arguments of Malthus against the public poor law, and the charity organization societies had carried on this "defeatist" attitude toward the obvious political abuses of public poor relief. But the situation was changing. The Depression had ended fantasies about the adequacy of private charity and raised the challenge of proper professional administration of the *public* programs.[16]

While Jane Hoey and her staff at the Bureau of Public Assistance could not dictate to the state legislatures an adequate level of assistance, still they could persuade Congress to broaden eligibility and increase the federal share of costs; then they could point out to state officials that their restrictive eligibility rules and low grant levels were losing them federal money, that if only the state were more generous (which it certainly should be for a truly adequate level of support) it would get more subsidy from Washington. In 1950 Congress authorized a new categorical program, Aid to the Permanently and Totally Disabled. This helped people who were too old for Aid to Dependent Children, too young for Old Age Assistance and not blind, but severely handicapped or disabled. Local assistance agencies could now get these people off general assistance and into a categorical program where the federal government would pay half the cost of their support up to the matching level. ("Permanent and total disabil-

16. On the reorganization of the poor law, see Edith Abbott, "Abolish the Pauper Laws," *Social Service Review*, 8 (March 1934): 1–16; Edith Abbott, *Public Assistance* (Chicago: University of Chicago Press, 1940), pp. 509–32; Sophonisba P. Breckinridge, *Public Welfare Administration*, rev. ed. (Chicago: University of Chicago Press, 1938), pp. 237–45, 773–80.

ity" proved not to be so absolute as it sounded; the category could stretch to include many who were somehow incapacitated.)

The goal of adequacy could be pursued only indirectly, but equity and efficiency were more potent guides to supervision. Most of the plan requirements—a program in operation throughout the state, a single state agency, participation by the state, fair hearings, payments in money rather than in kind—helped define a *right to public assistance*. They implied equal protection of the law and due process, both guaranteed by the federal Constitution; they applied both to state regulations and to administration. They were a weapon against prejudice toward particular groups or localities, against the extreme variations in administration where counties ran the programs. Equity meant similar treatment for people in similar circumstances. The principle lent itself to an explicit definition of procedures and standards—of budget and staffing, for example—and to enforcing uniformity of standards throughout the state. Efficiency of administration was judged by the quality of state supervision and control of its local officials, and especially by the quality of the staff. At first Congress had refused to give the Social Security Administration any power over who would be appointed, but in 1939 it imposed upon the states the requirement of a merit system, rather than the spoils system, for appointing staff, and thereafter federal supervisors oversaw the state classification of jobs and appointment and promotion practices.

The effect of this supervision of the categorical assistances, as it worked itself out over the years, was to improve equity and efficiency within a state but to allow much latitude to states in the plan, management, and outcome of the programs. Situations varied from state to state; contingencies played a large part. Perhaps the most common arrangement was that in which a state department supervised local (county) welfare departments; the federal government would pay about half the total cost and the state and county would divide the remainder. County politicians appointed the local administrator, a crucial position. These executives were likely to be responsive to local real estate and commercial interests and their persistent efforts to keep down the local property tax, which had also to meet a rapidly increasing demand for local schools, roads, and other services. They were also likely to reflect a moralistic and even punitive local opinion toward poor families that could not take care of themselves and had to fall on public assistance. But county officials had to deal with the state legislature and the state department, which were likely to be somewhat more liberal; "liberal" in this context meant respectful of the rights of welfare applicants and recipients, particularly the right to adequate and constructive relief. By that standard the federal legislation and supervision were liberal indeed, and the Bureau of Public Assistance and the American Public Welfare Association, together with allies in the private social-work agencies, encouraged a professional social-work ethos throughout the administration. It balanced and often overcame the charges of malingering and fraud that were so often laid upon the people who asked for help.

This tension between the layman's moralistic and punitive attitude toward reliefers and the more respectful view of welfare professionals grew in importance in the 1950s because the caseload changed. The aged, who were politically potent and organized in many states, such as Massachusetts and California, had won preferential treatment, and Old Age Insurance began to provide for much of their need. Meanwhile Aid to the Permanently and Totally Disabled brought into view a large group whose problems had to be evaluated on the social as well as the medical and financial side, many of whom might in fact be "rehabilitated" and made self-sufficient by proper medical care, casework, vocational training, and placement. The blind, who had relatively good organization and leadership and a sympathetic following, were also interested in a program that would not merely relieve financial need but help meet their social and vocational needs.

Larger and more difficult was the change in the caseload of Aid to Dependent Children. Among the prosperous working class Survivor's Insurance and private life insurance took care of many of the deserving widows for whom the program had been conceived. Meanwhile more generous eligibility rules, much encouraged by the Bureau of Public Assistance, made it possible to extend this program to mothers and children who were in popular thought less deserving because the fathers had never married the mothers or had deserted their children. In a moralistic view these mothers and fathers were misbehaving, and the public should not condone and support their ways but should somehow seek to deter and punish them. To complicate matters, a disproportionate number of these needy were black, so that racial prejudice was added to prejudice against paupers—a potent combination.

This complex surfaced in 1950 in the NOLEO (Notice to Law Enforcement Officials) amendment to the Aid to Dependent Children legislation, which required that public-assistance workers get from deserted mothers information about deserting fathers and give it to the district attorney, who might seek support by legal means. In the 1950s an enthusiasm spread for "suitable home" rules, which often made the birth of illegitimate children in itself evidence that the home was not suitable and authorized unannounced inspections, even "midnight raids," to reassure officials that the mothers were in fact deserted and that no man was around the house to share the grant that had been intended for the mother and children.

Social workers were quick to point to the impersonal or sociological factors of this changing ADC caseload. There was, for example, a general increase in family breakdown, an increase in illegitimacy and divorce. There was a technological revolution, a mechanization of agriculture, particularly in the South, and an automation of industry, that eliminated unskilled labor and put a premium on training and mobility. There was a great migration from rural to urban places and of poor people out of the South. Migration was nothing new, but many of these new migrants had the disadvantage of a non-European or nonwhite heritage. The rising and troublesome ADC caseload was made up largely of very poor people far from home, without many personal or neighborhood resources to rely on, living under trying conditions, often in poor health, physical and mental, victims of prejudice, disadvantaged, discouraged, and demoralized. It seemed in the 1950s that the ADC caseload varied inversely with employment; it went down when employment was high during World War II and the Korean War. This fact supported the belief that the program encouraged desertion; fathers who could not find work and whose families ordinarily received old-fashioned "general assistance" might do better by deserting so that their wives and children could get on the categorical program with its better standards of relief.

Beside this understanding of the impersonal factors of personal disorganization, there grew in the minds of social workers a much more hopeful view of human personality and a more constructive idea of the role of services. This attitude was rooted in Freudian psychology, although it bypassed the Master's stern pessimism, and it drew much on the "growth and development" course that had become a fixture of social-work education. It flowered in the casework of family service and child welfare agencies, which were increasingly preoccupied with the woes of respectable middle-class people. It went beyond a legal right to income maintenance to a sympathetic comprehension of the need for security in social and emotional life. As Charlotte Towle, professor of casework at Chicago, phrased it, in a little book written for the Social Security Administration in 1945 that was widely circulated among public-assistance agencies and translated into many foreign languages, all people had *Common Human Needs* that were essential in their growth toward the maintenance of personal and social responsibility. These needs were not only material—food, shelter, and clothing—but included opportunities for physical, mental, and spiritual growth and satisfying personal relationships. The infant came into the world self-centered and dependent, emotionally as well as physically; given the opportunity, he grew through familiar stages of childhood and adolescence to maturity, to a sort of reasonable autonomy and responsibility. The individual's struggle for personal growth and autonomy was trying enough in families that were normal in their stability and resources; it was much more difficult in families that were disadvantaged and discouraged, such as those that appeared so often in the public-assistance caseload. Here was no occasion for moralizing scorn or for deterrent or punitive tactics to humiliate or threaten these unfortunate people. They needed understanding, sympathy, help, not just money but self-respect and responsible self-determination, such as might come from asserting a rightful claim on a responsive and service-minded agency.

Professor Towle was particularly eager to distinguish the professional spirit, with its scientific basis and humane ethic, from "lay attitudes" that were moralistic and punitive, and her statement was only one of many in the 1940s and 1950s that confronted popular complacency in the affluent society. There were in this critical view three points, all of which had honored precedents in the history of social work:

1. From a moral point of view the problem was not in the misbehavior of people who were caught up in situations that were discouraging and even helpless but in the reluctance of society to provide a birthright of security and opportunity that it could well afford and that would, social workers believed,

strengthen and heal it in time. This point reaffirmed the traditional assertion of social responsibility in private charity and in the public poor law.

2. There were many policies and programs intended to help these people, not just income maintenance but also organizations for companionship, health and mental health, special education and reeducation or rehabilitation, and employment. These were private and public, and spread across all elements of the population, not just those on public assistance, although the latter stood in special need of help. But the provision and integration of such services were haphazard. This was the traditional problem of community organization.

3. People and families were all different and complex; help should be not only available but individualized so that the right resource was applied at the right place and time according to a plan conceived in the right spirit. This was the traditional problem of casework.

So in the 1950s interest grew in services and their delivery. In 1960 the conservative Eisenhower gave way to John Kennedy, who promised a more active federal policy. There was rising excitement as an advisory council met and reported.[17] The Columbia School of Social Work set up a project to gather together the wisdom of a variety of authorities and administrators on the subject of public welfare. There was little disagreement among these worthies, and their thoughts were summed up by Elizabeth Wickenden and Winifred Bell in a famous pamphlet, *Public Welfare: Time for a Change*. The change the experts had in mind was from the programs of the 1930s, with their emphasis on money and their inadequate, inequitable, and inefficient arrangements, which despite improvements were now so well documented, and toward a public welfare in which adequate and equitable assistance would combine with constructive services intended to help unfortunate people overcome the burden of deprivation and anxiety that society had hitherto misunderstood and tolerated. The idea would have a bright future in the 1960s, the more so because it was supported by developments in the direct services.

17. Advisory Council on Public Assistance, *Report*, January 1960, U.S. Senate, Misc. Docs., 86th Cong., 2d sess., no. 93.

Chapter

14

Direct Services, 1935–1961:
Toward Community Care

IN THE NINETEENTH century philanthropists, reformers, and social workers had looked upon organized provisions for the "dependent, defective, and delinquent classes" as parts of a common enterprise; this is why they came together in their conferences on "charity and correction" and conceived a "scientific philanthropy" and a profession of "social work" that would somehow address the whole predicament. In fact these notions—that the problems were related and that social science might apply to solving them—represented dim and hopeful insights. In a way they were profoundly true and kept recurring, but as a practical matter it often seemed that the best way to manage was to put aside the larger vision, to divide the problem or science into parts, and to address these in a specialized and rather myopic way. So some leaders in the progressive years expanded their perception of dependency (pauperism) to include poverty (relative deprivation). This line of thought led them to emphasize environmental conditions and legislation to improve health and safety at home and on the job; it encouraged the idea of social insurance to prevent poverty and pauperism. It drew its rationale from the developing academic discipline of economics, particularly "labor economics." Meanwhile other leaders tried to improve the practice of casework and community organization, getting what help they could from psychology and sociology.

The reforms of the New Deal years indicated a new consensus about many issues that had concerned the progressives. Protective legislation for health and working conditions was accepted, and the federal government joined the states in their regulation; it also established income maintenance programs and acted to counter depression and unemployment. Yet these great affairs were never the whole story and not even, for professional social workers, the most interesting part of social welfare. The competence of the professionals was in casework, group work, and community organization, and they found their main interest in what came to be called "direct services," in which personal relationships and helpfulness were somehow central.

The idea of direct services in social welfare did not usually include institutions for education and medical care, which had their own sovereign professions. Historically it involved two lines of work. One was the family and child welfare agencies, together with organizations that offered recreation and informal education, in the spirit of the settlement houses, and health care in the clinic or at home. These were sponsored by local people for local people, and traditionally they were a philanthropy for the needy or disadvantaged. The other was the great institutions for the mentally ill or retarded, delinquent, or handicapped, the heritage of the nineteenth century, which were run by the states and sometimes by populous counties. It was easy to see that community-based and institutional services were related, because the people in the institutions came from the community and might return to it; prevention and rehabilitation or aftercare were obviously tasks for local agencies. But to work this insight into a policy and a program was difficult indeed.

One complication was the diversity of sponsors and funding. Family and child welfare agencies often had religious ties, as did settlement houses and "community centers." These ties persisted even when funds were raised jointly through the community chest; they influenced the chest's allocation and other policies. Many agencies had clients that could and did pay fees—the YMCA, for example, or the adoption agency. On the other hand, prisons, reformatories, mental hospitals, and schools for the retarded were mostly paid for and directed by the state government, as were the aftercare or parole arrangements that had begun to appear by 1935; but even here there were—except for adult prisons—a few private institutions (notably for juveniles who were delinquent or mentally disordered). Already in 1935, however, local governments often sponsored and paid for services that duplicated or overlapped those of private philanthropy. Local outdoor relief might be run along the constructive lines of a charity organization or family welfare society. The local welfare department or some other public agency might help children who were neglected or abused or needed some substitute for their own family. The municipal general hospital had clinics for medical care that were free for the needy and sometimes offered a casework service for the nonmedical aspects of illness ("medical social work"). The public schools might have a few "visiting teachers" who helped with problems of attendance or difficult behavior ("school social work"). The juvenile court might offer casework to children and families that fell under its jurisdiction, and probation was the business of the county courts.

When the Social Security Act provided a foundation of income maintenance, it opened to these direct services an opportunity to concentrate on personal and social disorganization in our changing society. In the prosperous years after 1940 they received a lot more money, especially tax dollars. The trend was toward community care, to reduce the personal and financial costs of institutions and, beyond that, to try to improve social organization and enhance personal fulfillment. As expenditures went up, new problems of policy and administration became evident, but by 1961, when the Kennedy administration took office, the prospects looked bright for a bold new conception of social welfare and a new war on poverty.

Several circumstances influenced the demand for and supply of services. The most obvious was economic growth and prosperity. Already by 1940 the gross national product was as high as in the boom year 1929; it leaped ahead during the war (1941–1945) and then remained high, supported in part by large outlays for the cold war and foreign aid. Between 1940 and 1960 it increased five times. Qualify that figure for inflation, population increase, and rising standards of living; it was still impressive. In 1958 an influential book by the economist John Kenneth Galbraith gave a name to the phenomenon: *The Affluent Society*. Galbraith's purpose was not to praise but to criticize. He wanted to turn economic theory away from its preoccupation with production for the private market and to encourage a policy of greater investment in public services. The name stuck as a label for the 1950s; the argument pointed toward the excitement of the 1960s.

A second factor was increasing population. During the 1930s the birthrate had been low and immigration negligible; only 9 million people were added to the U.S. population in that decade. In the 1940s population grew by 21 million people; by 1960 an additional 30 million new faces brought the total to over 179 million. These increases were mostly because of higher birthrates, which reversed a long historic trend. Middle-class people in particular, who had usually delayed marriage and had few children, married younger and had more babies, prudently spaced. Among working-class families a fall in child mortality allowed more survivors, even though their high birthrate fell toward middle-class norms.

Economic boom and population growth were circumstances for great social and geographic mobility. Most immediately affected were families in the business and professional class. They had or sought the education that was the key to research and development and its marvels of technology. They were the organization men (and women, for middle-class women increasingly sought careers) who occupied the bureaucracies of industry, commerce, and government. In the conservative climate of the post war years their ideas and interests would dominate the provision of direct services. Part of the conservative climate was that they were so absorbed in their work, home, and families. They loved the suburbs, the communities of nice houses each on its own plot, the lawn and garden, the outdoor life, the shopping center, the fine new school and church. That was where they chose to raise their children. It was an old ideal, well established by the 1920s, but its appeal grew with affluence and among the broad overlapping class of prosperous skilled workers and white-collar functionaries who moved into the developments and tracts that lined the freeways. Poor people could not afford these communities—this was an attraction—and the residents were not directly involved with the traditional clientele of social work. They were interested in health and education, however, and they favored a scientific and professional spirit. When they did think about the poor, it was easy for them to conceive of the problems in terms of health and education. Whereas in the 1930s and before social welfare had usually been associated with labor legislation and the working class, after 1950 it was often linked to health and education, as in the federal Department of Health, Education and Welfare, established in 1953.

Meanwhile the migration of rural people to the metropolis, and particularly out of the South, also continued a pattern of the 1920s.

A large portion of the migrants were white—poor Okies and Arkies who moved west in the 1930s, for example, and Appalachian folk who moved into the Ohio River Valley and beyond. In large part their adjustment was favorable. They blended in, surfacing in their preference for country music, evangelical religion, and a southern temper in politics. Much more conspicuous were the blacks, and to a lesser extent the Mexican-Americans and Puerto Ricans, who filled up the cities as suburbanites moved out. They came, like other migrants, seeking opportunity and security, and in fact their situation was better than what they had left behind. Nevertheless they appeared disproportionately among the dependent, sick, mentally disordered, and delinquent. Their organizational resources were few at first. Their constructive ideas about their problems were simply mutual aid, in the traditional neighborly and religious way, and, among blacks, a growing movement for "civil rights"—an end to legal segregation and discrimination. They too were interested in education and health, but their first concern was access to the service, rather than its content or delivery.

So while the logic of direct services pointed toward an expansion of local programs, and while an affluent society could afford to pay for such expansion, there was lacking a sense of community that would encompass the suburbs and the city, the upward mobile and the poor migrants. Nor was there a sense of political urgency that would dramatize the problems of disorganization amid affluence. In this situation voluntary agencies played a more important role than anyone would have predicted in 1935.

Private philanthropy had flourished in America partly because of the benevolence of the pious and well-to-do and partly because public charity was afflicted with political abuse and corruption. By 1935 the gradual progress of political reform and of the civil service had much reduced the flagrant practice of the spoils system, and the government services gained public confidence during the emergencies of the Depression and the war. Meanwhile the rapid rise in taxes was a discouragement to givers. The government had taken over much of the work of income maintenance from private charity. Would it not do the same with services? Why should people voluntarily tax themselves, as it were, to pay for helping that the government might do just as well—might do better, with more resources and less condescension?

The traditional answer was that people had a personal religious obligation to give and to help, and a special responsibility toward those in their religious fellowship. This was the motive of the immigrant associations of the nineteenth century; it continued among working-class congregations as a sort of mutual aid and group identification. More prosperous people did not need the mutual aid or a narrow group identification, but they were open to appeals for help and to community spirit. If an appeal came along that they thought worthwhile and were willing to support, they could act. They did not have to endure the tedium of political decision, the negotiation and compromise among powerful vested interests; they could simply join with more or less like-minded people. Because the success of the appeal depended on their voluntary help, they were welcomed and urged to take part in the action. Because the sponsors were concerned and like-minded, they could act in ways that were politically infeasible or unpopular; they could take satisfaction in doing together what was good or right according to their own lights. Around that core of altruism gathered interests that were more self-regarding or prudential.

Perhaps the most remarkable showing of voluntary action after 1935 was the growth of national health organizations that followed the model of the National Foundation for Infantile Paralysis (1938). The Foundation had begun in 1934 as an effort by President Roosevelt, a polio victim, to raise funds for a treatment center in Warm Springs, Georgia in which he was interested. He set up an organization, headed by his friend Basil O'Connor, that sponsored annual Birthday Balls arranged by volunteer committees all around the country. These were successful and built up an association. Soon O'Connor moved away from his personal association with the President to an annual "March of Dimes" conducted, with great national publicity, by mothers to help defend children against the crippler (it was called the "Mothers' March"). He expanded his program to have local chapters distribute information about polio, help polio victims and their families, and work with health authorities in improving their efforts. The Foundation also arranged training courses for professionals, paid scholarships to recruit specialists, and funded research into the cause, prevention, and treatment of the disease. The ingredients were a core of interested people (families of polio victims and those who treated them), an effective national leadership and publicity that could use them to mobilize a much larger team, a big fund drive, and a continuing broad-gauge program of service.

Earlier organizations had something of this character, notably the National Tuberculosis Association (1904), with its Christmas seals, the American Cancer Society (1913), the National Society for Crippled Children (1921), the American Heart Association (1924), and the National Committee for Mental Hygiene (1909). O'Connor went beyond these with his intensive national publicity campaign, his appeal for mass participation and contributions, and his large program of service and research. He used the mass media, tapped a large potential of good will, and showed new possibilities for common effort. He, his staff, and his volunteers were rewarded when a polio vaccine was discovered in 1957. Within a few years new cases were practically eliminated and O'Connor led his team into a campaign against birth defects. Meanwhile his methods gave new vitality to the older organizations, especially Cancer and Heart, and fostered many new ones: for multiple sclerosis (1946), arthritis and rheumatism (1948), cerebral palsy (1948), and kidney disease (1950), among others. The National Committee for Mental Hygiene was reorganized as the National Association for Mental Health in 1950, and in 1953 local groups combined into the National Association for Retarded Children.[1] All these organizations took advantage of the prosperity and leisure of the business and professional class, who made large contributions of money and effort. Much of the practical work—counseling families around cases, getting people to work together, and bringing agencies for health, education, employment, and recreation to bear on their clients' needs—involved tasks that were familiar to professional social workers, who often found a place on the paid staffs of these associations.

Meanwhile private philanthropy found two new patrons, the business corporation and the labor union. In both cases the motive was frankly prudential or self-regarding. Well-to-do businessmen had always been a chief support of charity, but they and their families had given as individuals from their private purse. What was new in the

1. Richard Carter, *The Gentle Legions* (Garden City, N.Y.: Doubleday, 1961), is a general survey of these organizations.

1930s was corporation executives giving from the corporation treasury. Legally this money was not theirs to give; it belonged to the stockholders, who hired the management to make a profit on their investment. Accordingly, managers had to show that the gift was in the interest of the business and the investors. At first the benefit had to be specific, but in time the accepted rationale was that the gift would generally benefit the community in which the company was located, and therefore its workers, and would improve the company's "public relations"—a sort of institutional advertising. A second problem was whether such corporate gifts were tax deductible like gifts from private individuals. At first the Treasury was skeptical, but an important law of 1935 not only recognized the right of corporations to make gifts but also allowed them to deduct up to five percent of their taxable income for making such gifts.[2]

The Association of Community Chests and Councils had lobbied effectively for this law—it pointed to the great need of the chests in the depths of the Depression—and they were important beneficiaries of it, although in time the bulk of corporate donations went elsewhere, to colleges, hospitals, research institutes, and even cultural or artistic projects. The larger significance of the development was that it reflected a change in the thinking of influential businessmen. They recognized that the rise of the modern business corporation had separated ownership (the stockholders) from management, and they began to think of management as a profession. They saw executives as balancing the interests of owners, workers, and consumers, taking a long view of the profits and growth of the company, seeing them in relation to the development of the community and the nation. They were aware of the abuses among businessmen that had discredited private business and brought a hostile political climate. They talked about business ethics and social responsibility (not simply profit seeking). This doctrine of professional management spread from prestigious business schools, which were training young executives and rallying the business community, and it found support in a way in their courses (and research) in economics, administration, and law, in their training for information gathering and control, decision making, and planning. In short, the belief that professional managers should exercise a sense of social responsibility justified their

2. Morrell Heald, *The Social Responsibilities of Business: Company and Community, 1900–1960* (Cleveland: Press of Case Western Reserve University), chap. 6.

giving corporate funds to philanthropic enterprises, and while these enlightened executives were not afraid of government, they saw a value in private philanthropy as in private business enterprise, a freedom and pluralism that they wanted to maintain and promote.

For the unions the case was simpler. As they gained stability and power, particularly during the war years, their leaders were asked to support this or that service or cause. They could see that their members used many of the agencies supported by the community chest, for example, and that many philanthropic causes helped the working class, especially those who were poor and disorganized. They too had a public-relations problem, the widespread belief that they were corrupt or radical or at best self-seeking. They too recognized the difficulties and limitations of politics, and they were willing to join other groups in promoting the common good.

So management and labor were disposed to acknowledge the claim and potential of voluntary action and, in particular, to support the community chest. The number of chest campaigns steadily increased: 561 in 1940, 1,318 in 1950, 2,147 in 1960, with a proportionate rise in funds.[3] Moreover, the chests expanded the geographic area of their appeal to correspond to the metropolitan range of newspapers, radio, and TV and, it was hoped, to the metropolitan character of social problems and services. They were often called a United Fund or United Way. Because they were sponsored voluntarily by like-minded people they could combine across the political boundaries of cities and counties in a way that public agencies found very difficult. On the other hand, their voluntary character, their need for consensus, was also a limitation. Their sponsors had hoped for the convenience and efficiency of a single fund-raising drive and a well-considered allocation of funds. The great success of the health associations, with their national campaigns and legions of canvassers, contradicted this principle. The chests tried to get the health associations into a United Fund; sometimes they did, but the most successful of the health associations—the National Foundation for Infantile Paralysis, for example—saw no advantage in diluting their particular appeal in a more general cause and chose to go it alone. There was a similar problem within the chest; its officials must not offend Catholic Charities or the Jews or the YMCA, the Salvation Army or the

3. Scott M. Cutlip, *Fund Raising in the United States* (New Brunswick, N.J.: Rutgers University Press, 1965), p. 212.

Boy Scouts, groups that had a strong base of support and might decide to go it alone if they were not satisfied. Of course chest officials would not want to offend the businessmen who led the campaign, or even individuals or families who had given much money and effort.

Clearly the community chest and the agencies it funded—the local private direct-service agencies—were unlikely to foster strongly partisan causes or divisive political issues. On the other hand, they did have work to do, they wanted to improve it, they were glad to get what support they could, and volunteers gave them much time and effort as well as money. Partisans and political enthusiasts came and went, but the chests and agencies and their supporters had a stake in ongoing concerns: they hung in there.

In 1950 there were, according to the U.S. Bureau of Labor Statistics, 74,240 social workers in the United States. Sixteen percent of them had finished the two years of graduate work for the Master of Social Work (M.S.W.), the professional degree. An additional 24 percent had some graduate work. The largest occupational group (41 percent) was public assistance, in which only one of 25 workers had a professional degree. The M.S.W.'s were concentrated in local child welfare and family service agencies, but even there the proportion was not large: 29 percent and 42 percent, respectively. The most professional category was mental-hygiene clinics: these employed 1,071 workers, of whom 84 percent had the professional degree.[4] Even if one excluded public assistance, on the ground that its service was incidental to eligibility determination and review, most social workers in the direct services did not have formal professional qualifications.

Nevertheless professional social work was important because its practitioners set a standard of competence and their leaders and teachers thought more systematically and critically about the work than anyone else. Inevitably their thought turned to method: what to do, how to do it, how to do it better. In that perspective what was important was not who sponsored an agency or even the character of its clientele but whether workers were dealing with an individual (case-

4. U.S. Bureau of Labor Statistics, *Social Workers in 1950: A Report on the Study of Salaries and Working Conditions in Social Work* (New York: American Association of Social Workers, 1951).

work), a group (group work), or the representatives or organizers of groups (community organization).

A professional, it was said, was not simply a person with a sincere interest in helping or practical experience in some agency; he had learned a body of knowledge and a technique that was generic in the sense that it could apply to a large class of situations and relationships. There were other features of a "profession"—a sense of social responsibility, ethical self-discipline, an *esprit de corps* among practitioners—but the indispensable core was an idea of technical competence. In general, the professionals conceived of their method by analogy with that of the physician: they made a *diagnosis*—a systematic assessment of a situation—and applied a *treatment* or *intervention*. The analogy was flattering because of the great prestige of the medical profession, which was growing apace with the advances of the 1940s, but it was also suggestive for the training of social workers. The idea of diagnosis implied a pathology, and that implied a normal state. As physicians studied anatomy and physiology before they studied symptoms, so social workers might study psychology and sociology in order to understand the problematic situations they confronted. A more subtle relevance was that the physician did not make moral judgments the basis of treatment; social workers also wanted to avoid the quick, simple moral judgments that laymen made about behavior, which so often forestalled sympathy, understanding, and effective intervention.

So while professional social workers realized that the state of the art was very imperfect, still they enjoyed a sense of progress and a wish to improve, and while there were many skeptics in the public, vulgar and learned, no one tried to fault the aspiration. Two great trends in contemporary intellectual history gave it general support. One was the popularization of behavioral science—psychology, anthropology, and sociology—and its influence on the older social sciences, politics and economics. Theories emphasizing psychological and cultural compulsives came to the fore; they undermined the notion that behavior was mostly rational and the exaggerated sense of individualism and personal responsibility that had characterized the Protestant ethic. They spread through the colleges and into the high schools; they appeared in popular magazines and became available to all literate people.

These theories also influenced a religious revival that swept the nation between 1940 and 1960. In its outer dimension, church affil-iation rose from 49 percent to 69 percent of the population, and church construction amounted to around $5 billion.[5] Intellectually, the revival was complex. Its most conspicuous feature was a reasser-tion of Bible-believing fundamentalism, which won a response from displaced country people, especially southerners. Fundamentalists had no use for social-work theories. But in the congregations of the business and professional class and in the suburbs it was different. Like the evangelicals, they wanted to address their feelings of alien-ation, anxiety, and guilt; they found in religion a sense of belonging and direction and a beneficial association for their children. But among them salvation was not a convulsive conversion to Jesus but, in secular terms, a kind of good mental health. It was consistent with a scientific psychology; its advocates often used psychological lingo and adopted a scientific style of counseling. Among the plausible and popular statements of this attitude were those by the Rev. Harry Emerson Fosdick, *On Being a Real Person* (1943); Rabbi Joshua Loth Liebman, *Peace of Mind* (1946); the Rev. Norman Vincent Peale, *Guide to Confident Living* (1948) and *The Power of Positive Thinking* (1952); Harry Overstreet, *The Mature Mind* (1949); Bishop Fulton Sheen, *Peace of Soul* (1949); Smiley Blanton, *Love or Perish* (1956; Blanton, a psychiatrist and popularizer of Freud, was associated with Peale in a training program for pastoral counseling); and Eric Fromm, *The Art of Loving* (1956).

So the spiritual advisers of the affluent society sanctioned and helped spread a self-consciousness that was psychologically sophis-ticated. It could identify states like "anxiety" and "depression," and it could be candid about needs for security and love. It could recognize the role of professional counseling in clarifying and resolving per-sonal problems. Advice columns in the popular press spread the mes-sage in a concrete and secular form. Perhaps the most influential adviser of all in the years of the baby boom was Dr. Benjamin Spock's *Baby and Child Care* (1946), which brought out the psychol-ogical aspect of the child's development and of parenting.

When social workers in the 1940s and 1950s, pondering their methods, said that they ought to study behavior as a response to *com-mon human needs*, that they ought to look for the meaning of the be-

5. These statistics are from Sydney Ahlstrom, *Religious History of the American People* (New Haven, Conn.: Yale University Press, 1972), pp. 952f.

havior in order to help, and that they were likely to find that meaning in individual personal development and relationships—such doctrines found wide assent and support among educated people. The idea of casework as counseling akin to psychotherapy, already evident in the 1920s, took hold after the war not just because it fit the inclinations of social workers but also and especially because it made sense to the people who sponsored social agencies.

The psychological orientation, popular and professional, had a great effect on education for and practice of casework—the choice of 85 percent of students in professional schools and the occupation of most trained workers. It diverted students from public assistance, which was preoccupied with the problems of eligibility, and from probation and parole, which had an unwelcome element of authority and punishment. It turned them toward child and family welfare and especially toward "psychiatric social work," fields in which demand for their services was brisk and was reflected in relatively good salaries and working conditions. Many of these agencies were private, and most could be somewhat selective about their clientele—not with regard to religion or race (sectarian agencies funded by the community chests were open to all) but with regard to the appropriateness of the service or how helpable the client was. There were plenty of helpable clients—a family service agency or mental-health clinic usually had a waiting list that took weeks or months to pass through—but it was plain that these agencies were serving more people above the poverty line. A careful study of family service agencies in 1960 showed that 9 percent of applicants were upper class and 48 percent middle class. "This proportion is well in excess of that suggested by the out-of-date image that Family Agencies serve primarily the poor, the humble, and the unfortunate," the study's author commented. One reason was that middle-class people wanted casework whereas "lower-class" applicants had an "unrealistic expectation" for material aid and found it "hard . . . to conceive of being helped merely by a talking process."[6]

In the work of leisure and recreational agencies something similar took place. Such agencies—the settlements, the Y's, the Scouts—developed systematic programs and activities for different age groups that appealed to middle-class parents and children. The summer

6. Dorothy Fahs Beck, *Patterns in the Use of Family Agency Service* (New York: Family Service Association of America, 1962), pp. 26, 31.

camp, for example, which first appeared as a rural retreat for poor city kids, became in the 1940s a common childhood experience (the WPA and the CCC had built many facilities). Teachers were interested in informal education, and teachers of physical education were prepared to develop recreational games and sports. In the long run, however, people who were identified with social work pushed toward a generic conception of "group work," and in 1946 they organized as a specialty of professional social work. The first theorists, Grace Coyle and Wilbur Newstetter in the 1920s, had emphasized the political quality of participation: rightly guided, it was preparation for doing things together in a democratic society. The rise of developmental and social psychology directed attention toward the importance of group experience for individual "development" and "socialization" (this attracted the middle-class parents). In the 1950s Robert Vinter elaborated the therapeutic potential of group experience for the rehabilitation or resocialization of deviants or people with problems. These activities and theories rode a popular fascination with group psychology that would also flower in the self-help and encounter groups of the 1960s. (Alcoholics Anonymous, the model for many later self-help groups, was organized in 1935.)

As the demand for services rose in the middle class and social workers in private agencies turned toward the helpable types, the paradox arose that those who presumably needed help most were being ignored. A prospect opened for services on a much larger scale under public auspices.

There were, for example, specific services related to income maintenance. Public assistance and social insurance kept people out of the abhorrent almshouses and orphanages of earlier years. Moreover, they made it possible for recipients to live independent of the kinfolk who otherwise might have had to keep them. The income gave them dignity as well as sustenance. But it was low; they needed skill to manage. Often they lacked the skill. They needed friends, but what made them independent often left them isolated and vulnerable. Old folks getting feeble and confused, disabled people (including, as definitions broadened, the mentally ill or retarded)—these might need help in money management, housekeeping, or health care (to arrange or facilitate treatment). ADC mothers might need such help too; they might be newcomers to city ways; in any case they faced the perplexity of being single parents. Caseworkers in public assistance had no time for psychological counseling; their work was much too full of emergencies and errands. But beyond the emergencies was the prospect of constructive help, not just to relieve but to strengthen. Here were demands far beyond the means of private agencies.

In 1952 Bradley Buell published the very influential book *Community Planning for Human Services*. His organization, Community Research Associates, had made a comprehensive, intensive study of welfare work in St. Paul, Minnesota. Underwritten by the Grant Foundation, it was in the tradition of the surveys for community organization. He analyzed community provision, public and private, for four problems: dependency, ill health, recreation, and "maladjustment"—delinquency, mental disorder, and other failures in social living. His most striking finding was that 6 percent of the families studied suffered from such a compounding or vicious circle of problems that they absorbed well over half of the combined services of all agencies.[7] But the services were ineptly fragmented: each agency and worker saw only part of the problem; no one tried to put it all together. What was needed was a focus on families rather than simply on individuals, so that the various kinds of help would have a common rationale and direction. Beyond that, planners needed a systematic classification of problems and their occurrence, a sort of epidemiology that would help them define targets and establish priorities.[8] Buell thought that caseworkers were misguided by the analogy with the physician and the patient because it led them to think only of treatment skills with individuals. He thought they should also think in terms of public health, as it were, of a community-wide intervention directed toward a large class of cases.[9]

In the prosperity and high employment of the 1950s, Buell's concept of the "multiproblem family" flourished. Since dependency was almost always one of the problems, complicated by others, it reinforced the observation that the public-assistance clientele, particularly in ADC, was changing. Since physical or mental disability was often involved, it accorded with the hope for a sort of medical intervention. It was recognized that these hapless families were "hard to reach": they did not come looking for help and their helpers would

7. Bradley Buell, *Community Planning for Human Services* (New York: Columbia University Press, 1952), p. 9.

8. *Ibid.*, pp. 412–16.   9. *Ibid.*, pp. 270, 273.

need to provide active and persistent intervention. The main point was that the proper response to the "multiproblem family" was more services, better services, better community organization of services, and planning for prevention.[10]

In 1956 Congress amended the Social Security Act to clarify its purposes. Public assistance, it said, was intended to go beyond money payments to develop services. Public-assistance caseworkers should help the aged to achieve self-care, families with children to maintain and strengthen family life, the blind and disabled to attain self-care or self-support. They were to see that their clients got medical care, vocational rehabilitation, help with employment, or referral to other service agencies. Congress authorized larger federal expenditures to encourage state public-assistance officials to expand their efforts. It did not actually appropriate the money, but the thought and the promise were there. Charles Schottland, Commissioner of Social Security from 1954 to 1959, said in the latter year that the amendments "may well mark a turning point in . . . public welfare."[11] After 1960 officials of the Kennedy administration urged the idea upon Congress, and in 1962 Congress finally made substantial appropriations in order to realize the aspirations it had set down in 1956.

Provision for the mentally ill and retarded benefited in those years from the general progress of medical care and from the involvement of the federal government.

Between 1900 and 1960 the death rate dropped by almost half and infant mortality by three-quarters. Life expectancy at birth increased from 47 years to almost 70. These improvements were due partly to better living conditions, partly to control of infectious disease. In the 1940s the discovery of the antibiotic "wonder drugs," and then the antihistamines, was a sign of progress, as was the improvement in surgery.

With regard to welfare policy, the important question was more rational financing of the costs of care, which were a risk to economic

10. Bradley Buell, "Is Prevention Possible?" *Community Organization 1959: Papers presented at the 86th Annual Forum of the National Conference on Social Welfare* (New York: Columbia University Press, 1959), pp. 3–18.

11. Charles Schottland, "The Nature of Services in Public Assistance," *Casework papers 1959, from the National Conference on Social Welfare, 86th Annual Forum* (New York: Family Service Association, 1959), p. 19.

security and limited access to treatment. It was part of the more general question of income maintenance, and the answer, the experts said, was health insurance. The American Medical Association was strongly opposed. It did not have many votes, but it was well organized, it rallied its allies, its opinions were highly respected, and there was not much popular support for the experts. Health insurance was conspicuously absent from the Social Security Act of 1935. In 1948 President Truman raised the issue again. By this time the labor unions were potent and favorable and the case seemed ever clearer. Again the Medical Association won.

Meanwhile the government moved in other ways that the doctors could approve. The U.S. Public Health Service was the oldest federal welfare agency, established in 1798. Its first mission had been to establish marine hospitals for American sailors. It kept them off local poor relief in a day when hospitals were charitable institutions. It was in the Treasury Department because the Treasury had customs houses in seaports. In 1878 Congress gave it the job of checking immigrants for contagious disease and keeping them in quarantine. In 1887 it established a Hygienic Laboratory for research on cholera and other infectious diseases (doctors had learned about germs). In 1890 it undertook to curb interstate transmission of disease. It became a clearinghouse for state and local health departments as they came on the scene and expanded their functions from sanitary engineering to control of communicable disease. (Aided by the Rockefeller Foundation, the Johns Hopkins University set up the first professional school of public health in 1914; Harvard followed its example in 1918.) In 1935 the Social Security Act authorized the Service to make substantial grants-in-aid to states to help them improve their public health programs. It was not health insurance, but it was something.

The Act also funded two other grant-in-aid programs for public health. Both were administered by the Children's Bureau because their supporters came from child welfare rather than the medical profession. One of these programs was for maternal and child care. It helped support clinics for prenatal care, home nursing at time of birth, child health conferences, examinations in school to screen for medical and dental problems, advice about nutrition, special training for medical personnel, and interesting demonstration projects. (The Bureau had run a similar program under the Sheppard-Towner Act from 1921 to 1929.) The second program was for crippled children, for case finding, medical or surgical correction, and aftercare.

In 1939 both the Public Health Service and the Children's Bureau were transferred to a new organization, the Federal Security Agency, along with work relief, social insurance, public assistance, and the Office of Education. They continued their grant-in-aid programs, which were still quite small. In those days work relief and public assistance were the center of attention. This was soon to change. The Public Health Service began a major campaign against venereal disease. The discovery of penicillin, the first wonder drug, provided an effective cure, and the campaign received great support during World War II. At the end of the war the Service turned its attention to tuberculosis, which also succumbed to antibiotics.

These successes enhanced the high prestige of medical science and got across the notion that research pays off. In 1945 the Public Health Service had a modest research laboratory, developed over the years and then called the National Institute of Health. It had a second laboratory, the National Cancer Institute, authorized by Congress in 1939 and located in Bethesda, Maryland. Soon its leaders came forward with a proposal to build the greatest medical research facility in the world, also in Bethesda. Congress, although it was controlled in the postwar years by budget-cutting Republicans, was quite willing. In 1948 it created a National Heart Institute, a National Institute of Dental Research, a National Microbiological Institute, and an Experimental Biology and Medicine Institute. In 1949 came the National Institute for Mental Health, in 1950 the National Institute of Neurological Diseases and Blindness and the National Institute of Arthritis and Metabolic Diseases. Others appeared later. In 1945 federal appropriations for the National Institutes of Health totaled $2.8 million; in 1950, $52.1 million; in 1955, $81.3 million; in 1960, $430 million. Supporting these appropriations were the busy lobbying of professional and business groups and the voluntary health organizations and, ultimately, the confidence of the electorate. The money went not only to the labs around Washington but especially as grants to scientists in other institutes and universities around the country. An extensive list of review groups, made up of scientists, reviewed project applications in their special fields. This was known as "peer group review." After this screening an advisory committee made up of scientists made the decisions about the priorities of awards. The Institutes also awarded traineeships and fellowships to help build up scientific manpower.

In 1946 Congress passed something else the doctors could approve, the Hospital Survey and Construction (Hill-Burton) Act. Through the Public Health Service it offered to pay the states one-third to two-thirds of the cost of planning and expanding (but not operating) their health facilities. State health departments had to arrange a survey to bring out unmet needs in various areas of the state and various medical specialties, and establish a broad-based advisory body to determine priorities. Private and public organizations were eligible for grants. The Public Health Service set standards for the facilities it supported. The general idea was to build up a planning interest and capability, to diversify health services, and to make them available, especially in rural areas. (Like social services, medical care had been concentrated in the cities.)

Any survey of health needs brought out the problem of mental illness and retardation. Ironically, better survival and longer life would increase it by keeping alive severely retarded children who had once died of respiratory infections and by increasing the incidence of senility. The state services that were mainly responsible for these unfortunates had lost ground during the war, when their staff went to military duty or better-paying jobs and they were unable to maintain, let alone improve, their plant. Just after the war they fared badly: pay scales remained low and inflation eroded appropriations for construction. Increasingly overcrowded, understaffed, and dilapidated, the institutions sank to the terrible conditions described by Albert Deutsch in *The Shame of the States* (1948).

Meanwhile military psychiatry was encouraging. Army psychiatrists treated promising sorts of cases in a hopeful spirit. They saw familiar symptoms, but they knew their patients were mostly suffering from acute stress. They had the mission and the means to get them back to active duty. It was all quite different from the state hospital routine, the custodial care of people who often had histories of trouble running back to childhood. In 1946 Congress established the Department of Medicine and Surgery in the Veterans Administration. Its provision for mentally ill veterans offered staff and care that were far above what the states supplied. It set a new standard.

In addition to this care, the federal government began to offer inducements to the states to improve. In 1946 Congress passed the National Mental Health Act. Under it the Public Health Service offered grants for research and training, as it did for cancer and heart disease, but it went beyond that to offer the states a grant-in-aid to develop their community mental-health services. As in other grant-in-aid programs, the states had to designate an authority to receive the funds and the authority had to prepare an acceptable plan. In most states this authority turned out to be the state health department, not the agency that operated the state mental hospitals; the hope was to encourage people who were interested in community services and prevention in the public health tradition as distinct from those who were absorbed in the administration of asylums.

State governors were in a quandary. Their institutions were a scandal. The costs of bringing them up to standard were huge, especially because mental-health personnel were also sought by the VA and by community agencies. The prospect was for more building, more custodial care. In 1949 the Conference of State Governors arranged a major survey that brought out the overcrowding. In 1954 they held a conference that gave their support to research and training. That year Alfred Stanton and Morris Schwartz published *The Mental Hospital—A Study of Institutional Participation in Psychiatric Illness and Treatment*, which argued effectively that the organization and milieu of the traditional state mental hospital made patients worse.

Then came a breakthrough. The tranquilizing drugs, introduced on a large scale in 1954, much improved life on the wards and made it possible to discharge many cases. They were not cured, but they could manage, especially with help. In 1955 New York passed its Community Mental Health Services Act, which offered a state grant-in-aid to local mental-hygiene clinics. California, Minnesota, and New Jersey soon followed suit. A new prospect was in view. If states could discharge their hospital patients, they not only would save construction and high operating costs in state hospitals but also could put the ex-patients on public assistance—Aid to the Totally Disabled— and the federal government would pay about half of their maintenance. State taxpayers would pay less; local communities would have the advantage of a nearby agency; and it would probably be better for the patients. By 1957 most states had stabilized or reduced their mental-hospital populations, despite an increase in first admissions.

A similar trend benefited the mentally retarded; in that case the parents' movement, the core of the Association for Retarded Children, had much success in the 1950s in getting the public schools to improve their programs.

Meanwhile in 1955 Congress set up a Joint Commission on Mental Illness and Health that enlisted experts from 36 organizations and published 10 major research monographs plus its final report, *Action for Mental Health* (1961). It recognized the futility of the traditional state mental hospital and the need for research to better understand and treat the psychoses. It also recognized the high prevalence of psychological illness or maladjustment in the community that never got help (its researchers found that one in four adults felt they needed help at some time, and one in seven actually sought it). It proposed a reorganization of services to concentrate on what it called, in public health style, "secondary prevention"—early discovery of symptoms—and on immediate treatment in community mental-health centers or psychiatric wards in general hospitals. The state hospital appeared as a regional center for intensive treatment that would back up the local arrangements. Some patients would have to go on to hospitals for chronics, but most could return to the community for convalescence and rehabilitation. The Commission proposed that the federal government share the costs, with inducements to get the states and localities to meet adequate standards. It mentioned the VA mental hospitals as an adequate standard; they were spending an average of $12 per patient day in 1960, three times the average of state hospitals. This was a bold proposal, but it would seem tame in comparison with hopes for community mental health in the decade to come.[12]

In the field of correction the relationship between community agencies and state institutions, between sending deviants away from the community and returning them to it, was as plain as in the case of the mentally disordered. But its leaders were not able to identify their work with the hopefulness and prestige, the professional and scientific spirit of medical care, and the federal government was not much interested in their problems. An authority commenting on corrections in *The Book of the States* for 1952–1953 repeated the old

12. Joint Commission on Mental Illness and Health, *Action for Mental Health* (New York: Wiley, 1961), pp. 102f., 176; its recommendations are on pp. vii–xxiv.

lament of how politics debased the competence of personnel and administration.[13] He was referring to the persistence of the spoils system both in local public agencies—the police and the county courts, which often handled probation—and in those of the state. But there was a larger political difficulty that scholars brought to the fore in these years: the confusion between the spirit and policy of punishment and deterrence, on one hand, and reform or treatment on the other. These dispositions might point in the same direction—the "correctional system" supposed that they did—but well-informed and critical-minded people increasingly doubted it. Their studies brought out that much crime was a way of life and that much was an illegal business—gambling, prostitution, narcotics, various rackets—that was covertly supported by the community. The dominant scientific influence was sociology, divided into two parts: penology (focusing on punishment) and criminology (focusing on offenders). In a way penology corresponded to treating sick people and criminology corresponded to public health; the great interest in the 1950s in juvenile delinquency and its prevention corresponded to the movement for community mental health.

In fact the spoils system was declining and in many states and cities a professional spirit took hold, fostered by the American Prison (later Correctional) Association and the National Probation and Parole Association. Whatever the political confusion, correctional institutions lent themselves to bureaucratic rationalization. They had resources that an administrator might use to best advantage; their costs were measurable, as were their custodial effectiveness and to a lesser extent the behavior of their inmates when they left the institution. In the 1930s progressive administrators were interested in the "classification" of offenders for the purposes of security and program. They had an economic incentive because "minimum security" arrangements for convicts who were likely to be tractable were cheap. Program included medical care, work, education, recreation, and counseling; these elements might combine handily into a constructive plan for the inmate. As inmate population rose after the war— and as the state systems expanded—administrators were encouraged to think in more comprehensive terms: not an institution but a lot of institutions and services, not a crisis here or there but a common pol-

13. Council of State Governments, *The Book of the States*, IX (1952–1953), p. 373; a similar statement is in VIII (1950–1951), p. 380.

icy. Political or not, they had a job to do, they needed expert help, and they sought it. The federal correctional system, unified under the Bureau of Prisons in the Department of Justice (1930), was a leader and a model for professional administration.

While progressive administrators were pursuing bureaucratic rationality, *The Prison Community* (1940), by the sociologist Donald Clemmer, led to some sobering reflections. Studies in this tradition, notably *The Society of Captives* (1958), by Gresham Sykes, showed that the formal system of prison discipline, the bureaucratic program, was less important to the inmate than his relations with other prisoners and with guards in the routine of life. This was an old insight—that "prisons were schools for crime," for example—and the advocates of the "separate" and "silent" systems in the nineteenth century had tried to isolate the inmate from contamination by his fellows. In the reformatory tradition advocates of inmate self-government had hoped it would generate inmate self-discipline. The sociologists explained why the inmate social system was not likely to foster a sense of responsible conformity. They showed plainly how conflicts in values—between punishment and rehabilitation, for example—confused the correctional system, and they offered candid and sympathetic interpretations of the situation of inmates and guards.[14]

Skepticism about the consequences of imprisonment reinforced the interest in extramural treatment. In the 1950s perhaps two-thirds of convicted offenders were supervised in the community by probation or parole officers. This arrangement had the economic incentive that it cost much less than imprisonment—about one-tenth as much, according to a national survey.[15] Here were many opportunities for bureaucratic rationalization. The probation officer began his work by preparing a "presentence investigation" for the judge, a case study to help His Honor decide what to do with the convicted offender. He might put him on probation, with various conditions, or send him to one of several institutions. In either case it would be helpful to classify offenders so that probation officers as well as institutions might carry on in a deliberate way. It might be possible to provide central-

14. See, e.g., Richard Korn and Lloyd McCorkle, *Criminology and Penology* (New York: Holt, 1959), chaps. 21, 22.

15. President's Commission on Law Enforcement and Administration of Justice, *Task Force Report: Corrections* (Washington, D.C.: Government Printing Office, 1967), p. 28.

ized services to the officer who made the study, or perhaps to put the whole business in a "classification center." In 1940 the American Law Institute drafted a model Youth Authority Act that took sentencing away from judges and gave it to experts in a bureaucracy, who would also decide about parole. Among other advantages, the law was supposed to eliminate the gross inequities in the sentences of different judges. California enacted such a law in 1945, and other progressive states did so soon afterwards. In any case the state might set standards for probation service; it might establish a central parole agency, taking parole from the institution in which the convict had served time; it might combine probation and parole in a single statewide agency.

The presentence investigation began after guilt was determined, and probation was an alternative to confinement, but it might also be possible for the probation department to act before the trial and to arrange other alternatives. This was especially true for juvenile courts, whose probation office might run a "detention home" or "juvenile hall" or place children in foster care. It might make similar arrangements for neglected and dependent children, as the juvenile court might expand to handle domestic relations. "Highfields," the experimental and much discussed short-term residential treatment center established by the State of New Jersey and the New York Foundation in 1950, received delinquent boys as a condition of probation. It had no fences or guards but functioned as an alternative to a reformatory. At the other end of the sequence, the parole office might operate a residence in the community to help parolees make their way.

While administrators and social scientists thought about formal correctional institutions, other experts pondered the causes of crime and especially of juvenile delinquency. (The latter increased after 1945, along with the growing number of juveniles. The 1950s were a decade of fighting street gangs and vandalism.) The subject had a long history in child welfare. It had been the occasion for much speculation about "mental hygiene," for the "child guidance clinics" of the 1920s, in which psychiatric social work found a fertile field, and indeed for the founding of the American Orthopsychiatric Association (1924). In those days the focus was on the individual delinquent, individual psychopathology, and counseling. Conscientious experiments comparing delinquents who received that sort of diagnosis and treatment with others who did not showed that, whatever its other advantages, the procedure did not noticeably reduce delinquent behavior.[16]

In later years speculation was dominated by sociology. It focused first on the neighborhoods that seemed to foster delinquency and then on the groups or gangs that were so prominent in the delinquent behavior. The general investigation of urban sociology at the University of Chicago, led by Robert Park, had brought out certain "delinquency areas." Clifford Shaw, who had done the empirical work, believed that such neighborhoods suffered from a breakdown of spontaneous social controls—the ordinary expectations and sanctions that encourage responsible conformity. He thought the solution was to get the natural leaders of the neighborhood interested in helping their children and to encourage them to organize according to their indigenous traditions. He meant to contrast this approach with trying to get the neighbors to support a welfare agency that outsiders had established there. He raised some money from private foundations and from the State of Illinois, and in 1934 he began the Chicago Area Project. His workers were able to organize local leaders and help them find a direction, and delinquency did fall in three of the four areas where he tried his approach.[17]

Shaw's theory did not say how the breakdown of social control led to delinquency, and later investigators—William F. Whyte, in *Street Corner Society* (1943), for example—described a delinquent subculture, analyzed its values, rewards, and sanctions, and showed how boys learned it. In 1955 Albert Cohen brought together much speculation in *Delinquent Boys: The Culture of the Gang*. This line of argument suggested ways of dealing with the group, turning it toward positive ends. Authorities sent out "gang workers" to get to know the corner gangs and redirect them. "Group therapy" or "guided group interaction" in correctional institutions—Highfields was an example—also tried to direct the influence of the peer group.

16. W. Healy, A. Bronner, and M. Shimberg, "The Close of Another Chapter in Criminology," *Mental Hygiene*, 19 (October 1936): 208–22; Edwin Powers and Helen Witmer, *An Experiment in the Prevention of Delinquency* (New York: Columbia University Press, 1951), pp. 572f. (this book is an account of the famous "Cambridge–Somerville Youth Study").

17. Solomon Kobrin, "The Chicago Area Project, A 25-year Assessment," American Academy of Political and Social Science, *Annals*, 322 (March 1959): 20–29; Helen Witmer and Edith Tufts, *The Effectiveness of Delinquency Prevention Programs* (Washington, D.C.: U.S. Children's Bureau, 1954), pp. 11–17.

But Cohen had something deeper in mind. Lower-class boys rejected middle-class values and affirmed the delinquent subculture, he believed, because they were afraid of failure in the conventional middle-class struggle for status. The analysis of delinquent subcultures was carried forward by Lloyd Ohlin and Richard Cloward, sociologists associated with the Columbia University School of Social Work, in *Delinquency and Opportunity* (1960): if delinquency was a response to frustration, and if the frustration was a result of deprivation and lack of opportunity, the appropriate mode of prevention was to open legitimate avenues to success.

It happened that as Cloward and Ohlin worked out this view the leaders of the famous Henry Street Settlement came to them in 1958 to help formulate a research design for large-scale neighborhood programs that would attack the manifold problems of families in their area—one of the most deprived in New York—and in particular get at the underlying causes of juvenile delinquency. The National Institute of Mental Health was interested enough to give them a two-year planning grant, and later the Ford Foundation became a supporter. This was the origin of Mobilization for Youth, which gave form to ideas that would be a keynote of the national War on Poverty in 1964.

In January 1955, at the request of the International Conference of Social Work, the Russell Sage Foundation made a grant for the preparation of a summary account of industrialization in this country and its effects on social work for the family and community welfare. The authors were Harold Wilensky, an industrial sociologist, and Charles Lebeaux, a sociologist and professor of social work. Their report made a stir, and in 1958 they published a much-expanded revision called *Industrial Society and Social Welfare: The Impact of Industrialization on the Supply and Organization of Social Services in the United States.* In a cogent style they told how industrialization had created the peculiar problems of modern society—insecurity of income and social disorganization, for example—but had at the same time furnished great resources of wealth and organizational skill that might solve them. They showed how the "culture of capitalism" encouraged economic progress but frustrated its adaptation. They put social-welfare programs and the profession of social work into the context of this adaptation. Social work had a "liaison function," they said, among many bewildering services and agencies; it also had a planning function. They told how changes in the class structure changed the character of the clientele, bringing more middle-class people into it, and how class interests influenced the control of welfare bureaucracies. They saw the system at a great divide between a "residual conception" and an "institutional conception" of social welfare. According to the *residual conception*, families were supposed to provide their security by supporting themselves at paid employment and buying what they needed in the market. Welfare services provided for those who could not manage their family affairs or employment. The *institutional conception*—a version of the welfare state—took for granted that families would need a good deal of help outside the market, and provided it as a matter of right. Public assistance was residual, social insurance institutional; family service was residual, public education institutional.

In the spirit of the 1950s Wilensky and Lebeaux included a lengthy analysis of juvenile delinquency. They explained the various theories and favored Cohen's view that delinquency was largely a response to status anxiety; this put it into the context of the relative deprivation of the working class in industrial society and the problems of adapting the culture of capitalism, with its individualistic notions of social mobility. They recognized that there were other factors and that casework might have some limited benefit. But they thought "the greatest leverage" was "in changes in the social structure aimed at increasing equality (both in relative rewards going to the lowest stratum and the opportunities they [sic] have for moving up), coupled with . . . programs which, like work with gangs and neighborhoods, take account of the content and distribution of the delinquent subculture . . ."[18]

This was before Mobilization for Youth, but it pointed in the same direction. The "institutional conception" of social welfare would find much support among social workers. It brought income maintenance and direct services into a comprehensive view and pointed to problems of planning and coordination that would be a theme of the war on poverty.

18. Harold L. Wilensky and Charles N. Lebeaux, *Industrial Society and Social Welfare*, rev. ed. (New York: The Free Press, 1965), p. 228.

Chapter

15

National Action and Community

Organization, 1961–1966

BEFORE 1930 CONSTITUTIONAL doctrine and economic theory set narrow limits on how the federal government could act in domestic affairs. The Depression and the war removed these obstacles to positive national policies; Washington undertook to manage the economy and to provide income maintenance for important categories of the needy. An end to theoretical inhibitions did not resolve the practical question of when and how the federal government should act, however. President Truman (1945–1953) proposed to carry forward the activist tradition of the New Deal; he had strong support from labor and liberal elements, but a conservative coalition of Republicans and southern Democrats dominated Congress. President Eisenhower (1953–1961) accepted the reforms of the New Deal but opposed expanding the federal role in domestic policy. He was preoccupied by the diplomacy of the cold war. Liberal activist Democrats increased their strength in Congress, but they could not win against a dubious majority and a hostile President.

President Kennedy (1961–1963) put the power of the White House and the federal bureaucracy behind the activists, and President Johnson (1963–1969), following his initiatives and with a strong activist majority in Congress in 1965–1966, brought forth the most important welfare legislation in thirty years. Under these administrations the federal government both improved the income maintenance programs and stimulated the direct services that had formerly been left mostly to state and local governments. In 1966 the liberal group in

Congress suffered losses and a reaction set in. This was due in part to a disappointment in the new programs, in part to political divisions around black militance and the Vietnam War. The remarkable liberal consensus of the years 1964–1966 then confronted an impassioned radicalism and conservatism. The conservative Richard Nixon was able to win the Presidency in 1968 and 1972, but liberals remained strong in Congress.

Amid the partisan controversy of these years, there was with regard to welfare policy a somewhat technical issue. It began with the great number of programs: not only were these confusing and wasteful in their multiplicity but they were run by bureaucracies that often seemed self-serving, unresponsive, and unaccountable. On that point radicals—the New Left—and conservatives could agree, and they could agree too that the solution was a greater degree of local or community control. They differed on how to structure the community and arrange the control. Conservatives were pleased to put their trust in state and local government; this was the strategy of President Nixon's "New Federalism." Radicals thought that these governments were unrepresentative and in thrall to a status quo that forestalled a true humanist democracy; they put their faith in a counterculture that would create new forms of participation, responsibility, and self-realization.

So there was a contradiction. On one hand, the way to the welfare state seemed to require national initiatives, bureaucratic expertise and planning, and a professional spirit of service, the promise of technocracy; on the other hand, programs and services seemed to require a local support, initiative, and organization that was more intimate and comprehensive than an assortment of federal bureaucrats could manage. This chapter will describe the ascendancy of national action during the years 1961–1966; the next will outline some points of disenchantment during the years 1967–1972.

Underlying the consensus and even the contentions of the 1960s was a fundamental historical continuity: the reduction of the divisions that had earlier characterized American sociaty, the spread of a more homogeneous way of life. By 1960 foreign-born or non-English-speaking groups had been largely "acculturated"; they persisted here and there as ethnic neighborhoods in the cities and concentrations in the suburbs, but the tie was a matter of convenience and sentiment. The strong religious identifications that had once made Catholics and Jews seem somewhat un-American gave way to mutual respect and even ecumenical hopes. One feature of the religious revival of the 1950s was what sociologists called a "civil religion," an inclusive patriotic piety that played a part in affirming general American values during the cold war. The division between country and city folk, which had often corresponded to that between native- and foreign-born, was reduced along with the proportion of rural citizens; the newer division between central city and suburb was plainly comprehended in a "metropolitan area." The division between individual proprietors and capitalists and workers gave way to serried ranks of employees in bureaucracies. More and more clerical and semiskilled workers in "white-collar" jobs identified with the middle class, while more and more professionals envied or joined unions. It was hard to tell the government bureaucracies, rapidly growing, from those of profit-seeking capitalists. Union leaders supported the cold war. Rapid growth and migration of population tended to erase sectional differences. This was especially notable in the South, where the advance of commerce and industry brought in many outsiders, while poor workers, white and especially black, moved north and west seeking better opportunities.

Permeating these changes was a "mass culture," as the sociologists put it. Its main medium was television, appearing after 1945, but it rested too on the older media and on common experiences like formal education—generally extending now through high school and even into community (junior) college—and military service. Meanwhile the expansion of higher education and graduate schools was a base for sophisticated and critical-minded researchers. The social scientists among them, a flourishing tribe, tended to reduce the moral verities of the nation to an "ideology" of "WASPs," especially those of the middle class. They observed that there were in the country other groups and other ideologies; while all such ideologies were not without dignity, neither were they beyond reproach. It was often remarked that these social scientists, like other scholars, were loyal to their discipline, to a national or even international body of professionals, rather than to some more parochial place or group. In any case their analysis contributed to mutual understanding.

Along with the tendency toward a more homogeneous society, a mass popular culture, and a nationwide intellectual establishment, and especially important for social welfare, was the growth of public bureaucracies at all levels of government. In theory at least, they served all citizens alike; they were typically linked to some technical or professional expertise, and their workers, especially their experts and executives, found career lines that went from one place or level to another. In the political quiescence of the Eisenhower years, when there was no strong popular pressure for reform and politicians were deadlocked in "moderation," these bureaucratic leaders seemed to be an autonomous built-in force for criticism and change. There was, as Daniel Moynihan said in 1965 in a famous article, a "Professionalization of Reform."[1] Moynihan himself was of this type. A poor Irish lad from Manhattan who earned a Ph.D. in political science, he moved from academe to the staff of a Democratic governor of New York as a specialist in labor, then to Washington as Assistant Secretary of Labor when Kennedy took over. He had a zest to apply social science to policy, drawing freely on economics, sociology, psychology, and history to postulate and weigh alternatives, and he had a knack for being where the action was. Under Kennedy scores of such people arrived in Washington. In the Department of Health, Education and Welfare the most formidable was Wilbur Cohen, a disciple of John R. Commons who had helped write the Social Security Act of 1935 and had served long in its administration, who was a professor at the University of Michigan when he came to HEW in 1961 as Assistant Secretary for Legislation. It was as if the "Brains Trust" that had advised President Roosevelt was now diffused and institutionalized in the administrative agencies.

These people did not fit well into the picture of bureaucracy as myopic and self-serving—a picture they sometimes helped draw—and indeed it seemed a source of strength that they would consider problems in the aspect of a definite interest and ongoing programs. They were not ideologists, not capitalists or socialists, conservatives or radicals or true believers of any sort; they were problem solvers and innovators, somewhat detached from bureaucratic routines and rivalries, interested in what might get through the legislature and how it might work. They could bide their time, but it seemed that in the years 1961–1966 their time had come. These technicians of policy and innovation, rooted partly in interdependent administrative bu-

1. Daniel P. Moynihan, "The Professionalization of Reform," *The Public Interest*, 1 (Fall 1965): 6–16.

reaucracies and partly in the national communities of social scientists, were another force at work to create a more homogeneous national society and mass culture.

In social-welfare policy there were two key manifestations of this historic trend. The first was the increasing concern for equal rights. This was most conspicuous in the assertion of civil rights for black people, but it extended to the rights of recipients of public assistance, to poor people accused of crime, juvenile delinquents, mental patients, and retarded children, and in general to the individual beneficiaries of public programs. It was largely an enthusiasm of lawyers and courts, but it extended to bureaucratic administrators. Federal authorities were particularly involved, of course, and in their work they amplified the notion of national citizenship and rights against more limited parochial conceptions. The second indicator of the trend toward a more homogeneous society was the increasing number of federal grant-in-aid programs, which quadrupled during the decade. The essence of such programs was that Congress would define some common *national objective* and powerfully stimulate state and local governments to seek it. These programs often included some factor that tended to equalize the benefits among and within states, reducing to that extent the differences that separated places and people.

To President Kennedy and the activists in Congress, the main domestic problem was the economy. The prosperity of the 1950s had been marred by a series of "recessions," each of which left a larger residue of unemployed; some regions of the country (Appalachia, for example) were in a chronic depression, and economic growth, as measured by the gross national product, was rather sluggish. President Eisenhower's response was a conservative home truth: trust private enterprise and voluntary action (do not have the government, especially the federal government, do things for people that they should do for themselves); fight inflation (which bears down so hard on the poor) and stimulate private investment by reducing federal spending and balancing the budget. The argument appealed to the low-tax crowd in Congress and their constituents. Against it the activists presented a potent analysis, informed by Keynes. In part, they said, the slow growth was because of insufficient aggregate demand, as in the 1930s, and the cure was for the government deliberately to create deficits, as in the war years. In part the problem was "structural": there were jobs, but the unemployed did not have the needed skills or were in the wrong place; areas that had played out their resources needed some positive development to attract new enterprise.

Politically the structural problem was easier because the potential beneficiaries were well represented. Legislative remedies were offered in the 1950s, but they could not muster the two-thirds majority to overcome a presidential veto. Under Kennedy Congress passed (1) the Manpower Development and Training Act (1962), essentially an elaboration of vocational education to help the unemployed; (2) the Area Redevelopment Act (1961 and 1962), which offered advantageous loans to depressed areas to help public officials and private enterpreneurs get new enterprises going; (3) the Accelerated Public Works Act (1962), which provided grants-in-aid for public works in depressed areas, administered as part of area redevelopment; and (4) the Appalachian Regional Commission (1963), an alliance of eleven states funded by the federal government for technical assistance and coordination of development, with special loans and grants to suit the very severe problems of that area. In 1965 the area redevelopment and public-works programs were pulled together in a Public Works and Economic Development Act.

Stimulating aggregate demand was more difficult. Kennedy was reluctant to unbalance the budget, but he listened to Walter Heller, whom he had brought from the University of Minnesota to head his Council of Economic Advisers. He had to create a large deficit; he could either spend more money than the Treasury took in, on a big public-works program, perhaps, or he could maintain expenditures but cut the income tax, leaving a lot more money in taxpayers' pockets. The hope was that economic growth would leap forward (as it had during the war), employing the unemployed, raising incomes so that taxes would yield more even at lower rates, perhaps furnishing a surplus (a "fiscal dividend") that he could apply to desirable social programs. He chose the tax cut and set out to persuade the un-Keynesian multitude. Congress responded in 1964 (after his death), and for once economic science worked, even the prediction of a fiscal dividend.

As for income maintenance, for those who were not employed there were, it seemed, two big problems. The first was the growing

Aid to Dependent Children program. The problem was dramatized in 1961 when the city manager of Newburgh, near New York, baffled by strangers who appeared asking for relief, proposed directives that were frankly deterrent and punitive. The State Welfare Board quashed the plan, which would have put the state out of conformity with federal requirements and lost it the federal grant-in-aid, but the episode gave national publicity to the clash between popular and professional notions about public assistance. Kennedy's advisers, who were professionals, directed their attention toward two features of the problem. One was that the welfare caseload, particularly ADC, rose and fell with unemployment. An expansionist economic policy was medicine for this, but they also favored extending the period of unemployment insurance benefits at federal expense (this had been done in 1958 and was done again in 1961), subsistence allowances for unemployed workers in training (available under the Manpower Development and Training Act); and—something new—extending the ADC program to include families in which the father was unemployed (this would end the incentive to such men to desert their families to get them off local general relief and onto the more generous federally aided program). They might have advocated federal support for general relief—it occurred to them, of course—but that was too difficult politically, so they concentrated on expanding ADC into AFDC (Aid to Families with Dependent Children), enacted in 1961.

Beside the problem of unemployment, the professionals thought, was the problem of the changing caseload, the multiproblem, hard-to-reach family, the absence or inept fragmentation of constructive help. Eisenhower's administrators—Charles Schottland, for one—had pushed the idea of better services and won the verbal support of Congress in 1956, but Congress withheld funds until 1962. The "services amendments" of that year gave states an inducement by separating services from general administrative costs and offering to reimburse them for 75 percent of the expense (instead of the 50 percent for ordinary administration). To take advantage of the offer, states had to submit approved plans that would, among other features, accept the broad form of AFDC available to unemployed parents; set forth a broad definition of child welfare services, make them available in every county, and combine them with services for AFDC clients; prepare a "social study and plan for services" for every child on AFDC; and offer services to people not actually dependent but in danger of becoming so. The amendments authorized protective payments (for children whose parents were neglectful), foster-care payments to institutions (for children who had to be separated), "community work and training programs" (to help unemployed parents prepare for work), and grants for training social workers, for promising demonstration projects, and for research. The general idea was to change from merely giving needy people money to arranging with them a deliberate plan to make the best of their situation. The hope was that by concentrating on children and unemployed parents, by reaching out to families before they fell on relief and continuing with them after they left the rolls, the help would prevent or minimize dependency or make reliefers independent again. It would also build up the capability of the welfare department through its plans, training, demonstration, and research. The important thing was the spirit: the perfunctory or even punitive administration of financial relief would turn into a professional social-work service. Kennedy supported his advisers with the first presidential message for public welfare ever sent to Congress (on February 1, 1962), and when the measure passed, a new Bureau of Family Services drew up the specific regulations with professional astuteness and zeal.

Next to ADC, the great problem in income maintenance when Kennedy took office was paying for medical care. The American Medical Association had oppsed "third-party" arrangements that might put some skeptical interloper—some insurance adjuster, for example—between doctor and patient, judging the appropriateness of the fee or even of the treatment and thus threatening the confidence that doctors felt was essential and complicating the simple traditional direct payment of fees for service. Gradually the Association retreated. In 1950 Congress began to subsidize "vendor payments" by public-assistance agencies to hospitals and doctors who served welfare clients. Later the AMA accepted the principle of voluntary medical insurance (Blue Shield and similar contracts). Eisenhower favored this line.

Meanwhile the partisans of national health insurance focused on the toughest problem, health care of the aged. There were more and more old folks, they needed more and more care, and because they were retired on low incomes they could not afford it. Here the unions, worried about their retired members, could rally the organizations of the aged—a potent combination. In 1960, an election year, Congress enacted a program called Medical Assistance to the Aged (MAA) to help the "medically indigent"—those who could manage for themselves except for their medical bills: a help, but still a welfare program with a means test. Kennedy favored health insurance through social security. Opponents were able to stall action until the decisive liberal victory in 1964 after Kennedy's death. Then, in 1965, Congress enacted major health care legislation. It added Hospital Insurance (HI) to the OASDI program.

The general scheme was that wage and salary earners would pay a little extra in social-security taxes (matched by their employers, of course) and that *after they retired* (for either old age or disability) the program would pay substantial benefits for hospital and convalescent care. It was like a public Blue Cross policy for retirees, and in most places Blue Cross actually handled the business of payment. Another part of the law offered substantial payment for doctors' bills, especially for surgery. This was voluntary, and recipients paid for it out of their grants. Called Supplementary Medical Insurance (SMI), it was like a public Blue Shield program. Finally, the measure provided a much expanded program of Medical Assistance (Medicaid) to all public-assistance recipients and possibly to others who were not on public assistance but were medically indigent. This was a grant-in-aid program in which states shared the costs, and the states had a considerable option in what they would cover and for whom. The 1965 act thrust the government into the business of financing medical care for a large part of the population, and it practically ended the era of charity medicine in the United States.

As for direct services, President Kennedy put the federal government behind new activities in mental health and juvenile delinquency.

It was hard to define mental illness and therefore to measure its incidence, but the leaders in the National Institute of Mental Health (NIMH), who looked for such measurement, were sure that it was very high. They knew that 12 percent of the men examined for military service in World War II were rejected for neuropsychiatric reasons; of those accepted but later discharged, 37 percent had neuropsychiatric conditions. Other surveys, such as they were, indicated that 6 or 7 percent of the population was plainly afflicted, and of course the crowding of mental-hygiene clinics and state hospitals was obvious.[2] The Joint Commission on Mental Illness and Health, which reported on the last day of 1960, had emphasized community care to keep or get people out of the big state hospitals, but still it seemed to Dr. Robert Felix, head of the NIMH, to be "heavily weighted on the side of inpatient care." The report had pointed to the hard-core problem of hopeless schizophrenics on the back wards; Felix thought that it might have placed "considerably more attention . . . upon steps aimed at prevention of mental illnesses and upon maintenance of mental health."[3]

Felix and his associates thought that "people who become mentally ill usually become so in their homes, among their family members, or in their own neighborhoods." Their illness is related to this setting, and if so, "true recovery or even recovery to such an extent that they can function effectively, hinges upon adjustment to and in the community. By community is meant home, work, and neighborhood."[4] In his view community care, as a sort of *auxiliary* of medical and especially hospital treatment of the obviously sick, gave way to prevention. But public health experts recognized both primary and secondary prevention. "Primary" meant rooting out causes, in this case reducing disturbing influences and builiding positive ego strength; "secondary prevention" was early detection and treatment of symptoms. The Joint Commission Report had pointed its recommendations toward secondary prevention. "We must not repeat the mistake," it said, that was revealed in the history of the National Committee on Mental Hygiene, "of diverting attention to the more appealing and stimulating but as yet visionary prospect of true, or primary, prevention of mental illness."[5] But Felix thought that community practice should concern itself "with such problems as housing, unemployment, prejudice, and other sources of social and psychological tension in the neighborhood as well as in the home." A community itself was therapeutic or destructive; real prevention was to make it more therapeutic, not simply to take care of its problems.[6] The "visionary prospect of primary prevention" had, after all, distin-

2. Robert H. Felix, *Mental Illness: Progress and Prospects* (New York: Columbia University Press, 1967), pp. 28–31.

3. *Ibid.*, p. 66.   4. *Ibid.*, p. 67.

5. Joint Commission on Mental Illness and Health, *Action for Mental Health* (New York: Wiley, 1961), pp. 241f.

6. Felix, *Mental Illness*, p. 68.

guished proponents among psychiatrists, among them Dr. Karl Menninger, who published *The Vital Balance* in 1963, and Dr. Gerald Caplan, professor of public health and psychiatry at Harvard, who published *Principles of Preventive Psychiatry* in 1964. In time this view was called "community psychiatry" to distinguish it from efforts focused more on the hospital or the patient.

One principle of community psychiatry (and of community care) was that mental-health experts would consult and work with local agencies, particularly social agencies, and perhaps the most important of the ten research monographs authorized by the Joint Commission was *Community Resources in Mental Health*, by Reginald Robinson, David DeMarche, and Mildred Wagle (1960). It revealed that more than one-quarter of the counties in the nation did not have a full-time local public health unit, and one-fifth did not have public health nurses (who would actually find cases). Public assistance, which dealt with clients who were usually under great stress, was a mental-health hazard rather than a help because its benefits were so low and its administration so demeaning (this was the attitude that the services amendments of 1962 were intended to improve). Thirty-seven percent of the counties had no child welfare services of any sort, and half of the rest had no public child welfare services; since these dealt primarily with children who were separated or likely to become separated from their families, the deficiency was very serious. Probation and parole services were lacking in one-quarter of the counties, and where they existed the workers were too few and, usually, poorly prepared and paid. The public schools were perhaps in the best condition. They were universal and usually had some specialized capability, but even this fell far short of any reasonable standard, and of course wealthier districts did much better than poor ones. Two-thirds of the counties had no public recreation program; widespread private agencies like the Scouts and the Y's had a great but unrealized potential. Only 9 percent of the counties had a family service agency; fewer than one-quarter had mental health clinics. Only 9 percent of the counties had community welfare councils in which professionals might get together and plan, and only 18 percent had fund-raising bodies—community chests—with a year-round executive staff.[7]

7. Summary, in Joint Commission on Mental Illness, *Action for Mental Health*, pp. 111–122.

In a way this account was misleading, since a small portion of the counties held a large portion of the population, but still it was obvious that there was a great gap, and that even secondary prevention would require the energizing of workers in income maintenance, health, education, correction, and recreation, as well as the churches (which had a separate monograph in the Joint Commission series: Richard McCann, *The Churches and Mental Health*, 1962).

After he took office Kennedy appointed a cabinet-level committee to consider implementing the Joint Commission's recommendations. It worked for a year, consulting with NIMH and state leaders. Its report was never published, but on February 5, 1963 the President sent a message to Congress—another first—on mental health and mental retardation (the latter subject was of great interest to him because one of his sisters was retarded). In general, Kennedy followed the Joint Commission's recommendations—more funds for research and training and direct aid for construction and staffing—but it was clear that the NIMH leaders had made their point. The Mental Retardation Facilities and Mental Health Centers Construction Act of 1963 offered funds to public or voluntary groups that would build "community mental health centers," and it was plain that these were much more than outpatient clinics: the idea of a comprehensive service, including consultation, mental-health education, and community planning, stood beside the idea of continuity of care (diagnostic work, inpatient and outpatient services, and partial hospitalization). As in the Hill-Burton Hospital Construction Act (which was separate and did offer construction funds for traditional mental hospitals), the state had to make a plan, dividing the territory into regions and defining priorities for places and services; the centers had to serve a definite area encompassing from 75,000 to 200,000 people. Testimony at congressional hearings was favorable, even enthusiastic, except for that dread foe of socialized medicine, the AMA, which successfully opposed grants for staffing the new centers. However, when Congress got a liberal majority in 1965 the staffing grants were added.

Local planners had many options, but consultation and education were to some extent required, and given the leadership at NIMH there was no doubt that the advocates of community psychiatry and primary prevention would get a warm hearing. In 1963 *The Urban Condition*, edited by Dr. Leonard Duhl of the Professional Services

Branch of NIMH, drew together a variety of insights into how the "ecology" of city life and indeed modern civilization affected mental health and what broad-minded, farsighted, politically committed mental-health experts might do about it. It was enthusiastic stuff, celebrating "the hope of organizing the mad complexity that seems to be all around us," proposing a "constant effort to adapt and readapt to the complexities and ambiguities as they ebb and flow in the urban scene."[8] The widely read anthology, *Mental Health of the Poor*, edited by Frank Riessman, Jerome Cohen, and Arthur Pearl in 1964, began with the thought that the Community Mental Health Centers act "promised a tremendous break-through" and raised the question, "What adaptations and modifications of traditional treatment are needed?"[9] They too had plenty of ideas.

Meanwhile on May 11, 1961, shortly after he took office, President Kennedy created by executive order the President's Committee on Juvenile Delinquency. Its members included the Attorney General (his brother Robert), the Secretary of Labor, and the Secretary of HEW. Intended to make a high-level review of federal programs and potentialities, it was in fact a formality, but it had a good staff headed by David Hackett, a friend and political organizer for the Kennedys. Hackett was no expert, but he worked up the subject, talking with experts from NIMH and the Children's Bureau, and with officials of the Ford Foundation who were encouraging a broad way of dealing with the problems of urban disorganization and delinquency. He soon learned about Mobilization for Youth.

In spite of its later reputation for radicalism, Mobilization was a product of the establishment, of the Henry Street Settlement and other voluntary agencies, the Columbia University School of Social Work, the public services and the mayor's office, NIMH, and the Ford Foundation. Its governing board and staff were an example of the "professionalization of reform" in which many kinds of experts pulled together many interests—rather uneasily—and (an important point) many sources of substantial funds. Its efforts were directed toward an area on Manhattan's lower east side, small but populous, with over 100,000 people, of whom 20 percent were very poor. Its

8. Leonard Duhl, ed., *The Urban Condition: People and Policy in the Metropolis* (New York: Basic Books, 1963), p. xii.

9. Frank Riessman, Jerome Cohen, and Arthur Pearl, eds., *Mental Health of the Poor: New Treatment Approaches for Low-Income People* (New York: Free Press, 1965), p. viii.

significance was supposed to be not only in the people it helped but also in its influence as a demonstration. The experts on its board and staff, not to mention the funders at the NIMH and Ford, guaranteed that it would be scientific or at least rational: problems defined, goals set, strategies determined, performance checked.

Mobilization for Youth was in the first place a delinquency control project, of course; it was expected to reduce the number of offenses. It was an example of comprehensive planning involving relevant agencies. Its leaders were sure that the roots of delinquency lay in some general disorganization or malfunction that would require institutional (as distinct from personal) change, and they wanted to clarify and test the methods of institutional change. It was a scientific investigation of a social policy, a controlled and measured experiment in innovation. The program areas were familiar: services to individuals and families; group work and community organization with youth and the neighbors; special attention to education and work training. What appealed was the way they were put together around the theme of opportunity, building strengths, challenging racism and poverty, incarnating the aggressive and critical spirit that pushed aside complacent routine and resigned ineptitude.

Hackett caught the excitement from the lower east side, and it was central to the Juvenile Delinquency and Youth Offenses Control Act that his committee saw through Congress in 1961. The bill had been around in the Eisenhower years, and except for a new mention of the "opportunity theory" it did not seem tendentious. It provided federal support for demonstration projects like Mobilization, for training personnel to make possible better programs, and for technical assistance to localities interested in developing programs. The appropriation was small—$10 million a year for three years—but given the quality of its sponsors it was plainly a proving ground for better things to come. The President's Committee was supposed to link together the great federal departments represented on it. The staff work of receiving, reviewing, and approving applications was in a new Office of Juvenile Delinquency in HEW.

The staff wanted projects that were comprehensive, coordinated, and aimed at the social roots, the pervasive frustrations that, in their opinion, fostered delinquency. As they studied the plans that were offered them and talked to the local sponsors, they made severe judgments. Not only were local services, public and private, myopic in their vision, unwilling to change their ways to coordinate, but local leaders, even the professionals, did not understand the poor and their needs. To some extent the funders could get them together by offering the lure of a big, prestigious grant; they could insist that the plan include some formal apparatus for making decisions in which the various parties were represented. But increasingly they put their hope in the representation of people from the "target area," or the poor themselves. This notion had been central to the Chicago Area Project, the first effort at community control of juvenile delinquency, established in 1934, and Leonard Cottrell, a sociologist who had worked in that program, was the influential head of the Russell Sage Foundation when Mobilization took form. In Chicago the idea had been to build "community competence" as a way of overcoming social disorganization. In the 1960s the idea centered more on the involvement of the community as consumers and planners, working with the local bureaucracies, private and public, managing health, education, welfare, labor, the police, recreation, housing, and so forth—all the offices, officials, policies, and programs that had grown up in a generation of city life.

So the Kennedy administration and its advisers gave a national stimulus and a new turn to the idea of community care for the mentally disordered and delinquent. In the 1950s community care had been largely an enthusiasm of professionals in state departments of mental health and corrections; they had conceived it as an extension of their function and system; they had thought it would improve treatment and save money. In the 1960s the vision was bolder. "Community mental-health centers" would be more than outpatient clinics treating patients in an early or late phase of their disorder; they could deliberately reach out to "primary prevention," to reduce the social sources of mental disorder and build the foundations of mental health. Demonstration projects intended to be examples of delinquency control would not only deal with offenders but also mobilize the community, both the agencies and the "target population," to provide opportunity where there had been stupid fragmentation and mad complexity.

The various policy initiatives of 1961–1962, to stimulate the economy, improve income maintenance, and animate direct services, followed the lead of the 1950s. In 1962 *The Other America:*

Poverty in the United States, by Michael Harrington, put them in a new framework. Harrington had gone to Holy Cross, then to Yale Law School, and then, at age 21, got an M.A. in English literature from the University of Chicago. He joined Dorothy Day and the Catholic Worker movement and edited *The Catholic Worker* for two years, then worked on labor affairs for The Fund for the Republic, a venture of the Ford Foundation. A warmhearted man, a democratic idealist with an empiricist temper and a fresh, lucid prose style, he published in liberal intellectual journals of the 1950s, *Partisan Review, Commonweal, Commentary*. While experts and professionals started with functions and problems and moved on to policies and programs, he started with people, groups, or types of the poor and their life style. When he put together what various government investigations said about the distribution of income, he concluded that there were some 50 million poor people in the affluent society, perhaps one-quarter of the whole. But, he said, "I realized that I did not believe my own figures. The poor existed in Government reports; they were percentages and numbers in long, close columns . . . I could prove that the other America existed, but I had never been there."[10] His purpose was to explain why these people were invisible, to bring them into sight, and to analyze their situation.

So Harrington evoked the types that in the next few years became familiar in "profiles of poverty": the "rejects," his name for the structurally unemployed in the cities; the rural poor, especially the migrant workers; the blacks; the derelicts; the urban hillbillies; the aged. They were invisible partly because they were a minority, partly because they were in various ways segregated and their plight camouflaged. They often looked well fed, for example, they were generally well dressed, and urban renewal seemed to be replacing their slums with fine stores, apartment buildings, and public housing. They were outside the welfare state: if they were eligible for benefits, the benefits were small. But the main fact about their various life styles was that they were helpless and self-perpetuating. "There are two important ways of saying this," Harrington generalized: "The poor are caught in a vicious circle; or, the poor live in a culture of poverty."[11] The main feature of the vicious circle or culture of poverty was emotional

10. Michael Harrington, *The Other America: Poverty in the United States* (Baltimore: Penguin Books, 1963), pp. 10f.

11. *Ibid.*, p. 23.

or psychological. Its victims were isolated, alienated from American life; they were regarded as failures and tended to accept that judgment; they were fatalistic and pessimistic; they sought immediate gratification; they "acted out" their impulses without much self-control. "The poor," Harrington wrote in concluding a chapter on "The Twisted Spirit,"

> are not like everyone else. They are a different kind of people. They think and feel differently; they look upon a different America than the middle class looks upon. They, and not the quietly desperate clerk or the harried executive [two oft-limned types in the 1950s] are the main victims of this society's tension and conflict.[12]

Having urged a "moral obligation" for a "crusade against poverty," Harrington turned to practical steps. The "first and foremost" target, he said, was to "destroy the pessimism and fatalism that flourish in the other America"; this was not simply a matter of particular programs but required a comprehensive attack on the culture of poverty, the substitution of "a human environment for the inhuman one that now exists." Into this framework he put the familiar liberal proposals of the 1950s; only the federal government, moved by the New Deal coalition of middle-class liberals and labor unions, could do the job.[13] In short, he gave all the hopeful initiatives—for economic growth and manpower development, for income maintenance, for services to families and children, for the prevention of mental illness and juvenile delinquency, for the comprehensive organization of services—a clearer target—poverty—and a moral elan. His book was popular and influential.

The rapid increase in civil-rights demonstrations in the early 1960s gave a political urgency to this argument. In August 1963 civil rights leaders rallied over 200,000 people in Washington to demonstrate for jobs and freedom. Kennedy knew that the black vote was important for his cause. In December 1962 he had asked Walter Heller to work up material for a general policy on poverty. He reaffirmed his interest shortly before he was assassinated in November 1963. Shortly thereafter President Johnson affirmed the commitment and resolved to make it his own.

The "war on poverty," which Johnson heralded in a message of March 16, 1964, was partly embodied in the Economic Opportunity

12. *Ibid.*, p. 148.   13. *Ibid.*, pp. 178, 197, 185.

Act of the following August. It was planned by a task force of experts from various departments. Moynihan was among them, representing labor. He had in mind several training programs, like those in existence but tailored to special types of unemployment, as well as a stronger emphasis on full employment and income maintenace. Budget Bureau officials, a very influential group close to the President, thought unemployment was only part of the problem. They had other ideas. They had talked with David Hackett, and they were impressed with his advocacy of some comprehensive program that would get at the roots of the matter. They recognized the need to coordinate many different types of programs, both in their formulation at the federal and state levels and in their local delivery to the needy. They also liked the planning and rationality of the delinquency prevention projects, the experimental and demonstration feature. They wanted to see things tried and tested before they committed a lot of money; they wanted to invest what they realized would be a small appropriation in a way that brought long-run results.

Sargent Shriver, who was appointed after a few days to lead the task force, thought more about politics. He did not want a few demonstration projects with a long planning process that would employ mostly professionals. He wanted a program that would spread around so as to build a constituency, and he wanted efforts that would show results fast. Still, he liked the feature of the delinquency control (and community mental health) programs that brought forth local planning and control, the idea of participation by representatives of the residents, and "community action." This would not only needle the bureaucrats and build community competence but also minimize his need to define and carry out national programs by authorizing local responsibility for decisions.

So the Economic Opportunity Act took form. The federal government set up three new programs to improve economic opportunity for young people: (1) the Job Corps removed urban dropouts to a sort of residential school and offered them a controlled and wholesome life, with remedial help for medical and educational problems and training for semiskilled jobs. (2) the Neighborhood Youth Corps offered part-time jobs for young people who lived at home and attended school to motivate them to continue, and also some temporary public work that emphasized training. (3) The Work-Study Program helped poor students go to college. Title II of the act offered grants to communities that came forward with plans to mobilize their resources so as to promise a comprehensive attack on the causes of poverty. This was called the Community Action Program, and the local bodies that planned and administered it were called Community Action Agencies.

Other titles, less important, offered loans to poor farmers, provided incentives to businessmen to employ the poor and to poor people to go into business for themselves and funded work experience for people on relief. The act also established the Volunteers in Service to America (VISTA), which adapted the Peace Corps to the American scene. (Sargent Shriver had made his reputation by building the Peace Corps, which sent Americans, mostly enthusiastic college students, to foreign nations to do good deeds for little more than the cost of living.) An Office of Economic Opportunity (OEO) was set up in the President's Office, above the administrative departments as it were, the better to coordinate the manifold programs. The Office itself administered the Job Corps, the Community Action Program, and VISTA, but other new programs were located in existing departments, Neighborhood Youth Corps in Labor, for example, and the Agricultural Loan program in Agriculture. Congress passed the law without much discussion or criticism.

The coordinating function of the OEO became more necessary when the liberal Congress of 1965–1966, under Johnson's strenuous leadership, enlarged or enacted many important laws, including Medicare and Medicaid, Public Works and Economic Development, the Elementary and Secondary Education Act of 1965 (which, finessing at long last the opposition of southerners and Catholics, gave federal support to public schools), a new housing program and a Department of Housing and Urban Development to pull together programs for the cities, and major civil rights legislation. Business boomed. Promise filled the air.

Chapter

16

Disenchantment, 1967–1972

TO SOME PEOPLE the advances of 1961–1966 seemed little and very late. This occurred especially to blacks, who were, in the years after 1945, improving their group organizations and morale in a cumulative way. They were only a fraction of the poor, the sick, and the delinquent, but the fraction was out of proportion to their numbers. As long as they lived in the rural South, miserable but close to the land and intimidated by powerful whites, they were ignored, but when they moved to the cities they became conspicuous on relief, in the charity clinic, and in jail. They had a terrible grievance. Our religious tradition said that all individuals were equally precious to their Creator; it honored a long procession of philanthropists who had given form to that radical doctrine. The political tradition of liberalism rested on the belief that individuals had equal rights; it honored leaders who affirmed and extended those rights. Afro-Americans felt that they too were individuals in this Christian, European, liberal, and American sense. They were often told so. And yet on every hand their individuality and dignity were denied. They were dismissed because of their skin color. Most whites looked upon them as a type, a race, inferior in ability and even character, offensive or clownish in behavior. Prejudice and discrimination often led to an official policy of segregation: separate but equal. It was a travesty. Separate was not equal.

Many European immigrants had also suffered prejudice and de facto segregation. They, and many of their WASP compatriots, resented this injustice and advanced the notion of assimilation, acculturation, integration. Blacks and their white friends took the same line. People were all alike, they said, despite the accident of their pigmentation. Accept them and judge them as individuals. Fair employment, open housing, an end to segregation in schools and public accomodations, all followed from the spirit of integration. Then, in the 1960s, the idea of a "culture of poverty" moved beyond this older view. Already in 1894 Amos Warner had written about a "vicious circle" or cycle of poverty, and the thought had stimulated the environmental reforms of the progressive years. What was new seventy years later was the behavioral science implied in the term *culture*, the suggestion of a social-psychological determinism founded on intimate conditions of a social structure. The poor were not really like us, Michael Harrington said; they had a different psychology based on a different life style, imposed by a social organization that was beyond their will. For blacks, he said, the twisted spirit had an added twist, the peculiar and pervasive sense of race prejudice. They needed more than a way in; they needed a change in the society that could receive them.[1]

Harrington drew upon a substantial literature in his discussion of blacks, and in the next few years a number of sympathetic social scientists, black and white, described the pathology of the ghetto and the distinctive character of its residents. The picture was painful. *Dark Ghetto*, by the distinguished Negro social psychologist Kenneth Clark (1965), based on a two-year study of Harlem youth, brought out not only the frustration and despair but also the "pernicious self- and group-hatred, the Negro's complex and debilitating predudice against himself," the tendency of "middle-class Negroes . . . to accept the judgment . . . that [blacks] are responsible for their own troubles, that economic dependency is related directly to immorality."[2] Such upward mobile blacks, a source of leadership, were psychologically crippled by this racial shame even as they tried by their propriety to refute the stereotype.[3] Clark was also aware, however, of the "psychological safety" of the ghetto, the personal risk of integration (which he knew so well).[4] More than Harrington he emphasized the resentment and anger of the blacks; where Harrington had called upon liberals to awaken to crusade, Clark remarked acidly that racial

1. Michael Harrington, *The Other America: Poverty in the United States* (Baltimore: Penguin Books, 1963), p. 80.

2. Kenneth B. Clark, *Dark Ghetto: Dilemmas of Social Power* (New York: Harper & Row, 1965), pp. 64, 55.

3. *Ibid.*, pp. 55–62.   4. *Ibid.*, p. 19f.

injustice "could not exist without their acquiescence."[5] This theme came to a climax in *Black Rage*, by the Negro psychiatrists William Grier and Price Cobbs (1968), which showed with many clinical examples how "the dynamics of black self-hatred" confused not only group identification but the roles of womanhood and manhood. They postulated a "black norm . . . We submit that it is necessary for a black man in America to develop a profound mistrust of his white fellow citizens and of the nation . . . a *cultural paranoia*" and also a cultural depression, cultural masochism, and cultural antisocial attitude; these were, they said, adaptive devices, not in the circumstances pathological.[6]

Black churches, like their white counterparts, divided along class lines. Middle-class congregations were interested in civil rights and social reform, and often worked effectively with whites (Martin Luther King, Jr. was a hero among them), but the lower-class and storefront churches, like the first Christians in the Roman cities, turned away from a corrupt and sinful world to an ecstatic salvation. After 1945 the Black Muslims gained strength. They too preached strict asceticism in a sinful world, but they flatly rejected the European tradition of Christianity and liberalism in favor of an African heritage and racist black nationalism. Divided as they were, these movements all had an authentic insight and a contribution to a more positive identity. Black social scientists were for the most part in the liberal tradition. More clearly than the whites they could see the connection between the alienation and fecklessness of residents of the ghetto and their powerlessness, and conversely the likelihood of gaining a positive identification by asserting power. The HARYOU project, from which Kenneth Clark derived *Dark Ghetto*, had been funded by the President's Committee on Juvenile Delinquency, and the main thrust of the original report had been toward what became known as community action to give the poor, in this case the black youth of Harlem, a sense of collective strength and control of the programs that were supported to serve them.[7]

In short, the Community Action Program of the Office of Eco-

5. *Ibid.*, p. 229.

6. William H. Grier and Price M. Cobbs, *Black Rage* (New York: Basic Books, 1968), pp. 177–180.

7. Clark, *Dark Ghetto*, pp. xxii, 54.

nomic Opportunity coincided with the cresting of a tide of black militance, evident first in civil rights demonstrations in the South (1960–1963) and then in riots in cities of the North and West (1964–1967). The people in Washington who wrote and administered the act had regarded Community Action as a way of stimulating and coordinating local services. They had mandated "the maximum feasible participation of residents of the area," but they had looked upon participation as authorizing a voice for consumers, as it were, along with representatives of the public authorities and of private or philanthropic groups. They thought that it would encourage the training and employment of people from the neighborhood, as distinct from professionals from outside. In city after city they ran into trouble. As John Wofford, an administrator of the national program, remarked, first the civil rights leaders would protest that they were left out; when they were recognized, "more militant spokesmen—usually sparked by white and Negro clergy" would organize in opposition to the established black leadership; when *they* got on board, another committee might start. When a local group or faction did not get what they wanted they went to the press and their congressman. Sometimes OEO backed elections for "poverty representatives," including funds for campaigning; the results were "pitiful," a 2 to 5 percent turnout to decide among the contentious militants.[8] Even strong partisans acknowledged that it was difficult to arrange meaningful participation; often the "more articulate, militant, and forceful residents . . . pushed the less aggressive into minor roles;" organizers were "not prepared for the hard work of obtaining real resident involvement."[9] The mayors got angry. They really won elections; they really had responsibility; they were mostly Democrats; and they protested to President Johnson.

In April 1966 a self-appointed Citizens' Crusade Against Poverty assembled representatives of the poor in Washington to support the OEO and particularly the Community Action Program against its critics. But radicals among them booed and hooted Sargent Shriver out of the hall. "I don't know where we go from here," said Jack

8. John Wofford, "The Politics of Local Responsibility: Administration of the Community Action Program—1964–1966," in James L. Sundquist, ed., *On Fighting Poverty: Perspectives from Experience* (New York: Basic Books, 1969), pp. 80, 83.

9. Sanford Kravitz, "The Community Action Program—Past, Present, and Its Future," *idem.*, p. 63.

Conway, an official of the United Auto Workers who had gone to work for OEO and had organied the Citizens' Crusade. "They're wrecking the meeting. They have turned on the people who wanted to help them."[10] The Economic Opportunity Act of 1966 sharply limited Community Action. It was signed on election day as the Republicans gained 51 seats in Congress, mostly from liberal Democrats.

While blacks grew militant against injustice and scornful of those who acquiesced in it, they found unexpected allies among many children of the middle class. These appeared in Harrington's book (1962) as "the only humorous part of the other America . . . the poor who are intellectuals, bohemians, beats," a "subculture of poverty . . . that is at times spirited, ebullient, enthusiastic."[11] They would soon get a new name—hippies—, many more recruits, many, many more sympathizers, as the babies of the 1940s reached college age; and the status of a national emergency. It was easy to perceive them as spoiled and self-indulgent. Harrington was unsympathetic: "They strive or pose. . . . They reject the working world because it does not give them time. They spend their entire life making time. . . . At best, they return sheepishly to the conventional world from whence they came; at worst, they simply vegetate."[12] Others were more sympathetic, Paul Goodman, for one, in his prescient *Growing up Absurd: Problems of Youth in the Organized Society* (1960). He saw the disaffected young as rebels against pervasive and evil features of American life: its competitiveness, its role playing (as opposed to authenticity), its public relations (as opposed to candor or even truth). They rejected boredom, loneliness, canned (market-oriented) culture, and they were "achieving a simpler fraternity, animality, and sexuality than we have had . . . in a long, long time."[13] When Goodman and Harrington wrote, the flower children were cultural dropouts, not politically involved—that is what Harrington had against them. At their deepest, perhaps, they saw in the hypocrisy and anxiety of their parents a striving after status measured in material things, and they envisioned a "counterculture" that would be

10. Quoted in John C. Donovan, *The Politics of Poverty* (New York: Pegasus, 1967), p. 69.

11. Harrington, *The Other America*, p. 91.

12. *Ibid.*, pp. 91, 96.

13. Paul Goodman, *Growing Up Absurd: Problems of Youth in the Organized Society* (New York: Random House, 1960), p. 240.

humane and communal, peaceful, loving, enlivened by their own art, song, dance, and poesy.

Then in 1965 President Johnson decided to escalate the war in Vietnam. He had in mind the global strategy of the Cold War, but the action was never popular and in time it seemed wrong, even diabolical, to the young, who became liable to the draft. The political among them had already been concerned with peace, disarmament, and civil rights. The war on poverty had appealed to them, and they grew angry when military involvement pushed it aside. Gathering together around the campuses, they learned to dignify their sentiments with radical doctrines, a New Left, a counterculture. They were aggressively interracial, and nonwhites were increasingly numerous among them. Nonwhite minorities did not get along well back in their home neighborhoods, but around the campuses blacks could make common cause with Puerto Ricans, Mexicans, Native Americans, and Asians, all of whom appeared in significant numbers. They all discovered a common identity as victims of racial prejudice and affirmers of ethnic cultures, threatened in a society that professed to be cosmopolitan but was, they believed, European and racist. On the international scene they felt a relationship to the emerging nations of the Third World, which they felt were victims of European and racist imperialism. These views confirmed the belief that American society was hypocritical, complacent, and materialist, badly in need of a New Left and a counterculture. The students and their friends, including many of their professors, became master demonstrators against war and racism, for "liberation" from all sorts of conventions and oppressions.

Student demonstrators, like ghetto militants, were in the late 1960s big news and the delight of pundits, but they did not win elections. They stirred much resentment in the working class, an antiintellectual reaction that found spokesmen in George Wallace and Spiro Agnew, a New Right to balance the New Left. Both the New Left and the New Right eroded the consensus that President Johnson had tried to maintain in the Democratic party and contributed to the victories of President Nixon in 1968 and 1972. Presidential initiative and the influence of federal agencies took a more conservative turn.

In the conservative tradition, Nixon disapproved of federal involvement in services to individuals and communities. He preferred self-help and individual responsibility, or voluntary or private action, or intervention by the state or local government. This doctrine supported the popular argument for keeping federal spending and taxes down. Nixon also cultivated a popular sentiment, nationalistic, anticommunist, honoring the conventional religion and proprieties, hostile to what he regarded as an elitist and liberal intellectual establishment that subverted the national interest. In welfare policy this sentiment tended to be moralistic and punitive toward people on public assistance, suspicious of "welfare fraud," and racist. Ironically, it shared a moralistic and punitive spirit with the New Left, which also denounced big bureaucracies, professional elites, educational institutions, and the mass media; the radicals sympathized with the victims of this order, however, and laid their ire on the faults and hypocrisy of the privileged classes, if not the intrigues of a "power structure." The Old Left had had a program: democratic socialism, the planned economy, nationalization of industry. The New Left rejected it; it implied elite planners, big bureaucracies, and perhaps the police state tactics of Stalinism. They favored participatory democracy, devices to give power to workers and consumers, to free human potential. As for social welfare, they favored expanding programs that would tax the wealthy to benefit the poor and the disadvantaged; in running the programs they favored more opportunities and influence for "paraprofessionals," workers who had little formal training but were close to the disadvantaged groups that the programs were supposed to serve. While they favored bigger and better social services, they rejected the view, so prominent in the 1950s, that the services were essentially agencies in which professionals or qualified experts efficiently undertook a task. They thought of the services as opportunities for jobs and collective power as well as technical functions, or rather, they wanted to transfer the power that was exercised by an elite in the interest of a status quo to people who needed not only help but social change. What Right and Left had in common was an irritable suspicion of the growing consensus and professionalization of reform that had seemed so promising before riots, war, and demonstrations pushed people toward extremes.

Meanwhile the technocrats and professional reformers were themselves calling for humility, as it became clear that their hopeful projects were not working well.

Economists who sought to manage the economy proposed to use

monetary and fiscal policy to stimulate economic growth while avoiding a destructive inflation on the one hand and destructive stagnation and unemployment on the other. Sometimes, they thought, it was necessary to stop inflation, even though that action would increase unemployment. It seemed that such a time had come in 1968 and 1969, but as a practical matter it was not clear when the moment arrived, what the restraint should be, or how it was working. Even if the technical information had been clear, there were political factors, for example, the wish to sustain an unpopular war that fed the inflation. As it happened, the restraints Nixon applied reduced employment but did not much reduce inflation. Economists wondered whether his actions were inept or whether there was some fundamental change in the economy that they had not accounted for. As unemployment rose after 1969, the manpower programs intended to reduce structural unemployment among specially vulnerable groups did not seem effective. The results were in any case hard to evaluate and, hence, to justify.

Inflation cut down the value of social-insurance benefits, but Congress raised them 7 percent in 1965, 13 percent in 1967, 50 percent between 1968 and 1971, and 20 percent in 1972. It also added an expensive medicare program in 1965. To fund these (and other) improvements, it raised the tax, from 3.625 percent on the first $4,800 of wages in 1965 to 5.85 percent of the first $12,000 in 1974 (employers contributed a like amount). As the bite got bigger, criticism grew. The tax was regressive: the *rate* was the same whether you earned $4,000 or $12,000; the *total tax* paid was the same whether you earned $12,000 or $22,000. The future looked dim because the birthrate fell rapidly in the 1960s, so that in time to come fewer workers would have to support more dependents. To make the financing sound, it seemed, might involve supplementing social security with general taxes, thereby putting it more into politics; in any case the growth of expenditures and taxes dramatized the question of how much social insurance people were willing to pay for.

In public assistance there were two problematical developments, the growing importance of in-kind assistance and the increase in the AFDC caseload. The in-kind benefits were food, shelter, and medical care. The oldest food program, surplus commodities distribution, began in 1933. It was a way to dispose of agricultural products that the federal government had bought to keep up the market price. It gave them away to needy people, who presumably were not in the market. The commodities included peanut butter, dried milk, flour, and a few others. Recipients lined up at a warehouse to pick up a month's supply, which was often bulky. Food stamps were supposed to be less demeaning and more convenient. People on relief purchased them and benefited because the face value was much greater than the purchase price. They could spend them as needed, on food products they preferred, at their participating local grocery. The program ran from 1939 to 1943, and Democrats tried but failed to reenact it in the Eisenhower years. Kennedy expanded the surplus commodity program with his first executive order and in 1961 signed a law authorizing food stamps. He also increased the school lunch program, in which surplus and other commodities were made available cheap to school districts and needy children were entitled to free or low-cost lunches.

These programs were devices to increase the income of recipients and make sure that it was spent on nutrition. It was somewhat embarrassing when it appeared that only one-fifth of the eligible families signed up for food stamps. (In the 1960s these were available, where the county accepted the program, to all low-income people, not just those on relief.) They were too proud, it was said ("the program was demeaning"), or too poor to afford stamps even though they would save in the long run, or they found it too inconvenient. Food programs got a boost in 1968 when several investigations, dramatized on TV, revealed widespread hunger in the nation. Publicity increased their acceptance and use. By 1972 the annual expenditure on food stamps was $1.9 billion; the other food programs amounted to $1.6 billion.

The oldest federal effort to help the needy get better shelter was public housing (1937). The U.S. Housing Authority paid construction costs, so that renters had only to pay operating costs. Many could not even afford that. Little public housing was built in the 1950s, and that was concentrated in slum areas, where huge apartment buildings replaced old tenements. To avoid this concentration and open more housing, Congress enacted a rent supplement program in 1965. The idea was that instead of building, local housing authorities would lease private apartments and the federal government would pay them the difference between the rent and one-quarter of the tenant's income. A 1968 act made possible low-interest loans to builders of low-income housing or to potential homeowners among the poor. By 1972 the annual expenditure on shelter programs was about $2 billion.

Medical care was more expensive. Medicaid, passed in 1965 for people on public assistance (and, if a participating state chose, the "medically indigent" among low-income groups), cost $3.3 billion by 1972, and other programs, notably for veterans and for maternal and child health, cost another billion. Medicare, the insurance program (HI), cost another $1.8 billion. Many medicare beneficiaries were among the poor.

In short, these outlays for food, shelter, and medical care for the poor, which had been negligible before 1960, amounted by 1972 to over $9 billion a year, compared with about $11 billion in cash assistance. Such in-kind programs, enacted without attention to others, complicated planning for relief of poverty.

Meanwhile AFDC had grown larger and more difficult. In the prosperous years between 1963 and 1969, when employment was high and the caseload was expected to fall, it doubled; in the recessions that followed, it grew more rapidly. In 1972 it served 11 million recipients, including 7.9 million children, or about one in ten in the nation. In 1962 the Kennedy administration had hoped that services would reduce their number. This seemed to follow from the findings about "hard-core" and "multiproblem" families in the 1950s. The new emphasis cost a lot of money, to train and hire workers, reduce caseloads, and keep account of the services, and by 1967 Congress thought it did not work. The enthusiasm that year was "work incentives" (WIN): a carrot and a stick to get recipients to go to work. The stick was that they had to face a test for work potential; if they passed, as it were, they had to accept job training and placement if it were offered to them. One might suppose that they would want this help, but Congress gave them no choice. The carrot was that authorities would provide day care for children of trainees and that those in the program could expect to improve their income because they could get the benefit of expenses related to work—clothing and transportation—and could keep the first $30 that they earned in a month and one-third of the rest. This was called the "thirty-and-a-third" provision. Before it, if recipients went to work, the amount they earned was deducted from their welfare grant. Now people on relief, especially AFDC mothers, might see an advantage in preparing themselves for breaking into work, and they would presently launch themselves into self-sufficiency.

The plan did not work well. Work training and especially day care cost a lot of money, and employment was uncertain. It often seemed that it was cheaper and better simply to give assistance. From the recipient's point of view AFDC, especially with "thirty-and-a-third" and in-kind benefits—food stamps, school lunches, housing assistance, and medicaid—was likely to be better than low-pay jobs. The problem of the "notch" arose: if a worker earned a few dollars more, he or she was likely to lose more in benefits than was gained in disposable income. An AFDC mother with three children in New York City in 1972 would have to earn $7,000 a year to have real income equivalent to welfare, even if she did not have subsidized housing.[14]

By 1969, when President Nixon took office, the welfare problem was plainly AFDC. It had three dimensions: adequacy (not just low payments but their patchwork supplementation with in-kind benefits); equity (some states—like New York—paid much better than others, and in them people on welfare might fare better than those who were self-supporting); and incentives (to encourage families to become self-supporting). There were three general types of proposals for reform. One, the report of the Advisory Council on Public Welfare to the Secretary of HEW in 1966, which represented professional social work, was to improve the existing system by a federal minimum in all states or perhaps by outright federalization, and to expand the AFDC-unemployed parent program. A second, also favored by social workers, more radical and much more expensive, was to grant children's allowances to all parents, whether they were on welfare, poor, or affluent; it would avoid the stigma of public assistance and aid the working poor as well as those on welfare, and it could be made taxable so that the affluent would pay back much of their share in income taxes. A third, much more radical and favored by some economists, was for the federal government to guarantee everyone a minimum income and to tax income above it at a rate that would make work still worthwhile. This was called a "negative income tax"

---

14. Blanche Bernstein et al., "Income-Tested Social Benefits in New York: Adequacy, Incentives, and Equity," *Studies in Public Welfare, Paper no. 8,* U.S. Congress, Joint Economic Committee, Subcommittee on Fiscal Policy, 93d Cong., 1st sess., 1973 (Washington, D.C.: Government Printing Office, 1973), pp. 138–140.

because breadwinners submitted an income tax form, and if you were below the minimum, the Treasury sent you a check. Ironically, it was first advocated by Milton Friedman, an influential economist at the University of Chicago, who based it on his "conservative" inclination to minimize bureaucracy and make the transfer from prosperous to poor as obvious and direct as possible. The catch was that the minimum was likely to be very low, much below social workers' notions of adequacy.

Realists supposed that the negative income tax was too radical, but this was the option the President chose in a famous speech on the welfare crisis on August 11, 1969. He followed the advice of Daniel Moynihan, whom he appointed as a counselor; Moynihan worked with planners in HEW (he had at first favored a children's allowance). Nixon proposed a minimum benefit from the federal government to all families with children, whether or not the head was working. The amount was on a scale that offered $1,600 a year for a family of four. The first $720 of earnings would be tax free; thereafter there would be a 50 percent tax, in the sense that the $1,600 benefit would be reduced by 50 percent of the amount that was earned up to a "breakeven point" at which the family would be fully self-supporting; above that it would pay income taxes instead of receiving a benefit. Of course the minimum benefit was much below existing AFDC benefits in many states, and the bill provided that such states would have to supplement the federal minimum so that no families would lose. On the other hand, all recipients had to register for work or training.

The measure passed the House, lost in the Senate, and was introduced again in a more liberal form in 1971, with the same fate. It was defeated by a combination of liberals who thought it was too little and conservatives who thought it was too much. A fragment did pass in 1972; it put all the "adult categories"—Old Age Assistance, Aid to the Blind, and Aid to the Disabled—into one and established a federal minimum benefit in it. It was called Supplemental Security Income (SSI); the name suggested that it was to supplement the main social-insurance program, OASDHI. The federal government offered to administer the program through its Social Security offices. States that had paid higher than the federal minimum had to continue to pay up to their standard, so no one lost income. To that extent, at least, the idea of a federal minimum and federal administration was realized. As for the family program, it was widely recognized that an effort to relieve poverty had to extend beyond those who were in immediate need of assistance to the much larger number of families whose breadwinners worked but still could not maintain their dependents at a decent level.

How fared the war on poverty? A careful study reported that the portion of people in families below the official poverty line fell from 21 percent in 1962 to 11.9 percent in 1972. These figures were adjusted for changing prices. They took account of cash income but ignored in-kind benefits; if those were figured in—a difficult calculation—the portion living in poverty in 1972 fell to 5.4 percent. Radicals challenged these conclusions on two grounds: (1) the "official poverty line" was set too low, and (2) in any case the proper measure was not a definite sum of money but income relative to that of other people, in other words, the overall distribution of income; by that standard—the portion of total income that went to the lowest income groups—there was no reduction in "poverty" during the decade.[15]

As services proliferated in the 1960s, the high cost challenged skeptics and critics. They often focused on "accountability." Congress (and the federal administrative agency) wanted to be sure that operating agencies properly spent its grants-in-aid. This checkup might involve simply an audit of records, but it might—in public assistance, for example—extend to quality of administration. Increasingly executives and legislatures looked at budgeting in a constructive way, as making rational decisions about how to allocate their resources: they wanted to know about the outcomes of the program, not just whether it was honestly run. The enthusiasm for community action and citizen participation suggested that programs should be directly responsive to their users as well as indirectly responsible by way of elected officials. While officials wanted to know what the program did for taxpayers, users wanted to know what it did for beneficiaries. Their interest was based on the increasing sensitivity to legal rights— to service, in these cases—and it corresponded to the rise of "consumerism" in the private economy.

By these standards of accountability the Social Services Amend-

15. Robert Plotnick and Felicity Skidmore, *Progress Against Poverty: A Review of the 1964–1974 Decade* (New York: Academic Press, 1975), pp. 82, 85, 174–176.

ments of 1962 did not fare well. They were intended to help welfare clients, to prevent further trouble by improving their functioning, and, it was hoped, to enable them to become self-supporting. The law did not define services, but the Bureau of Family Services (formerly the Bureau of Public Assistance), which administered it, understood that "services" meant primarily casework in the social-work tradition. They began with eligibility determination and proceded to a social diagnosis. Each case had a peculiar set of strengths and weaknesses; each individual had a distinctive personality that gave balance and direction to his behavior. In theory the caseworker did not just help in particular concrete ways but in the process of helping tried to sustain and build the client's personal strengths, his self-confidence and social relationships, for example. Eligibility determination, in this view, was a way to "test reality."

There were both moral and practical objections to this notion. The moral problem arose because the worker had (1) the power to make or adjust the grant and (2) a degree of discretion. He could say, in effect, "Behave as I wish or I'll hurt you." To be sure, the social worker's professional ethic affirmed a right to relief and a client's right to "self-determination"; as a practical matter the client's willing cooperation and responsibility were what casework wanted to develop. But still there was a problem, especially when workers were untrained— as they were, mostly, in public assistance—and when middle-class white workers dealt with poor minority group clients.

The practical difficulty was how to measure the service and its outcome. Concrete acts of help were easy to list, but the crucial psychological involvement and development were more obscure. Theoretically, talking or counseling, together with concrete acts, helped the client to a degree of insight, relief, resolution, and better functioning. It was plausible, but insight, relief, and resolution are hard to standardize or to relate to any particular intervention. Systematic efforts to define the process and its outcomes were generally disappointing and fostered doubts about the whole enterprise.

Planners who contemplated this enigma began to distinguish between "soft" and "hard" services. "Soft" applied to casework that was supposed to reorient behavior but that one could not define or measure easily. "Hard" applied to actions that were specific and measurable, like homemaker service or day care for children of working mothers; they did not involve esoteric skills and usually saved money (a homemaker service was much cheaper than foster-home care, for example). Given an emphasis on hard services, carework fell under a cloud, but vocational rehabilitation prospered, and the star of Mary Switzer rose in HEW.

Switzer had come to Washington in 1921, fresh out of Radcliffe, and soon went to work in the Treasury Department. She became an expert on the Public Health Service (then in the Treasury) and went with it to the new Federal Security Agency in 1939. She was appointed head of the Office of Vocational Rehabilitation in 1950. The program was old and solid, but small. It had begun in 1920 as a grant-in-aid to help states provide for disabled industrial workers (disabled veterans had a separate arrangement; much of the general support for rehabilitation was for them). At first it was linked to education, a partner to an early grant-in-aid for vocational education. In 1943, during the wartime demand for labor, it was reorganized and expanded to include medical treatment and job placement and development for the mentally as well as physically handicapped.

Compared with public assistance, vocational rehabilitation had many administrative advantages. It had a clear objective: to make disabled workers employable. It was selective. Eligibility depended on whether the disability could reasonably be repaired and the worker placed. This judgment was made by a specialist, usually called a counselor, who also managed the case. Much of his job was like casework, but much of it was arranging for "hard services" with specialists—surgeons, physical therapists, speech therapists, homemakers, teachers of vocational education or recreation, for example. It helped only a fraction of its potential clientele. There matters stood in 1950. Switzer knew how governments worked and how treasurers thought. She could see the possibilities. She worked up cost-benefit analyses that showed that every federal dollar invested in vocational rehabilitation paid back many dollars in taxes and savings on relief. She answered the question, Do social services really work? They named a building after her.

In 1967, when Congress was concerned about AFDC, disappointed in services, and hopeful about employment, Switzer seemed to have the answer. A major reorganization in HEW made over the Welfare Administration into the Social and Rehabilitation Service (SRS). The Bureau of Family Services was divided to correspond to a new division of functions: a new Assistance Payments Administration supervised state arrangements for relief payments and pressed to make them simple and to minimize discretion; a new Community Services Administration supervised the social-work services, which were now to be strictly voluntary. State agencies were told to separate payments from services in their administration. This was supposed to clarify the right to public assistance, on one hand, and to concentrate social-work services to best advantage, on the other. Switzer presided over this new grouping, and "vo rehab" personnel were important in its work.

The Children's Bureau also came under SRS. Since 1935 it had worked to bring proper social-work standards to rural areas that did not have private agencies. Now it had to look after AFDC children, a much different lot, and it was expected to develop day care and head start programs, which had a hard-services and somewhat antiprofessional quality. The new chief was Jule Sugarman, no social worker but an executive who had helped develop the head start program in the Office of Economic Opportunity. Child welfare agencies generally faced a new situation. They had traditionally served families who came to them voluntarily for casework with their children, in the pattern of family service, or they had exercised a legal mandate to help children who were neglected and abused. Their resources had been so limited that they dealt with the extremes of the voluntary or legally liable client. As their resources grew they, like the family agencies, encountered many new clients, neither eager for help nor legally neglectful, whose notions of child care might differ from middle-class norms and whose parental rights had to be respected. This new clientele was harder to help.

Community mental health had grave problems of accountability. The traditional mental-hygiene clinic services were familiar, but skeptics doubted whether individual psychotherapy worked, especially with the working class and the poor. The public health perspective and "community psychiatry" that fostered the Community Mental Health Centers were an example of this skepticism. But the leaders at NIMH found it difficult to communicate their enthusiasm for public health to their followers in the local centers. The notion of "primary prevention" coincided with the doctrine of "community action"; here and there radicals tried to rally the neighborhoods for democracy, social justice, and good mental health. The outcomes offended politicians and puzzled planners; they knew that psychiatrists generally were as skeptical about the techniques of "primary prevention" as the public health crowd was of individual therapy.

Meanwhile, however, most people who staffed most community centers did what they were trained to do: they tried to help people who came to them. As the centers took form—there were 325 by 1972—the state mental hospitals were discharging patients to the community. Many were aged; most lived in boarding homes. They needed supporting services; the community mental-health centers might have rallied these but did not. The situation threatened to become a scandal like the asylums had been. Meanwhile the federal funds were intended as seed money and NIMH expected that local communities would pick up the costs in a few years. The communities were very reluctant. By 1972 the program was in trouble. Its mission was unclear, its performance dubious, its support failing. The Nixon administration was negative. A report by a Ralph Nader study group that undertook to represent the "consumer interest" in community mental health was very critical. The centers, said Nader, "have been neither accountable backward to the National Institute of Mental Health . . . nor forward to the consumers and citizens in the community they allegedly serve. They have often become . . . windfalls for psychiatrists who have systematically ignored the program's directives to serve the poor and . . . blue-collar workers."[16]

In correctional services the doubts were deeper than in community mental health. For two centuries enlightened authorities had wanted to replace cruel punishment with programs that were intended to reform or rehabilitate offenders. For a century social science had cast doubt upon the notion of free will and guilt and tried to relate crime to impersonal or unconscious factors. This line of thought also suggested more subtle ways to treat and rehabilitate offenders. The main problem, it seemed, was the persistence of punitive and moralistic sentiments that frustrated more scientific and humane work.

The main finding of the 1960s, however, was that efforts to reform or rehabilitate did not work and that the process actually might be more punitive than a simple, definite punishment. The concepts of juvenile delinquency, the juvenile court, and the juvenile correctional institutions, for example, were intended to foster

16. Ralph Nader, "Introduction," in Franklin Chu and Sharland Trotter, *The Madness Establishment* (New York: Grossman, 1974), p. xiii.

favored, humane, and constructive arrangements different from those for older criminals. In fact "juveniles" were often charged with offenses that would be ignored in adults—incorrigibility and truancy, among others—and in effect might be punished more severely. They might go to reform school for nine months for an offense that would put an adult in jail for 15 or 30 days. In 1967, in *In re Gault*, the Supreme Court affirmed the legal rights of juveniles, particularly due process in the courtroom, even though it rested on old-fashioned assumptions about moral responsibility and an adversary procedure to determine guilt.

The Court's decision was one of many that affirmed the rights of the accused and convicts and, conversely, the responsibilities of correctional authorities. Meanwhile, however, public opinion moved in another direction. The rising crime rate, riots, and demonstrations of 1964–1967 made "law and order" a popular conservative slogan. Conservatives criticized the courts and correctional authorities for being *too easy* with criminals, ignoring the rights and protection of the community. In 1968 Congress established the Law Enforcement Assistance Administration in the Department of Justice; like the Institutes of Health, it conducted and funded research, promoted efforts to improve personnel, and encouraged demonstration projects in all phases of the criminal justice system. Between 1969 and 1972 its budget rose from $60 million to almost $700 million. But better research did not help the partisans of rehabilitation. In 1971 Robert Martinson, a sociologist, summarized research findings about various correctional strategies: nothing worked. He favored community-based programs, not because they were more effective at reducing recidivism than custodial institutions but because they were no worse, they were cheaper, and they were less onerous to the offender. He also favored more research into whether old-fashioned deterrence might work better.[17]

That year—1971—the American Friends Service Committee published an influential report, *Struggle for Justice*. It said that the 200-year experiment with the penitentiary, which Quakers had begun, had failed.[18] Like other criticisms of rehabilitation, it focused

17. Robert Martinson, "What Works?—Questions and Answers About Prison Reform," *The Public Interest*, 34 (Spring 1974): 48–50. This was the first report of his investigation.

18. *Struggle for Justice: A Report on Crime and Punishment in America Prepared for the American Friends Service Committee* (New York: Hill & Wang, 1971), p. v.

on the indeterminate sentence, according to which judges and parole boards waited for evidence of behavior change that was dubious and made decisions that were arbitrary. It called for a return to the fixed sentence that more or less fit the crime; this too was arbitrary, but at least similar crimes were similarly punished. The argument soon won many converts.

One ironic consequence of the new emphasis on punishment and deterrence was a move to "decriminalize" many offenses, not only the misbehavior of juveniles but also vagrancy, drunkenness, prostitution, and minor drug offenses; the idea was to divert these from the criminal justice system so that it could concentrate on more serious crimes. The Law Enforcement Assistance Administration favored projects of this sort and also measures for prevention. So the notion of treatment was not entirely surrendered; it was to some extent separated from the traditional business of criminal justice and punishment, and it was approached in a more skeptical, speculative, and experimental way.

Whether one set out to help multiproblem families, the mentally disordered, or delinquents, it was plain that as a practical matter one had to involve workers in many different programs—public assistance, medical care, education, employment, and recreation, among others—and that these workers had interests and concerns, professional and bureaucratic, that put them to some extent at cross-purposes. This was the old problem of charity organization, of the community chest and welfare council, the persistent effort to rationalize, organize, and control the services. What was new in the 1960s was the increasing investment, stimulated and directed by federal agencies. In 1971 the Law Enforcement Assistance Administration took the lead in an Interdepartmental Council to Coordinate All Federal Juvenile Delinquency Prevention Programs. It included ten major federal agencies. It discovered that 130 federal programs affected its interests.[19] The same complexity appeared in efforts to help any other group—the aged or children, the sick or unemployed. It appeared in state and local governments, and it included private or voluntary interests at all levels. It was a major intellectual challenge,

19. U.S. Department of Justice, Law Enforcement Assistance Administration, *Sixth Annual Report*, 1974, p. 43.

central and vital to the well-being of a free society. Where "community organization" had once suggested a few philanthropists and a secretary, or a few local executives getting together, it now involved people with power—presidents, governors, or mayors—and the soothsayers of "administration" and "policy science."

In general, these worthies pushed in two directions: to improve management at the top and to coordinate "service delivery" at the bottom. Thinking about management, they often made a distinction between "generalists" and "program specialists." Program specialists were engineers or military officers, or in the case at hand social workers, teachers, or doctors, who had become administrators and had to plan and advocate program changes. They had technical education and connections, definite preferences or values, and rational arguments. Politically they had informal but potent ties with legislative committees and client groups. The most notorious connection was the "military-industrial complex," as President Eisenhower called it, and the Departments of Treasury, Defense, and State, but in fact others were much clearer and stronger, in agriculture, rivers and harbors (traditionally the "pork barrel"), and veterans' affairs, for example. In a healthy agency the program-specialist administrator knew what he was doing and why and had a strong constituency: a tough combination.

"Generalists" were a new breed. They were either politicians who got rewarded with top appointive jobs or, more usually, advisers to the top officials. Of the advisers, some were civil servants who had learned on the job (like Mary Switzer), while others were specially trained in public or business administration; many were lawyers, but others were economists or political scientists. By the 1960s academic students of business administration and public administration realized that generalists had much in common. Executives, whether in government or business, managed large organizations and made and implemented decisions. There was a political element in business decisions—a balancing of interests—and a business element in political decisions, in the sense that government services had a cost and intended a benefit. In theory the civil servants, those who actually carried out the programs, were politically neutral. They followed the leadership of their executives, who were appointed by the President. The President appointed people in sympathy with his aims to execute what he thought was his mandate. The President (or governor or mayor) was a generalist because he was elected by a general appeal and had somehow to coordinate all the particular programs.

The significance of the distinction was that *program specialists* focused on a particular problem and a particular set of means and ends; *generalists* looked in a comparative way at a variety of problems, ends, and means. There was no fundamental conflict between the two views, but there were certainly vested interests that stood to lose or gain. The general movement toward the welfare state—toward a national minimum of income and, latterly, services and opportunity—had appeared first as somewhat technical questions within charities and correction or social work. What was the proper role of public and private agencies? of volunteers and professionals? of case treatment and preventive efforts? of punishment and rehabilitation? The movement toward better income security and community-based programs for deviants took form among program specialists, as it were, against a background of popular apathy or suspicion, often against the opposition of those who were self-consciously conservative or radical. This was part of the "professionalization of reform" that Moynihan had noted. Moynihan, however, was one of the generalist advisers who deliberately tried to cut across institutionalized problems and services, the technical and political, to think in a large way.

To the generalist the budget was a key to analysis and control, and scientific management leaped forward when President Kennedy appointed Robert McNamara Secretary of Defense in 1961. McNamara, who had been a professor at the Harvard Business School and president of the Ford Motor Company, brought in young management experts to confront the military experts and applied the planning programming, budgeting system (PPBS). He used PPBS to organize the department's business strictly around objectives, so that the parts were plainly related to the whole, and to collect and sort out information in relation to those objectives; to define the objectives in terms of measurable effects; and to measure their effectiveness. He also wanted systematic speculation about different ways to attain the objectives by altering various elements of the situation, and he wanted long-run estimates.

In 1965 President Johnson ordered the system installed in all the federal departments, and soon a new Assistant Secretary appeared in HEW with a small staff for coordination, planning, and evaluation.

"Until the advent of PPB," said Alice Rivlin, a political scientist who took part in this work, "budgets in HEW had been made by building on the previous year's base and adding additional funds where administration priorities, Congressional interest, or the bargaining power of program managers dictated. New legislation was handled separately, usually after the budget was put to bed, with little explicit consideration of trade-offs between funding old programs and adding new ones."[20] The programs set forth in the traditional appropriations budget were the work of various committees (and committee chairmen), the concern of various friends and foes and vested interests; each had its peculiar legislative history. The program budget rearranged them all around objectives and attempted a judgment about their effectiveness. In this moment of truth, nobody knew. "Indeed," she said, "it may be that the most important result of the PPB effort in HEW so far (after three years) has been the discovery of how little is really known, either about the status of the Nation's health, education, or welfare, or about what to do to change it."[21] The discovery stimulated speculation about "social indicators" analogous to those that were so important in economy policy. As it happened, President Nixon discarded the PBB system, but he approved its spirit, and before long two HEW undersecretaries from the Harvard Business School worked out a system of "management by objectives" that they called the "operational planning system."[22]

While generalists and policy planners tried to animate the bureaucracies from the top, Community Action Agencies were to coordinate and adapt the services at the point of delivery. They had resources from OEO and a structure that brought together political and professional leaders and residents of the area. By 1969 there were a thousand of them, and despite the angry exchanges between militants, city hall, and agency executives, their ventures were mostly reasonable: neighborhood service centers and head start (preschool) programs were the most prominent. Perhaps more important were a

20. Alice Rivlin, "The Planning, Programming, and Budgeting System in the Department of Health, Education and Welfare: Some Lessons from Experience," in *The Analysis and Evaluation of Public Expenditures: The PPB System*, U.S. Congress, Joint Economic Committee, 91st Cong., 1st sess., 1969 (Washington, D.C.: Government Printing Office, 1969), III, 919.

21. *Ibid.*, p. 917.

22. Rufus Miles, *The Department of Health, Education and Welfare* (New York: Praeger, 1974), p. 274.

spirit and practice of advocacy that sought out benefits that were technically available to the poor but were ignored by agencies that chose to keep their expenditures down. Recipients of public assistance in big cities found support in "welfare rights organizations." In the long run the most important OEO-funded venture was an expansion of legal aid in which young lawyers helped poor consumers, debtors, and tenants guard their interests, and often developed important test cases and "class actions" that won a liberalization of the law (ending the residence requirement for public assistance, for example).

Community Action Agencies, where they existed, gave a voice to the poor and the residents, but as they became absorbed in operating programs they became part of the problem, another service agency rather than a mobilizer and coordinator of agencies. In 1966 Congress established the Model Cities Program to try again to coordinate. The Department of Housing and Urban Development (itself established in 1965) offered funds to selected "demonstration cities" that took initiative in getting their resources together. The projects were aimed at poor neighborhoods, and residents were represented in their planning and administration, but responsibility was definitely with the mayor. The new structure was more stable than the Community Action Agencies—it sometimes coexisted with them—but it was subject to the same basic strain between neighborhood militants and city hall.

President Nixon had a different idea. Like Kennedy and Johnson before him, he encountered the inertia of the bureaucracies. It bothered him more than them because he knew the bureaucrats were predominantly Democrats and favorable to the continued expansion of the federal government. His proposal was to get the federal government out of the grant-in-aid business, with its great federal apparatus for formulating goals and supervising performance, its hodgepodge of vested interests. Instead he would take the money that went into federal grants-in-aid and give it to the states and cities. Let them look within themselves instead of to Washington; let them discuss their priorities and fight out decisions; let them develop their local publics and constituencies. "Revenue sharing" was a key to the "New Federalism" (or "New American Revolution") that would Nixon hoped, reverse the long trend toward a huge federal establishment. The idea of revenue sharing itself had been proposed first by the liberal economist Walter Heller and had much liberal support, but as a supplement to grants-in-aid, not a substitute for them. The thought also appeared in the proposal for "block grants," which would combine a number of related "categorical grants" so as to give state or local authorities more discretion.

Nixon got part of what he wanted in the State and Local Financial Assistance Act of 1972; after his landslide electoral victory in 1972 he moved vigorously to cut back many social programs of the 1960s against stiff resistance from Congress, the bureaucracy, and organized beneficiaries. His administration was soon demoralized by the Watergate scandal, but it was plain that thinking about social-welfare policy faced a change. For forty years progress had depended on the development of national goals, formulated in grant-in-aid programs and by attention to national human rights, implemented by a professionalization of reform and a managerial logic most influential in the federal government. Now conservatives were affirming their traditional solicitude for state and local government, and radicals too were preaching participatory democracy and community control and criticizing the pretensions and vested interests of bureaucrats, managers, professionals, and experts generally.

In the excitement of these years social workers appeared both as technical workers in the programs and as executives or planners. In a way their professional interests were deeply in tune with the times, but they also felt the confusion and divisions of the period as problems of professional identity.

Chapter

17

Professional Identity in Social Work:

Historical Reflections

THE EVIDENCE THAT professional social workers were in tune with the times in the 1960s was first of all the great increase in investment in and political salience of the welfare programs in which they were employed. More specifically, it appeared in the support for training grants and research in the professional schools. Much of this came from NIMH. The Institute was medical, interested in hospitals, clinics, doctors, and nurses, but the commitment of its leaders to "community mental health" and "primary prevention" opened the way to substantial support for many disciplines and activities. The Services Amendments of 1962 gave federal financial grants to public-assistance agencies for training to improve the qualifications of their workers, and the military gave support to its social workers seeking advanced degrees. There were grants for training and research from many public and private agencies concerned with special groups—children, the aged, delinquents, the handicapped or retarded, medical patients and their families, alcoholics and other drug abusers.

The work appealed to the young. It appeared to address the problems of alienation and communal values that interested the counterculture and the New Left, to tap the spirit of service that appeared in the Peace Corps. It was something one could do with the popular college majors in psychology, sociology, and anthropology. To people from "minority groups" it was a channel of social mobility that would capitalize on their experience and aid their people.

Pull joined to push and professional schools that once had difficulty filling their classes grew crowded. In 1962, 56 schools of social work enrolled 6,039 students in M.S.W. programs; in 1973, 79 enrolled 16,099.[1] The 1973 figures do not include programs in Canada or undergraduate majors, many of which were professional. In short—a growing, diverse, and spirited student body looking toward a growing, diverse, and challenging market. What did they get? What did they need? Here was the problem of professional identity at its core.

Historically education for social work had changed in important ways. In 1919 the fifteen schools then in existence had joined in an Association. Nine of them were linked with universities, six with operating agencies, in the fashion of a nursing school based on a hospital rather than a college. (The highly esteemed New York School of Philanthropy was of the latter type.) By 1932 they had agreed on a minimum curriculum and a procedure for formal accreditation. By 1939 they had agreed that proper social-work education was two years of graduate professional study leading to the M.S.W. (The New York School had affiliated with Columbia University.) There was still much support in the Midwest for a program of undergraduate professional education looking to staff the public bureaucracies as the teachers' colleges staffed the public schools, but it faded. In the 1940s the academic content of graduate professional education was the "basic eight" fields: the methods of social casework, group work, and community organization plus social administration, public welfare, social research, medical information, and psychiatric information. By 1959, when there was a major study of curriculum, the various fields were often conceived as *foundation courses* in human behavior, social organization, social research, and history, programs, and policy (whence this book), on one hand, and *methods* courses, on the other. The newer formulation reflected the increasing importance of clinical and social psychology and sociology and a desire to combine knowledge and skill courses in a more systematic way.

Whatever the changes, most students came for and got casework with a strong therapeutic slant. There was a market for their services in agencies that helped children, families, delinquents, and the mentally disordered; the work answered to the ever-growing popular inter-

1. *Encyclopedia of Social Work, Seventeenth Issue* (New York: National Association of Social Workers, 1977), II, 1669.

est in "mental health" after 1940. Even group workers in the 1950s came to look upon their efforts as therapeutic, and found work in institutions. To emphasize this clinical and therapeutic interest, fully half of the M.S.W. curriculum, which many thought the best half, was not academic at all but consisted of supervised field work. "Methods courses" related directly to it, and the field supervision involved elaborate reflection not only on the problems of clients but also on the feelings and responses of the worker; it aimed in part at a self-knowledge that was undeniably fascinating.

There was always a party in social-work education that criticized the overwhelming emphasis on casework with a therapeutic slant. As the 1960s dawned, it grew apace. Some people pointed to outcome studies that showed that casework (like other psychotherapy) was not measurably effective in changing behavior. Others observed that however it appealed to the middle-class type of client it was not relevant to the needs or problems of many poor people or minority groups. Some of these critics favored political solutions, others a particular mode of intervention called "behavior modification" or "operant conditioning," which was derived from the psychological theory of behaviorism rather than dynamic psychology and claimed more scientific rigor and success. Another party observed that M.S.W.'s usually moved quickly into supervisory or administrative positions, and argued that professional education should prepare them for that work. They favored organizing education around problems or fields of practice, training specialists in mental health or child welfare rather than casework or group work.

The method called "community organization" (CO) advanced in the excitement of the period. It had developed in a small way around the wish of community chests or welfare councils to hire staff prepared for research and administration. Now the Mobilization for Youth spirit and community action generally suggested a much more active and political function: the community organizer would be a resource or guide for the militant spirit, helping the disadvantaged articulate their discontents or needs and organize around them. Another, and very different, type of community organizer, however, would respond to the managerial spirit in the executive and legislative areas and rise to the tasks of policy analysis and planning. These organizers represented the "professionalization of reform"; in the social-work curriculum their preparation would be for "indirect services"—administration, policy analysis, planning—as distinct from the "direct services" of conventional or "clinical" social work.

The activist sort of community organization had some support and much sympathy, but its practitioners were often skeptical about academics and professionalism, and it did not lend itself to academic preparation. Policy analysis, planning, and administration did invite academic training. Traditionally the policy course in social-work education had discussed the rationale of income maintenance programs or the legal bases of child welfare legislation. But in the 1940s economists and sociologists worked out a general type of analysis. Its central concepts were system and model. A "system" was a conceptualization of a situation or process as parts related to a whole. Its heuristic use was to alert observers to elements, factors, or relationships that they might otherwise ignore or take for granted. A "model" was a very abstract, simplified, and explicit formulation of a system that made its relationships definite and clear. Analysts often tried to make the model as abstract as a mathematical formula, with inputs and outputs specified and quantified and relationships clarified by elaborate statistical analysis. PPBS was of this type. This was quite a stretch for old-fashioned CO. Its practitioners had to learn a range of systems theory that was very different from the growth-and-development-and-deviant-behavior pabulum that was thought central to the direct services. The difference raised a question as to whether the two—"direct" and "indirect" services—belonged together in a single profession.

Meanwhile there was another question, that of how M.S.W.'s fitted into the direct services. It was obvious by mid-decade that there would never be enough M.S.W.'s to staff all direct-service positions. The number of M.S.W.'s in practice doubled over the 1960s, from 26,000 to 52,000, but they remained one-fifth or less of the total employed in social agencies.[2] It was plausible to think that they might supervise teams of workers with lesser credentials. In 1970 the Council on Social Work Education began to approve undergraduate professional programs and the National Association of Social Workers recognized such "Bachelors of Social Work" as professionals. Meanwhile the two-year colleges, a mighty host with a strong vocational

2. Henry J. Meyer, "Profession of Social Work: Contemporary Characteristics," in *Encyclopedia of Social Work*, Sixteenth Issue (New York: National Association of Social Workers, 1971), II, 961f.

orientation, were developing Associate of Arts curricula to train "social-work technicians."

Just what was the difference in training and skill between these three levels? It was hard to say. It depended on a standardization of jobs and tasks that did not exist. It was reasonable to suppose that employers would want to standardize the job market and that social-work education would adapt to the situation. Meanwhile it stood to gain from the great increase in research competence in the social and behavioral sciences and from the Ph.D.'s who joined its faculties; by 1971, 21 of the 75 accredited professional schools had advanced programs, most of them emphasizing research. The main historical fact behind the confusion about curricula and boundaries—behind the problem of professional identification—was that a knowledge base and practice that had been parochial—mainly casework in professionalized agencies—was expanding in a timely and flexible way to try to encompass a lot of different jobs and demands. Amid the confusion and uncertainty of this transition, it is helpful to take a historical bearing.

Professional social work had its origin in a voluntary association that undertook to criticize and reform the class of institutions known then as "charities and correction." Its nucleus was a small group of people associated with the "state boards of charities" whose business was to advise elected officials about the work of a variety of state institutions that were coming into existence. The state boards were also interested in local jails, almshouses, and outdoor poor relief and in the question of state subsidies for private—mostly religious—charities. They came together as a section of the Social Science Association, and in 1874 they became a separate Conference of Charities and Correction. In 1880 they were joined by partisans of "charity organization." This group wanted to improve the administration of local private charities, but it too was interested in the local public agencies, which duplicated much of the work. Members of the two groups had in common the facts that they came from the business and professional class and that most of them had been active in founding local charities or serving on their boards. They and their associations were then identified by the term *philanthropists*. "Society ladies" were prominent among them. They could see a relationship in the work of the local and state, public and private agencies, the need for a common policy, and they could see too that there were relationships among the unfortunate people that the agencies cared for, who were then classified as "dependent, defective, and delinquent."

The constructive idea that brought and held these people together was, in the idiom of the time, "scientific charity" or "scientific philanthropy." The words *charity* and *philanthropy* had a strong religious connotation, the ancient Christian assertion of a personal and communal responsibility to help the forlorn and outcast. Most "philanthropists" were very pious; many were clergymen. By "scientific" they meant rational and efficient, in contrast with practices that were, in their opinion, self-defeating. Specifically, they criticized a private charity that was casual and sentimental—a coin to a beggar, for example—and a public charity that was routine and perfunctory. They wanted to establish a clearer and more efficacious relationship between the means and ends of helping. In their minds rationality took three forms. First, they accepted the liberal theory of political economy as it had developed in England. Like the political economists, they believed that lax administration of public charity (the poor law) was self-defeating inasmuch as it encouraged pauperism. Second, they upheld the doctrine of the Scottish clergyman and charity reformer (and political economist) Thomas Chalmers, that there were certain informal and "natural" agencies of helping among family, neighbors, and religious congregations, and that a wise charitable administration ought to discover and animate these rather than weaken or supplant them with an institution that was necessarily more impersonal and lacked the intimate sense of responsibility on the part of both helper and helped. Finally, they were busy collectors and classifiers of statistics, hoping in this way to analyze the causes of trouble and the effects of intervention. Their observations were directed in a naive and moralistic way toward the personal characteristics of the cases they counted, but they did bring out impersonal and environmental conditions—public health hazards, genetic factors of behavior, and the momentous researches of Charles Booth into poverty as well as pauperism.

The volume *American Charities*, by Amos Warner (1894), summarized the first generation of this movement in a lasting way. Scientific charity (Warner suggested the term *philanthropology*) focused on specific agencies and issues, but its advocates stood at a watershed in

American history. The traditional religion that had sanctioned charity had been gravely challenged by the rise of science, and one response among well-educated people—people in the business and professional class—was to redeem religion by emphasizing its ethical character and making it more relevant to social problems. That way lay "modernist" (as opposed to "fundamentalist") Protestantism and the social gospel. At the same time, the liberal policy of *laissez faire*, which had centered on protecting property rights, was giving way to an assertion of the police power—the power of the state to protect the health, safety, and morals of the citizenry. That way lay the political movement called progressivism and its legislation to protect vulnerable and disadvantaged groups. So the proponents of scientific charity or philanthropy, who were concerned in a technical way with institutions that were supposed to help the dependent, defective, and delinquent, were about to find a wide and interested audience.

A sign of things to come was the arrival in the Conference of the settlement house workers in 1896. The first American social settlement had appeared in 1886, and many others had followed. The settlers differed from the earlier groups in that they were not interested in the administration of particular institutions. They were from the same class of people, however—they were mostly college graduates, and the first generation of college women was conspicuous among them—and in their way they were interested in scientific philanthropy. They were mostly very pious and looked upon their settlements as outposts of a "Christian sociology" or "practical sociology" or "applied ethics" that was then very popular in the colleges. At first they were likely to be dubious about existing institutions and formal charity. They wanted to be of service, but they favored a spontaneous neighborliness rather than institutionalized helping. Nevertheless they did identify with the Conference and with more organized efforts to help people in need or trouble, and ironically they themselves very soon developed the institution of the neighborhood or community center, with its clubs and activities. They showed a spirit that the progressive movement would write large.

When the first generation of scientific philanthropists had thought about politics, what had struck them most forcibly was the abuse of local public charities under the spoils system. They had hoped that the private charities and state institutions in which they were interested would circumvent such abuse. But their scientific interest in the causes of dependency and delinquency and their growing appreciation of environmental and impersonal factors suggested the possibility of preventive legislation, and they often became leaders in obtaining municipal and state enactments for better labor conditions; more wholesome sanitation, food supply, and housing; more and better education; control of saloons, gambling, and vice; and reforms intended to confound boss rule and political corruption. By 1912 many of these enthusiasms had found a more general rationale—prevention of poverty through the establishment of legal minima of well-being— and substantial political support.

While the search for causes and the hope for preventive legislation gave some experts in charity and correction a role in the politics of the progressive period, the scientific spirit was also working to improve day-to-day administration. It began with the belief that each person in need or trouble was different and that an effective response depended on correctly individualizing the case. In the early practice of charity organization the individualizing had three parts: (1) an "investigation" by a district secretary—a paid worker—who would make sure that the application was not fraudulent and would refer the applicant to such relief societies as seemed appropriate; (2) a "case conference" of representatives of such agencies and others, who would reflect on the applicant's situation and formulate a comprehensive plan of help; and (3) a follow-up by a "friendly visitor," who would give the advice and moral support of a sincere and knowledgeable friend. In fact much of the work of these agencies proved to be with broken families, and there was much overlap with child-saving agencies, which were also interested in individualization.

After 1900 the idea of individualized "casework," as it came to be called, spread to many institutional settings: probation (attached to the courts); helping hospital patients and their families (medical social work); helping difficult students in school and their families (truant officers or visiting teachers); aftercare for patients from mental hospitals (psychiatric social work); and among executives of institutions, who undertook to classify their wards in many ways in order to provide a more individualized program for them. To individualize a case properly, workers needed to know not only about personality, family, and associations but also about laws and available agencies and practices, not just for material relief but also for law enforcement, health, education, industrial labor, and immigration. Caseworkers needed to know how to find significant facts about their clients and how to form these into a rational plan and activity, how to follow up the case and cumulate its social significance. The necessary learning and skills might come haphazardly from experience, but by 1900 experiential learning was being channeled into an organized course of instruction—usually called a School of Philanthropy—and into a systematic rationale for "social diagnosis" and "casework."

With regard to their practical work, charity organizers and scientific philanthropists entered two currents of our general history. One was the growing spirit of professionalism in the labor force, the other a popular interest in scientific psychology. The mark of a "profession" was advanced formal academic training and certification, which ordinarily implied a career commitment. Its first great expansion in the nineteenth century was in the engineering and technical schools—the Institutes of Technology and A. and M.'s—which took advantage of scientific progress in chemistry, physics, and biology. Medical schools were improving their instruction because of the great advances in physiology and bacteriology. Around them grew special schools for dentists, optometrists, pharmacists, and nurses. There were "normal schools" (later "teachers' colleges") for instructors of the young and "graduate schools" for future college professors and researchers. There were business colleges, secretarial schools, and schools for librarians, journalists, and fine and commercial artists. The idea of a professional curriculum in scientific philanthropy was part of this emerging pattern.

But there was a subtler aspect of a "profession" that was also important and appealing: it involved not just technical know-how but trustworthiness in its application, a spirit of service and a professional ethic. This ethical feature had been especially important in the traditional professions of lawyers, clergymen, and physicians, who often made grave decisions about people in crisis; practitioners of scientific charity also had to help people in personal and family crisis, people who were, moreover, likely to be particularly disadvantaged and vulnerable. The original idea of scientific charity or philanthropy had rested on the theological doctrine that charity was a service to God, that Christ was there in "the least of these my brethren." As that kind of theological doctrine faded in the rise of scientific naturalism, in part changing to the amiable humanitarianism of the social gospel, the idea of a professional service, a professional altruism, took its place. By 1910 the word *charity* had the connotation of the well-to-do patronizing the poor, and in that context the notion of a professional service offered to clients seemed less snobbish and more democratic.

Psychology entered the picture because scientific charity had to deal with emotions and morals—feelings and ideas about good and bad, right and wrong, hope and fear, guilt and pride, dependency and autonomy. Traditional charity had understood these phenomena in religious terms: faith was the source of duty and forgiveness, inspiration and consolation. As the theology faded, people turned toward naturalistic psychologies. But academic psychologists, who were just setting up their labs, were not very helpful. They were interested in the mechanism of the mind, the stimulus and response. Insofar as they were practical, they were interested in how we learn—an important matter for the teachers' colleges, which had a professional interest in how we teach. The concerns of scientific philanthropists fell under the rubric of "abnormal psychology," partly because the mentally ill and retarded were classed among the "defective." These unfortunates were more of interest to clinical psychiatry than to academic psychology, and as it happened thought about them turned more and more to the provocative theories of Dr. Sigmund Freud. Academic psychologists, and most psychiatrists for that matter, thought that he was really unscientific, but to people interested in family relations and "mental hygiene" for children his doctrines were suggestive. Caseworkers in particular were intrigued by his thoughts about therapy, which put their relationship with clients in a new light. As Freudian ideas spread among well-educated people in the 1920s, caseworkers seemed to be riding a rising tide.

The fascination of casework somewhat obscured the earlier interest in systematic coordination and direction of various agencies, but this level of administration also found a scientific support, in the theories about business administration and public administration that addressed the interests of funders and executives.

By 1930, then, the original sense of identity that rallied people under the banners of "scientific philanthropy" and "charities and correction" had developed in two directions. One looked beyond particular institutions toward predisposing conditions or circumstances and supported the political demand for preventive legislation. Its advocates appeared regularly in the National Conferences and other forums—*Survey* magazine, for one—and attracted a good deal of attention, but their institutional support was weak. They were board members or executives of associations that advocated good causes. They were few in number, divided, and conspicuously lacking in mass support, even among the people they intended to help, for example in the areas of child labor and social insurance. They hoped for a revival of the Progressive party or, better, something like the British Labor party. These hopes were not well founded, and in the absence of a more powerful constituency they turned to their friends in the philanthropic community.

The second direction was toward professionalism in practical work. Its advocates had much stronger institutional support. There were an ever-increasing number of agencies and jobs, a growing constituency of funders, public and private, among local elites, and a growing network of professional associations and training schools to focus their attention. They came to dominate the National Conference, which changed its name from Charities and Correction to Social Work in 1917. But the professionals also were weak. Many executives doubted whether formal professional training was necessary; the training schools differed on whether to require an undergraduate degree of their students, to relate primarily to agencies or to universities, to emphasize general principles or specific skills. They too could see that even good professional skill would not affect the more basic problems that they encountered in their work.

Obviously there was some link between preventive legislation and professional practice, but it was not clear. Professionals might plausibly argue for laws to end a public subsidy to orphanages or to enact civil-service status for probation officers; or they might look a little deeper and champion laws to keep children out of the factories and in the schoolrooms, or to compensate the victims of industrial accidents; or they might look still deeper and advocate laws to close down saloons, restrict immigration, set up social insurance, remain neutral in the World War, or enact woman suffrage. All these and many other causes had claimed to deal in a preventive way with basic problems and therefore to deserve the professional's support. Of course professionals should be concerned with preventive legislation, but this generalization did not indicate which preventive legislation or even how to advocate it.

Unemployment in the depression of the 1930s was certainly a

basic problem, obvious, pressing, and plainly related to relief. It occurred to many well-informed and thoughtful people then that those were not ordinary hard times but that the capitalist system and liberalism itself were in their death throes. This opinion had a strong echo among professional social workers, some of whom thought that the class war was at hand and that they should enlist in it. Plainly a day for preventive legislation had arrived, and many reforms for which the progressives had campaigned at the state level—against child labor and for minimum wages, maximum hours, and better labor conditions—were now enacted at the federal level, along with social insurance against the risks of old age, unemployment, and loss of the breadwinner. From a narrowly professional point of view the most important enactments were the public-assistance and child welfare provisions of the Social Security Act. The public-assistance laws practically put an end to private poor relief and required accountable agencies in all 48 states and over 3,000 counties; the child welfare legislation helped build up public agencies and services, especially in rural areas. Professional social workers could give some advice and leadership during these changes, but there were too few professionals to staff the new agencies, even at the higher levels. It was feared that the direct services—social work in family service, mental hygiene, hospitals and schools, probation and parole, and neighborhood centers—might decline during the emergency, but they held fast and even grew.

Popular political support for major legislation ended in 1938 (well before the problem of unemployment was solved), but the process of professionalism moved on then and in the prosperous years that followed the war. The Council on Social Work Education, established in 1952, provided more vigorous leadership than earlier accrediting bodies. In 1955 seven associations of specialists in social work joined together in a single National Association of Social Workers (NASW), much strengthening their lobbying capability and introducing many useful professional publications and services. In the 1950s professional social workers were in a position to respond to the popular concern about child and family welfare, health and mental health, and juvenile delinquency. Private agencies expanded and enlisted professional direction; the great network of Catholic charities, growing with the parishes, reorganized along professional lines, and the Jewish agencies were the envy of the professional community. Every state government had its departments of public assistance, child welfare, health and mental health, and corrections, working usually with county or municipal agencies. In these agencies social workers did not have the sort of monopoly or authority that M.D.'s had in medical practice or lawyers in the courts, but it was widely acknowledged that the work they did was worth doing and that they had special qualifications to do it. Funds increased for training and research.

As of 1963 the basic historical trend seemed clear. For ninety years there had been a steady elaboration of welfare institutions and a steady strengthening of the professional sentiment and organizations of social workers. At the same time, there was a recurrent feeling that professional social workers had some larger charge than the efficient administration of the institutions and programs in which they were employed; they ought to look beyond such formal helping to some preventive action in the community, much as physicians looked from treating patients to action for public health. But the etiology of the dependent, defective, and delinquent classes was not so definite as the etiology of illness. There were impersonal or environmental forces or influences, but authorities did not agree on them. The difficulties were both technical and moral. Technically it was not clear what was amiss or what to do about it; morally it was *not* clear what a professional social worker ought to do about it or how. It *was* felt, however, that professional commitment extended beyond the technical responsibilities of administration to the ethical and political responsibilities of society at large.

Events of the 1960s dramatized this problem of identity. Social workers faced in the first place the familiar technical and administrative problems of income maintenance (especially public assistance) and direct services, the familiar gaps between theory and practice, promise and performance, needs and resources. The political enthusiasm of the decade aimed at poverty and racism, and it was plausible that these were "basic" problems, that there was a culture of poverty that was deeper than public assistance, probation, or mental-health clinics could reach, that racial prejudice frustrated the administration of many helpful programs and, more seriously, reduced the ability of its victims to respond. Beyond those problems were noticeable changes in the life style of the affluent and dominant majority, a malaise about personal relationships and work that was reflected in the much-discussed "generation gap" and the idea of a "countercul-ture." Some people envisioned a grand liberation, others a break-down of morality and authority. Beyond that, there were new inter-national problems, the cold war and relations with the Third World. In these circumstances the doubt about professional identity often came up. The gap between theory and practice, promise and perfor-mance raised questions of technical competence that were central to the administrative and professional core of social work. But even if caseworkers and group workers had a proper competence, should social workers put their efforts into helping individuals adapt to cir-cumstances, or should they turn rather to "institutional changes?" If so, which changes? And how? Should they take their place beside the union organizer or the civil rights leader and help them organize a following? If these leaders were divided, which side should they sup-port? What was the relation between movements for change in the United States and in other nations? Questions of technical compe-tence and of strategy and tactics in institutional change necessarily in-volved conceptions of professional identity and mission.

While in 1963 the issue of professional identity seemed much like that during the Progressive years and the New Deal, circum-stances had changed significantly. These included the institutional framework of social services, the organization and employment of the profession, the research capability in departments of social science, not to mention social agencies, and the changing constellation of people interested in the services as sponsors and users. When critics said in 1963 that institutions were not working well and might be improved, they had in mind a much different picture than people who made the same observation in 1933 or 1903. Obviously the in-stitutional framework was much bigger and more ramified, not just the income maintenance and direct-service programs that were classed under "social welfare" but also those in education, health, and labor. The argument in 1963 was not that there ought to be such institutions but that, having been created, they were not well con-ceived or effective. The critical judgments reflected a cumulation of knowledge, insight, and critical skill in pondering social problems and social organizations. The war on poverty began in the reflections of economists on improved statistics of the distribution of income and the variables associated with low income. The campaign against racism, which had once been entirely moral and constitutional, drew in the 1960s on an understanding of how racial discrimination contributed to personal and social disorganization. The argument that social-service bureaucracies were not accountable to their users—the argument for a degree of community control or consumer participation—rested not simply on claims of justice or entitlement but on a better understanding of administration and its tendencies. The demand that these bureaucracies be accountable to their funders rested on improvements in the formulation of objectives (policy analysis) and on better evaluative research.

When Porter Lee made his perceptive analysis of the identity problem in 1929, "Social Work as Cause and Function," he was thinking of the situation in the preceding decades: the "cause" he had in mind was a small group of philanthropists advocating a child labor law or a social-insurance program; the functionaries were an executive, a few supervisors, and a small work force of caseworkers or inspectors. When Daniel Moynihan outlined "The Professionalization of Reform" in 1965, *he* had in mind the institutionalization of expertise to improve managerial decisions and processes, what social workers would refer to as "indirect" or staff, as opposed to line, services. Into the traditional confrontation between the new cause and the vested interest stepped policy analysts and budget officers with their technical questions about costs and benefits or effectiveness; often it appeared that the vested interest was not a greedy capitalist but a myopic program manager. It was the President's Bureau of the Budget that supported community action in the war on poverty. Politically it was significant that many "causes" of the progressive years, child labor legislation and social insurance, for example, not to mention Prohibition, had little support among the people they were supposed to help, whereas the labor movement in the 1930s and the civil rights movement of the 1960s provided a broader political base.

The elaboration of programs in the 1960s gave added significance to the distinction made by Wilensky and Lebeaux in 1958 between the "residual" and "institutional" conceptions of social welfare. The idea of preventive legislation had in practice been pretty much limited to a "residual" conception. "Prevention" was related to particular agencies or programs. While its proponents said "Let's treat causes, not symptoms," they usually had in mind a public health analogy in which symptoms had a specific etiology and prevention would intervene in it. By implication, the "institutional" conception went much beyond this; it addressed not the prevention of symptoms, the correction of some particular circumstance or condition, but the general functions of the social system. It was somewhat as if a physician were more interested in measures to promote good health than in measures to treat illness. So, for example, if people were unemployed, the answer was not simply temporary relief, a public-works project, or unemployment insurance but an employment policy that had many parts: action deliberately to stimulate investment and create jobs, labor market arrangements to bring supply and demand together, and unemployment insurance and training grants to maintain income. This sort of thinking about unemployment would have been unlikely in 1933 because theoretical understanding of the economic system was rudimentary and so were the relevant institutional frameworks. It drew upon speculation about economic development in the Third World and the process of modernization, which brought out the reciprocal influences and trade-offs that planners had to understand and encompass. The same type of thinking appeared in the notion of "primary prevention" in forestalling mental illness, and in the scheme to open opportunities as a strategy to diminish delinquency. In 1971 the sociologist and social worker John Romanyshyn, in a textbook entitled *Social Welfare*, substituted the term *developmental* for *institutional* and organized the variety of interests and programs around the functions "social provision," including income maintenance; "socialization," including the programs for the family, education and recreation; and "social development," or community organization for social change.[3]

The significance of an institutional or developmental conception of social welfare for the problem of professional identity is that it much expands the subject matter and role of scientific and technical understanding in contemplating, deciding on, implementing, and evaluating programs, and it indicates a continuum between the kinds

3. John M. Romanyshyn, with the assistance of Annie L. Romanyshyn, *Social Welfare: Charity to Justice* (New York: Random House, 1971), pp. 4–5, 51–58. Romanyshyn does not emphasize the development of "indirect services" out of community organization in the way that I do; for that story see Ralph H. Kramer and Harry Specht, *Readings in Community Organization Practice*, 2d ed. (Englewood Cliffs, N.J.: Prentice-Hall, 1975), pp. 1–14, and the six articles on aspects of "Social Planning and Community Organization" in the *Encyclopedia of Social Work*, Seventeenth Issue (New York: National Association of Social Workers, 1977), II, 1404–53.

of knowledge needed and used at different levels of intervention. To some extent this continuum is institutionalized in professional instruction in "indirect services" and employment in management, policy analysis, and evaluative research as well as in "direct service." Of course professional social workers will have no monopoly on knowledge or skill at any particular point in the continuum, but it seems likely that there will be much work for people who are to some degree prepared to look at the whole, to parlay with different kinds of experts, and to act in different sorts of situations.

It may be objected that the knowledge base, as social workers put it, is so confused at any point along the continuum that the prospect of pulling the insights together is dubious, and it is certainly true that the interventions and practice skills at any level do not seem to be very effective. But the burden of this history is that social-welfare institutions and the profession of social work did not grow into their present prominence because of their theoretical elegance or practical success. They took form because a powerful and growing group in society—the urban business and professional class—was willing to support them. Its support was persistent, but never united or strong; it was a feeling that, despite confusions and frustrations, social work was on the right track. The right track was essentially the idea that if people were in trouble or need, someone ought to help, and that insofar as helping was organized—insofar as it took the form of a social agency—it ought to be rational, with a scientific elucidation of means and ends.

The record is clear enough to reject two simple historical interpretations of social work: that its proponents and practitioners were essentially agents of the status quo whose business was social control for prudential reasons, or that they were somehow political representatives of the poor and disadvantaged in a struggle for social justice. My interpretation is that the development of our welfare programs and professional social work institutionalized in an American setting certain assumptions of a quasi-religious character in historic liberalism.

The theory of liberalism, as it took form in the seventeenth century, held that society was a collection of individuals, each more or less selfishly pursuing his own interests and goals, and that it was quite proper for individuals to formulate and pursue their own goals, to enjoy "life, liberty, and the pursuit of happiness" as they saw fit.

This doctrine might have justified a self-seeking anarchy, a war of all against all, but that tendency was supposed to be limited by enlightened self-interest, a rational quality in human nature that might rise above immediate desires and conflicts to envision common interests and objectives. Government, in this theory, had the functions of both protecting individual interests and providing a machinery for negotiating and implementing common interests. To rational people politics and negotiation were a substitute for force, and the machinery of a liberal government—constitutions, elections, legislatures, courts—was a set of devices by which powerful people and interests might persuade and negotiate to mutual advantage.

There were obviously religious assumptions in this doctrine—in the importance ascribed to the privacy, integrity, and autonomy of the individual, for example—and formal religion also put the pursuit of happiness into a larger context, both the theological drama of salvation by faith in God and the implications of Christian doctrine for social life. The religious tradition recognized the evil aspect of the individuality of people and the predominance of their self-interested and self-seeking (sinful) motives, but it also held that there were in human personality unselfish motives, of fellow-feeling and self-sacrifice, of personal and communal responsibility for the well-being of others, as if society were not a collection of selfish individuals but more like a big family. It held that these motives were a touch of divinity.

The idea of scientific charity or philanthropy brought together these two motives—a rational self-interest or prudence and a feeling of sympathy and helpfulness. So the tradition of social work has been to recognize and assert the dignity and poignancy of individual existence and the personal responsibility of those who help and those who are helped; but it has also consistently tried to build up the bonds of mutual sympathy and responsibility in the family, in the neighborhood, and among the larger divisions of classes and groups in the community.

In the 1970s the problem has taken on a new dimension. Liberal economics, the foundation of the welfare state, always put its trust in increased production; the stresses of poverty and inequality would be relieved by that remedy. Ecologists now argue, however, that natural resources are strictly limited and that we shall have to do with less and share it more. Moreover, liberalism was a political economy of the national state; each historic welfare state developed more or less in political isolation. Now the depletion of resources in wealthy nations is much complicated by the dangers of overpopulation in the Third World; as a nation (or group of nations) we shall have to share more with others. The problems that appeared in our social development, and that are by no means solved, now become obvious on a global scale. The aspiration of social work to deal with characters and events in a humane and scientific way faces an even greater test than it has received in the society of its origin.

References and Guide
to the Literature

I USUALLY REFER to publications by author and date; for full citation see
the bibliography.

Primary sources include publications and archives of agencies that administered programs, records of groups that tried to influence or determine
policy, and papers of individuals. There is a significant difference in locating
records of private and public agencies and groups. Materials about private
efforts are scattered and hard to find. Clarke Chambers' article on "Archives
of Social Welfare" mentions many library collections, and Chambers has
gathered material from many national voluntary associations and leaders
into the Social Welfare History Archives at the University of Minnesota.
Other likely places to look are divinity school libraries, which often have
documents from the late nineteenth century related to charity or "Christian
sociology," and schools of agriculture, which may have valuable material on
rural problems. Schools of social work have M.S.W. theses that go back to
the 1930s or before; whatever their merits as academic psychology, political
science, or sociology, they are often good description, much better than formal reports, personal recollections, or popular journalism. Doctoral disserta-
tions in social work and social welfare are abstracted in the *Social Service
Review* (September issues, 1954–1974) and thereafter in *Social Work Research and Abstracts* (formerly *Abstracts for Social Workers*).

Public records have been collected more systematically than those of
private associations and individuals, especially in recent years. They divide
into local, state and federal, legislative, executive, and judicial (court decisions or attorney generals' opinions are sometimes especially illuminating).
In general, they are accessible through well-established finding aids for
public and legal documents and archives. Before 1930 they are generally
scattered and incomplete. For the nineteenth century the tomes of Adelaide

359

Hasse provide remarkable bibliographies for the thirteen states she surveyed (California, Delaware, Illinois, Kentucky, Maine, Massachusetts, New Hampshire, New Jersey, New York, Ohio, Pennsylvania, Rhode Island, and Vermont), in which state welfare institutions are usually included under the rubric of "maintenance." State labor bureaus, which appeared on the scene after 1869, often inquired into social problems and welfare agencies in their early years; these documents are accessible in the *Index of All Reports Issued by Bureaus of Labor Statistics in the United States Prior to 1902*, published by the U.S. Department of Labor in 1902. The "Subject Index of Bulletins of the Bureau of Labor Statistics," *Bulletin* 174 of the U.S. Bureau of Labor Statistics (1915) refers to summaries in the *Bulletin* of worthwhile reports by state bureaus. Beginning in 1915 the *Public Affairs Information Service* (PAIS), an invaluable finding aid, picks up many public documents of all kinds at all levels, as well as a wide range of nongovernmental publications.

The quality of public records improves after 1930, when the federal government got involved in relief, social insurance, and services. A good starting point is Abe Bortz's *Social Security Sources in Federal Records, 1934–1950;* it both mentions specific material and suggests the variety of documents that may be available. In federal grant in-aid programs, which played so large a part after 1935, the "feds" supervised the states and (usually) the states supervised the counties. The records of supervisory officials, where they can be recovered, may be rich in information and insights about local problems and politics as well as administration. My own interest in these records of social insurance and public assistance has been to study the development of welfare programs, but I suppose that in the long run their great use will be to illuminate the lives of recipients or clients in the agenda of social history.

While agency records are likely to be scattered and hard to manage, several serial publications furnish readily available primary sources. The most important is the annual proceedings of the National Conference on Social Welfare, earlier called National Conference on Charities and Correction (1874–1917) and National Conference of Social Work (1918–1948). There are indexes in 1906 and 1933. Bruno's survey (1957) rests on these proceedings and gives them some background and thematic continuity. *Survey* magazine (1909–1952) was for decades the liveliest journal of social reform and the closest to social workers. It also has excellent pictures. Professor Chambers has its papers in the Social Welfare History Archives, and they are the basis of his biography of Paul Kellogg, its editor. Other widely available periodicals are *Mental Hygiene* (1917–　　), published by the National Association for Mental Health (originally National Committee for Mental Hygiene); *Social Casework* (1920–　　), published by the Family Service Association and originally called *The Family; The Social Service*

Review (1927–   ), a scholarly journal published by the University of Chicago School of Social Service Administration ("Forty-Year Index, 1927–1966," in vol. 42, March 1968). Beginning in 1927 the *Social Work Yearbook* presented brief, authoritative articles and bibliography on many subjects, with a helpful directory. It appeared every two or three years until 1960, when it was succeeded by a more elaborate *Encyclopedia of Social Work* in 1965, 1971, and 1977. *Child Welfare*, published by the Child Welfare League of America, begins in 1931; *Public Welfare*, published by the American Public Welfare Association, in 1943; and the *Social Security Bulletin*, issued by the Social Security Board, in 1938.

A number of volumes present sources. *Public Welfare Administration* (1927, rev. ed. 1938), edited by Sophonisba Breckinridge, brings together historical documents on state and local agencies and programs with comment and bibliography; the 1938 edition is a reprint with a large new section on the New Deal years. Grace Abbott's *The Child and the State* (2 vols., 1938), includes many historical documents and clear, authoritative essays on legislation about children. It is supplemented broadly, but not supplanted, by *Children and Youth in America: A Documentary History*, edited by Robert Bremner (1970–1974) which includes material on family life, education, health, and minority groups, with valuable introductions and bibliography. *Public Assistance* (1940), edited by Edith Abbott, contains many historic documents that focus on the issues of the 1930s, particularly the right to relief, and it has an excellent section on financing medical care.

A few collections of documents are teaching tools: *The Heritage of American Social Work*, by the Pumphreys (1961), emphasizes professional development to 1940; Roy Lubove gathered together some important nineteenth-century English documents on poor relief and medical care in *Social Welfare in Transition* (1966); his *Poverty and Social Welfare in the United States* (1972) brings together articles around issues of the 1960s, as does *On Their Own*, by the Rothmans. The Arno Press has an ambitious program of reprinting significant books in the history of social welfare; see its announcements, with helpful bibliographical notes, for the series "Children and Youth," "Criminal Justice," "Mental Illness," "Poverty," and "Social Problems."

The survey histories of the field and the profession are disparate in their focus and interpretation, reflecting the state of historical thought on the subject. Still, they each have some peculiar value. Nathan Cohen's (1958) is a primary source for what well-informed social workers of that decade thought was their significant past, with judicious comment on the years after 1930. Woodroofe (1962) brings together events in England and the United States, with some attention to professionalization, whereas Mencher (1967), relates policy developments about income maintenance in the two nations. Coll

(1969) focuses on poor relief before 1930. Trattner (1974) is strong on child welfare and public health; Axinn and Levin (1975) make an interesting comparison between policy toward veterans and toward blacks. Sir Ernest Barker's little book (reprinted 1945), which deserves to be more widely read, puts the international story in a different framework, the general rationalization of the European state system as it appeared to a political scientist in the 1920s, when political science was largely constitutional history. Rimlinger (1971) puts events in the perspective of economic development as conceived by an economist.

Articles on the history of social welfare are abstracted in *Social Work Research and Abstracts*.

Chapter 1: American Society, 1815–1845: The Rural Democracy

Starting points in history are more or less arbitrary. Since my opening theme is how the problems, interests, and ideas of city people impinged on an agrarian order, I begin with a tableau of the preindustrial way of life. This interpretation suggested itself in my work on state institutions and reflected the divisions apparent in state politics; it was in accord with my earlier study of labor statistics and legislation and with an interpretation of the Jacksonian period that dominated the 1950s, in works such as those of Curti (1943, rev. ed. 1964), Gabriel (1956), and Tyler (1944), and drew much from Alexis de Tocqueville, *Democracy in America* (first published 1835). The picture of an ebullient equalitarian yeomanry has been sharply challenged by Edward Pessen (1973), who presents impressive data about the existence and persistence of great extremes of wealth during these years. His data refer mostly to New York (city), which was not typical of the ordinary distribution of wealth, and my notion of the homogeneous democratic society includes much more than economic equality. Two important books point to a significant transition at the end of the colonial period: Raymond Mohl, *Poverty in New York*, 1783–1825 (1971), uncovers a surprising amount of dependency and relief, which, he says, turned benevolent humanitarians into punitive moralists. David Rothman, *Discovery of the Asylum* (1971), taking a broader view, relates the characteristics of nineteenth-century institutions to a sense of disorder in the wake of the breakdown of the hierarchical social structure of colonial times. In my view the main successor to the colonial social structure was what I call the rural democracy, not the anxious city people he writes about; what he sees as the end of an earlier process I see as the beginning of a new one.

Meanwhile economic historians have been doing much interesting work on the transition from an agrarian to an industrial order under their rubrics of economic development and productivity. Much of the interest in their work is its relationship to economic theory, and their writing is obscure to laymen. On the earlier period I found especially helpful George Taylor's "American Economic Growth Before 1840" (1964) and Lebergott's *Manpower in Economic Growth* (1964).

Representative contemporary statements about the relationship of non-European minorities to social problems in the 1830s are Tocqueville, vol. I, ch. 18; Thomas Sedgwick, *Public and Private Economy* (1836), pp. 257–59; and Alexander Everett, *New Ideas About Population* (1826), 29–32, 75–80. Sedgwick was a Jacksonian radical, Everett a conservative. There is no survey of philanthropic and self-help institutions among black Americans. Bremner (1970–1974) has documents and references about child welfare among minorities in the later period, and Billingsley (1972) has an interpretation of black self-help efforts for child welfare. On black history generally Franklin's survey (1964) is full and scholarly; he has an article on public welfare in the South during the Reconstruction (1970). Other helpful publications on black institutions are Pease (1963), Diner (1970), Moran (1971), Lide (1973), and Rabinowitz (1974). Olds's dissertation (1966) is the fullest account of the welfare work of the Freedmen's Bureau.

On policy toward Native Americans see Sar Levitan, *Indian Giving* (1975). The Council on Social Work Education has published bibliographies for social workers of materials on minority groups. These are mostly current but include some historical items: on blacks, Dunmore (1970); on Native Americans, Brennan (1972); on Chicanos, Navarro (1971); and on Asian-Americans, Kitano (1971). Gossett (1963) is a general history of the idea of race in the United States.

Chapter 2: Religious Ideas About Social Welfare, 1815–1845

Religious encyclopedias have good articles on the Jewish and Christian doctrines of charity in a theological framework. Brian Tierney's *Medieval Poor Law* (1959) gives a sympathetic statement of the charitable tradition and commentators on it. Sydney Ahlstrom's *Religious History of the American People* (1972) is a comprehensive account of American churches and teachings. American experience tended toward extremes: passionate revivalism on one hand and liberal Unitarianism on the other. Two books are important for the eighteenth-century background: Heimert (1966) brings out the democratic implications of its religious revival and Sydney James (1963) discusses the ideas of the Quakers, who dominated Pennsylvania and were leaders in much practical work in the early nineteenth century (and later). On the general ideas of the religious revival of the Jacksonian years and its significance for "benevolence," philanthropy, and social reform, see Timothy Smith (1957), Charles I. Foster (1960), Charles C. Cole, Jr. (1954), Clifford Griffin (1960), and D. G. Mathews (1969).

Summaries of the scholarly debate over the Protestant ethic are Robert W. Green (1973) and Reinhard Bendix (1967). Two important books about its significance in the English background are by R[ichard] H. Tawney (1926) and W[ilbur] K. Jordan (1959). See also Jordan's article, "The English Background of Modern Philanthropy" (1961). Miyakawa (1964) shows the significance of the discipline of the Protestant ethic on the frontier but ignores its implications for mutual aid. McClelland (1961) relates it to the "Achieving Society." *The Elements of Moral Science*, by Francis Wayland (1837, reprinted 1963), a college textbook that was very popular for a generation, states in a direct, clear way the association between the responsibilities and spirit of the so-called "Protestant ethic" and "benevolence" or charity.

Chapter 3: Secular Ideas About Social Welfare, 1815–1845

On liberalism in its European context I know nothing better than Ruggiero (1927), Thomas Marshall (1964), and Sabine (1961). General outlines of American political thought appear in Curti (1964) and Gabriel (1956). Three reflective elucidations are by Hartz (1955), Boorstin (1953), and Handlin (1961); they differ greatly, but the differences do not bear on my argument. Dorfman's five-volume *Economic Mind in American Civilization* (1946–1959) is comprehensive and detailed. Among primary sources on the reception of European liberalism, I found Sedgwick (1836) and Everett (1826) especially illuminating.

Tocqueville's analysis of American individualism and social action is in *Democracy in America*, vol. I, second book, chs. 2–5. Constance Smith (1972) is a bibliographical essay on voluntary institutions and their significance. Emerson's "Politics" is in his *Essays: Second Series* (1844). Gabriel's chapter on the Concord worthies is especially good. On the relation between highbrow social theory and popular notions about the self-made man and success, I follow the excellent work of Cawelti (1965).

Chapter 4: The Poor Law, 1815–1845

The poor law is the main topic of the historiography of social welfare. Most writing about it, reflecting English conditions and ideas, has emphasized its faults, earlier authors holding that it was too lax and more recent ones that it was too punitive. My interpretation is that in the period under consideration, and generally in rural society, it was a reasonable assertion of community responsibility and standards. The standards were certainly low in relation to those of city-bred business and professional people, but not in relation to those of hard-scrabble farmers. Blum (1971) sketches the early history of the European agricultural village. The best statement of the traditional rural arrangement and its decline in America is in Berthoff, part 1 (1971); like Rothman (1971), Berthoff emphasizes change and disorder rather than the persistence of the ideal of neighborly helpfulness; see his study of terrible conditions in the anthracite region (1965). The association between the religious inspiration of most of the "utopian communities" and the form of the rural village appears most clearly in their own presentations: Noyes's *History of American Socialisms* (1875, reprinted 1961) seems to me to have the best insight into their spirit. A recent history of the Mormons that emphasizes their social programs is Arrington (1976). The literature on the English poor law is large. Tierney (1959) puts its origin into the context of canon law; the initial legislation of 1536 is clarified in Fideler's "Christian Humanism and Poor Law Reform in Early Tudor England" (1974). The main reference is still the relevant volumes of the Webbs' great work on *English Local Government, The Old Poor Law* [before 1834] (1927), and *The Last Hundred Years* (1929). Recent interpretations are handily summarized and annotated in J. D. Marshall (1968) and M. Rose (1972).

A few items of special interest are Nassau Senior's article (1865, first published 1836), which gives the historical sense of the reformers of 1834; Polanyi's famous *Great Transformation* (1944) and Poynter (1969) interpret the argument leading up to the reform. De Schweinitz, *England's Road to Social Security* (1943), is a popular survey illuminated by a professional social worker's reflections on administration; it also suggests what partisans of social security in the 1930s thought was their usable past.

On the poor law in America, Klebaner's dissertation (1951; now printed by Arno Press) is a compendium based on statutes; it puzzles me that he did not find more difference between northern and southern states; Wisner's *Social Welfare in the South* (1970) pays more attention to administration and does make some distinctions, but a more thorough and analytical study of southern arrangements ought to be a high research priority. Bridenbaugh gives attention to poor relief in his accounts of colonial cities (1938, 1955), and Mohl (1971) is full on New York for the years 1783–1825.

Here is a list of histories of state poor law and welfare administration, arranged alphabetically by state. Most of these are chronicles of the law, with little background in social or intellectual (or for that matter political) history. The most analytical are those on California, Rhode Island, New

York, and New Jersey; those on Massachusetts and Pennsylvania are important because those states were important; that on North Carolina is interesting for the South; on Iowa for the midwest.

CALIFORNIA: Helen Valeska Bary and Frances Cahn, *Welfare Activities of Federal, State and Local Governments in California, 1850–1934* (Berkeley: University of California Press, 1936).

CALIFORNIA: James Leiby, "State Welfare Administration in California, 1879–1929," *Pacific Historical Review*, 41 (May 1972).

CALIFORNIA: James Leiby, "State Welfare Administration in California, 1930–1945," *Southern California Quarterly*, 55 (Fall 1973).

CONNECTICUT: Edward Capen, *The Historical Development of the Poor Law of Connecticut* (New York: Columbia University Press, 1905).

ILLINOIS: Sophonisba P. Breckenridge, *The Illinois Poor Law and Its Administration* (Chicago: University of Chicago Press, 1939).

INDIANA: Alice Shaffer, *The Indiana Poor Law* (Chicago: University of Chicago Press, 1936).

IOWA: John L. Gillin, *History of Poor Relief Legislation in Iowa* (Iowa City: State Historical Society of Iowa, 1914).

KANSAS: Grace A. Browning, *The Development of Poor Relief Legislation in Kansas* (Chicago: University of Chicago Press, 1935).

KENTUCKY: Emil McKee Sunley, *The Kentucky Poor Law 1792–1936* (Chicago: University of Chicago Press, 1942).

LOUISIANA: Elizabeth Wisner, *Public Welfare Administration in Louisiana* (Chicago: University of Chicago Press, 1930).

MASSACHUSETTS: Martha Derthick, *The Influence of Federal Grants: Public Assistance in Massachusetts* [1935–1969] (Cambridge, Mass.: Harvard University Press, 1970).

MASSACHUSETTS: Robert W. Kelso, *The History of Public Poor Relief in Massachusetts, 1620–1920* (Boston: Houghton Mifflin, 1922).

MICHIGAN: Isabell C. Bruce, *The Michigan Poor Law* (Chicago: University of Chicago Press, 1936).

MISSOURI: Fern Boan, *History of Poor Relief and Administration in Missouri* (Chicago: University of Chicago Press, 1941).

MONTANA: F. R. Veeder, *The Development of the Montana Poor Law, 1938* (Chicago: University of Chicago Press, 1941).

NEW JERSEY: James Leiby, *Charity and Correction in New Jersey: A History of State Welfare Institutions* (New Brunswick, N.J.: Rutgers University Press, 1967)

NEW YORK: David M. Schneider and Albert Deutsch, *The History of Public Welfare in New York*, 2 vols. (Chicago: University of Chicago Press, 1938–1941).

NORTH CAROLINA: Roy M. Brown, *Public Poor Relief in North Carolina* (Chapel Hill: University of North Carolina Press, 1928).
OHIO: Aileen E. Kennedy, *The Ohio Poor Law and Its Administration* (Chicago: University of Chicago Press, 1934).
PENNSYLVANIA: William C. Heffner, *History of Poor Relief Legislation in Pennsylvania, 1682–1913* (Cleona, Pa.: Holzapfel, 1913).
RHODE ISLAND: Margaret Creech, *Three Centuries of Poor Law Administration: A Study of Legislation in Rhode Island* (Chicago: University of Chicago Press, 1936).
WASHINGTON: Marion Hathway and John A. Rademaker, *Public Relief in Washington, 1853–1933* Washington Emergency Relief Administration, Pub. no. 1 (Olympia, Wash., 1934).

McMaster's old survey (1924) gives a good narrative account of efforts to reform poor relief in 1815–1830, based on newspaper accounts (IV, 522–49). Rothman (1971, ch. 7, 8) analyzes the hopes and plans of the reformers, as does Coll (1955). Breckinridge (1927) and Pumphrey give extracts from original resources, including those I cite in my text; others are in the Arno Press volumes, *The Almshouse Experience* (1971) and *The Jacksonians on the Poor* (1971). Abbott (1940) includes clear analysis of the legal questions.

Chapter 5: The Promise of the Institution, 1815–1845

Rothman (1971) has general accounts of the penitentiary, the insane asylum, the almshouse, and the orphanage and children's refuge; my book on New Jersey describes the range of institutions in that state from the perspective of state political interests.

Beaumont and Tocqueville's *On the Penitentiary System in the United States* (1833, reprinted 1964) is the best contemporary survey; their section on the refuges is on pp. 108–30. They do not deal with rural police and the rural jail; my sketchy reconstruction is inferred from court records and the comments of later reformers who wanted to set up special correctional institutions and reduce the political resources of the sheriff. Bruce Smith's *Rural Crime Control* (1933) has some historical information. On the penitentiary see the works of Negley Teeters (1935, 1957) and W. David Lewis (1965). General histories of corrections are Orlando Lewis (1922) and Blake McKelvey (1936). Recent histories of the children's refuge are Pickett (1969) and Mennel (1973). Hawes (1971) is a broad survey of the treatment of juvenile delinquency, with references to fiction and criminology. On programs in residential boarding schools for children of the elite, see MacLachlan (1970); on programs in the common schools, Michael Katz (1968).

I base my discussion of special education for the deaf and blind on the works of Harry Best (1914, 1919) and on Schwartz's biography of Samuel Gridley Howe (1956). Farrell (1956) is a general history of responses to the blind. M. Rosen (1976) collects many documents about the history of care of the mentally retarded.

The history of medicine is a well-developed field. For a general introduction see the books by Shryock (1947, 1960). George Rosen's book on public health (1958) is important for the early period. On the hospital I found especially useful Rosen's article (1963), Eaton's study of the origin of Massachusetts General Hospital (1957), and Charles Lawrence's *History of the Philadelphia Almshouses and Hospitals* (1905), which includes the story of "Old Blockley" (my references to the sale of cadavers from the almshouse and the "Board of Buzzards" are from pp. 198 and 352).

The history of provision for the mentally ill is also well developed. Foucault's interpretation of the European origins of moral treatment (1965) is stimulating but, I believe, misleading. Kathleen Jones (1972) is conventional and full on English developments. For the United States Henry Hurd's hospital-by-hospital account (4 vols., 1916) is still useful. Deutsch (1949) brought a journalist's pen and a reformer's temper to his survey, which embodies the hopes of the 1940s. A medical—that is, psychiatric—view is the collection of essays published by the American Psychiatric Association on its centennial, *One Hundred Years of American Psychiatry* (1944). There is a biography of Benjamin Rush by Goodman (1934). The life of Dorothea Dix by Helen Marshall (1937) does not supplant the older biography by Tiffany (1891). Dain (1964) describes changing concepts of insanity in the United States to 1860 and Grob (1966, 1973) the development of policy and institutions to 1875. These are careful, well-informed studies and interpretations. Less successful is Caplan (1969), which draws heavily on the recent enthusiasm for community mental health. On phrenology see J. Davies (1955).

The notion that the "humanitarian" and "benevolent" reforms of the new republic were really "conservative" efforts at "social control" touches much of the recent literature I have mentioned—Mohl (1971), W. David Lewis (1965), M. Katz (1968), Rothman (1971). Lois Banner's essay (1973) criticizes it, at least as far as it relates to religious benevolence, and Heale (1975, p. 321n.) has a bibliography and judicious comment. Grob's article "The Political System and Social Policy in the Nineteenth Century" (1976) has interesting observations and reflections about how the organization of political activity affected legislation and policy; his findings undermine the social control thesis. I believe that the history of the "humane" movement— for the protection of animals—throws light on the general motives of reformers; Harrison (1973) analyzes that activity in England.

Chapter 6: Urban Charities, 1845–1900

Historians of religion have written much about the "urban impact" on the churches, but their themes have been mostly intellectual history and the rise of the social gospel (which I discuss in chapter 9) rather than the practical charity of congregational life. Nelson Burr's extensive bibliography of religion in America (1961) scarcely mentions these good works; nor do the three volumes published by the National Council of Churches, *The Churches and Social Welfare* (1955–1956), which focus on activities at the denominational level. Historians of labor have not inquired into the ways working-class congregations helped their members who were in need. Technically this is *unorganized* charity, neighborly and ad hoc, but it is plainly a matrix in which helping by formal organizations arose. One gets a sense of its importance in the fact that both Charity Organization Societies and settlement houses wanted to animate and improve it; the institution of friendly visiting and the notion that personal considerations and relations are somehow central in helping came from this source.

Abell (1943) offers a good general view of Protestant social services. Carroll Smith Rosenberg (1971) presents a sympathetic picture of the city missionary movement in New York, 1812–1870. Dunstan (1966), on the City Missionary Society of Boston, pays attention to more recent years. Biographies that bring out the association between missionary work and social service include those of Joseph Tuckerman, by McColgan (1940), and of Charles Loring Brace, by his daughter Emma (1894). The YMCAs have had good historians: Howard Hopkins (1951) and Whiteside (1951). (The Young Women's Christian Association—YWCA—was organized in 1866 and performed similar services for working girls in the city: see Sims [1936].) On the Salvation Army, see the published dissertation by Lamb (1909) and the general survey by Wisbey (1955); Wisbey also has a history of the Volunteers of America (1954), which separated from the Army in 1896 and carried on a somewhat different type of service. Heasman (1962) appraises the social work of English evangelicals in this period.

My interpretation of immigrant religious and mutual-aid agencies draws largely on the works of Handlin (1941 [rev. 1972] and 1954), which present them as examples of group solidarity in the process of group identification. A good contemporary account is in *Charities* (magazine) for May and December 1904. O'Grady's *Catholic Charities* (1930) is a chronicle and survey. On the National Conference of Catholic Charities, see Gavin (1962). McColgan's *Century of Charity* (1951), on the St. Vincent de Paul Society, affords a good general picture of Catholic interests and ideas. There is a biography of Thomas Mulry, Catholic lay leader, by Helmes (1938).

In my text I do not differentiate Jewish charities except, later on, in their role in federated financing. Bogen (1917) is old but useful; Solomon (1956) tells about formative efforts among the Jewish community of Boston, Lurie (1961) about the Jewish federation movement.

Bremner (1970–1974) has extensive selections on issues in the care of dependent children (II, 247–438). Old but still useful summaries are Folks (1902) and Warner (1894). F. Lane (1932) describes institutional care. Brace's *Dangerous Classes of New York* (1872) is a good introduction; note that the classes in question are neglected youth, not proletarian workers, and the danger is their affinity for criminal and political corruption, not class war. On the placing-out system, see Langsam (1964). On the question of state subsidies to charity and public education in New York, see Pratt (1967). An interpretation of church–state relations and subsidies in social welfare is Coughlin (1965).

Warner (1894) gives a contemporary description of municipal charities from the reformer's point of view, as does Julia Lathrop's article, "The Cook County Charities," in *Hull-House Maps and Papers* (1895); see also James Brown (1941) and Lawrence (1905). McKelvey (1963) gives a general picture of urban institutions, with many references. Zink's study of urban bosses (1930) notes that "generosity to the poor" was their most typical quality (p. 63), and Handlin (1954, ch. 7) presents a sympathetic picture. The generous boss speaks for himself in Riordan's *Plunkitt of Tammany Hall* (1963). Pratt's article, "Boss Tweed's Public Welfare Program" (1961), shows how the boss used public funds to subsidize private charities. Forthal's "Relief and Friendly Service by Political Precinct Leaders" (1933) reports a scholarly inquiry into the Chicago machine.

Chapter 7: Philanthropy and Science, 1850–1900: State Institutions

There is a sketch of the (British) National Association for the Promotion of Social Sciences in Abrams, *Origins of British Sociology, 1863–1914* (1968); the volume as a whole is valuable background for American developments. Luther and Jessie Bernard have a full account of the American Social Science Association (1943). Betty Broadhurst's dissertation (1971), available through University Microfilms, gives an account of the Social Science Association in the context of the development of academic instruction in the subject, particularly at Johns Hopkins University; focusing on Herbert B. Adams, Richard T. Ely, Amos Warner, and Franklin Sanborn, Broadhurst brings out many interesting features and relationships of the movement. Furner (1975) describes the professionalization of American Social Science. Bremner's *From the Depths* (1956) is a broad survey of philanthropic and reform-minded responses to urban poverty, with particularly valuable discussions of statistical investigations and of imaginative literature; see also his article "Scientific Philanthropy" (1956). My own interpretation is based mostly on primary sources that are rich and provide many good introductions. Alexander Johnson's memoirs, *Adventures in Social Welfare* (1923), shows very well the underlying spirit of and relations between state institutions and boards and charity organization societies. So does Amos Warner's classic survey, *American Charities* (1894); Broadhurst has biographical detail on Warner, and my article (1963) analyzes his leading ideas and later editions of his survey (finally revised in 1930); the volume has a good contemporary bibliography. Other contemporary surveys include the volumes of the U.S. Census of 1880 and 1890 on the subject "Dependent, Defective, and Delinquent Classes," which have admirable introductions and analyses by Frederick Wines. The Catalog of U.S. Census publications (1945) gives many other references. Many statistics, from both the Census and Labor Bureaus, are summarized handily and interpreted judiciously in Carroll Wright's *Practical Sociology* (rev. ed., 1909). The National Conference of Charities and Corrections in 1893 has brief authoritative surveys of the work of its first twenty years. Other items of interest on scientific philanthropy include Sanborn's recollections, "The First State Boards of Charities" (1904); Frederick Wines's account of the growth of the National Conference (1905); and the Conference proceedings for 1895, where relationships between academic social science and practical work were a focus. Bliss, *Encyclopedia of Social Reform* (1908), is a helpful contemporary reference. Franklin, "Public Welfare in the South During the Reconstruction Era" (1970), emphasizes relief. James Bryce (1871) gives an English view of American poor relief that did not get into his *American Commonwealth*.

My account ignores the influence of the Civil War, which stimulated philanthropy: Bremner's article (1960) lays out these efforts and their practical significance. Olds's dissertation describes the work of the Freedmen's Bureau. Fredrickson's *Inner Civil War* (1965) builds up an interpretation of the postwar relationship between philanthropy and science that differs from mine. A full interpretation of the significance of science for social reform in these years should include the thinking behind labor statistics (see Leiby [1960]), public health (Trattner [1974] has a good chapter and Rosenkrantz [1972] is a good interpretation with a full bibliography), and education (Cremin [1961] is a start). Current interpretations seem to me to be misleading inasmuch as they look at the nation as a whole; the picture I get is of particular metropolitan cultures that were rather self-contained and distinctive, and of course the significant locus of legislation in the late nineteenth century was the state capital. In fact historians tend to give leaders in New York and Boston more influence than they had; this is why, in my text, I emphasize how few were the partisans of scientific philanthropy and how unusual was their concern amid the complacent multitudes. Gettleman

(1963, 1975), Hall (1974, 1975), and Naylor (1975) are Marxist interpretations, full of dark thoughts about philanthropy.

The State Boards of Charities dominated the National Conference for many years, and its proceedings give authoritative statements about both organizational and substantial problems. Breckinridge (1938) examines their history and work and reprints many important documents. Many histories of state poor laws describe the work of the boards: see especially Schneider and Deutsch on New York (1941) and mine on New Jersey (1967) and California (1972, 1973). Josephine Shaw Lowell has a sympathetic biographer in Stewart (1911), with documents; see also Taylor's article on her (1963). Sanborn's autobiography (1909) dwells on his association with the transcendentalists of Concord rather than his later work in social science and administration. Alexander Johnson contributes an "appreciation" of Sanborn's later career to *Survey*, March 10, 1917.

On corrections after the Civl War, see, in addition to the general surveys cited in chapter 5, Enoch C. Wines and Theodore W. Dwight, *Report on the Prisons and Reformatories of the United States and Canada* (1867), Frederick Wines's *Report* for the Census of 1880 and his later volume (1919); and Charles Henderson's four-volume work for the Russell Sage Foundation in 1910. On convict labor in the South see Fletcher Green (1969). Roger Lane has a critical interpretation of local crime statistics (1968) and a book with critical bibliography on the development of local police (1967), a subject I pass by in my text.

President Pierce's veto of federal aid for state insane asylums is excerpted with discussion in Breckinridge (1938), and there is some analysis in Marshall (1937). Grob's survey of mental health policy (1973) carries the story to 1875; his history of the Worcester State Hospital goes forward to 1930. For the rest, I have relied on the general works cited for chapter 5 and my own studies of state institutions in New Jersey (1967). There is a biographical notice of Dugdale by Edwin Shephard (1884). Hofstadter's *Social Darwinism* (1959) brings out the connection with eugenics. There were several types of state institutions that I do not mention in my text, for Civil War veterans, their orphans and, toward the end of the period, inebriates, epileptics, and the tuberculous.

Chapter 8: Charity Organization and Social Settlements, 1877–1920

On English developments see Young and Ashton (1956) and Woodroofe (1962).

Because the poor law reformers of the 1830s and the charity organizers of the 1870s ignored the impersonal pressures toward personal disorganization and because their notion of science was uncritical, they have fared poorly with twentieth-century historians. De Schweinitz (1943) has sympathetic chapters, and McColgan's biography of Joseph Tuckerman (1940)—the American Chalmers—is favorable; so are Watson's book on the COS (1922), which has a good deal of historical information; Margaret Rich's history of the family welfare association (1956); and Florence Waite's story of the Cleveland agency (1960). But these accounts are uncritical when not inept. To recapture the consciousness of the charity organizers, their battle against obtrusive complacency, self-defeating sentimentality, and political corruption, and for personal and community responsibility, one best turns to their own works. For the English background, Mackay's history of the poor law (1899) defends the reformers of 1834; Loch's *Charity and Social Life* (1910) is a brief, cogent history of charity that supports the COS view; Bosanquet's history of the London Charity Organization Society (1914) is candid and forceful. Recent unsympathetic interpretations by professional historians are the volumes by Mowat (1961) and Huggins (1971) and the chapters in Woodroofe (1962) and Lubove (1965).

On the American side, the matrix of charity organization in the good works of good women is sketched in Treudley (1940) and Melder (1967); I have found particularly helpful the essays by Heale, "From City Fathers to Social Critics: Humanitarianism and Government in New York, 1790–1860" (1976) and "Patterns of Benevolence: Organized Philanthropy in the Cities of New York, 1830–1860" (1976), which give a different picture of New York from that of Mohl (1970, 1971). On the Association for the Improvement of the Condition of the Poor, a predecessor of the New York COS, see Rosenberg (1971) and the hard-to-find but excellent manuscript by Lillian Brandt (1942). On a predecessor of charity organization in Chicago, see Otto Nelson (1966) and Naylor (1971—a Marxist view). There are articles on Louisa Lee Schuyler, an important woman around New York, by Cross (1961) and Trattner (1967), biographies of Josephine Shaw Lowell by Stewart (1911) and Margaret Rich (1956), and an article on her by Lloyd Taylor (1963). On Gurteen, who introduced the COS into the United States, see Verl Lewis (1966), which is based on his doctoral dissertation (1954). On Oscar McCulloch, and more generally the situation in Indiana, see Weeks (1965, 1976).

On the COS in the United States, Lowell (1884) is essential; the Proceedings of the National Conference of Charities and Correction are full of material, and the summaries by contemporaries, particularly the Conference of 1893, Warner (1894), and Alexander Johnson (1923), are a good start. Robert Woods (1895) is a contemporary survey of urban poverty and its relief. Devine (1939) is an interesting reminiscence of the New York scene.

As for secondary accounts of particular cities, I know of only two—Waite on Cleveland (1960), by a social worker, and Huggins on Boston (1971), by a historian writing in the spirit of the 1960s. Weeks (1965, 1977) includes much about Indianapolis, as does Seeley (1957). More such researches might prove interesting and useful.

On the transiton from charity organization to professional social work, the main secondary work is Lubove (1965). It is much less sympathetic than the interpretation in my text: Lubove thinks the professional demiurge was status rather than service, "bureaucratic imperatives" rather than the urgency of helpfulness. Brackett's contemporary account (1903) is more favorable to professionalism, as is Rich's (1956); I have also found the articles on the friendly visitor by Dorothy Becker (1963, 1964) helpful, and on Mary Richmond I have followed the excellent dissertation by Pumphrey (1956). Richmond's publications are central; fortunately she wrote well and her important articles are collected in *The Long View* (1930), with good annotations. See also Klein's article (1931). On Francis McLean, I follow Ormsby's biography (1970). Cannon (1952) recounts the origin of medical social work, which I ignore in my text.

Because of their association with progressive politics, the settlement houses have gotten more attention than any topic in this history. *Spearheads for Reform*, by Allen Davis (1967), is the leading work in this genre, with a full bibliography. Davis also has a good brief account of Hull House (1969) and an excellent biography of Jane Addams (1973); for different interpretations of Addams' career see Levine (1971) and the selection of her works edited by Lasch (1965). Settlement house leaders spoke very well for themselves—Addams, Graham Taylor, Robert Woods, Lillian Wald, and Mary Simkovitch among them—but neither they nor their enthusiastic chroniclers dealt much with the technical side of settlement work that interests me. A partial exception is Louse Wade's excellent biography of Graham Taylor (1964). Pacey, *Readings in the Development of Settlement Work* (1950), is some help, but I have relied mainly on the writings of Robert Woods. His "Social Work: A New Profession" (1905) is an early statement; *The Settlement Horizon* (1922) and *Neighborhood in Nation Building* (1923) are comprehensive and critical. There is a biography by his wife, Eleanor Woods (1929). Hunter (1902) makes a contemporary statement of the relationship between the COS and the settlement house, and Addams' *Democracy and Social Ethics* (1909)—an important book—has a good chapter on the problems of the charity worker. Urwick (1914) compares the movement in Britain and the United States.

On the peculiar attraction of the settlements for women, see Rousmaniere (1970) and Conway (1971, 1972).

On settlement houses in the Depression, see Trolander (1975).

Chapter 9: The Progressive Years, 1900–1919

On the changes in liberalism, see the surveys by Sabine (1961) and Ruggiero (1959); Girvetz (1963) is specific on the American scene, Hofstadter (1959) on social Darwinism. Mann (1956) notes British influences on American social reform. Abell (1943) and May (1949) put the social gospel into the context of responses to urban problems; Handy (1966) is a recent anthology, and Ahlstrom (1972) has a good chapter that puts the social gospel into the context of religious liberalism (not the same as political or social liberalism) and of the continuing strength of more orthodox or fundamentalist views. Gavin (1962) tells how American Catholics, following the papal encyclicals, lent organized support to social legislation that was also supported by the social gospelers. General intellectual histories, such as Curti (1964) and Gabriel (1956), have interpretations of the relationship between social science, religion, and social reform.

On the specific subject of ideas about and programs for poverty in the late nineteenth century and the progressive period, Bremner's *From the Depths* (1956) is the best starting point. My interpretation emphasizes more than his the distinction between pauperism and poverty, the significance of the idea of minima, and the technical interests of the reformers. On the significance of Charles Booth, see Abrams (1968) and Simey (1960). In my text I do not mention the important (English) social survey by Seebohm Rowntree (1902): see Asa Briggs's biography (1961). On the association between the National Conference of Charities and Correction and the Progressive party of 1912, see Chambers's biography of Paul Kellogg (1971) and Davis' *Spearheads for Reform* (1967). Father Ryan's autobiography (1941) is interesting.

Bremner's collection of sources, *Children and Youth* (1970–1974), has documents and annotations on all aspects of child welfare. Folks's early book (1902) is still useful, as is Thurston's (1930). Trattner's biography of Folks (1968) is the best view on the White House Conference, and it puts the many interests of Folks's career in perspective. Trattner's volume on child labor (1970) covers the technical and political sides of that question through the 1920s. Goldmark's biography of Florence Kelley (1953) is in part a personal reminiscence; the later volume by Blumberg (1966) deals with Kelley's early years. On the Children's Bureau see the unpublished dissertation by Weiss (1974).

My interpretation of the origin of the juvenile court follows the conventional line in the sources cited in my text; see also Flynn (1954) and Judge Ben Lindsey's story of his work (1925). A revisionist view in the spirit of the 1960s is Platt (1969).

Davis (1967) and Chambers (1971) show how social workers looked on the war; my interpretation of its actual impact is based mostly on the primary sources cited in the text. Bremner (1960) has a good chapter on the general wartime philanthropic effort; on the Red Cross see Dulles (1950). On "home service" see Richmond's article in *The Long View* (1930) and Watts's article (1964).

Three important reforms in which social workers were interested, which I omit from my text for reasons of space, are housing reform (see Lubove [1962], the effort to eliminate tuberculosis (see Shryock [1957]), and the special efforts to help disadvantaged immigrants and blacks (see Davis [1967] and, on the National Urban League, Parris and Brooks [1971] and Weiss [1974]).

Chapter 10: The 1920s: Constructive Ideas

The picture of the 1920s as a conservative period in the history of social welfare between two eras of reform is well presented in Clarke Chambers' *Seedtime of Reform* (1963) and his biography of Paul Kellogg (1971) as well as Trattner's history of the Child Labor Committee (1970). Other important monographs from this point of view are Bernstein's history of labor (1960) and Lemons' study of "social feminism" (1973), or what women did when they got the vote. These and many similar interpretations have in common the facts they they find their main continuity in national politics—the transition from progressivism to New Deal—and their sources in the writings of individuals and associations interested in social legislation. My interpretation is built up largely from primary sources related to other interests, specifically, public and private welfare organization at the state and local levels, professional schools and associations, and business and private philanthropy; these are different parts of the picture and, I believe, show much constructive work.

Some of these sources are readily available. One is the 1930 edition of Amos Warner's oft-reissued text *American Charities*, revised by Stuart Queen and Ernest Harper. Queen had had substantial experience in welfare administration and social-work education; both he and Harper were well-known scholars, and he would become president of the American Sociological Association. The book, written from a definite historical and professional perspective that I try to evoke in my text, is comprehensive and critical, with a good bibliography. Another helpful survey text is *Poverty and Dependency* (1926), by John L. Gillin, a sociologist who had also had practical experience. The *Annals* of the American Academy of Political and Social Science are an excellent source in this period. The *Social Work Yearbook* (beginning 1927) gives brief, authoritative articles and bibliography. On general developments, *Recent Social Trends* (1933), published by the President's Research Committee on Social Trends, gives authoritative and factual presentations; Karl has an interesting article (1969) that gives the Committee's background in the "technological optimism" of the Hoover years. See also Hawley (1974) on Hoover's work as Secretary of Commerce. *The Encyclopedia of Social Science* (15 vols., 1930–1934) is an excellent source for contemporary thought and developments.

With regard to secondary works on the economy, I found that George Soule (1947) held up well. On scientific management, see Haber (1964); on personnel management, Eilbert (1950); on "industrial welfare," Brandes (1976).

Bremner's brief history of American philanthropy (1960) opens up the primary sources on foundations; particular foundations often have histories, for example, that of the Russell Sage Foundation by Glenn et al. (1947) and of the Commonwealth Fund (1963). My general interpretation of the interests of businessmen draws on Morrell Heald, *The Social Responsibilities of Business* (1970). On fund raising generally, see Cutlip's useful history (1965), which has a chapter on the 1920s. Lubove (1965) has an insightful chapter on fund raising and community chests; see also the good contemporary book by Norton (1927).

On the rise of public administration and its importance, see Dahlberg (1966) and Schiesl (1977). My discussion of public welfare draws on my own publications (1967, 1973) and on oral history interviews with Frank Bane (1965) and Helen Valeska Bary (1972). Important contemporary works are by Odum (1923) and Breckinridge (1938).

On professional social work in the 1920s, Warner (1930) is a full contemporary statement, Lubove (1965) a modern analysis that brings out the influence of psychiatry. Works on special subjects include Dillick on community organization (1953), Chute on probation (1956), and Cannon on medical social work (1952). There are interesting autobiographies by Bertha Reynolds (1963) and Daisy Lee Worcester (1964); Virginia Robinson has a good biography of Jessie Taft (1962), the doyenne of the Philadelphia school, and Konopka of Lindemann (1958). An important part of this story is the history of professional education. There are accounts of the New York School by Meier (1954), of the Cleveland School by Campbell (1967), of the Catholic University School by Lawler (1951), and of the Simmons (Boston) School by Channing (1954). On the Chicago School see the reminiscences about Sophonisba Breckinridge by Edith Abbott and others (1948); of Edith Abbott by Wisner (1958); and the article by Helen Wright (1954). Edith Abbott (rev. ed., 1942) presents her views on professional education and other subjects. More work along this line would be illuminating, particularly about the Chicago School. As for the supposed "psychiatric deluge" that overtook social work and social-work education in the 1920s, see the careful article by Alexander (1972).

Chapter 11: Social Insurance and Pensions Before 1930

I have found no general history of the idea of insurance that relates its various forms. My account of the rise of commerical insurance is pieced together from secondary sources too numerous and fragmentary to detail. Some are company histories; others are about types of contracts. Nelli (1971) is an annotated bibliography. For a brief general interpretation related to economic and social history, I found nothing better than the article by Alfred Manes in the *Encyclopedia of the Social Sciences*, VIII, 94–98.

On friendly societies and fraternals in England, see Gosden (1961); there is no comparable work on those in the United States.

Bismarck's program of social insurance in Germany has received surprisingly little attention, in English at least. Dawson's old account (1912) is the most valuable; Braun's (1956) is a more modern analysis but brief. On England, De Schweinitz (1943) is brief and simple; Bentley Gilbert (1966) is very good on the political interests at stake; and T. H. Marshall (1975) puts the income maintenance programs in the larger perspective of the rise of the welfare state in England.

This chapter parallels Lubove's well-researched volume, *The Struggle for Social Security in America*, 1900–1935 (1968). His interpretation emphasizes the resistance that lay in the American tradition of voluntarism; I bring out the ethical and practical interest in the institutions in relation to the tradition of charity and the importance of the ethnic heterogeneity of the population. (Jane Addams thought our ethnic divisions were an important obstacle to social insurance; see her thoughtful remarks in that good book, *Newer Ideals of Peace* [New York: Macmillan, 1907], pp. 151f.). Rubinow (1934) and Epstein (rev. ed., 1938) are detailed contemporary histories by men who were leaders in the movement for modern income maintenance programs; Rubinow's is particularly lucid and interesting, Epstein's more technical. E. S. Corwin has a characteristically perceptive article on constitutional problems (1917). On the debate over unemployment insurance, Daniel Nelson's illuminating study (1969) is much more favorable to the Wisconsin point of view than is Lubove. Paul Douglas's autobiography (1972) has many firsthand comments on the campaign for social insurance.

The importance of veterans' legislation in the history of social welfare has not been sufficiently recognized. The President's Commission on Veterans' Pensions *Report* (1956) has an authoritative staff report on "The Historical Development of Veterans' Benefits in the United States." Useful interpretative histories include Glasson (1918) and M. Dearing (1952).

On "widow's pensions" see, in addition to the surveys by Lubove, Rubinow, and Epstein, the sources collected in Bremner (1970–1974), II, 369–97. Mary Richmond's articles on the subject are reprinted in *The Long View* (1930). On pensions for the blind, see Best (1919), and on services for the blind generally, Farrell (1956).

Chapter 12: Relief and Social Security, 1930–1946

On Hoover's policies, see Warren (1959) and Romasco (1965). Chambers (1963) and Trattner (1968) have good chapters on how the Depression appeared to social workers. Some basic statistics on the relief problem are in Newcomer (1941) and Geddes (1937).

The New Deal story begins in New York: Freidel's biography of Franklin Roosevelt (1952–1973) is detailed, as is Bellush's monograph on his term as governor (1955). Particularly interesting are Frances Perkins' *The Roosevelt I Knew* (1946) and the excellent biography of Perkins by Martin (1976); the biography of Senator Robert F. Wagner by Huthmacher (1968); and the memoirs of Senator Douglas (1972), a scholar in politics. Harry Hopkins defends his relief work (1936). Two biographers discuss his administration, Charles (1963) and Kurzman (1974); neither is very satisfactory. Robert Sherwood's older biography (1948) is fine, but dwells on Hopkins's later years in diplomacy.

The general political history of these years is told in lively style by Schlesinger (1957–1960). With regard to the problem of relief, the crucial technical issue was relations with the states, well discussed by Patterson (1969). Braeman et al. (1975) consider the impact of New Deal policies. On particular states see Schneider and Deutsch on New York (1941), my book on New Jersey (1967) and article on California (1973), and Derthick (1970) on Massachusetts. A contemporary history of unemployment relief is Feder (1936).

Schlabach's biography of Witte (1969) describes the writing and defense of the Social Security Act. There is no other major secondary literature on the subjects of relief and social security, and I built my interpretation out of contemporary accounts, which are, however, voluminous. In general, I follow the well-informed and excellent book of Josephine Brown, *Public Relief, 1929–1939* (1940), and the masterful report of the U.S. National Resources Planning Board on *Security, Work and Relief Policies* (1943), plus the work of Breckinridge (1938) and Grace Abbott (1941) and Edith Abbott

(1940). The Lynds (1937) draw a detailed picture of one local relief effort. In 1936 the American Association of Social Workers published the proceedings of a conference, entitled *This Business of Relief*, which state their hopes for regularizing the FERA and their doubts about the reorganization. Macmahon (1941) describes the organization of federal work relief; Howard (1943) is a favorable view by a social worker. Salmond (1967) has a monograph on the Civilian Conservation Corps, the most widely approved of the federal work relief programs. Very critical of work relief is Lewis Meriam, *Relief and Social Security* (1946). Later publications of interest are "Work relief . . . A Current Look," Public Assistance Report No. 52, Bureau of Family Service, U.S. Department of Health, Education and Welfare (1962) and Gartner (1973) on "public service employment." The Social Science Research Council published in 1937 a series of thirteen "Research Memoranda" called "Studies in the Social Aspects of the Depression": one of these, by Clyde and Mary White, was on relief policies. Others were on social work, by F. Stuart Chapin and Stuart A. Queen, and on health, rural life, crime, recreation, internal migration, the family, and minority peoples; Arno Press has published the set. On the Townsend movement see Holtzman (1963) and Putnam (1970).

Edwin Witte, secretary of the committee that drew up the Social Security Act, published a record of its work (1962); see also his essays (1962) and Schlabach's biography (1969). Arthur Altmeyer, who helped formulate the Act and later administered it, presents his version (1966). McKinley and Frase give a fascinating firsthand story of *Launching Social Security* (not published until 1970). The Social Security Board published valuable readings, *Social Security in America* (1937), and its successor, the Social Security Administration, occasionally revised it as *Basic Readings in Social Security* (most recently in 1970). Hirshfield has a monograph (1970) on the defeat of health insurance. I have benefited from Parker's dissertation on the origin of the public-assistance provisions of the Act (1972) and from the insightful article by Burns (1944) on social insurance. *Regulating the Poor* (1971), by Cloward and Piven, offers a dubious cyclical interpretation by social scientists who attribute motives by deductive speculation rather than by studying what people actually thought and said.

On the later history of the New Deal, Bernstein (1970) and Derber and Young (1957) deal with organized labor. Patterson (1967) describes the rise of the conservative coalition in Congress, and Moore (1967) carries the story forward to 1945. The influence of Keynes on the New Deal is outlined in two articles in the *American Economic Review* for May 1972, by Sweezey and Jones; be sure to read the commentary that follows. Stein (1969) is a general account.

Charles Merriam, the leading figure in the National Resources Planning Board, describes its work in 1944; a critical review of the Report by Elizabeth Brandeis appeared in 1943. Otis Grahame has published a history of national planning beginning with the Board (1976).

The National Conference of Social Work is very rich on professional developments in these years, as are successive issues of the *Social Work Yearbook*. Bremner et al. (1970–1974) have much material on child welfare; Trolander has a book on the settlement houses (1975), and Davis (1969) sketches in the later history of Hull House; Weiss (1974) describes the Depression-year activities of the National Urban League. On the "rank-and-file movement," see Reynolds (1963) and Haynes (1975).

Chapter 13: Income Maintenance, 1935–1960

Improving income maintenance programs was a central concern of what came to be called, about 1948, the "welfare state." Schottland's collection of articles on that subject (1967) presents many points of view; other works I have found helpful are Marwick (1967), on the role of the labor party in the British welfare state; Krieger's history of the idea (1963); T. H. Marshall's sociological interpretation (1961); Wilensky's introduction to the paperback edition of *Industrialism and Social Welfare* (1965); and Myrdal (1960). Philosophical analyses of welfare and the welfare state—very different in their perspectives—are Frankel (1962) and Rescher (1972). Grahame's history of national planning in the United States (1976), interesting in itself, does not deal with welfare programs.

There are no historical surveys of income maintenance since 1935. I have pieced my story together from contemporary records and accounts by participants and social scientists that are somewhat retrospective. These are mostly descriptive; that is, they present the facts about laws, policies, and programs—an essential and demanding job in itself, especially since these facts change every day. If they go on to analyze the ideas that informed policy and administration or the circumstances that influenced decisions and practice, they do so with regard to theories of economics, sociology, or political science without much critical attention to the matrix and context of social and intellectual history.

The basic published primary source, widely available and easy to use, is the *Social Security Bulletin*, published by the Social Security Administration (originally Board), which presents data on operations, interesting studies about target populations and other relevant subjects, legislative histories, bibliographies of current publications, official and otherwise (a valuable feature), and much more. The Social Security Administration's regular reports give this sort of material some continuity and interpretation. Schlitz's study of "Public Attitudes Toward Social Security 1935–1965" (1970) is one of many interesting monographs done for it. For an account of its research, see Ida Merriam (1968). For an independent and more critical view, with a contemporary bibliography, see the articles on public assistance and social insurance in successive editions of the *Social Work Yearbook*, which provide glimpses and running commentary.

Altmeyer's *Formative Years of Social Security* (1966) is a vigorous defense of his administration (from the start until 1956), including a bibliography. Schlabach's biography of Witte (1969) has an interesting chapter on Witte's later years as "defender of the faith," and Robert Lampman has edited a collection of Witte's essays (1962). Two other books by veterans of the early years that give a somewhat personal view of issues and events are Douglas Brown, *The American Philosophy of Social Insurance* (1972), and A. Delafield Smith, *The Right to Life* (1955), by the legal counsel of the Social Security Administration. Miles (1974) is a brief, authoritative history of the Department of Health, Education and Welfare by its senior administrator. Also in the category of veteran is Eveline Burns, the foremost academic commentator in my opinion, whose works demonstrate great analytical and expository skill and a perceptive sense of historical continuities: *The American Social Security System* (1949) and especially *Social Security and Public Policy* (1956); see also her important articles "Social Insurance in Evolution" (1944) and "Social Security in Evolution: Toward What?" (1965). A bibliography of her publications is in Jenkins (1969).

Of the many textbooks economists have written on "economic and social security," the best exposition of theory and general historical development is by Carlson (1962). I have found helpful the books of readings by Haber and Cohen (1948, 1960) and the general text by Turnbull, Williams, and Cheit (several editions). Adams (1971) is a history of public attitudes toward unemployment insurance. Economists have done most of the writing about voluntary economic security programs or "fringe benefits"; there are chapters in Carlson (1962) and Turnbull (1967). In addition to the monographs I cite by Dearing (1954) and Muntz (1967), see Allen (1964) and Babson (1974). The general significance of these programs in relation to public provision is brought out in an important work by Titmuss (1958). Incidentally, what economists call "welfare economics" is not about income maintenance or other "welfare" programs but about how economic planners can decide questions of allocation of resources.

Public assistance attracted scholarly attention in these years mostly because of its state–federal administrative structure and the question of eligibility. Burns (1956) has a cogent chapter, Vasey (1958) a helpful description, and Leyendecker (1955) a more extended analysis. H. Taylor (1962) is clear on the "right to public assistance." The articles I cite by Parsons (1962) and Hale (1945, 1957) suggest possibilities for administrative history. See also Bell (1967) on the history of "relatives' responsibility." There is surprisingly little general work by political scientists on public assistance: Steiner wrote the most extensive work, *Social Insecurity* (1965), because, he said, he could not find anything similar; he focuses on congressional deliberations and decisions. Derthick's study of public-assistance administration in Massachusetts (1970) puts the problems into a better historical and practical context. Lansdale (1961) describes the impact of the Social Security Act in the South. In my text I do not mention an interesting line of inquiry that relates "welfare outcomes" in the states to various political and economic factors: see Dawson and Robinson (1965), Dye (1966), and the review article by Koehler (1971).

On social work in public assistance see, in addition to Towle (1945) and her bibliography, the articles by Jane Hoey (1937, 1945, 1949, 1953), Schottland (1959), Altmeyer (1955), Ida Merriam (1962), and Wiltse (1954). Richman's dissertation (1969) is a history of policy about services in public assistance. Bell (1965) and McKeany (1960) analyse problems in the administration of ADC in the 1950s. Viswanathan's dissertation on the role of the American Public Welfare Association in formulating welfare policies (1961) gives the views of administrators.

Chapter 14: Direct Services, 1935–1961: Toward Community Care

Social statistics got steadily better after 1935, and reflections on them and their significance for direct services appear more and more frequently in the articles and bibliography of the *Social Work Yearbook*. Wilensky and Lebeaux (1958) present one contemporary interpretation; the 1965 edition has a new introduction that continues and elaborates its analysis of social trends. Friedlander's textbook (1955 and subsequent editions) gives more conventional and comprehensive coverage of the various services, with an excellent bibliography. My material on religious views and their sociology comes from Ahlstrom (1972), McGloughlin (1959), McGloughlin and Bellah (1968—a helpful collection of essays), and Greeley (1972).

Bremner (1960), Cutlip (1965), and Heald (1970) carry the story of financing voluntary welfare agencies through this period. Bornet's survey (1960) has several interesting and sympathetic chapters on voluntary agencies; for current problems see Manser (1976). A popular but well-informed history of voluntary fund-raising groups like the National Foundation for Infantile Paralysis is Carter (1961); on the psychology of such organizations see Sills (1957). On the foundations, see Nielsen (1972); on voluntary organizations generally, Constance Smith (1972). Seeley (1957) is a sociological analysis of the Indianapolis Community Chest with a historical background. Waite's history of the family service agency of Cleveland (1960) reaches into this period. Bremner (1970–1974) carries the story of child welfare, in all its dimensions, into the 1950s, with a good bibliography. Levin (1964) gives a brief, well-informed view of the history and prospects of family and children's agencies. Katz (1976) is full on the self-help agencies, such as Alcoholics Anonymous. On particular services, the *Social Work Yearbooks* give authoritative, brief accounts. On professional education and interests generally, see Hollis and Taylor (1951) and the fourteen volumes of the *Project Report of the Curriculum Study* published by the Council on Social Work Education (1959). Of course the *Social Work Yearbooks* are full on developments in particular methods and target groups. Diner's history of the *Social Service Review* (1977) throws light on professional development. Zimbalist (1977) has an account of the research into the multiproblem family.

For a brief, readable account of the changes in health care I know nothing better than the relevant chapters of Somers (1961). Miles (1974) has three excellent chapters on the increasing federal involvement in health services, including good, brief discussions of the Hill-Burton Act and the National Institutes of Health. The Report of the Joint Commission on Mental Health (1961) sums up the thought of the 1950s and opens the way to its ten scholarly monographs; for a more extended historical treatment see Ridenour (1961). Clear and authoritative pictures of services in that decade are Stevenson (1956) on mental health and Davies (1959) on the mentally retarded. Leiby (1967) has chapters on state services for the mentally ill and retarded in historical perspective.

In the text I mention some important works in thinking about crime and corrections during the decade; my work on New Jersey (1967) has a chapter on administration in a state that was supposed to be a leader in the field. The overview is well presented in many textbooks, of which I found most useful Korn and McKorkle (1959) and Tappan (1951). Weller (1944) and Meyer (1952) detail the rise of the federal probation system. On the origin and significance of Mobilization for Youth, see the opening chapters of Marris and Rein (rev. ed., 1973). The Mobilizers tell their own story in Weissman (1969).

Chapter 15: National Action and Community Organization, 1961–1966

Basic demographic, economic, and program statistics are conveniently compiled in the statistical appendix of the *Encyclopedia of Social Work* (1977), with sources and an excellent article on the statistical literature and its development. Basic political, especially congressional, data are assembled in *Politics in America, 1945–1970*, one of a series of fact books issued by Congressional Quarterly Service (1971). My analysis of political issues follows Sundquist (1968), Schlesinger (1965), and Reagan (1972). On the general subject of national planning, see Grahame (1976), and on relations between the federal government and cities, an important question I ignore in my text, see Gelfand (1975). Karl (1976) considers the research, planning, and bureaucracy of the 1960s in historical prespective. An interesting perspective on the excitements of the 1960s is the report of the President's Commission on National Goals (1960), which Eisenhower appointed. On the Services Amendments of 1962, C. Gilbert (1966) is a legislative history; Steiner (1966) has a discussion related to policy about AFDC; Derthick (1970) describes some problems of implementation. These accounts by political scientists overlook the general professional speculation about the "multiproblem family," which I emphasize. It is worthwhile to read the primary sources, especially the hearings of the House Committee on Ways and Means, "Public Welfare Amendments of 1962," and President Kennedy's Message of February 1, 1962 (available in the Presidential Papers). DeForest (1970) is a valuable legislative history of the Aid to Dependent Children Program, done for the Office of Economic Opportunity, published in process form, and not widely available; there is a copy in the library of the Institute for Governmental Studies, University of California, Berkeley. Steiner (1971) has discussions of food stamps, housing, and certain veterans' benefits that parallel public assistance. Drew (1967) has an interesting account of the potent lobby for health and mental-health measures. On mental health see, in addition to the works I cite in my text, Connery (1968), a political scientist's review of efforts to implement the policy of community mental health. On corrections in the 1960s, see the many publications of the President's Commission on Law Enforcement and Administration of Justice, which include summary volumes on crime and juvenile delinquency (1968), nine "task force reports" (one of which is on juvenile delinquency and another, on "Corrections," includes a good account of probation and parole), and scores of consultant's reports, most published in process form and not widely available. The *American Journal of Corrections* for September-October 1970 prints much historical material and a stock-taking of the centennial meeting of the American Correctional Association, including interesting personal reminiscences.

Ritz (1966) tells how Newburgh officials tried to get tough with public assistance. Harrington's *The Invisible Poor* (1962) was followed by a deluge of books about poverty and the larger subject of income distribution. His notion of a "culture of poverty" was not rigorous (nor is my exposition of it); for a brief and more technical presentation see Lewis (1966), and for a vigorous technical criticism, Valentine (1968) (both men are anthropologists). The most important item in this literature is the report of the President's Commission on Income Maintenance (1969), with its supplementary *Background Papers* (an excellent description of programs and issues) and *Technical Papers*. Of the many textbook-style presentations, I think the best is the knowledgeable and lucid work of Wilcox (1969). See also the President's National Advisory Commission on Rural Poverty (1967). On the war on poverty itself: Knapp and Polk (1971) describe in detail its relationship to the President's Committee on Juvenile Delinquency; Silberman (1964) and Rainwater and Yancy (1967) evidence the rising concern about civil rights (the latter gives a history of the "Moynihan Report" on the Negro family [1964] and reprints the report and many comments on it). Donovan (1967) is a narrative history based largely on newspapers. Especially useful is the collection by Sundquist (1969), including many reminiscences of officials. Reich's seminal article, "The New Property" (1964), was the start of a new effort to identify and protect the legal rights of the poor, which is developed in Ten Broek, *The Law of the Poor* (1966) and O'Neil (1970).

Some works on special subjects are Pechman (1968) on OASDHI, Gartner (1973) on public-service employment, Crook and Rose (1969) on VISTA, and Johnson on the OEO legal-services program (1974). Richard Harris (1969) tells the story of the campaign for medicare and medicaid in an interesting way; Stevens (1975) is a "case study" of medicaid. In 1968 the Department of HEW published "Accomplishments, 1963–1968, Problems and Challenges and a Look to the Future," by Wilbur Cohen, the outgoing secretary, which summarizes the record in a sympathetic light.

Chapter 16: Disenchantment, 1967–1972

The literature on civil rights, race relations, and social welfare is very large; for references and summaries, see many relevant articles in the *Encyclopedia of Social Work* and the bibliographies published by the Council on Social Work Education for social-work students; on blacks, Dunmore (1970); on Asians, Kitano (1971); on Chicanos, Navarro (1971); and on Native Americans, Brennan (1972). Parris and Brooks (1971) carry the story of the National Urban League to 1968. On the history of black protest thought, see Meier, Rudwick, and Broderick (1971). In addition to the important primary works cited in my text, by Clark (1965) and Grier and Cobbs (1968), *Black Power*, by Carmichal and Hamilton (1967), popularized the concept of "institutional racism," and the *Report of the National Advisory Commission on Civil Disorders* (Kerner Commission) (1968) gave strong support to the militants by its condemnation of white racism. Cloward and Piven (1971) argue that the war on poverty was a response to militancy. Brager and Purcell (1967), Moynihan (1969), and Sundquist (1969) present diverse views of the Community Action Program in the war on poverty. Roszak (1969) is a sympathetic portrayal of the "counterculture" and the hippies; Diggins (1973), Bacciocco (1971), and Unger (1975) are studies of the New Left. On the Welfare Rights Organization, Jackson and Johnson (1974) tell the story for New York City and Bailis (1974) for Massachusetts; Steiner (1971) mentions its significance and impact on national politics. Romanyshyn's textbook (1971) pulls together a great deal of the literature, empirical and speculative, in psychology and social science, that testified to the sense of crisis and emergency in the late 1960s.

On the disenchantment with the war on poverty, see the articles collected in Moynihan (1969) and by Ginzberg and Solow (1974, an issue of *The Public Interest*, a journal that became a vehicle for this sentiment). The great hope for research on policy questions ("If we can send a man to the moon why can't we eliminate poverty?") is authoritatively discussed in a publication of the National Academy of Sciences, "Policy and Program Research in a University Setting: A Case Study" (1971) and Richard Nelson, "Intellectualizing the Moon-Ghetto Metaphor: A Study of the Current Malaise of Rational Analysis of Social Problems" (1974). Steiner (1971) is part of this literature; his account of AFDC, food stamps, and housing goes forward to 1969. Review essays on such accounts are by Henry Cohen (1972) and Dale Marshall (1974). On President Nixon's Family Assistance Plan see Moynihan (1973) and Burke (1974), a journalistic presentation that is well researched and sees the business through to 1972. Disillusion with the results is forcefully put in *The State of the Cities: Report of the Commission on the Cities in the '70's* (1972), edited by Senator Fred Harris and Mayor John Lindsay, with many staff papers. Recent collections of articles that bring out the disenchantment: on corrections, Ohlin (1973), and on community mental health, Denner and Price (1973). The Comptroller General's report to Congress on "How Federal Efforts to Coordinate Programs to Mitigate Juvenile Delinquency Proved Ineffective" (1975) is effective. Steiner (1976) describes federal efforts to devise a policy for child health and development and the bureaucratic changes that led to the demise of the U.S. Children's Bureau. On day care, which I ignore in my text, see Steingels (1973). The story of Mary Switzer and the internal reorganization of the Bureau of Family Services of the Department of HEW I draw from Miles (1974), who has interesting reflections on "program specialists" and "generalists" in administration. Rivlin (1971) is a readable statement of the new importance of accountability in its connection with policy, planning, and evaluative research. On later efforts to reorganize welfare administration in HEW, see the journal *Policy Analysis* for Spring 1975, edited by Lynn.

Kramer and Specht (1975) assemble articles on the recent developments in community organization. On the important Services Amendments of 1972, which much altered the federal funding and supervision of social services, see the legislative history by Mott (1976). On revenue sharing there is a large literature: Caputo and Cole (1974) is a balanced history and analysis, with some early data on results in cities. Well-informed reviews of the continuing effort to reduce poverty are Plotnick and Skidmore (1975), Levitan and Taggart (1976), and the helpful reference material in the fact book "Future of Social Programs," published by Congressional Quarterly in 1973.

Chapter 17: Professional Identity in Social Work: Historical Reflections

Brief, authoritative accounts of all professional concerns in the 1960s, with copious bibliography and useful statistics, are readily available in *The Encyclopedia of Social Work*, published in 1965, 1971, and 1977. More recent is not necessarily better, so it pays to look at all the editions. Readily available published primary sources include the journal of the National Association of Social Work, *Social Work* (1956–   ), and the periodicals of the Council on Social Work Education, *Journal of Education for Social Work* (1965–   ) and *Social Work Education Reporter* (1953–   ).

Three collections of interpretive essays on professional concerns, with a good deal of contemporary history, are edited by Cora Casius (1954) and Alfred J. Kahn (1959 and 1973). A critical history of social research in American social work is Zimbalist (1977). Greenwood has a summary of research for the decade ending 1957 (1957), and Maas has edited two useful volumes of essays in which experts summarize recent research in their several fields (1966, 1971). Other articles that discuss the historical role of research in professional development are Briar (1971) and Germain (1970), on methods, and Diner (1977), on the history of *The Social Service Review*, the foremost academic journal of the profession.

An interesting historical interpretation of what I call the direct services is in the volumes by the English sociologist Paul Halmos (1966, 1970), Rieff's *Triumph of the Therapeutic* (1966) analyzes the general problem of moral responsibility during the decline of Christianity. *Social Welfare and Social Development*, by Eugen Pusic (1972), has many thoughtful historical interpretations from an international perspective, as does the older work of Myrdal (1960).

Romanyshyn's textbook (1971) sums up much activist thought of the 1960s. Recent analyses and interpretations from a radical perspective are by Galper (1975), on American social services and social work, and George and Wilding (1976), on the ideology of the welfare state in England.

Bibliography

Abbott, Edith. "Abolish the Pauper Laws," *Social Service Review*, 8 (March 1934): 1–16.

—— *Public Assistance*. Chicago: University of Chicago Press, 1940.

—— *Social Welfare and Professional Education*. Rev. ed. Chicago: University of Chicago Press, 1942.

—— "Sophonisba Preston Breckinridge: Over the Years," *Social Service Review*, 22 (December 1948): 417–23. (Part of a memorial issue on Breckinridge.)

Abbott, Grace. *From Relief to Social Security*. Chicago: University of Chicago Press, 1941.

Abell, Aaron I. *Urban Impact on American Protestantism, 1965–1900*. Cambridge, Mass.: Harvard University Press, 1943.

Abrams, Philip. *The Origins of British Sociology, 1834–1914: An Essay with Selected Papers*. Chicago: University of Chicago Press, 1968.

Adams, Leonard P. *Public Attitudes Toward Unemployment Insurance: A Historical Account with Special Reference to Alleged Abuses*. Kalamazoo, Mich.: W. E. Upjohn Institute for Employment Research, December 1971.

Addams, Jane. *Democracy and Social Ethics*. New York: Macmillan, 1902.

—— *Newer Ideals of Peace*. New York: Macmillan, 1907.

—— *The Second Twenty Years at Hull House, September 1909 to September 1929, with a Record of a Growing World Consciousness*. New York: Macmillan, 1930.

—— *Twenty Years at Hull House, with Autobiographical Notes*. New York: Macmillan, 1910.

Addams, Jane et al. *The Child, the Clinic and the Court: A Group of Papers*. New York: New Republic, 1925.

—— *Philanthropy and Social Progress*. New York, 1893.

Ahlstrom, Sydney E. *A Religious History of the American People*. New Haven, Conn.: Yale University Press, 1972.

Alexander, Leslie B. "Social Work's Freudian Deluge: Myth or Reality," *Social Service Review*, 46 (December 1972): 517–38.

Allen, Donna. *Fringe Benefits: Wages or Social Obligation? An Analysis with Historical Perspectives*. Ithaca, N.Y.: Cornell University Press, 1964.

The Almshouse Experience: Collected Reports. New York: Arno Press, 1971.

Altmeyer, Arthur. "The Dynamics of Social Work," National Conference on Social Welfare, *Social Welfare Forum,* 82 (1955): 98–111.

———— *The Formative Years of Social Security.* Madison: University of Wisconsin Press, 1966.

American Association of Social Workers. *This Business of Relief: Proceedings of the Delegate Conference . . . February 14–16, 1936.* New York, 1936.

American Psychiatric Association. *One Hundred Years of American Psychiatry.* New York: Columbia University Press, 1944.

Arrington, Leonard J., Feramorz Y. Fox, and Dean L. May. *Building the City of God: Community and Cooperation Among the Mormons.* Salt Lake City, Utah: Deseret, 1976.

Axinn, June and Herman Levin. *Social Welfare: A History of the American Response to Need.* New York: Dodd, Mead, 1975.

Babson, Stanley. *Fringe Benefits—the Depreciation, Obsolescence, and Transience of Man . . .* New York: Wiley, 1974.

Bacciocco, Edward J., Jr. *The New Left in America: Reform to Revolution, 1956 to 1970.* Stanford, Calif.: Hoover Institution Press, 1974.

Bailis, Lawrence N. *Bread or Justice.* Lexington, Mass.: Lexington Books, 1974.

Bane, Frank. "Public Administration and Public Welfare." Typed transcript of tape-recorded interviews conducted in 1965 by James R. W. Leiby for the Regional Oral History Office, Bancroft Library, University of California, Berkeley.

Banner, Lois. "Religious Benevolence as Social Control: A Critique of an Interpretation," *American Journal of History,* 60 (June 1973): 23–41.

Barker, Sir Ernest. *The Development of Public Services in Western Europe, 1660–1930.* London: Oxford University Press, 1945.

Bary, Helen Valeska. "Labor Administration and Social Security: A Woman's Life." Typed transcript of taped interviews conducted in 1972–1973 by Jacqueline K. Parker for the Regional Oral History Office, Bancroft Library, University of California, Berkeley.

Beaumont, Gustave and Alexis de Tocqueville. "On the Penitentiary System in the United States and its Application in France," translated by Francis Lieber. Philadelphia, 1833.

Beck, Dorothy F. *Patterns in Use of Family Agency Services.* New York: Family Service Association of America, 1962.

Becker, Dorothy. "Early Adventures in Social Casework: The Charity Agent 1880–1910," *Social Casework,* 44 (May 1963): 255–61.

———— "Exit Lady Bountiful: The Volunteer and the Professional Social Worker," *Social Service Review,* 38 (March 1964): 57–72.

Bell, Winifred. *Aid to Dependent Children.* New York: Columbia University Press, 1965.

———— "Relatives Responsibility: A Problem in Social Policy," *Social Work,* 12 (January 1967): 32–39.

Bellush, Bernard. *Franklin D. Roosevelt as Governor of New York.* New York: Columbia University Press, 1955.

Bendix, Reinhard. "The Protestant Ethic Revisited," *Comparative Studies in Society and History,* 9 (April 1967).

—— Work and Authority in Industry; Ideologies of Management in the Course of Industrialization. New York: Wiley, 1956.

Bernard, L[uther] L. and Jessie Bernard. Origins of American Sociology. New York: Russell & Russell, 1965; reprint of 1943 ed.

Bernstein, Irving. The Lean Years: A History of the American Worker, 1920–1933. Boston: Houghton Mifflin, 1960.

—— Turbulent Years: A History of the American Worker, 1933–1941. Boston: Houghton Mifflin, 1970.

Berthoff, Rowland. "The Social Order of the Anthracite Region, 1825–1902," Pennsylvania Magazine of History and Biography, 89 (July 1965).

—— An Unsettled People: Social Order and Disorder in American History. New York: Harper & Row, 1971.

Best, Harry. The Blind: Their Condition and the Work Being Done for Them in the United States. New York: Macmillan, 1919.

—— The Deaf: Their Position in Society and the Provision for Their Education in the United States. New York: Thomas Y. Crowell, 1914. (Also: 1943 ed., new title: Deafness and the Deaf in the United States . . .).

Billingsley, Andrew and Jeanne M. Giovannoni. Children of the Storm: Black Children and American Child Welfare. New York: Harcourt Brace Jovanovich, 1972.

Bliss, W[illiam] D. P., ed. The New Encyclopedia of Social Reform. New York: Funk & Wagnalls, 1908.

Blum, Jerome. "The Euopean Village as a Community," Agricultural History, 45 (July 1971): 157–85.

Blumberg, Dorothy R. Florence Kelley: The Making of a Social Pioneer. New York: Augustus Kelley, 1966.

Bogen, Boris D. Jewish Philanthropy: An Exposition of Principles and Methods of Jewish Social Service in the United States. New York: Macmillan, 1917.

Boorstin, Daniel J. The Genius of American Politics. Chicago: University of Chicago Press, 1953.

Bornet, Vaughn D. Welfare in America. Norman: University of Oklahoma Press, 1960.

Bortz, Abe. Social Security Sources in Federal Records, 1934–1950. U.S. Department of Health, Education and Welfare, Social Security Administration, Research Report no. 30. Washington, D.C.: Government Printing Office, 1969.

Bosanquet, Helen. Social Work in London, 1869 to 1912: A History of the Charity Organization Society. London: J. Murray, 1914.

Bowen, Louise de Koven. Speeches, Addresses and Letters of Louise de Koven Bowen, Reflecting Social Movements in Chicago . . . Mary E. Humphrey, ed. Ann Arbor, Mich.: Edwards Bros., 1937.

Brace, Charles Loring. The Dangerous Classes of New York and Twenty Years' Work Among Them. New York: Wynkoop & Hallenbeck, 1872.

Brace, Emma, ed. The Life of Charles Loring Brace: Chiefly Told in His Own Letters . . . London: Low, Marston, 1894.

Brackett, Jeffery R. Supervision and Education in Charity. New York: Macmillan, 1903.

Bradbury, Dorothy E. Five Decades of Action for Children: A History of the Chil-

dren's Bureau. U.S. Department of Health, Education and Welfare, Social Security Administration, Children's Bureau Publication no. 358. Washington, D.C.: Government Printing Office, 1962.

Brager, George A. and Francis P. Purcell, eds. *Community Action Against Poverty: Readings from the Mobilization Experience*. New Haven, Conn.: College and University Press, 1967.

Brandeis, Elizabeth. "Security Policies and the National Resources Planning Board Report," *Social Service Review*, 17 (September 1943): 335–39.

Brandes, Stuart D. *American Welfare Capitalism, 1880–1940*. Chicago: University of Chicago Press, 1976.

Brandt, Lillian. *Growth and Development of AICP and COS*, Report to the Committee on the Institute of Welfare Research. New York: Community Service Society of New York, 1942.

Braun, Heinrich. *Industrialization and Social Policy*. Koen and Berlin: Carl Heymans Verlag K.G., 1956, pp. 73–81.

Breckinridge, Sophonisba. *Public Welfare Administration*. Chicago: University of Chicago Press, 1927; rev. ed., 1938.

Bremner, Robert. *American Philanthropy*. Chicago: University of Chicago Press, 1960.

—— *From the Depths: The Discovery of Poverty in the United States*. New York: New York University Press, 1956.

—— "The Impact of the Civil War on Philanthropy and Social Welfare," *Civil War History*, 12 (December 1966): 293–303.

—— " 'Scientific Philanthropy,' 1873–93," *Social Service Review*, 30 (June 1956): 168–73.

Bremner, Robert, ed. *Children and Youth in America: A Documentary History*, 3 vols. in 5. Cambridge, Mass.: Harvard University Press, 1970–1974.

Brennan, Jere L. *The Forgotten American—American Indians Remembered*. New York: Council on Social Work Education, 1972.

Briar, Scott. "Social Casework and Social Group Work: Historical and Social Science Foundations," *Encyclopedia of Social Work: Sixteenth Issue*. New York: National Association of Social Workers, 1971, II, 1237–45.

Bridenbaugh, Carl. *Cities in Revolt: Urban Life in America, 1743–1776*. New York: Knopf, 1955.

—— *Cities in the Wilderness: The First Century of Urban Life in America, 1625–1742*. New York: Ronald Press, 1938.

Briggs, Asa. *Social Thought and Social Action: A Study of the Work of Seebohm Rowntree, 1871–1954*. London: Longmans, 1961.

Broadhurst, Betty Page. "Social Thought, Social Practice, and Social Work Education: Sanborn, Ely, Warner, Richmond." Unpublished dissertation, Columbia University, June 1971.

Brown, J. Douglas. *An American Philosophy of Social Security: Evolution and Issues*. Princeton, N.J.: Princeton University Press, 1972.

Brown, James. *The History of Public Assistance in Chicago, 1833 to 1933*. Chicago: University of Chicago Press, 1941.

Brown, Josephine C. *Public Relief, 1929–1939*. New York: Holt, 1940.

Bruno, Frank J. *Trends in Social Work, 1874–1956: A History Based on the Proceedings of the National Conference of Social Work*, 2d ed. with additional chapters. New York: Columbia University Press, 1957.

Buell, Bradley. "Is Prevention Possible?" In *Community Organization 1959: Papers Presented at the 86th Annual Forum of the National Conference on Social Welfare*. New York: Columbia University Press, 1959, pp. 3–18.

Buell, Bradley and associates. *Community Planning for Human Services*. New York: Columbia University Press, 1952.

Burke, Vincent J. and Vee Burke. *Nixon's Good Deed: Welfare Reform*. New York: Columbia University Press, 1974.

Burns, Eveline M. *The American Social Security System*. Boston: Houghton Mifflin, 1949.

———— "Social Insurance in Evolution," *American Economic Review Supplement*, 34 (March 1944).

———— *Social Security and Public Policy*. New York: McGraw-Hill, 1956.

———— "Social Security in Evolution: Toward What?" *Social Service Review*, 39 (June 1965): 129–40.

Burr, Nelson R., ed. *A Critical Bibliography of Religion in America*. Princeton, N.J.: Princeton University Press, 1961.

Bryce, James. "American Experience in the Relief of the Poor," *Macmillan's Magazine*, 25 (November 1871): 54–65.

Campbell, Thomas F. *SASS: Fifty Years of Social Work Education: A History of the School of Applied Social Sciences, Case Western Reserve University*. Cleveland: Press of Case Western Reserve University, 1967.

Cannon, Ida M. *On the Social Frontier of Medicine: Pioneering in Medical Social Service*. Cambridge, Mass.: Harvard University Press, 1952.

Caplan, Ruth B., in collaboration with Gerald Caplan. *Psychiatry and the Community in Nineteenth-Century America: The Recurring Concern with the Environment in the Prevention and Treatment of Mental Illness*. New York: Basic Books, 1969.

Caputo, David A., and Richard L. Cole. *Urban Politics and Decentralization*. Lexington, Mass.: Heath, 1974.

Carlson, Valdemar. *Economic Security in the United States*. New York: McGraw-Hill, 1962.

Carmichael, Stokely, and Charles Hamilton. *Black Power*. New York: Random House, 1967.

Carter, Richard. *The Gentle Legions*. Garden City, N.Y.: Doubleday, 1961.

Cawelti, John G. *Apostles of the Self-Made Man*. Chicago: University of Chicago Press, 1965.

Chambers, Clarke A. "Archives of Social Welfare." In *Encyclopedia of Social Work, Seventeenth Issue*, 2 vols. Washington, D.C.: National Association of Social Workers, 1977, I, 80–84.

———— *Paul U. Kellogg and the Survey: Voices for Social Welfare and Social Justice*. Minneapolis: University of Minnesota Press, 1971.

———— *Seedtime of Reform: American Social Service and Social Action, 1918–1933*. Minneapolis: University of Minnesota Press, 1963.

———— "Social Service and Social Reform: A Historical Essay," *Social Service Review*, 37 (March 1963): 76–90.

Channing, Alice. "The Early Years of a Pioneer School [Simmons College School of Social Work]," Social Service Review, 28 (December 1954): 430–40.

Chapin, F. Stuart and Stuart A. Queen. *Research Memorandum on Social Work in the Depression*. New York: Social Service Research Council, 1937.

Charles, Searle F. *Minister of Relief: Harry Hopkins and the Depression*. Syracuse, N.Y.: Syracuse University Press, 1963.

Chute, Charles Lionel and Marjorie Bell. *Crime, Courts, and Probation*. New York: Macmillan, 1956.

Clark, Kenneth B. *Dark Ghetto: Dilemmas of Social Power*. New York: Harper & Row, 1965.

Cloward, Richard, and Frances Fox Piven. *Regulating the Poor: The Functions of Public Welfare*. New York: Random House, 1971.

Cohen, Harry. "Poverty and Welfare: A Review Essay," *Political Science Quarterly*, 87 (December 1972).

Cohen, Nathan E. *Social Work in the American Tradition: Field, Body of Knowledge, Process, Method and Point of View*. New York: Dryden Press, 1958.

Cohen, Wilbur J. *Health, Education and Welfare: Accomplishments 1963–1968, Problems and Challenges, and a Look to the Future*, A Report to President Lyndon B. Johnson. U.S. Department of Health, Education, and Welfare. Washington, D.C.: Government Printing Office, 1968.

Cole, Charles C., Jr. *The Social Ideas of the Northern Evangelists, 1826–1860*. New York: Columbia University Press, 1954.

Coll, Blanche D. "The Baltimore Society for the Prevention of Pauperism, 1820–1860," *American Historical Review*, 61 (October 1955): 77–87.

———— *Perspectives in Public Welfare, A History*. Washington, D.C.: Government Printing Office, 1969.

Commonwealth Fund. *The Commonwealth Fund: Historical Sketch, 1918–1962*. New York: 1963.

Conference on Unemployment, Committee on Recent Economic Changes. *Recent Economic Changes in the United States*. New York: McGraw-Hill, 1929.

Connery, Robert et al. *The Politics of Mental Health*. New York: Columbia University Press, 1968.

Conway, Jill. "Women Reformers and American Culture, 1870–1930," *Journal of Social History* (Winter 1971–1972).

Corwin, E. S. "Social Insurance and Constitutional Limitations," *Yale Journal of Law*, 26 (April 1917): 431–43.

Coughlin, Bernard J. *Church and State in Social Welfare*. New York: Columbia University Press, 1965.

Council on Social Work Education. *Project Report of the Curriculum Study*, 14 vols. New York, 1959.

Cremin, Lawrence A. *The Transformation of the School: Progressivism in American Education, 1876–1957*. New York: Knopf, 1961.

Crook, William H. and Thomas Rose. *Warriors for the Poor: The Story of Vista . . .* New York: William Morris, 1969.

Cross, Robert. "The Philanthropic Contributions of Louisa Lee Schuyler," *Social Service Review*, 35 (September 1961): 290–301.

Curti, Merle E. *The Growth of American Thought*. 3d ed. New York: Harper & Row, 1964.

Cutlip, Scott M. *Fund Raising in the U.S. Its Role in America's Philanthropy*. New Brunswick, N.J.: Rutgers University Press, 1965.

Dahlberg, Jane S. *The New York Bureau of Municipal Research, Pioneer in Government Administration*. New York: New York University Press, 1966.

Dain, Norman. *Concepts of Insanity in the United States, 1789–1865*. New Brunswick, N.J.: Rutgers University Press, 1964.

Davies, John D. *Phrenology: Fad and Science*. New Haven, Conn.: Yale University Press, 1955.

Davies, Stanley P. *The Mentally Retarded in Society*. New York: Columbia University Press, 1959.

Davis, Allen F. *American Heroine: The Life and Legend of Jane Addams*. New York: Oxford University Press, 1973.

—— *Spearheads for Reform: The Social Settlements and the Progressive Movement, 1890–1914*. New York: Oxford University Press, 1967.

Davis, Allen F. and Mary Lynn McCree, eds. *Eighty Years at Hull-House*. Chicago: Quadrangle Books, 1969.

Dawson, Richard, and James Robinson. "The Politics of Welfare." In Jacob Herbert and Kenneth Vines, eds. *Politics in the American States: A Comparative Analysis*. Boston: Little, Brown, 1965.

Dawson, William H. *Social Insurance in Germany, 1883–1911* . . . London: Unwin, 1912.

Dearing, Charles. *Industrial Pensions*. Washington, D.C.: Brookings Institution, 1954.

Dearing, Mary. *Veterans in Politics: The Story of the G.A.R.* Baton Rouge: Louisiana State University Press, 1952.

DeForest, Paul et al. *Legislative History of the Aid to Dependent Children*. Washington, D.C.: Bureau of Social Science Research, 1970.

Denner, Bruce and Richard Price, eds. *Community Mental Health: Social Action and Reaction*. New York: Holt, Rinehart & Winston, 1973.

Derber, Milton, and Edwin Young, eds. *Labor and the New Deal*. Madison: University of Wisconsin Press, 1957.

Derthick, Martha. *The Influence of Federal Grants: Public Assistance in Massachusetts*. Cambridge, Mass.: Harvard University Press, 1970.

—— *Uncontrollable Spending for Social Service Grants*. Washington, D.C.: Brookings Institution, 1975.

DeSchweinitz, Karl. *England's Road to Social Security: From the Statute of Laborers in 1349 to the Beveridge Report of 1942*. Philadelphia: University of Pennsylvania Press, 1943.

Diggins, John P. *The American Left in the Twentieth Century*. New York: Harcourt, Brace, Jovanovich, 1973.

Dunmore, Charlotte. *Poverty, Participation, Protest, Power, and Black Americans*. New York: Council on Social Work Education, 1970.

Dunstan, J. Leslie. *A Light to the City: 150 Years of the City Missionary Society of Boston, 1816–1966*. Boston: Beacon Press, 1966.

Dye, Thomas. *Politics, Economics and the Public*. New York: Rand McNally, 1966.

Eaton, Leonard K. *New England Hospitals, 1790–1833*. Ann Arbor: University of Michigan Press, 1957.

Eilbert, Henry. "The Development of Personnel Management in the United States," *Business History Review*, 33 (1959): 345–64.

Epstein, Abraham. *Insecurity, A Challenge to America: A Study of Social Insurance in the United States . . .* New York: Random House, 1938.

Everett, Alexander H. *New Ideas in Population, with Remarks on the Theories of Malthus and Godwin*. New York: 1826. (Reprinted New York: Augustus Kelley, 1970.)

Farrell, Gabriel. *The Story of Blindness*. Cambridge, Mass.: Harvard University Press, 1956.

Feder, Leah H. *Unemployment Relief in Periods of Depression*. New York: Russell Sage Foundation, 1936.

Felix, Robert H. *Mental Illness: Progress and Prospects*. New York: Columbia University Press, 1967.

Fideler, Paul. "Christian Humanism and Poor Law Reform in Early Tudor England," *Societas*, 4 (Autumn 1974): 269–85.

Flynn, Frank T. "Judge Merritt W. Pinckney and the Early Days of the Juvenile Court in Chicago," *Social Service Review*, 28 (March 1954): 20–30.

Folks, Homer. *The Care of Destitute, Neglected, and Delinquent Children*. New York: Macmillan, 1902.

Follett, Mary Parker. *The New State: Group Organization the Solution of Popular Government*. New York: Longmans, Green, 1918.

Forthal, Sonya. "Relief and Friendly Service by Political Precinct Leaders," *Social Service Review*, 8 (December 1933): 608–18.

Foster, Charles I. *An Errand of Mercy: The Evangelical United Front, 1790–1837*. Chapel Hill: University of North Carolina Press, 1960.

Foucault, Michael. *Madness and Civilization: A History of Insanity in the Age of Reason*. New York: Pantheon Books, 1965.

Frankel, Charles. *The Democratic Prospect*. New York: Harper & Row, 1962.

Franklin, John Hope. *From Slavery to Freedom: A History of Negro Americans*. New York: Knopf, 1967.

——— "Public Welfare in the South During the Reconstruction Era," *Social Service Review*, 44 (December 1970): 379–92.

Fredrickson, George M. *The Inner Civil War: Northern Intellectuals and the Crisis of the Union*. New York: Harper & Row, 1965.

Freidel, Frank B. *Franklin D. Roosevelt*. 4 vols. Boston: Little, Brown, 1952–1973.

Friedlander, Walter A. and Robert Z. Apte. *Introduction to Social Welfare*. 4th ed. Englewood Cliffs, N.J.: Prentice-Hall, 1974.

Furner, Mary O. *Advocacy and Objectivity: A Crisis in the Professionalization of American Social Science 1865–1905*. Lexington, Ky.: University Press of Kentucky, 1975.

Gabriel, Ralph H. *The Course of American Democratic Thought: An Intellectual History Since 1815.* 2d ed. New York: Ronald Press, 1956.

Galper, Jeffrey H. *The Politics of Social Services.* Englewood Cliffs, N.J.: Prentice-Hall, 1975.

Gartner, Alan, comp. *Public Service Employment: An Analysis of Its History, Problems and Prospects.* New York: Praeger, 1973.

Gavin, Donald P. *The National Conference of Catholic Charities, 1910–1960.* Milwaukee: Catholic Life Publications, 1962.

Geddes, Anne E. *Trends in Relief Expenditure, 1910–1935,* U.S. Works Progress Administration, Division of Social Research, Research Monograph no. 10. Washington, D.C.: Government Printing Office, 1937.

Gelfand, Mark J. *A Nation of Cities: The Federal Government and Urban America.* New York: Oxford University Press, 1975.

George, Vic, and Paul Wilding. *Ideology and Social Welfare.* London: Routledge & Kegan Paul, 1976.

Germain, Carel. "Casework and Science: A Historical Encounter." In Robert W. Roberts and Robert H. Nee, eds. *Theories of Social Casework.* Chicago: University of Chicago Press, 1970.

Gettleman, Marvin. "Charity and Social Classes in the U.S.," *American Journal of Economics and Sociology,* 22 (April, July 1963): 313–29, 417–26.

——— "Philanthropy as Social Control in Late Nineteenth-Century America: Some Hypotheses and Data on the Rise of Social Work," *Societas,* 5 (Winter 1975): 49–59.

Gilbert, Bentley. *The Evolution of National Insurance in Great Britain: The Origins of the Welfare State.* London: Joseph, 1966.

Gilbert, Charles. "Policy-making in Public Welfare: The 1962 Amendments," *Political Science Quarterly,* 81 (June 1966): 196–224.

Gillin, John L. *Poverty and Dependency: Their Relief and Prevention.* Rev. ed. New York: Century, 1926.

Ginzberg, Eli and Robert M. Solow, eds. "The Great Society: Lessons for the Future," *The Public Interest,* 34 (Winter 1947): entire issue.

Girvetz, Harry. *The Evolution of Liberalism.* Rev. ed. New York: Collier Books, 1963.

Glasser, Melvin. "The Story of the Movement for a Single Professional Association," *Social Work Journal,* 33 (July 1949).

Glasson, William H. *Federal Military Pensions in the United States.* New York: Oxford University Press, 1918.

Glenn, John M., Lilian Brandt, and F. Emerson Andrews. *Russell Sage Foundation,* 2 vols. New York: Russell Sage Foundation, 1947.

Goldmark, Josephine. *Impatient Crusader: Florence Kelley's Life Story.* Urbana: University of Illinois Press, 1953.

Goodman, Nathan G. *Benjamin Rush, Physician and Citizen, 1746–1813.* Philadelphia: University of Pennsylvania Press, 1934.

Goodman, Paul. *Growing Up Absurd: Problems of Youth in the Organized System.* New York: Random House, 1960.

Gosden, P. H. J. H. *The Friendly Societies in England, 1815–1875.* Manchester (England): Manchester University Press, 1961.

Grahame, Otis L. *Toward a Planned Society. From Roosevelt to Nixon.* New York: Oxford University Press, 1976.

Greeley, Andrew M. *The Denominational Society: A Sociological Approach to Religion in America.* Glenview, Ill.: Scott, Foresman, 1972.

Green, Fletcher M. "Some Aspects of the Convict Lease System in the Southern States." In J. Isaac Copeland, ed., *Democracy in the Old South and Other Essays.* Nashville, Tenn.: Vanderbilt University Press, 1969.

Green, Robert W. *Protestantism, Capitalism, and Social Science: The Weber Thesis Controversy.* 2d ed. Lexington, Mass.: Heath, 1973.

Greenwood, Ernest. "Social Work Research: A Decade of Reappraisal," *Social Service Review,* 31 (March 1957): 311–315.

Grier, William H. and Price M. Cobbs. *Black Rage.* New York: Basic Books, 1968.

Grob, Gerald N. *Mental Institutions in America: Social Policy to 1875.* New York: Free Press, 1973.

—— "The Political System and Social Policy in the Nineteenth Century: Legacy of the Revolution," *Mid-America,* 58 (January 1976): 5–19.

—— *The State and the Mentally Ill: A History of Worcester State Hospital in Massachusetts, 1830–1920.* Chapel Hill: University of North Carolina Press, 1966.

Haber, Samuel. *Efficiency and Uplift: Scientific Management in the Progressive Era, 1890–1920.* Chicago: University of Chicago Press, 1964.

Haber, William and Wilbur J. Cohen, eds. *Readings in Social Security.* New York: Prentice-Hall, 1948.

—— *Social Security: Programs, Problems, and Policies: Selected Readings.* Homewood, Ill.: Irwin, 1960.

Hale, Mark. "The Process of Developing Policy for a Federal-State Grant-in-Aid Program as Illustrated by the Work of the Social Security Board, 1935–1946," *Social Service Review,* 31 (September 1957): 290–310.

—— "Some Aspects of Federal-State Relations," *Social Service Review,* 28 (June 1954): 126–36.

Hall, P. D. "The Model of Boston Charity: A Theory of Charitable Benevolence and Class Development," *Science and Society,* 38 (Winter 1974–1975): 464–77.

Halmos, Paul. *The Faith of the Counsellors: A Study in the Theory and Practice of Social Case Work and Psychotherapy.* New York: Schocken Books, 1966.

—— *The Personal Service Society.* New York: Schocken Books, 1970.

Handlin, Oscar. *Boston's Immigrants, 1790–1880: A Study in Acculturation.* New York: Antheneum, 1972.

—— *The Uprooted: The Epic Story of the Great Migrations That Made the American People.* Boston: Little, Brown, 1951; rev. ed., 1973.

Handlin, Oscar and Mary F. Handlin. *The Dimensions of Liberty.* Cambridge, Mass.: Belknap Press of Harvard University Press, 1961.

Handy, Robert T., ed. *The Social Gospel in America, 1870–1930: Gladden, Ely, Rauschenbush.* New York: Oxford University Press, 1966.

Harrington, Michael. *The Other America: Poverty in the United States.* New York: Macmillan, 1962.

Harris, Fred R., and John V. Lindsay, eds. *The State of the Cities: Report of the Commission on Cities in the '70s.* New York: Praeger, 1972.

Harris, Richard. *A Sacred Trust.* Baltimore: Penguin Books, 1969.

Harrison, Brian. "Animals and the State in 19th Century England," *English Historical Review,* 88 (October 1973): 786–820.

Hartz, Louis. *The Liberal Tradition in America.* New York: Harcourt, Brace, 1955.

Hasse, Adelaide R. *Index of Economic Material in Documents of States of the United States . . .* 13 vols. in 16. Washington, D.C.: Carnegie Institute of Washington, 1907–1922. (Vols. on the following states: California, Delaware, Illinois, Kentucky, Maine, Massachusetts, New Hampshire, New Jersey, New York, Ohio, Pennsylvania, Rhode Island, Vermont.)

Hawes, Joseph M. *Children in Urban Society: Juvenile Delinquency in Nineteenth Century America.* New York: Oxford University Press, 1971.

Hawley, Ellis W. "Herbert Hoover, the Commerce Secretariat and the Vision of an 'Associative State,' 1921–1928," *Journal of American History,* 61 (June 1974): 116–40.

Haynes, John Earl. "The 'Rank and File Movement' in Private Social Work," *Labor History,* 16 (Winter 1975): 78–98.

Heald, Morrell. *The Social Responsibilities of Business: Company and Community, 1900–1960.* Cleveland: Press of Case Western Reserve University, 1970.

Heale, Mark J. "The Formative Years of the New York Prison Association, 1844–1862," *New York Historical Society Quartelry,* 49 (October 1975): 320–47.

——— "From City Fathers to Social Critics: Humanitarianism and Government in New York, 1790–1860," *Journal of American History,* 43 (June 1976): 21–41.

——— "Humanitarianism in the Early Republic: The Moral Reformers of New York 1776–1825," *Journal of American Studies,* 2 (October 1968): 161–75.

——— "The New York Society for the Prevention of Pauperism," *New York Historical Society Quarterly,* 55 (April 1971): 153–76.

——— "Patterns of Benevolence: Associated Philanthropy in the Cities of New York, 1830–1860," *New York History,* 57 (January 1976).

——— "Patterns of Benevolence: Charity and Morality in Urban and Rural New York," *Societas,* 3 (Autumn 1973): 337–50.

Heasman, Kathleen. *Evangelicals in Action: An Appraisal of Their Social Work in the Victorian Era.* London: Bles, 1962.

Heimert, Alan E. *Religion and the American Mind from the Great Awakening to the Revolution.* Cambridge, Mass.: Harvard University Press, 1966.

Helmes, J. W. *Thomas M. Mulry, A Volunteer's Contribution to Social Work.* Washington, D.C.: Catholic University Press, 1938.

Henderson, Charles R. *Correction and Prevention.* 4 vols. Prepared for 8th International Prison Conference. New York: Russell Sage, 1910.

Hegner, H. "Scientific Value of Social Settlements," *American Journal of Sociology,* 3 (September 1897) 171–82.

Hirshfield, Daniel S. *The Lost Reform: The Campaign for Compulsory Health Insurance in the United States from 1932 to 1943.* Cambridge, Mass.: Harvard University Press, 1970.

Hoey, Jane. "The Contribution of Social Work to Government." In *National Conference of Social Work, Proceedings, 1945.* New York: Columbia University Press, 1945, pp. 3–17.

—— "The Federal Government and Desirable Standards of State and Local Administration." In *National Conference of Social Work, Proceedings, 1937.* Chicago: University of Chicago Press, 1937, pp. 440–44.

—— "Next Steps in Public Assistance." In *National Conference of Social Work, Proceedings, 1945.* New York: Columbia Univeristy Press, 1945, pp. 148–160.

—— "Public Welfare—Burden or Opportunity," *Social Service Review,* 27 (December 1953): 377–84.

Hofstadter, Richard. *Social Darwinism in American Thought.* New York: Braziller, 1959.

Hollis, Ernest V. and Alice L. Taylor. *Social Work Education in the United States.* New York: Columbia University Press, 1951.

Holtzman, Abraham. *The Townsend Movement: A Political Study.* New York: Bookman Associates, 1963.

Hoover, Herbert C. *The New Day: Campaign Speeches . . .* Stanford, Calif.: Stanford University Press, 1928.

Hopkins, Harry. *Spending to Save: The Complete Story of Relief.* New York: W. W. Norton, 1936.

Hopkins, Howard C. *History of the Y.M.C.A. in North America.* New York: Association Press, 1957.

Howard, Donald S. *The WPA and Federal Relief Policy.* New York: Russell Sage Foundation, 1943.

Huggins, Nathan I. *Protestants Against Poverty. Boston's Charities 1870–1900.* Westbrook, Conn.: Greenwood, 1971.

Hunter, Robert. *Poverty.* New York: Macmillan, 1904.

—— "The Relation Between Social Settlements and Charity Organization." In *National Conference of Charities and Correction, Proceedings,* 1902, pp. 302–14.

Hurd, Henry M. et al. *The Institutional Care of the Insane in the United States and Canada,* 4 vols. Baltimore: Johns Hopkins University Press, 1916–1917.

Huthmacher, J. Joseph. *Senator Robert F. Wagner and the Rise of American Liberalism.* New York: Antheneum, 1968.

Jackson, Larry and William A. Johnson. *Protest by the Poor.* Lexington, Mass.: Heath, 1974.

The Jacksonians on the Poor: Collected Pamphlets. New York: Arno Press, 1971.

Jenkins, Shirley, ed. *Social Security in International Perspective: Essays in Honor of Eveline M. Burns* (includes bibliography of Burns' writings, 1923–1968). New York: Columbia University Press, 1969.

Johnson, Alexander. *Adventures in Social Welfare.* Fort Wayne, Ind.: Published by the author, 1923.

——"An Appreciation [of Franklin B. Sanborn]," *Survey,* May 10, 1917.

Johnson, Earl. *Justice and Reform: The Formative Years of the OEO Legal Services Program.* New York: Russell Sage Foundation, 1974.

Joint Commission on Mental Illness and Health. *Action for Mental Health, Science Editions.* New York: Wiley, 1961.

Jones, Byrd L. "The Role of Keynesians in Wartime Policy and Postwar Planning," *American Economic Review,* 62 (May 1972).

Jones, Kathleen. *A History of the Mental Health Services* [Great Britain]. Boston: Routledge & Kegan Paul, 1972.

Jordan, Wilbur K. "The English Background of Modern Philanthropy," *American Historical Review,* 66 (January 1961): 401–408.

—— *Philanthropy in England, 1480–1660.* New York: Russell Sage Foundation, 1959.

Kahn, Alfred J., ed. *Issues in American Social Work.* New York: Columbia University Press, 1959.

—— *Shaping the New Social Work.* New York: Columbia University Press, 1973.

Karl, Barry. "Philanthropy, Policy Planning, and the Bureaucratization of the Democratic Ideal," *Daedalus* (Fall 1976), pp. 129–149.

—— "Presidential Planning and Social Science Research: Mr. Hoover's Experts," *Perspectives in American History,* 3 (1969): 347–409.

Kasius, Cora, ed. *New Directions in Social Work.* New York: Harper, 1954.

Katz, Alfred and Eugne Bender. *The Strength in Us: Self Help Groups in the Modern World.* New York: New Viewpoints, 1976.

Katz, Michael B. *Irony of Early School Reform: Educational Innovation in Mid-Nineteenth-Century Massachusetts.* Cambridge, Mass.: Harvard University Press, 1968.

Kitano, Harry H. L. *Asians in America: A Selected Bibliography for Use in Social Work Education.* New York: Council on Social Work Education, 1971.

Klebaner, Benjamin J. *Public Poor Relief in America, 1790–1860.* Ph.D. dissertation, Columbia University, 1951. Printed by Arno Press, New York, 1975.

Klein, Philip. "Mary Richmond's Formulation of a New Science." In Stuart Rice, ed., *Methods in Social Science.* Chicago: University of Chicago Press, 1931.

Knapp, Daniel and Kenneth Polk. *Scouting the War on Poverty: Social Reform Politics in the Kennedy Administration.* Lexington, Mass.: Heath, 1971.

Koehler, Gustav. *Economics, Politics, and Welfare Outcome: A Review Essay,* University of California, Davis, Institute for Government Affairs, Research Reports, no. 20. Davis, Calif., April 1971.

Konopka, Gisela. *Eduard C. Lindemann and Social Work Philosophy.* Minneapolis: University of Minnesota Press, 1958.

Korn, Richard and Lloyd McKorkle. *Criminology and Penology.* New York: Holt, 1959.

Kramer, Ralph M. and Harry Specht. *Readings in Community Organization Practice.* 2d ed. Englewood Cliffs, N.J.: Prntice-Hall, 1975.

Krieger, Leonard. "The Idea of the Welfare State in the United States and Europe," *Journal of the History of Ideas,* 24 (October 1963).

Kurzman, Paul. *Harry Hopkins and the New Deal.* Fair Lawn, N.J.: Burdick, 1974.

Lamb, Edwin G. *Social Work of the Salvation Army*. New York: Columbia University Press, 1909.

Lane, Francis Emmet. *American Charities and the Child of the Immigrant. A Study of Typical Child Caring Institutions in New York and Massachusetts Between the Years 1845 and 1880*. Washington, D.C.: Catholic University Press, 1932.

Lane, Roger. "Crime and Criminal Statistics in 19th Century Massachusetts," *Journal of Social History*, 2 (Winter 1968): 156–63.

—— *Policing the City: Boston, 1822–1885*. Cambridge, Mass.: Harvard University Press, 1967.

Langsam, Miriam Z. *Children West: A History of the Placing-Out System of the New York Children's Aid Society, 1853–1890*. Madison: State Historical Society of Wisconsin for University of Wisconsin, Department of History, 1964.

Lansdale, Robert T. "The Impact of the Federal Social Security Act on Public Welfare Programs in the South," Florida State University, Institute for Social Research, Research Reports, vol. 4, no. 1. Tallahassee, Florida, February 1961.

Lasch, Christopher, ed. *The Social Thought of Jane Addams*. Indianapolis: Bobbs-Merrill, 1965.

Lathrop, Julia. "The Cook County Charities." In *Hull-House Maps and Papers . . .* New York: 1895, pp. 131–61.

Lauck, W[illiam] Jett. *The New Industrial Revolution and Wages . . .* New York: Funk & Wagnalls, 1929.

Lawler, Loretto. *Full Circle: A Story of the National Catholic School of Social Service, 1918–1947*. Washington, D.C.: Catholic University Press, 1951.

Lawrence, Charles. *History of the Philadelphia Almshouses and Hospitals . . .* Philadelphia: compiled and published by the author, 1905.

Lebergott, Stanley. *Manpower in Economic Growth: The American Record Since 1800*. New York: McGraw-Hill, 1964.

Lee, Porter R. *Social Work as Cause and Function, and Other Papers*. New York: Columbia University Press, 1937.

Leiby, James. "Amos Warner's *American Charities*, 1894–1930," *Social Service Review*, 37 (December 1963): 441–55.

—— *Carroll Wright and Labor Reform: The Origins of Labor Statistics*. Cambridge, Mass.: Harvard University Press, 1960.

—— *Charity and Correction in New Jersey: A History of State Welfare Institutions*. New Brunswick, N.J.: Rutgers University Press, 1967.

—— "Social Work and Social History: Some Interpretations," *Social Service Review*, 43 (September 1969): 310–15.

—— "State Welfare Administration in California, 1879–1929," *Pacific Historical Review*, 41 (May 1972): 169–87.

—— "State Welfare Administration in California, 1930–1945," *Southern California Quarterly*, 55 (Fall 1973): 303–18.

Lemons, J. Stanley. *The Woman Citizen: Social Feminism in the 1920's*. Urbana: University of Illinois Press, 1973.

Levin, Herman. "The Future of Voluntary Family and Children's Social Work: A Historical View," *Social Service Review*, 38 (June 1964): 163–73.

Levine, Daniel. *Jane Addams and the Liberal Tradition.* Madison: State Historical Society of Wisconsin, 1971.

Levine, Murray and Adeline Levine. *A Social History of the Helping Services: Clinic, Court, School and Community.* New York: Appleton-Century-Crofts, 1970.

Levitan, Sar. *Programs in Aid of the Poor for the 1970s.* Rev. ed. Baltimore: Johns Hopkins University Press, 1973.

———— *The Promise of Greatness.* Cambridge, Mass.: Harvard University Press, 1976.

Levitan, Sar and William B. Johnston. *Indian Giving: Federal Programs for Native Americans.* Baltimore: Johns Hopkins University Press, 1975.

Lewis, Orlando. *The Development of American Prisons and Prison Customs, 1776–1845.* [Albany]: The Prison Association of New York, 1922.

Lewis, Oscar. "The Culture of Poverty," *Scientific American,* 215 (October 1966): 19–25.

Lewis, Verl S. "The Development of the Charity Organization Society Movement in the United States 1875–1900." Unpublished dissertation, Case Western Reserve University, 1954.

———— "Stephen Humphreys Gurteen and the American Origins of Charity Organization," *Social Service Review,* 40 (June 1966): 190–201.

Lewis, W. David. *From Newgate to Dannemora: The Rise of the Penitentiary in New York, 1796–1848.* Ithaca, N.Y.: Cornell University Press, 1965.

Leyendecker, Hilary M. *Problems and Policy in Public Assistance.* New York: Harper, 1955.

Lide, Pauline. "The National Conference on Social Welfare and the Black Historical Perspective," *Social Service Review,* 47 (June 1973): 171–207.

Lindsey, Benjamin B. *Twenty-five Years of the Juvenile and Family Court of Denver.* Denver: Ben B. Lindsey, 1925.

Loch, Sir Charles S. *Charity and Social Life.* London: Macmillan, 1910.

Lowell, Josephine Shaw. *Public Relief and Private Charity.* New York: Putnam's, 1884.

Lubove, Roy. *Poverty and Social Welfare in the United States.* New York: Holt, Rinehart & Winston, 1972.

———— *The Professional Altruist; The Emergence of Social Work as a Career, 1880–1930.* Cambridge, Mass.: Harvard University Press, 1965.

———— *The Progressives and the Slums.* Pittsburgh: University of Pittsburgh Press, 1962.

———— *The Struggle for Social Security, 1900–1935.* Cambridge, Mass.: Harvard University Press, 1968.

Lubove, Roy, ed. *Social Welfare in Transition: Selected English Documents, 1834–1909.* Pittsburgh: University of Pittsburgh Press, 1966.

Lurie, Harry. *A Heritage Affirmed: The Jewish Federation Movement in America.* Philadelphia: Jewish Publication Society of America, 1961.

Lynd, Robert S. and Helen M. Lynd. *Middletown in Transition: A Study in Cultural Conflicts.* New York: Harcourt, Brace, 1937.

Lynn, Laurence E., Jr. and John M. Seidl. "Policy Analysis at HEW: The Story of the Mega Proposal," *Policy Analysis*, 1 (Spring 1975): entire issue.

McClelland, David. *The Achieving Society*. Princeton, N.J.: Van Nostrand, 1961.

McColgan, Daniel T. *A Century of Charity: The First One Hundred Years of the Society of St. Vincent de Paul in the United States*. Milwaukee: Bruce, 1951.

—— *Joseph Tuckerman: Pioneer in American Social Work*. Washington, D.C.: Catholic University of America Press, 1940.

McGloughlin, William G. *Modern Revivalism: Charles Grandison Finney to Billy Graham*. New York: Ronald Press, 1959.

McGloughlin, William G. and Robert M. Bellah, eds. *Religion in America*. Boston: Houghton Mifflin, 1968.

MacKay, Thomas. *A History of the English Poor Law*. Vol. III, *From 1834 to the Present Time*. New York: Putnam's, 1899.

McKeany, Maurine. *The Absent Father and Public Policy in the Program of Aid to Dependent Children*. Berkeley: University of California Publications in Social Welfare, 1960.

McKelvey, Blake. *American Prisons, A Study in American Social History Prior to 1915*. Chicago: University of Chicago Press, 1936.

—— *The Urbanization of America, 1860–1915*. New Brunswick, N.J.: Rutgers University Press, 1963.

McKinley, Charles and Robert W. Frase. *Launching Social Security: A Capture-and-Record Account*. Madison: University of Wisconsin Press, 1970.

McLachlan, James. *American Boarding Schools: A Historical Study*. New York: Scribner's, 1970.

MacMahon, Arthur et al. *The Administration of Federal Work Relief*. Chicago: Published for the Committee on Public Administration Service, 1941.

McMaster, John Bach. *History of the People of the United States, From the Revolution to the Civil War*, 8 vols. New York: Appleton, 1898–1913.

Maas, Henry S., ed. *Five Fields of Social Service: Reviews of Research*. New York: National Association of Social Workers, 1966.

—— *Research in the Social Services: A Five-Year Review*. New York: National Association of Social Workers, 1971.

Mann, Arthur. "British Social Thought and American Reformers of the Progressive Era," *Mississippi Valley Historical Review*, 42 (March 1956).

Manser, Gordon. *Voluntarism at the Crossroads*. New York: Family Service Association, 1976.

Marris, Peter and Martin Rein. *Dilemmas of Social Reform: Poverty and Community Action in the United States*. 2d ed. Chicago: Aldine, 1973.

Marshall, Alfred. *Principles of Economics*, 2 vols. London: MacMillan, 1890.

Marshall, Dale R. "Implementation of Federal Poverty and Welfare Policy: A Review Essay," *Policy Studies Journal*, 2 (Spring 1974): 152–57.

Marshall, Helen. *Dorothea Dix, Forgotten Samaritan*. Chapel Hill: University of North Carolina Press, 1937.

Marshall, J. D. *The Old Poor Law, 1795–1834*. London: MacMillan, 1968.

Marshall, Thomas Humphrey. *Class, Citizenship and Social Development: Essays*. Garden City, N.Y.: Doubleday, 1964.

———— *Social Policy in the 20th Century.* 4th ed., rev. Atlantic Highlands, N.J.: Humanities Press, 1975.

———— "The Welfare State, A Sociological Interpretation," *European Journal of Sociology,* tome II, 1961, no. 2.

Martin, George. *Madame Secretary: Frances Perkins.* Boston: Houghton Mifflin, 1976.

Martineau, Harriet. *Society in America,* 2 vols. New York, 1837.

Marwick, Arthur. "The Labour Party and the Welfare State in Britain, 1900–1948," *The American Historical Review,* 73 (December 1967): 380–403.

Mathews, D. G. "The Second Great Awakening as an Organizing Process, 1780–1830: An Hypothesis," *American Quarterly,* 21 (Spring 1969): 23–43.

May, Henry. *Protestant Churches and Industrial America.* New York: Harper, 1949.

Melder, Keith. "Ladies Bountiful: Organized Women's Benevolence in Early 19th Century America," *New York History,* 48 (July 1967): 231–74.

Meier, August, Elliott Rudwick, and Francis L. Broderick, eds. *Black Protest Thought in the Twentieth Century.* 2d ed. Indianapolis: Bobbs Merrill, 1971.

Mencher, Samuel. *Poor Law to Poverty Program: Economic Security Policy in Britain and the United States.* Pittsburgh: University of Pittsburgh Press, 1967.

Mennel, Robert M. *Thorns and Thistles: Juvenile Delinquents in the United States, 1825–1940.* Hanover, N.H.: University Press of New England, 1973.

Meriam, Lewis. *Relief and Society Security.* Washington, D.C.: Brookings Institution, 1946.

Merriam, Charles. "National Resources Planning Board," *American Political Science Review,* 38 (December 1944): 1075–88.

Merriam, Ida. "The Relations of Social Security and Social Welfare Services," *Social Security Bulletin,* 25 (February 1962): 7–14.

———— "Three Decades of Social Security Research Publishing," *Social Security Bulletin,* 31 (March 1968): 33–38.

Meyer, Charles. "Half-century of Federal Probation and Parole," *Journal of Criminal Law,* 42 (March/April 1952): 707–28.

Miles, Rufus E. *The Department of Health, Education and Welfare.* New York: Praeger, 1974.

Miyakawa, Tetsuo Scott. *Protestants and Pioneers: Individualism and Conformity on the American Frontier.* Chicago: University of Chicago Press, 1964.

Mohl, Raymond. "Humanitarianism in the Preindustrial City: The New York Society for the Prevention of Pauperism, 1817–1823," *Journal of American History,* 57 (December 1970): 576–99.

———— *Poverty in New York, 1783–1825.* New York: Oxford University Press, 1971.

Moore, John R. "The Conservative Coalition in the U.S. Senate, 1942–1945," *Journal of Southern History,* 33 (August 1967): 368–76.

Moran, Robert. "The Negro Dependent Child in Louisiana, 1800–1935," *Social Service Review,* 45 (March 1971): 53–61.

Mott, Paul. *Meeting Human Needs: The Social and Political History of Title XX.* Columbus, Ohio: National Conference on Social Welfare, 1976.

Mowat, Charles L. *The Charity Organization Society, 1869–1913.* London: Methuen, 1961.

Moynihan, Daniel P. *Maximum Feasible Misunderstanding: Community Action in the War on Poverty.* New York: Free Press, 1969.

—— *The Politics of a Guaranteed Income: The Nixon Administration and the Family Assistance Plan.* New York: Random House, 1973.

Moynihan, Daniel P., ed., *On Understanding Poverty.* New York: Basic Books, 1969.

Munts, Raymond. *Bargaining for Health: Labor Unions, Health Insurance and Medical Care.* Madison: University of Wisconsin Press, 1967.

Musto, David. "Whatever Happened to 'Community Mental Health'?" *Public Interest*, 39 (Spring 1975): 53–79.

Myrdal, Gunnar. *Beyond the Welfare State: Economic Planning and Its International Implications.* New Haven, Conn.: Yale University Press, 1966.

National Academy of Sciences, Advisory Committee for Assessment of University-Based Institutes for Research on Poverty. *Policy and Program Research in a University Setting: A Case Study.* Washington, D.C.: National Academy of Science, 1971.

National Council of the Churches of Christ in the U.S.A. *The Churches and Social Welfare.* 3 vols. New York: National Council, 1955–1956.

Navarro, Eliseo. *The Chicano Community.* New York: Council on Social Work Education, 1971.

Naylor, T. "Responding to the Fire: The Work of the Chicago Relief and Aid Society," *Science and Society*, 39 (Winter 1975).

Nelli, Humbert O. *A Bibliography of Insurance History.* Atlanta: Georgia State University, Bureau of Business and Economic Research, 1971.

Nelson, Daniel. *Unemployment Insurance: The American Experience, 1915–1935.* Madison: University of Wisconsin Press, 1969.

Nelson, O. M. "The Chicago Relief and Aid Society, 1850–1874," *Journal of the Illinois State Historical Society*, 59 (Winter 1966): 48–66.

Nelson, Richard R. "Intellectualizing About the Moon-Ghetto Metaphor: A Study of the Current Malaise of Rational Analysis of Social Problems," *Policy Sciences*, 5 (December 1974): 375–414.

Newcomer, Mabel. "Fifty Years of Public Support of Welfare Functions in the United Statss," *Social Service Review*, 15 (December 1941): 651–60.

Nielsen, Waldemar. *The Big Foundations: A 20th Century Fund Study.* New York: Columbia University Press, 1972.

Norton, William J. *The Cooperative Movement in Social Work.* New York: Macmillan, 1927.

Noyes, John Humphrey. *History of American Socialisms.* New York: Hillary House Publications, 1961. (First published 1875.)

Odum, Howard, ed. "Public Welfare in the United States," The American Academy of Political and Social Science, *Annals*, 105 (June 1923): entire issue.

O'Grady, John. *Catholic Charities in the United States: History and Problems.* Washington, D.C.: National Conference of Catholic Charities, 1930.

Ohlin, Lloyd, ed. *Prisoners in America: Perspectives on Our Correctional System.* Englewood Cliffs, N.J.: Prentice-Hall (Spectrum), 1973.

Olds, Victoria. "The Freedmen's Bureau as a Social Agency." Unpublished D.S.W. dissertation, Columbia University, June 1966.

O'Neil, Robert. *The Price of Dependency: Civil Liberties in the Welfare State.* New York: Dutton, 1970.

Ormsby, Ralph. *A Man of Vision: Francis H. McLean, 1869–1945.* New York: Family Service Association of America, 1970.

Pacey, Lorene. *Readings in the Development of Settlement Work.* New York: Association Press, 1950.

Parker, Jacqueline Kay. "Shaping the Social Security Act: Social and Political Bases of the Public Assistance Provision." Unpublished D.S.W. dissertation, University of California, Berkeley, December 1972.

Parris, Guichard and Lester Brooks. *Blacks in the City: A History of the National Urban League.* Boston: Little, Brown, 1971.

Parsons, Jack. "The Origins of the Income and Resources Amendment to the Social Security Act," *Social Service Review,* 36 (March 1962): 51–61.

Patterson, James T. *Congressional Conservatism and the New Deal: The Growth of the Conservative Coalition in Congress, 1933–1939.* Lexington: For the Organization of American Historians (by) University of Kentucky Press, 1967.

—— *The New Deal and the States.* Princeton, N.J.: Princeton University Press, 1969.

Pease, William and Jane Pease. *Black Utopia: Negro Communal Experiments in America.* Madison: University of Wisconsin Press, 1963.

Pechman, Joseph et al. *Social Security: Perspectives for Reform.* Washington, D.C.: Brookings Institution, 1968.

Perkins, Frances. *The Roosevelt I Knew.* New York: Viking Press, 1946.

Pessen, Edward. *Riches, Class and Power Before the Civil War.* Lexington, Mass.: Heath, 1973.

Pickett, Robert S. *House of Refuge. Origins of Juvenile Reform in New York State, 1815–1857.* Syracuse, N.Y.: Syracuse University Press, 1969.

Platt, Anthony M. *The Child Savers: The Invention of Delinquency.* Chicago: University of Chicago Press, 1969.

Plotnick, Robert and Felicity Skidmore. *Progress Against Poverty: A Review of the 1964–1974 Decade.* New York: Academic Press, 1975.

Polanyi, Karl. *The Great Transformation.* New York: Rinehart, 1944.

Poynter, John R. *Society and Pauperism: English Ideas on Poor Relief, 1795–1834.* Toronto: University of Toronto Press, 1969.

Pratt, John W. "Boss Tweed's Public Welfare Program," *New York Historical Society Quarterly,* 45 (October 1961): 396–411.

—— *Religion, Politics, and Diversity: The Church–State Theme in New York History.* Ithaca, N.Y.: Cornell University Press, 1967.

President's Research Committee on Social Trends. *Recent Social Trends in the United States.* New York: McGraw-Hill, 1933.

Pumphrey, Muriel W. "Mary Richmond and the Rise of Professional Social Work in Baltimore: The Foundations of a Creative Career." Unpublished D.S.W. dissertation, Columbia University, 1956.

Pumphrey, Ralph E. and Muriel W. Pumphrey. *The Heritage of American Social Work.* New York: Columbia University Press, 1961.

Pusić, Eugen. *Social Welfare and Social Development.* The Hague, the Netherlands: Institute of Social Studies, 1972.

Putnam, Jackson K. *Old Age Politics in California: From Richardson to Reagan.* Stanford, Calif.: Stanford University Press, 1970.

Rabinowitz, Howard N. "From Exclusion to Segregation: Health and Welfare Services for Southern Blacks, 1865–1890," *Social Service Review,* 48 (September 1974): 327–54.

Rainwater, Lee and William L. Yancey. *The Moynihan Report and the Politics of Controversy.* Cambridge, Mass.: M.I.T. Press, 1967.

Reagan, Michael. *The New Federalism.* New York: Oxford University Press, 1972.

Reich, Charles A. "The New Property," *Yale Law Journal,* 73 (April 1964): 732–87.

Rescher, Nicholas. *Welfare: The Social Issues in Philosophical Perspective.* Pittsburgh: University of Pittsburgh Press, 1972.

Reynolds, Bertha. *An Uncharted Journey: Fifty Years of Growth in Social Work.* New York: Citadel Press, 1963.

Rich, Margaret E. *A Belief in People: A History of Family Social Work.* New York: Family Service Association of America, 1956.

———— *Josephine Shaw Lowell.* New York: Family Service Association of America, 1954.

Richardson, Anne B. "Women in Philanthropy." In *National Conference of Charities and Correction, Proceedings, Nineteenth Annual Session, 1892,* pp. 216–23.

Richman, Harold. "Alms and Friends: The Relationship Between Social Services and Financial Assistance in Public Welfare Policy." Unpublished Ph.D. dissertation, University of Chicago, March 1969.

Richmond, Mary E. *The Long View: Papers and Addresses.* Joanna C. Colcord and Ruth Z. S. Mann, eds. New York: Russell Sage Foundation, 1930.

———— *Social Diagnosis.* New York: Russell Sage Foundation, 1917.

———— *What Is Social Case Work? An Introductory Description.* New York: Russell Sage Foundation, 1922.

Ridenour, Nina. *Mental Health in the United States. A Fifty Year History.* Cambridge, Mass.: Published for the Commonwealth Fund by Harvard University Press, 1961.

Rieff, Philip. *The Triumph of the Therapeutic: The Uses of Faith After Freud.* New York: Harper & Row, 1966.

Riessman, Frank, Jerome Cohen, and Arthur Pearl, eds. *Mental Health of the Poor: New Treatment Approaches for Low Income People.* New York: Free Press, 1964.

Riordan, William. *Plunkitt of Tammany Hall.* New York: Dutton, 1963.

Rimlinger, Gaston V. *Welfare Policy and Industrialization in Europe, America, and Russia.* New York: Wiley, 1971.

Ritz, Joseph P. *The Despised Poor: Newburgh's War on Welfare.* Boston: Beacon Press, 1966.

Rivlin, Alice M. "The Planning, Programming and Budgeting System in the Department of Health, Education, and Welfare: Some Lessons from Experience." In U.S. Congress, Joint Economic Committee. *The Analysis and Evaluation of Public Expenditures: The PPB System.* 91st Cong., 1st sess., 1969, III, 909–22.

———— *Systematic Thinking for Social Action.* Washington, D.C.: Brookings Institution, 1971.

Robinson, Virginia P., ed. *Jessie Taft: Therapist and Social Work Educator*. Philadelphia: University of Pennsylvania Press, 1962.

Romanyshyn, John M., with the assistance of Annie L. Romanyshyn. *Social Welfare: Charity to Justice*. New York: Random House, 1971.

Romasco, Albert U. *The Poverty of Abundance: Hoover, the Nation, the Depression*. New York: Oxford University Press, 1965.

Rose, Gordan. *Struggle for Penal Reform*. Chicago: Quadrangle Books, 1961.

Rose, Michael E. *The Relief of Poverty, 1834–1914*. London: Macmillan, 1972.

Rosen, George. *History of Public Health*. New York: MD Publications, 1958.

———— "The Hospital: Historical Sociology of a Community Institution." In Eliot Freidson, ed., *The Hospital in Modern Society*. New York: Free Press, 1963.

Rosen, M. et al. *The History of Mental Retardation: Collected Papers*. 2 vols. Baltimore: University Park Press, 1976.

Rosenberg, Carroll Smith. *Religion and the Rise of the American City. The New York City Mission Movement, 1812–70*. Ithaca, N.Y.: Cornell University Press, 1971.

Rosenkrantz, Barbara G. *Public Health and the State: Changing Views in Massachusetts 1842–1936*. Cambridge, Mass.: Harvard University Press, 1972.

Roszak, Theodore. *The Making of a Counter Culture*. Garden City, N.Y.: Doubleday, 1969.

Rothman, David. *The Discovery of the Asylum: Social Order and Disorder in the New Republic*. Boston: Little, Brown, 1971.

Rothman, David J. and Sheila M. Rothman, eds. *On Their Own: The Poor in Modern America*, Reading, Mass.: Addison-Wesley, 1972.

Rousmaniere, John P. "Cultural Hybrid in the Slums: The College Woman and the Settlement House, 1889–1894," *American Quarterly*, 22 (Spring 1970): 45–66.

Rowntree, Benjamin Seebohm. *Poverty: A Study of Town Life*. 2d ed. London: Macmillan, 1902.

Rubinow, I[saac] M. *The Quest for Security*. New York: Holt, 1934.

———— *Social Insurance, with Special Reference to American Conditions*. New York: Holt, 1913.

Ruggiero, Guido. *The History of European Liberalism*. Boston: Beacon Press, 1959.

Ryan, John A. *Social Doctrine in Action: A Personal History*. New York: Harper, 1941.

Sabine, George. *A History of Political Theory*. 3d ed. New York: Holt, Rinehart & Winston, 1961.

Salmond, John A. *The Civilian Conservation Corps, 1933–1942: A New Deal Case Study*. Durham, N.C.: Duke University Press, 1967.

Sanborn, Franklin B. "The First State Boards of Charities," *Charities*, 13 (November 5, 1904): 115–20.

———— *Recollections of Seventy Years*. Boston: Badger, 1909.

Schiesl, Martin. *The Politics of Efficiency: Municipal Administration and Reform in America, 1880–1930*. Berkeley: University of California Press, 1977.

Schlabach, Theron F. *Edwin E. Witte, Cautious Reformer*. Madison: State Historical Society of Wisconsin, 1969.

Schlesinger, Arthur M., Jr. *The Age of Roosevelt*. Vols. 1–3. Boston: Houghton Mifflin, 1957–1960.

——— *A Thousand Days: John F. Kennedy in the White House.* Boston: Houghton Mifflin, 1965.

Schlitz, Michael E. "Public Attitudes Toward Social Security, 1935–1965," U.S. Department of Health, Education and Welfare, Social Security Administration, Research Report no. 33. Washington, D.C.: Government Printing Office, 1970.

Schneider, David M. *The History of Public Welfare in New York State, 1609–1866.* Chicago: University of Chicago Press, 1938.

Schneider, David M. and Albert Deutsch. *The History of Public Welfare in New York State, 1867–1940.* Chicago: University of Chicago Press, 1941.

Schottland, Charles. "The Nature of Services in Public Assistance." In *National Conference on Social Welfare, 86th Annual Forum, 1959; Casework Papers.* New York: Family Service Association, 1959.

Schottland, Charles, ed. *The Welfare State: Selected Essays.* New York: Harper & Row, 1967.

Schwartz, Harold. *Samuel Gridley Howe, Social Reformer, 1801–1876.* Cambridge, Mass.: Harvard University Press, 1956.

Scudder, Vida D. *On Journey.* New York: Dutton, 1937.

Seager, Henry R. *Social Insurance: A Program of Social Reform.* New York: Macmillan, 1910.

Sedgwick, Theodore. *Public and Private Economy.* New York, 1836.

Seeley, John R. et al. *Community Chest: A Study in Philanthropy.* Toronto: University of Toronto Press, 1957.

Senior, Nassau. "English Poor Laws." In *Historical and Philosophical Essays.* London, 1865.

Shepard, Edwin M. *The Work of a Social Teacher* [Richard L. Dugdale], Society for Political Education, Economic Tracts, no. XII. New York, 1884, pp. 1–14.

Sherwood, Robert E. *Roosevelt and Hopkins: An Intimate History.* New York: Harper, 1948.

Shryock, Richard. *The Development of Modern Medicine: An Interpretation of the Social and Scientific Factors Involved.* Rev. ed. New York: Knopf, 1947.

——— *Medicine and Society in America, 1660–1860.* New York: New York University Press, 1960.

——— *The National Tuberculosis Association, 1904–1954: A Study of the Voluntary Health Movement in the United States.* New York: National Tuberculosis Association, 1957.

Silberman, Charles. *Crisis in Black and White.* New York: Random House, 1964.

Sills, David L. *The Volunteers.* Glencoe, Ill.: Free Press, 1957.

Simey, T[homas] S. and M. B. Simey. *Charles Booth, Social Scientist.* London: Oxford University Press, 1960.

Simkovich, Mary K. *Neighborhood: My Story of Greenwich House.* New York: Norton, 1938.

Sims, Mary S. *The Natural History of a Social Institution—the Y.W.C.A.* New York: Women's Press, 1936.

Smith, Arthur Delafield. *The Right to Life.* Chapel Hill: University of North Carolina Press, 1955.

Smith, Bruce. *Rural Crime Control*. New York: Institute of Public Administration, 1933.

Smith, Constance E. and Anne Freedman. *Voluntary Associations: Perspectives on the Literature*. Cambridge, Mass.: Harvard University Press, 1972.

Smith, Timothy L. *Revivalism and Social Reform in Mid-Nineteenth Century America*. New York: Abingdon Press, 1957.

Solomon, Barbara M. *Pioneers in Service: The History of the Associated Jewish Philanthropies of Boston*. Boston: Associated Jewish Philanthropies, 1956.

Somers, Herman M. and Anne R. Somers. *Doctors, Patients and Health Insurance: The Organization and Financing of Medical Care*. Washington, D.C.: Brookings Institution, 1961.

Soule, George H. *Prosperity Decade, from War to Depression: 1917–1929*. New York: Rinehart, 1947.

Stein, Herbert. *The Fiscal Revolution in America*. Chicago: University of Chicago Press, 1969.

Steiner, Gilbert Y. *Social Insecurity: The Politics of Welfare*. Chicago: Rand McNally, 1966.

———— *The State of Welfare*. Washington, D.C.: Brookings Institution, 1971.

Steiner, Gilbert Y., with the assistance of Pauline H. Milius. *The Children's Cause*. Washington, D.C.: Brookings Institution, 1976.

Steinfels, Margaret O'Brien. *Who's Minding the Children? The History and Politics of Day Care in America*. New York: Simon & Schuster, 1973.

Stevens, Robert B. and Rosemary Stevens. *Welfare Medicine in America: A Case Study of Medicaid*. New York: Free Press, 1974.

Stevenson, George S. *Mental Health Planning for Social Action*. New York: McGraw-Hill, 1956.

Stewart, William R., ed. *The Philanthropic Work of Josephine Shaw Lowell* . . . New York: Macmillan, 1911.

Struggle for Justice: A Report on Crime and Punishment in America. Prepared for the American Friends Service Committee. New York: Hill & Wang, 1971.

Sundquist, James L. *Politics and Policy: The Eisenhower, Kennedy and Johnson Years*. Washington, D.C.: Brookings Institution, 1968.

Sundquist, James L., ed. *On Fighting Poverty: Perspectives from Experience*. New York: Basic Books, 1969.

Sweezey, Alan. "The Keynesians and Government Policy, 1933–1939," *American Economic Review*, 62 (May 1972).

Tappan, Paul W. *Contemporary Corrections*. New York: McGraw-Hill, 1951.

Tawney, R[ichard] H. *Religion and the Rise of Capitalism: A Historical Study*. London: Murray, 1926.

Taylor, George R. "American Economic Growth Before 1840: An Exploratory Essay," *Journal of Economic History*, 24 (December 1964).

Taylor, Graham. *Chicago Commons Through Forty Years*. Chicago: University of Chicago Press, 1936.

Taylor, Hasseltine B. "The Nature of the Right to Public Assistance," *Social Service Review*, 36 (September 1962): 265–67.

Taylor, Lloyd C. "Josephine Shaw Lowell and American Philanthropy," *New York History*, 44 (October 1963): 336–64.

Tead, Ordway and Henry C. Metcalf. *Personnel Administration: Its Principles and Practice*. New York: McGraw-Hill, 1920.

Teeters, Negley K. *The Cradle of the Penitentiary: The Walnut Street Jail at Philadelphia, 1773–1835*. Philadelphia [Pennsylvania Prison Society], 1935.

Teeters, Negley K. and John D. Shearer. *The Prison at Philadelphia, Cherry Hill: The Separate System of Prison Discipline, 1829–1913*. New York: Published for Temple University Publications by Columbia University Press, 1957.

Ten Broek, Jacobus, ed. *The Law of the Poor*. San Francisco: Chandler, 1966. [First published in *California Law Review*, 54 (May 1966).]

Thurston, Henry W. *The Dependent Child: A Story of Changing Aims and Methods in the Care of Dependent Children*. New York: Columbia University Press, 1930.

Tierney, Brian. *Medieval Poor Law*. Berkeley: University of California Press, 1959.

Tiffany, Francis. *Life of Dorothea Lynde Dix*. 4th ed. Boston: Houghton Mifflin, 1891.

Titmuss, Richard M. *Commitment to Welfare*. New York: Pantheon, 1968.

—— *Essays on "The Welfare State."* London: Allen & Unwin, 1958.

Tocqueville, Alexis de. *Democracy in America*. Phillips Bradley, ed. 2 vols. New York: Knopf, 1945.

Towle, Charlotte. *Common Human Needs*. New York: National Association of Social Workers, 1957.

Trattner, Walter I. *Crusade for the Children: A History of the National Child Labor Committee and Child Labor Reform in America*. Chicago: Quadrangle Books, 1970.

—— *From Poor Law to Welfare State: A History of Social Welfare in America*. New York: Free Press, 1974.

—— *Homer Folks: Pioneer in Social Welfare*. New York: Columbia University Press, 1968.

—— "Louisa Lee Schuyler and the Founding of the State Charities Aid Association," *New York Historical Association Quarterly*, 51 (July 1967): 233–48.

Treudley, M. B. "The 'Benevolent Fair': A Study of Charitable Organizations Among American Women in the First Third of the Nineteenth Century," *Social Service Review*, 14 (September 1940): 509–22.

Trolander, Judith Ann. *Settlement Houses and the Great Depression*. Detroit: Wayne State University Press, 1975.

Turnbull, John G., C. Arthur Williams, Jr., and Earl F. Cheit. *Economic and Social Security*. 3d ed. New York: Ronald Press, 1967.

Tyler, Alice Felt. *Freedom's Ferment: Phases of American Social History to 1860*. Minneapolis: University of Minnesota Press, 1944.

Unger, Irwin. *The Movement: A History of the American New Left, 1959–1972*. New York: Dodd, Mead, 1975.

U.S. Advisory Council on Public Assistance. *Public Assistance: Report*. Washington, D.C.: Government Printing Office, 1960.

U.S. Bureau of the Census. *Defective, Dependent, and Delinquent Classes of the Population, 1880*. Washington, D.C.: Government Printing Office, 1888.

—— *Report on Crime, Pauperism, and Benevolence, 1890*. Washington, D.C.: Government Printing Office, 1895.

U.S. Bureau of Labor Statistics and National Social Welfare Assembly. *Salaries and Working Conditions of Social Welfare Manpower in 1960*. New York, n.d.
—— *Social Workers in 1950: A Report on the Study of Salaries and Working Conditions in Social Work, Spring, 1950*. New York: American Association of Social Workers, 1950.
—— *Bulletin* no. 250 (February 1919). "Welfare Work for Employees in Industrial Establishments in the United States."
U.S. Commission on Industrial Relations. *Final Report*, 11 vols. Washington, D.C.: Government Printing Office, 1916.
U.S. Committee on Economic Security, Social Security Board. *Social Security in America: The Factual Background of the Social Security Act . . .* Washington, D.C., 1937.
U.S. Comptroller General. *Report to the Congress: How Federal Efforts to Coordinate Programs to Mitigate Juvenile Delinquency Proved Ineffective*. April 21, 1975.
U.S. Department of Health, Education, and Welfare, Bureau of Family Services. *Work Relief . . . A Current Look*, Public Assistance Report no. 52. March 1962.
U.S. House of Representatives. Committee on Ways and Means. *Hearings, Public Welfare Amendments of 1962*. 87th Cong., 2d sess., 1962.
U.S. National Advisory Commission on Civil Disorders (Kerner Commission). *Report*. New York: Bantam Books, 1968.
U.S. National Advisory Committee on Rural Poverty. *The People Left Behind*. Washington, D.C.: Government Printing Office, 1967.
U.S. National Resources Planning Board. *Security, Work and Relief Policies*. Washington, D.C.: Government Printing Office, 1943.
U.S. President's Commission on Income Maintenance (Heineman Commission). *Poverty Amid Plenty: The American Paradox*. Washington, D.C.: Government Printing Office, 1969; *Background Papers*. Washington, D.C.: Government Printing Office, 1970; *Technical Studies*. Washington, D.C.: Government Printing Office, 1970.
U.S. President's Commission on Law Enforcement and Administration of Justice. *Crime in a Free Society*. Belmont, Calif., 1968.
—— *Juvenile Delinquency in a Free Society*. Belmont, Calif., 1968.
U.S. President's Commission on National Goals. *Goals for Americans*. New York: Prentice-Hall, 1960.
U.S. President's Commission on Veterans' Pensions. *Report*, 3 vols. *Findings and Recommendations*, "Staff Report No. 1: The Historical Development of Veterans Benefits in the U.S." Washington, D.C.: Government Printing Office, 1956.
U.S. Senate. Committee on Finance. *Public Assistance Act of 1962, Hearings*. 87th Cong., 2d sess, 1962.
U.S. Social Security Administration, Office of Research and Statistics. *Basic Readings in Social Security*. Washington, D.C., 1970.
Urwick, E. J. "The Settlement Movement in England and America," *Quarterly Review* (England), 221 (July 1914): 216–24.

Valentine, Charles. *Culture and Poverty*. Chicago: University of Chicago Press, 1968.

Vasey, Wayne. *Government and Social Welfare*. New York: Holt, 1958.

Viswanathan, N. "The Role of the American Public Welfare Association in the Foundation and Development of Public Welfare Policies in the United States, 1930–1960." Unpublished D.S.W. dissertation, Columbia University, June 1961.

Wade, Louise. *Graham Taylor, Pioneer for Social Justice, 1851–1938*. Chicago: University of Chicago Press, 1964.

Waite, Florence T. *A Warm Friend for the Spirit: A History of the Family Service Association of Cleveland and Its Forebears, 1830–1952*. Cleveland: Family Service Association of Cleveland, 1960.

Wald, Lillian. *The House on Henry Street*. New York: Holt, 1915.

Warren, Harris G. *Herbert Hoover and the Great Depression*. New York: Oxford University Press, 1959.

Watson, Frank D. *The Charity Organization Movement in the United States*. New York: Macmillan, 1922.

Watts, Phyllis. "Casework Above the Poverty Line: The Influence of Home Service in World War I on Social Work," *Social Service Review*, 38 (September 1964): 303–15.

Wayland, Francis. *The Elements of Moral Science*. Cambridge, Mass.: Harvard University Press, 1963. (Reprint of 1837 edition.)

Webb, Sidney and Beatrice Webb. *English Local Government: English Poor Law History*, pt. I, *The Old Poor Law* [before 1834]; pt. II, *The Last Hundred Years*. New York: Longmans, Green, 1927, 1929.

Weeks, Genevieve C. *Oscar Carleton McCulloch, 1843–1891: Preacher and Practitioner of Applied Christianity*. Indianapolis: Indiana Historical Society, 1976.

—— "Oscar C. McCulloch: Leader in Organized Charity," *Social Service Review*, 39 (September 1965): 209–21.

—— "Religion and Social Work as Exemplified in the Life of Oscar C. McCulloch," *Social Service Review*, 39 (March 1965): 38–52.

Weiss, Nancy. *The National Urban League, 1910–1940*. New York: Oxford University Press, 1974.

—— "Save the Children: A History of the Children's Bureau, 1903–1918." Unpublished Ph.D. dissertation, University of California, Los Angeles, 1974.

Weissman, Harold H., ed. *Individual and Group Services in the Mobilization for Youth*. New York: Association Press, 1969.

—— *Justice and the Law in the Mobilization for Youth Experience*. New York: Association Press, 1969.

Weller, Miriam Damick. "The Development of the Federal Probation System," *Social Service Review*, 18 (March 1944): 42–58.

White, R. Clyde and Mary White. *Research Memorandum on Social Aspects of Relief Policies*. New York: Social Service Research Council, 1937.

Whiteside, William. *The Boston Y.M.C.A. and Community Need: A Century's Evolution, 1851–1951*. New York: Association Press, 1951.

Wilcox, Clair. *Toward Social Welfare*. Homewood, Ill.: Irwin, 1969.

Wilensky, Harold L. and Charles N. Lebeaux. *Industrialism and Social Welfare.* New York: Russell Sage Foundation, 1958; rev. ed., New York: Free Press, 1965.

Wiltse, Kermit. "Social Casework Services in the Aid to Dependent Children Program," *Social Service Review,* 28 (June 1954): 173–88.

Wines, E[noch] C., and Theodore W. Dwight. *Report on the Prisons and Reformatories of the United States.* Albany, N.Y., 1867.

Wines, Frederick H. "The Growth of the National Conference," *Charities,* 14 (July 1905): 892–95.

—— *Punishment and Reformation.* New York: T. Y. Crowell, 1919.

Wisby, Herbert A., Jr. *History of the Volunteers of America.* New York [Volunteers of America], 1954.

—— *Soldiers Without Swords: A History of the Salvation Army in the U.S.* New York: Macmillan, 1955.

Wisner, Elizabeth. "Edith Abbott's Contributions to Social Work Education," *Social Service Review,* 32 (March 1958): 1–10.

—— *Social Welfare in the South, from Colonial Times to World War I.* Baton Rouge: Louisiana State University Press, 1970.

Witmer, Helen L. and Edith Tufts. *The Effectiveness of Delinquency Prevention Programs.* Washington, D.C.: U.S. Department of Health, Education, and Welfare: Children's Bureau, 1954.

Witte, Edwin E. *The Development of the Social Security Act.* Madison: University of Wisconsin Press, 1962.

—— *Social Security Perspectives: Essays by Edwin E. Witte,* Robert J. Lampman, ed. Madison: University of Wisconsin Press, 1962.

Woodroofe, Kathleen. *From Charity to Social Work in England and the United States.* London: Routledge & Kegan Paul, 1962.

Woods, Eleanor. *Robert A. Woods: Champion of Democracy.* Boston: Houghton Mifflin, 1929.

Woods, Robert A. *The City Wilderness.* Boston: Houghton Mifflin, 1918.

—— *The Neighborhood in Nation Building.* Boston: Houghton Mifflin, 1923.

—— "Social Work: A New Profession," *International Journal of Ethics,* 16 (October 1905): 25–39.

—— "University Settlements as Laboratories in Social Science." In *International Congress of Charities, Correction, and Philanthropy, Chicago 1893,* sec. VII, pp. 31–44.

—— "University Settlements: The Point and Drift," *Quarterly Journal of Economics,* 14 (November 1899): 67–86.

Woods, Robert A. and Albert Kennedy. *The Settlement Horizon: A National Estimate.* New York: Russel Sage Foundation, 1922.

Woods, Robert A. et al. *The Poor in Great Cities: Their Problems and What Is Being Done to Solve Them.* New York: Scribner's, 1895.

Worcester, Daisy Lee. *Grim the Battles: A Semi-Autobiographical Account of the War Against Want in the United States During the First Half of the Twentieth Century.* New York: Exposition Press, 1954.

Wright, Carroll D. *Outline of Practical Sociology.* 7th ed. rev. New York: Longmans, Green, 1909.

Wright, Helen R. "Three Against Time: Edith and Grace Abbott and Sophonisba P. Breckinridge," *Social Service Review*, 38 (March 1954): 41–53.

Young, A. F. and E. T. Ashton. *British Social Work in the Nineteenth Century*. London: Routledge & Kegan Paul, 1956.

Zimbalist, Sidney E. *Historic Themes and Landmarks in Social Welfare Research*. New York: Harper & Row, 1977.

Zink, Harold. *City Bosses in the U.S.* New York: AMS Press, 1968.

Index